I0810975

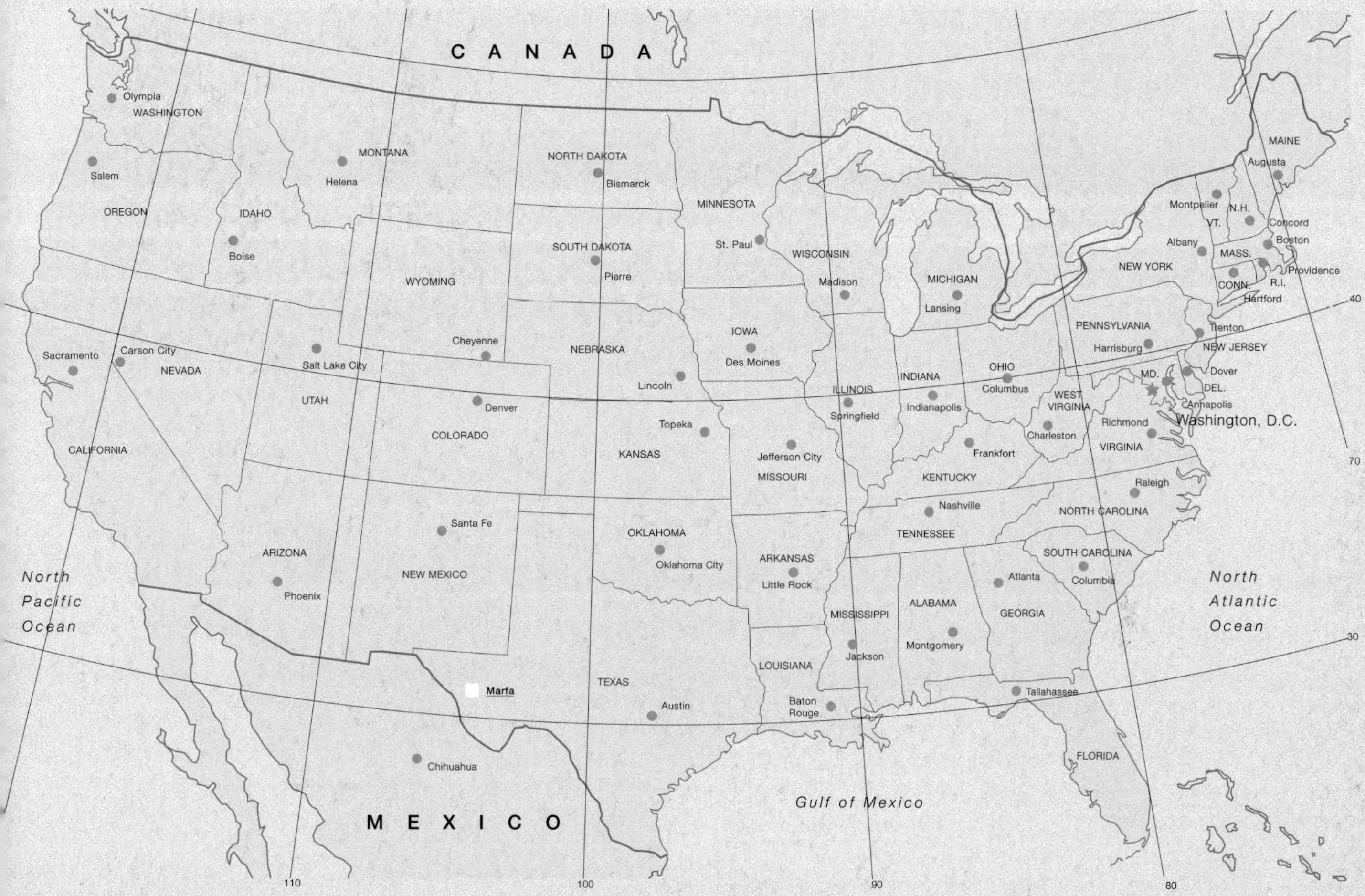

Map of the United States of America

Karte der Vereinigten Staaten von Amerika

Albers Equal – Area Projection
standard parallels 28° 30'N and 45° 30'N

805 Kilometers
0
500 Miles

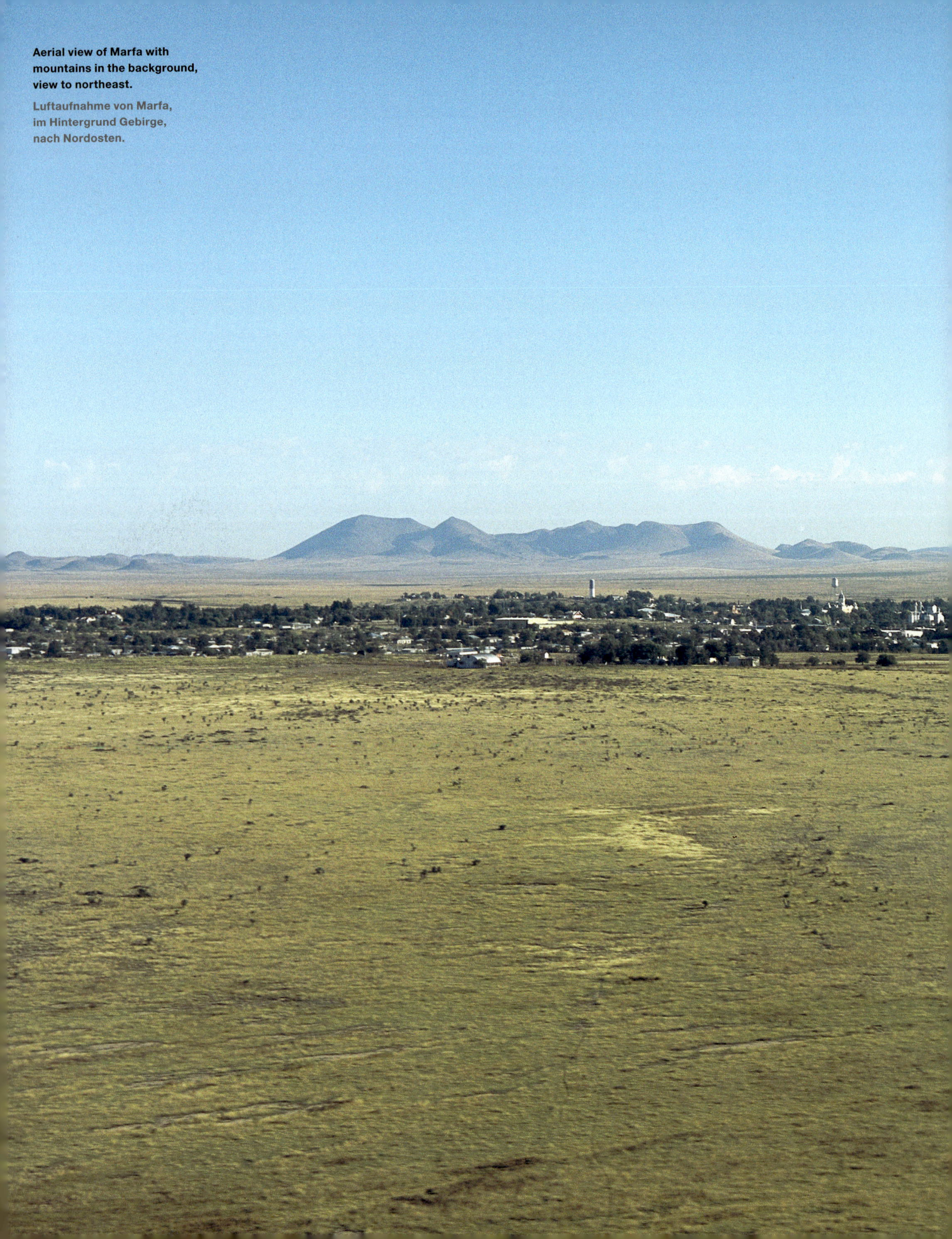

Aerial view of Marfa with mountains in the background, view to northeast.

Luftaufnahme von Marfa, im Hintergrund Gebirge, nach Nordosten.

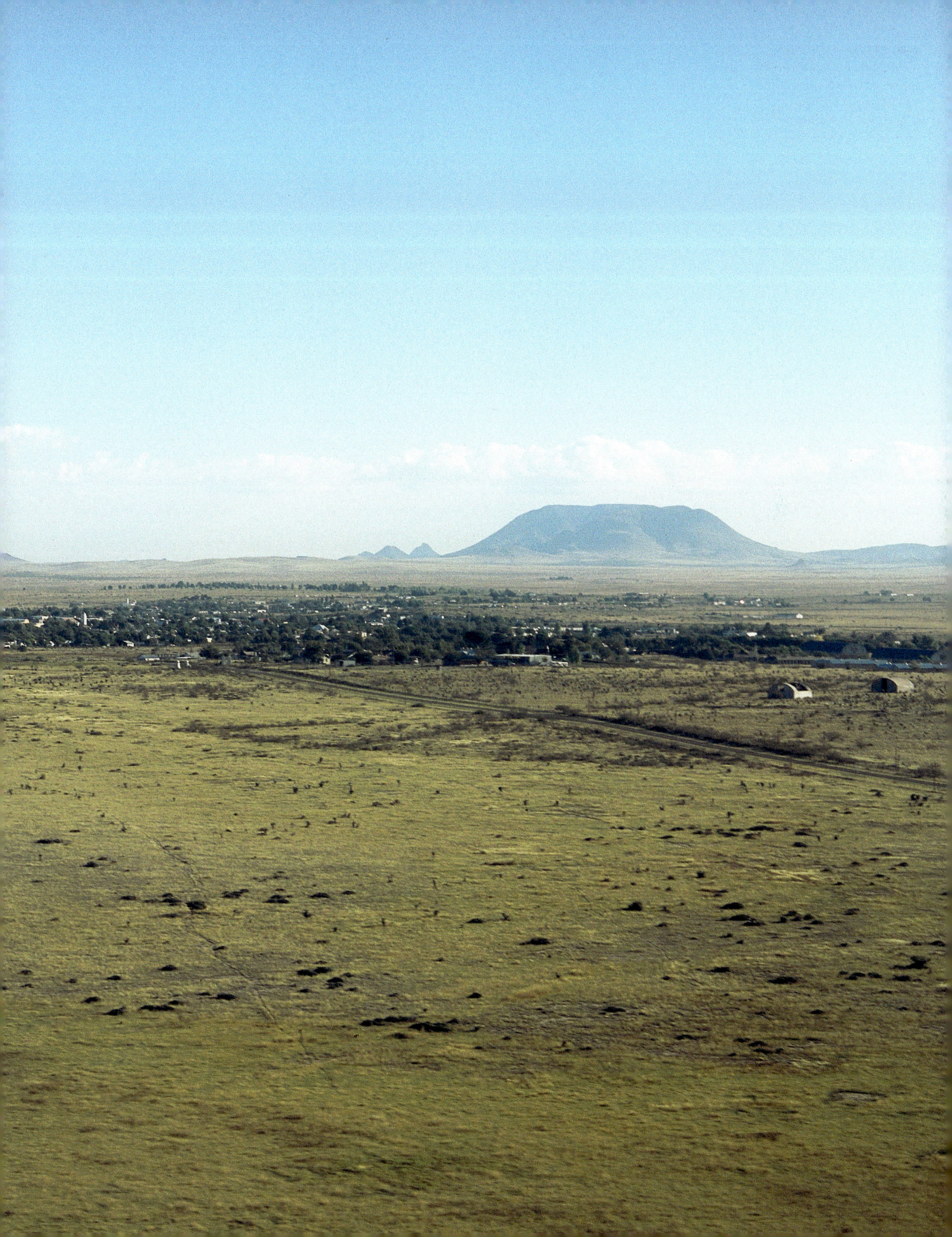

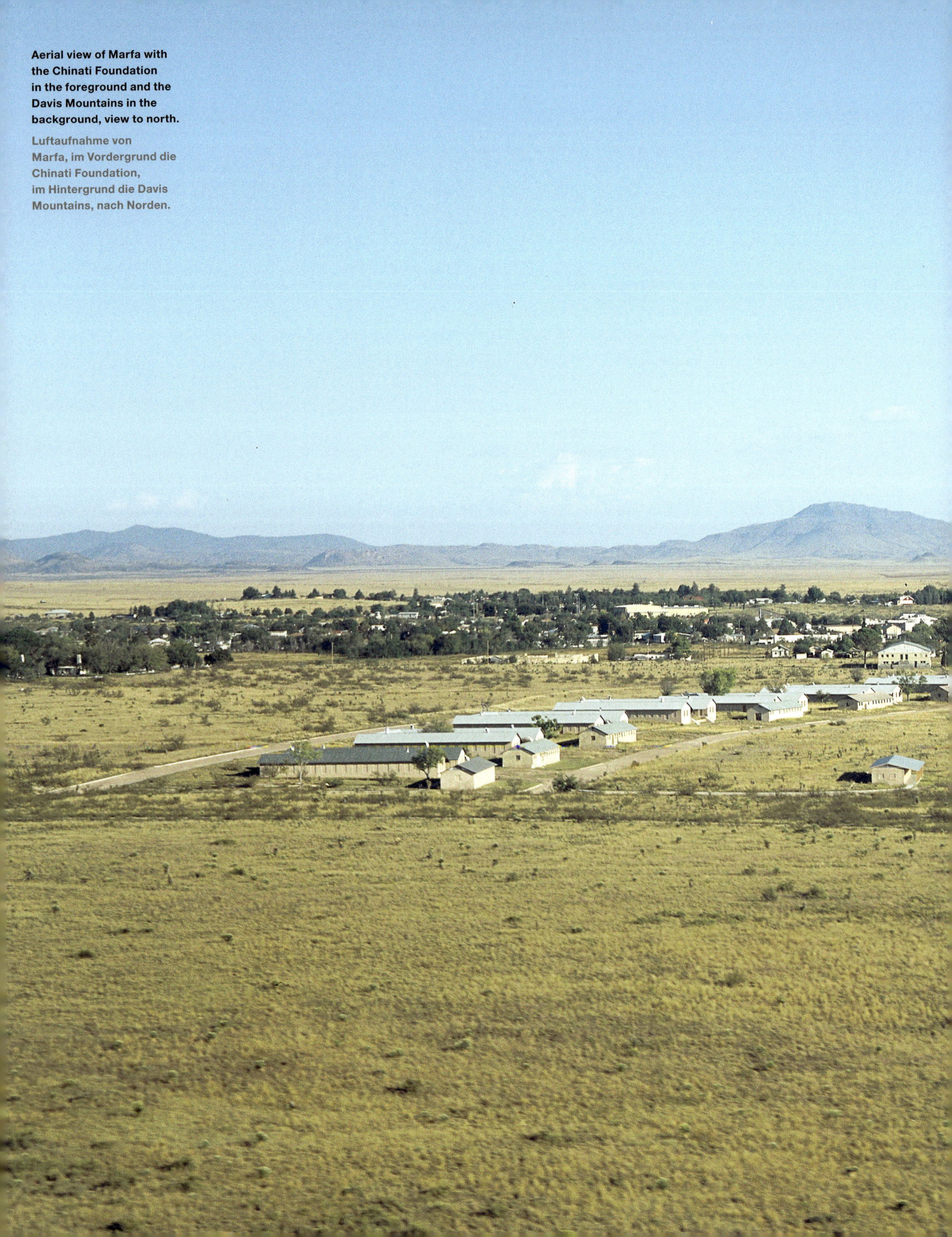

Aerial view of Marfa with the Chinati Foundation in the foreground and the Davis Mountains in the background, view to north.

Luftaufnahme von Marfa, im Vordergrund die Chinati Foundation, im Hintergrund die Davis Mountains, nach Norden.

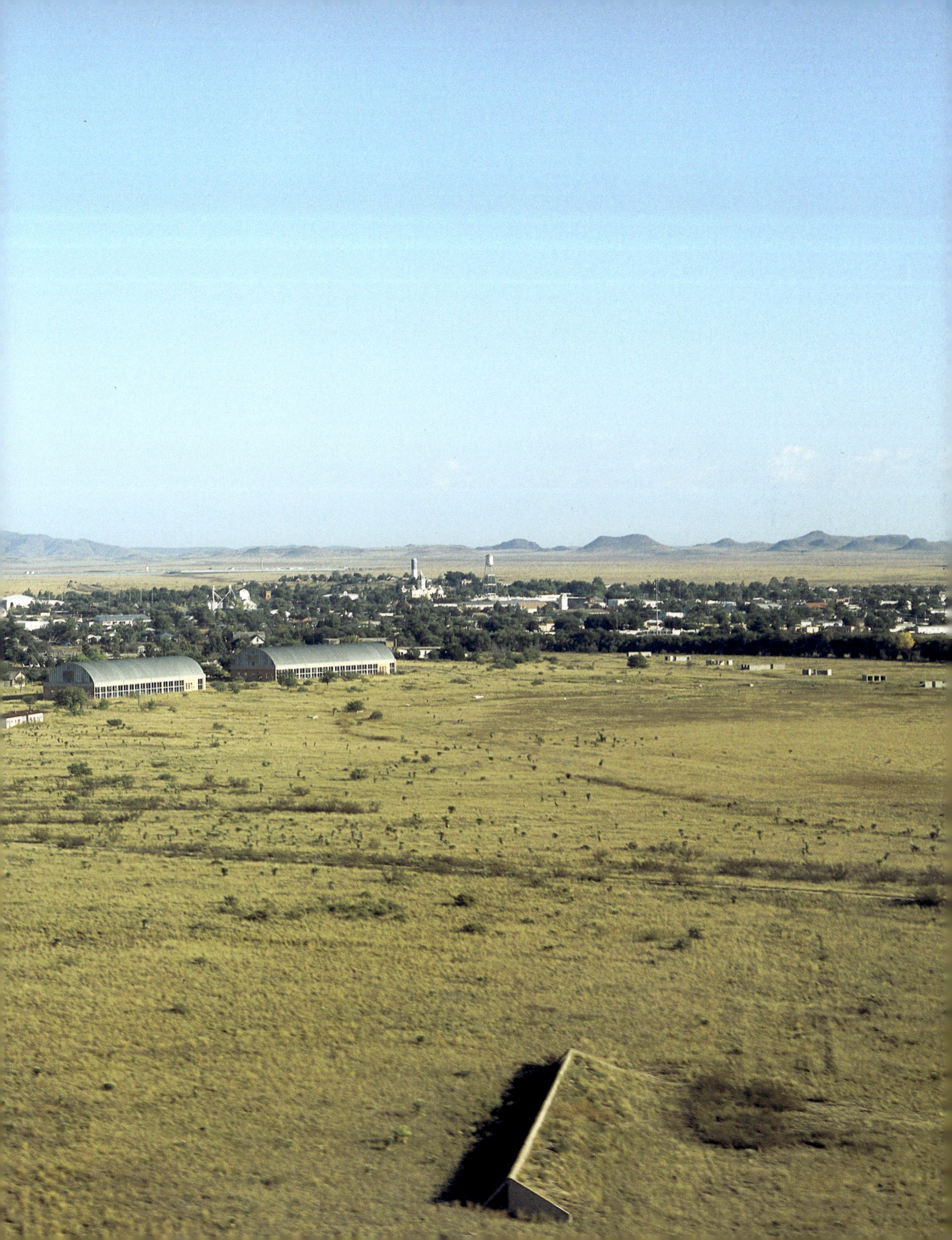

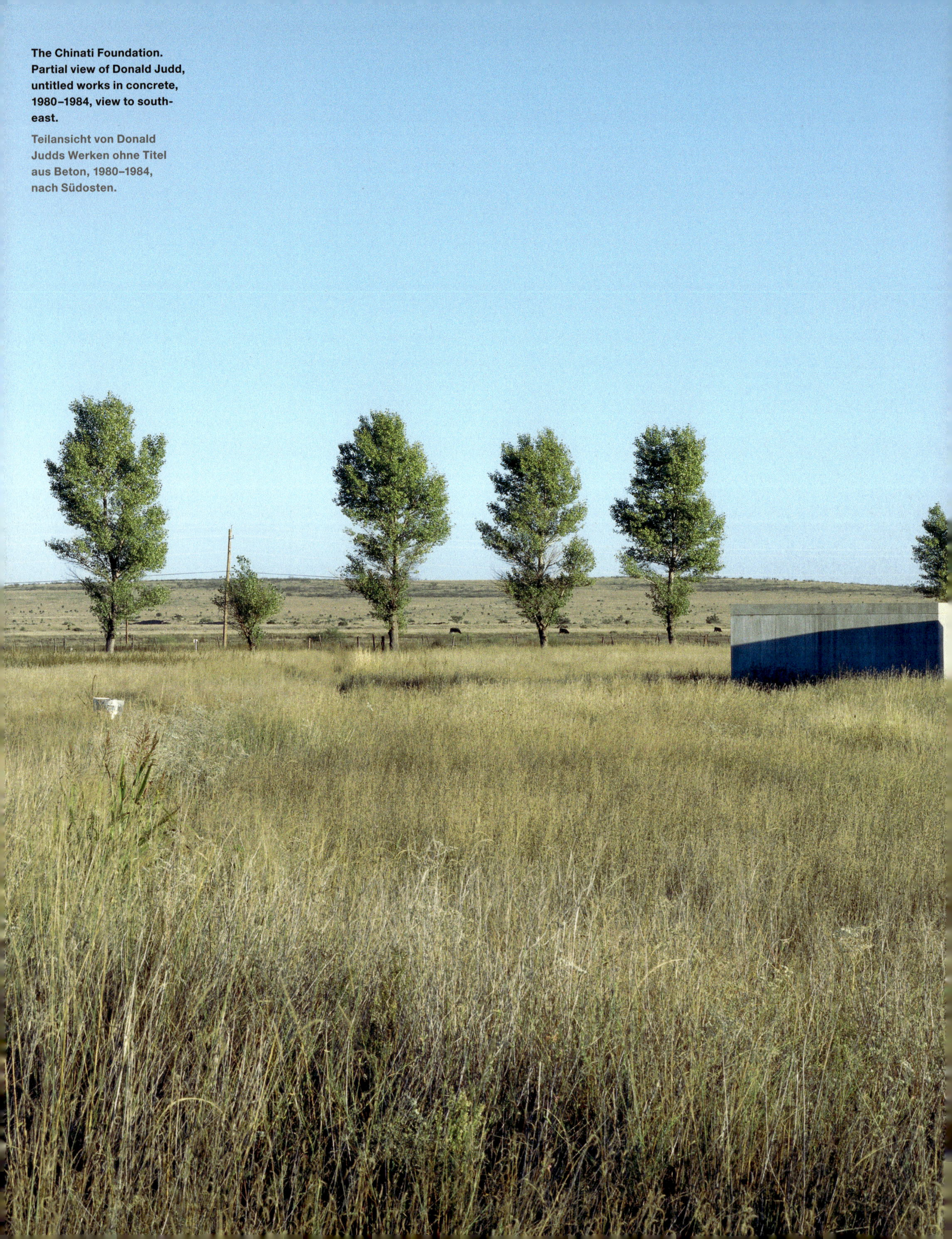

The Chinati Foundation. Partial view of Donald Judd, untitled works in concrete, 1980–1984, view to south-east.

Teilansicht von Donald Judds Werken ohne Titel aus Beton, 1980–1984, nach Südosten.

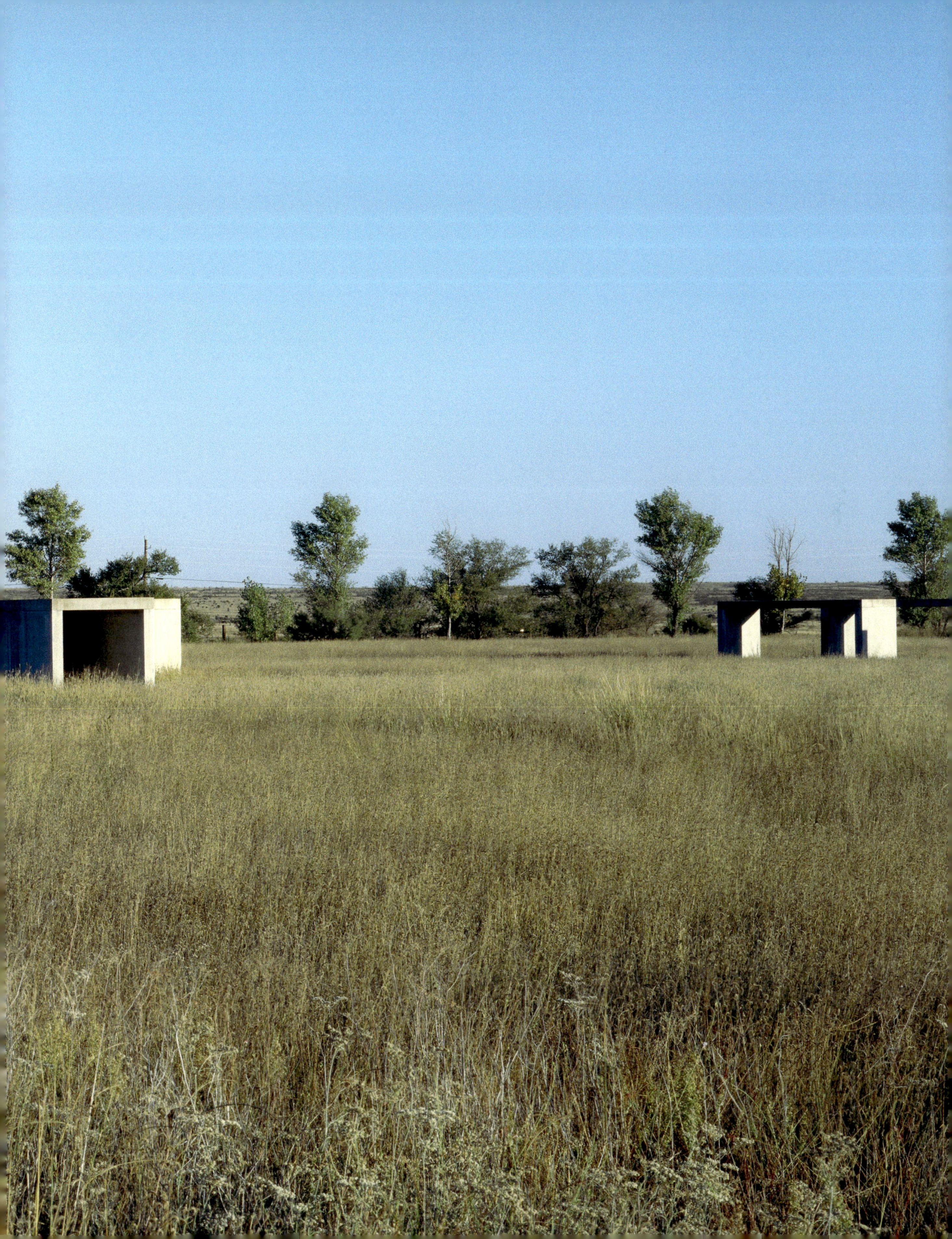

The Chinati Foundation. Partial view of Donald Judd, untitled works in concrete, 1980–1984, view to north.

Teilansicht von Donald Judds Werken Ohne Titel aus Beton 1980–1984, nach Norden.

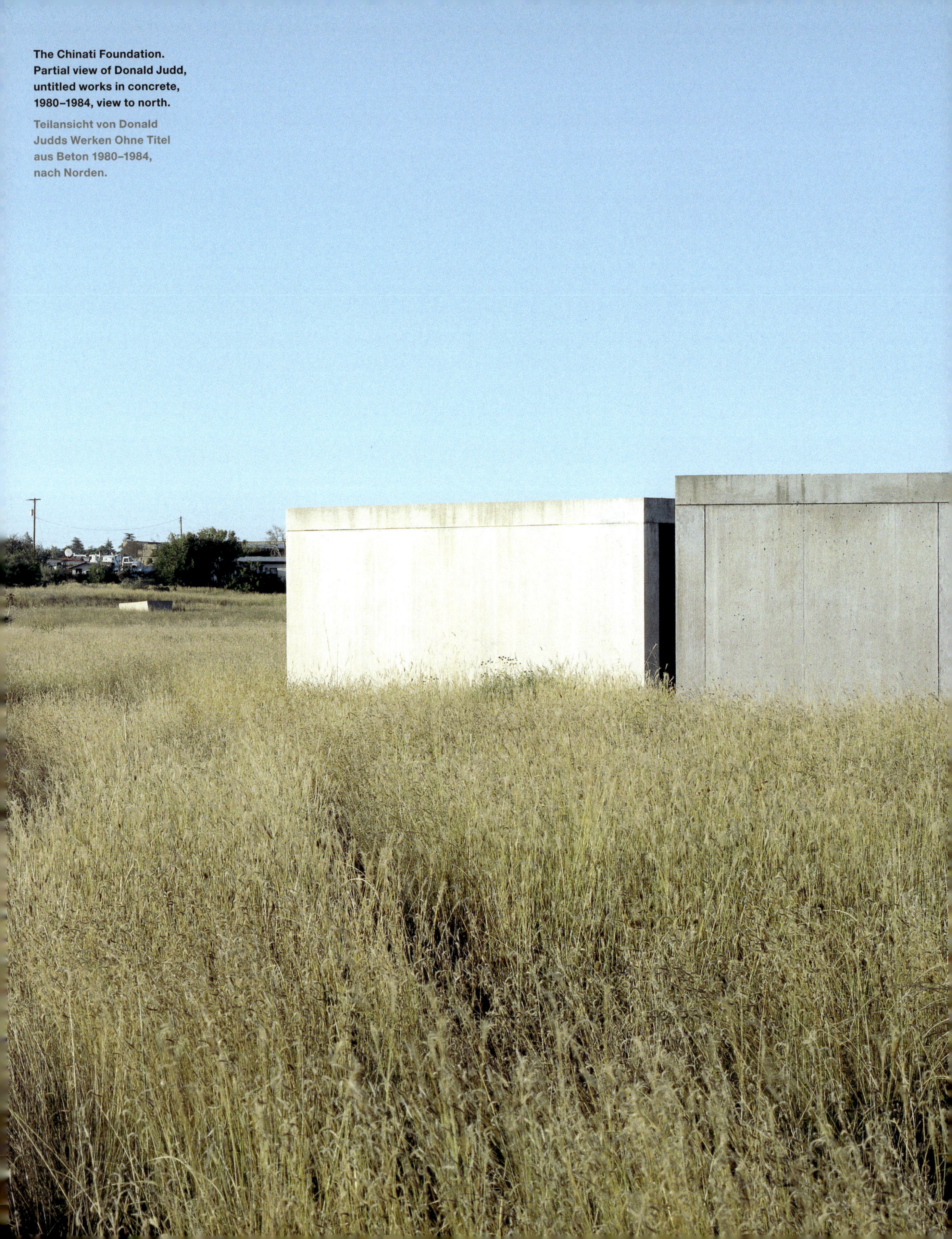

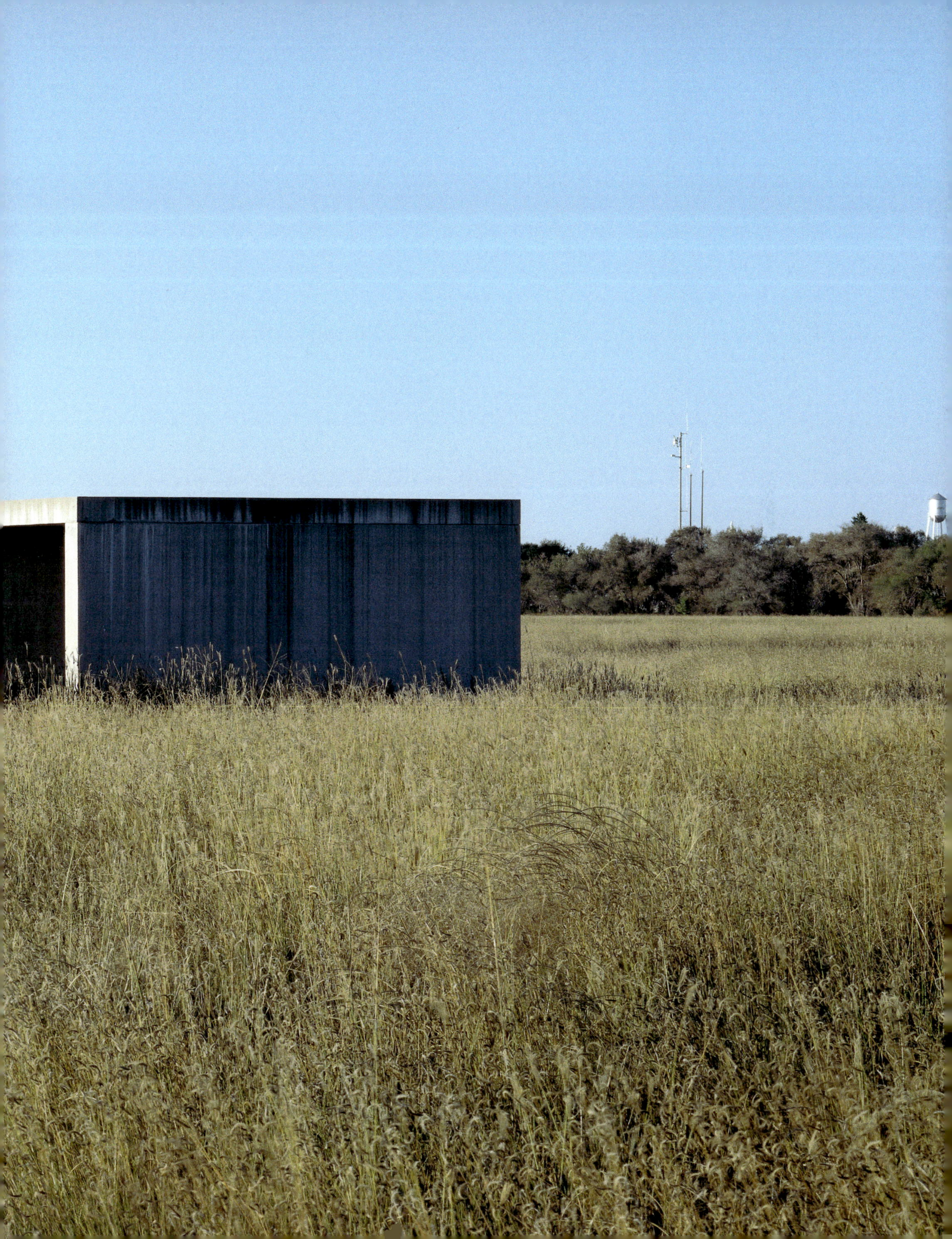

DONALD JUDD
ARCHITECTURE IN MARFA, TEXAS

URS PETER FLÜCKIGER

2ND EXPANDED EDITION
BIRKHÄUSER
BASEL

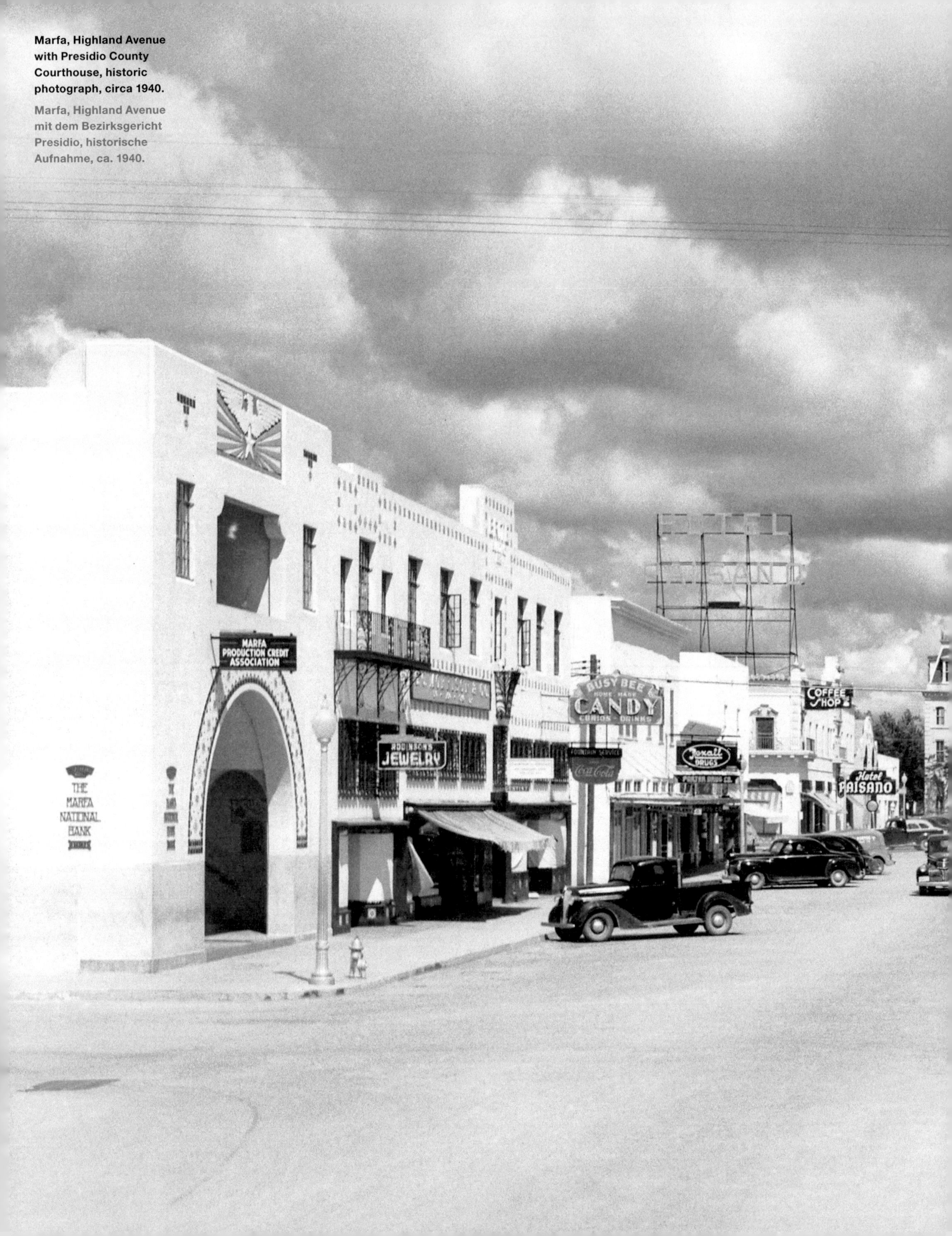

Marfa, Highland Avenue with Presidio County Courthouse, historic photograph, circa 1940.

Marfa, Highland Avenue mit dem Bezirksgericht Presidio, historische Aufnahme, ca. 1940.

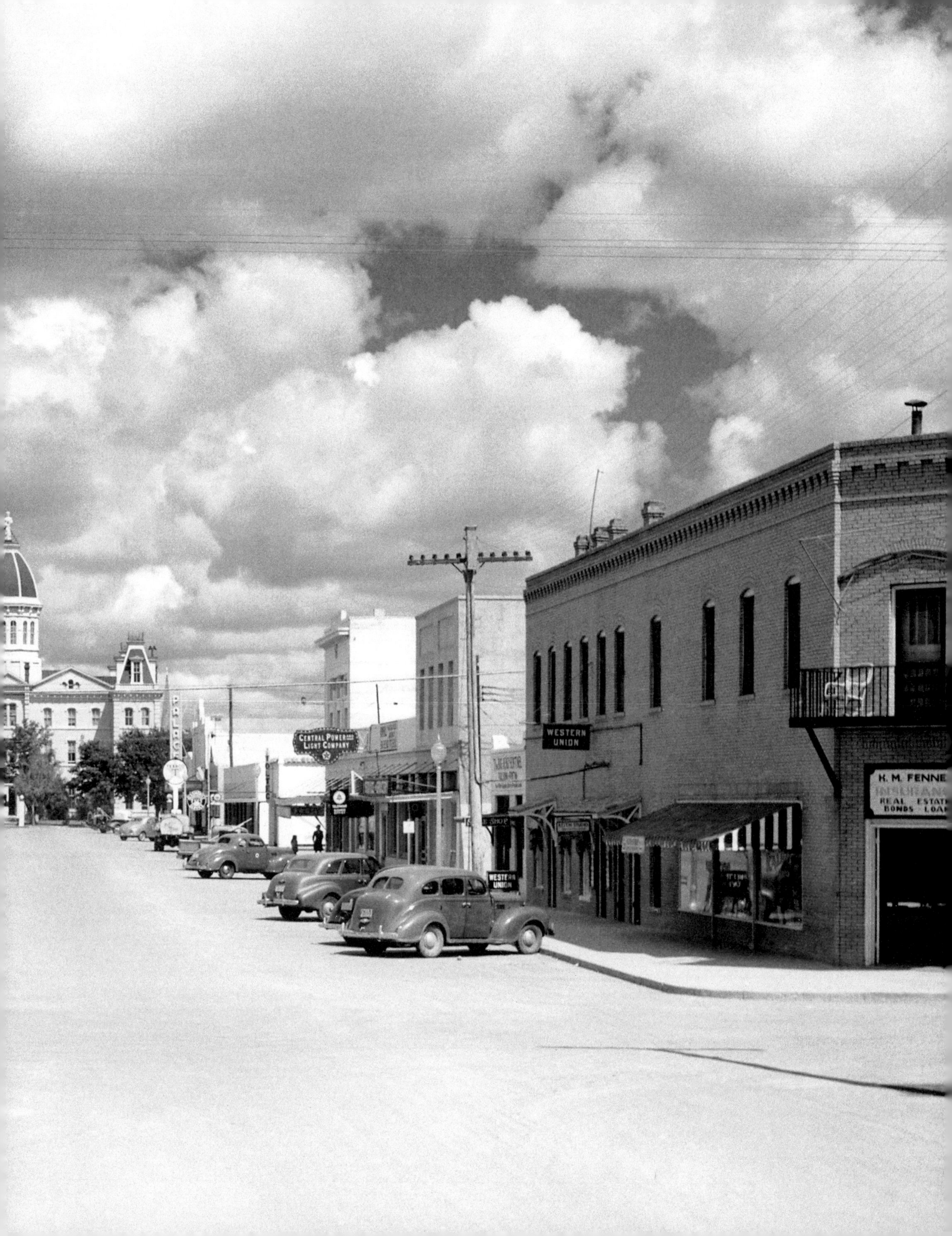
CENTRAL POWER
LIGHT COMPANY
WESTERN
UNION
WESTERN
UNION

PLAN OF MARFA LAGEPLAN VON MARFA

1 **LA MANSANA DE CHINATI** LA MANSANA DE CHINATI
(JUDD FOUNDATION)

2 **THE ARENA** DIE ARENA
(THE CHINATI FOUNDATION)

3 **ARTILLERY SHED 1** ARTILLERIE-HALLE 1
(THE CHINATI FOUNDATION)

4 **ARTILLERY SHED 2** ARTILLERIE-HALLE 2
(THE CHINATI FOUNDATION)

5 **THE CHAMBERLAIN BUILDING** CHAMBERLAIN-GEBÄUDE
(THE CHINATI FOUNDATION)

6 **ARCHITECTURE STUDIO** ARCHITEKTURSTUDIO
(JUDD FOUNDATION)

7 **The Gatehouse** Pförtnerhaus
(JUDD FOUNDATION)

8 **The Cobb House** Haus Cobb
(JUDD FOUNDATION)

9 **THE WHYTE BUILDING** WHYTE-GEBÄUDE
(JUDD FOUNDATION)

10 **The Art Studio** Kunstatelier
(JUDD FOUNDATION)

11 **The Architecture Office** Architekturbüro
(JUDD FOUNDATION)

12 **The Ranch Office** Ranchbüro
(JUDD FOUNDATION)

13 **The Locker Plant** Schlachterei
(THE CHINATI FOUNDATION)

14 **The Ice Plant** Eisfabrik
(THE CHINATI FOUNDATION)

15 **The Print Building** Grafikgebäude
(JUDD FOUNDATION)

16 **15 untitled works in concrete** 15 Werke ohne Titel aus Beton
(THE CHINATI FOUNDATION)

17 **The Concrete Buildings** Die Beton-Gebäude
(THE CHINATI FOUNDATION)

18 **Row of Cottonwood Trees** Reihe von Pappeln

Note capitalized titles are represented in this publication.

Die mit Großbuchstaben bezeichneten Objekte
sind in dieser Publikation dargestellt.

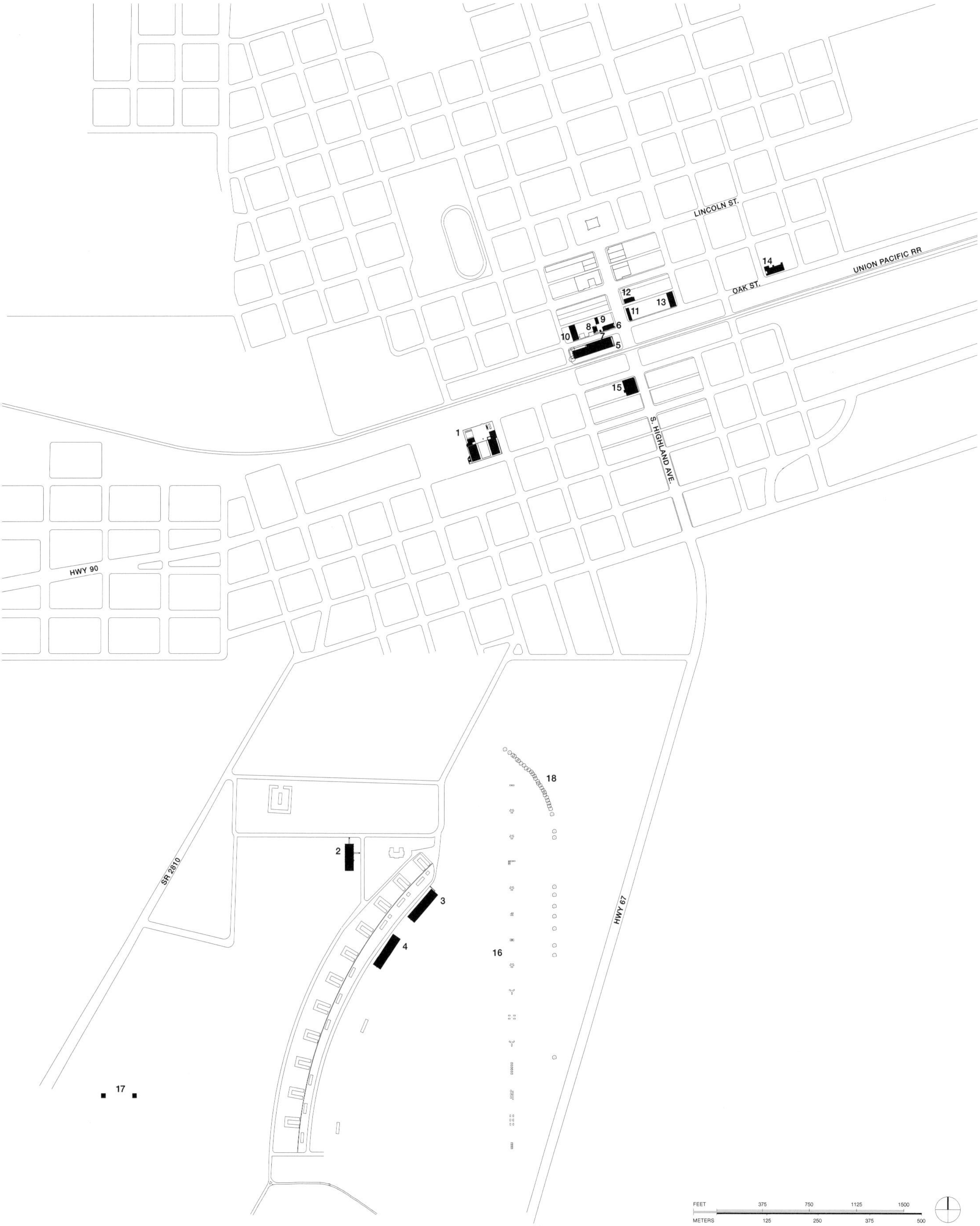

LINCOLN ST.
OAK ST.
UNION PACIFIC RR
S. HIGHLAND AVE.
HWY 90
SR 2810
HWY 67
1
2
3
4
5
6
7
8
9
10
11
12
13
14
15
16
17
18
FEET
375
750
1125
1500
METERS
125
250
375
500

For Carol and Lucas

"The first step in architecture would be to do nothing whatsoever."
Donald Judd[1]

1 Judd, Donald. Guest lecture at the School of Architecture, University of Texas, Austin, Texas, March 9, 1992. Audio Recording. University of Texas at Austin School of Architecture archives, Alexander Architectural Archives, University of Texas Libraries, The University of Texas at Austin

INHALTSVERZEICHNIS

19 VORWORT: PROPORTION ALLER BELANGE, W. MARK GUNDERSON

25 EINFÜHRUNG: DONALD JUDDS ARCHITEKTUR IN MARFA, TEXAS

50 LA MANSANA DE CHINATI / THE BLOCK

74 DIE ARTILLERIE-HALLEN

86 DIE ARENA

98 DAS CHAMBERLAIN-GEBÄUDE

110 DAS ARCHITEKTURSTUDIO

119 DAS WHYTE-GEBÄUDE

128 CASA MORALES, OF AYALA DE CHINATI

145 CASA PEREZ, OF AYALA DE CHINATI

162 LAS CASAS, AYALA DE CHINATI

178 NACHWORT URS PETER FLÜCKIGER

ANHANG

210 DONALD JUDD, BIOGRAFISCHE NOTIZ

210 CHRONOLOGISCHES VERZEICHNIS DER ARCHITEKTONISCHEN WERKE

213 ANMERKUNGEN ZU DEN ZEICHNUNGEN

214 ÜBER DEN AUTOR

215 DANK 2. AUFLAGE

215 ABBILDUNGSNACHWEIS

Die Rechte für alle Kunstwerke und Architektur von Donald Judd liegt bei der Judd Foundation/Artist Rights Society (ARS) New York

TABLE OF CONTENTS

19 FOREWORD: PROPORTION OF CONCERNS, W. MARK GUNDERSON

25 INTRODUCTION: DONALD JUDD'S ARCHITECTURE IN MARFA, TEXAS

50 LA MANSANA DE CHINATI / THE BLOCK

74 THE ARTILLERY SHEDS

86 THE ARENA

98 THE CHAMBERLAIN BUILDING

110 THE ARCHITECTURE STUDIO

119 THE WHYTE BUILDING

128 CASA MORALES, OF AYALA DE CHINATI

145 CASA PEREZ, OF AYALA DE CHINATI

162 LAS CASAS, AYALA DE CHINATI

178 AFTERWORD URS PETER FLUECKIGER

APPENDIX

210 DONALD JUDD, BIOGRAPHICAL NOTE

210 CHRONOLOGICAL INDEX OF DONALD JUDD'S ARCHITECTURAL WORK

213 A NOTE ABOUT THE DRAWINGS

214 ABOUT THE AUTHOR

215 ACKNOWLEDGEMENTS 2ND EDITION

215 PHOTOGRAPHIC CREDITS

All art and architecture by Donald Judd is copyrighted by Judd Foundation/Artist Rights Society (ARS) New York

W. MARK GUNDERSON

VORWORT: PROPORTION ALLER BELANGE

FOREWORD: PROPORTION OF CONCERNS

„… tiefe Gedanken, einfach ausgedrückt“[1]
Vincent van Gogh, 1883

Der erste Akt der Orientierung und Bewertung besteht im sinnlichen und kritischen „Aufnehmen“ von Informationen, einem „Abschätzen“, wenn man so will, dem „Lesen“ der räumlichen Gegebenheiten oder des physischen und konzeptionellen Kontexts, um daraus ein Verständnis zu generieren. Dies kann als intuitiver Akt betrachtet werden, als Synthese aus früheren Erfahrungen und Erkenntnissen. Danach beginnt man zu überlegen und abzuwägen, zu denken und zu handeln. Erst einatmen, dann ausatmen. Ein funktionierendes Rahmenkonzept zu erstellen, im wahrsten Wortsinn „den Sinn zu erkennen“, ist elementar und unentbehrlich für das Grundverständnis eines Ortes oder einer Situation. Christopher Norris schrieb in *Deconstruction, Omnibus Volume*, dass es ohne eine Vorstellung von Struktur, Architektur, Bauen oder Konstruktion nahezu unmöglich sei, sequenziell zu denken. Beim Bauen wird mit Schnurgerüsten, heutzutage mit Lasern, ein Gitter erstellt; in der Archäologie wird ein Raster über einen Fundort gelegt. Beide Vorgehensweisen beruhen auf der Schnurvermessung mit verknoteten Seilen im alten Ägypten. Das englische Wort „survey“ für „Vermessung“ leitet sich aus dem lateinischen Begriff für „sehen“ oder „überblicken“ ab. Bei der Vermessung werden wichtige Punkte mit Nägeln markiert. So schafft man eine Bezugshöhe – eine Art der Strukturierung, die das Wesen der Architektur ist und es ermöglicht, Daten zu sammeln und zueinander in Beziehung zu setzen. Im Bauwesen wird damit die Gestaltung des Projekts ermöglicht. Auch ein Arzt führt beim ersten Besuch eines Patienten zunächst einige allgemeine Untersuchungen, Tests und Messungen durch. Erst diese Bezugswerte ermöglichen es ihm, einen sinnvollen Behandlungsplan zu erstellen.

Das Messen als eine Form der Beschreibung ist womöglich die einzige Art der Darstellung, die Donald Judd als philosophisch valide oder integer bezeichnen würde – eine Beschreibung mittels Messung und Mathematik statt durch die ungenaue Sprache. Das simple numerische Notieren der wichtigsten physischen Eigenschaften in Form von Maßen beinhaltet eine Vielzahl an Informationen. Belegt wird diese Tatsache dadurch,

"… profound things said in a plain way."[1]
Vincent van Gogh, 1883

The first act of orientation and assessment is a sensual and critical "taking in" of information—to "size something up" in colloquial terms—to "read" the extant spatial conditions or the physical and conceptual context in order to attempt to orient and understand it. This might be considered an intuitive act, the synthesis of prior actual experience and understandings. One begins then to consider and deliberate; to think and act. Inhale, then exhale. The establishment of a working conceptual framework, literally "making sense", is rudimentary and essential to the initial understanding of a place or situation. Christopher Norris wrote in *Deconstruction, Omnibus Volume* that "Without some notion of structure, architectonic, building or construction, it's virtually impossible to think in a sequential way". In construction a grid is laid out with string and batter boards, set now by lasers; in archeology a string grid is laid over a site. Both have ancient precedent in Egyptian "rules of the cord" measurement by knotted rope. In survey work (the word "survey" is derived from Latin for "seeing" or "overseeing") pins are located at the salient points. This creation of reference datum—an act of structuring and therefore at the essence of architecture—provides for collecting evidence and then relating that data. In construction, it allows "lay out" of the project. A first visit to a doctor begins with a "baseline" set of scans, tests and measurements. Such a reference enables meaningful thought towards a plan of action.

Mensuration as a form of description might be the only form of delineation that Donald Judd would find philosophically valid or of integrity—measurement and mathematics as description versus the imprecision of language. The simple numerical notation of the salient physical features by dimension contains considerable information. Judd's use of dimensional references such as 50 × 50 × 100 gives evidence of this respect, particularly as he refused to "name" work in order to avoid other references or allusions.

Language and poetry have more accuracy within a certain realm—of emotion for example—but the concision and economy of number as fixed information in the delineation of physical

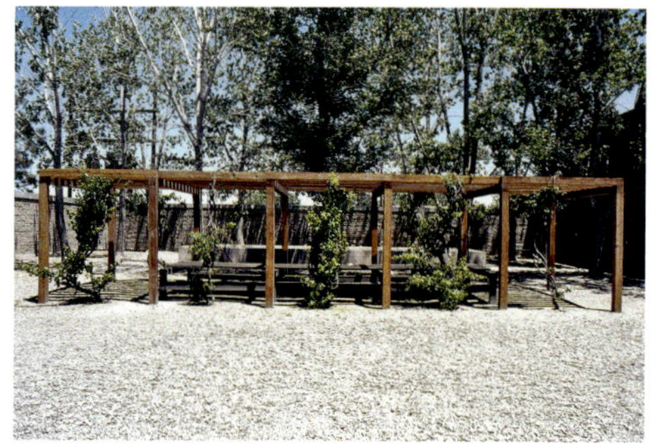

FIG./ABB. 01

Pergola at La Mansana de Chinati / The Block, Judd Foundation, Marfa, Texas

Pergola in La Mansana de Chinati / The Block, Judd Foundation, Marfa, Texas

dass Judd Maßreferenzen wie 50 × 50 × 100 für seine Werke verwendete. Er lehnte es ab, diese in Worten zu beschreiben, um Missverständnisse oder Deutungen zu vermeiden.

Sprache und Poesie sind in bestimmten Bereichen, beispielsweise wenn es um Gefühle geht, präziser einsetzbar, während bei der Beschreibung physischer Formen und Räume die Präzision und Prägnanz von Zahlen als feste Informationseinheiten objektiv und nachhaltig sind. Der intrinsische Wert von Zahlen als Mittel der Beschreibung liegt darin, dass sie langfristig nicht verfälscht beziehungsweise missverstanden werden können. Und die ausgedruckten Pläne mit Grundrissen und Schnitten sind dauerhafter als ihre digitalen Pendants, deren Daten stets ein geeignetes Speichersystem benötigen. Die Nutzung von Tinte auf Papier hat hingegen schon seit Jahrtausenden Bestand.

Die akkuraten Computerzeichnungen – hauptsächlich Grundrisse und Schnitte –, die Flückiger mit seinen Studierenden vor Ort aus analogen/händischen Messungen (statt mit modernen Scanning-Technologien) erstellt hatte, wurden anschließend in ein digitales CAD-Format überführt. Seit ihrer Fertigstellung bilden sie präzise ab, welche Intentionen Judd mit seiner Anordnung der Werke im Raum verfolgte. Eine solche Dokumentation ist als historische Ressource sowie als Grundlage für ein kritisches Verständnis von unschätzbarem Wert. Und ihre Publikation in Form eines realen, gedruckten Buchs durch ein renommiertes Verlagshaus stellt einen signifikanten Beitrag zur künftigen Bewertung von Judds Gesamtwerk dar.

Der Künstler selbst hat viel über den Unterschied zwischen Kunst und Architektur geschrieben und dabei seine Gründe erläutert, warum er die Grenze zwischen den beiden nicht verwischen möchte. Gleichwohl ist seine Sensibilität, seine „Stimme“, in beiden Disziplinen ohne Weiteres erkennbar und lesbar, und es gibt klare und schlüssige formale Assoziationen zwischen seinen Werken in beiden Bereichen, die die Bedeutung des Umfelds hervorheben, in dem ein oder mehrere Werke innerhalb eines Raums, den Judd ebenfalls bearbeitet hat, angeordnet sind. Die „Funktion“ stellte für Judd das grundlegende Unterscheidungsmerkmal dar. In einem frühen Kommentar begründete er seine Entscheidung, eher Künstler als Architekt zu sein, damit, dass ein Architekt mit der Öffentlichkeit interagieren müsse.

form and space is objective and lasting. The intrinsic value of data as description is this—that it cannot be contaminated over time or misconstrued. And the printed drawing with such plans and sections may far outlast their digital equivalent, whose data is constantly over time “chasing” a storage system. Ironically, ink on papyrus has endured for thousands of years.

Thus it is that these accurate computer drawings—primarily plans and sections—produced by Flueckiger and students *in situ* from analog/hand measurement (as opposed to newer digital scanning technologies) were then transposed to digital CAD format. In the years from their creation they have, and will, show with accuracy Judd’s intentions in placement and in the relationships between work and space. Documentation such as this is invaluable as a historic resource and as basis for critical understanding. And their publication in the form of a tangible, printed book by a renowned publisher is a significant and meaningful contribution to the continued future assessment of Judd’s body of work.

There is much written by the artist as to the distinction between art and architecture, and his reasons for not blurring the line between them. At the same time his sensibility, his “voice”, is readily evident and legible in both disciplines, and there are clear and compelling formal associations between his works in each which enhance the situations in which a work, or several, are placed within a space he has also dealt with. The issues related to “function” provide the primary distinction for Judd. An early comment described his decision to be an artist as opposed to an architect because of the need for an architect to deal with the public.

Obwohl er sich in Texas wegen staatlicher Zulassungsvorschriften nie offiziell als „Architekt“ bezeichnen durfte, war es offensichtlich, dass er sich in seiner Arbeit mit Gebäuden und Bauformen architektonischen Belangen widmete, und zwar auf einem geistigen Niveau, das viele zugelassene Architekten nie erreichen würden. Judds „Hilfsmittel“ waren seine Ideen; ganz besonders sein Feingefühl für die richtige Platzierung und sein Sinn für Nützlichkeit und Angemessenheit. Seine Schwäche – in baulicher Hinsicht – war sein fehlendes Verständnis (oder auch Interesse) für jene Aspekte der architektonischen Komposition und Logik, die Wetter und Witterung betreffen; soll heißen: die Notwendigkeit, Wasser aus dem Gebäudeinneren fernzuhalten oder das Gebäude durch sorgfältige Detailausbildung vor dem Verfall zu schützen. Die Form wurde nach Judds Auffassung von anderen Faktoren bestimmt. Tatsächlich ist es diese Nichtbeachtung oder auch dieses Unverständnis, auch was die Bauausführung angeht, das den Erhalt und die Pflege seines Werkes bis heute schwierig macht.

Dass sich Judd in Marfa bestehende Bauwerke aneignete und diese umnutzte, spricht für seine Art der pragmatischen und respektvollen (wenn nicht sogar sinnvollen) Inbesitznahme und belegt sein fehlendes Interesse an gezielter architektonischer Gestaltung. Seine Eingriffe waren wohlüberlegt und rücksichtsvoll, wobei er vorhandene Elemente bewahrte, wenn er sie für geeignet erachtete. Aber hauptsächlich entfernte er unausgereifte Komponenten und hob insbesondere Struktur, Proportion, Raum und Form deutlich hervor. Seine Bemühungen, Raum und Werk als „Tatsachen“ zu etablieren, waren bemerkenswert. Über die Spring Street 101 sagte Judd: „... jedwede Veränderung musste mit der ursprünglichen Situation im Einklang stehen. Für mich war wichtig, dass ich in dem Haus leben und arbeiten konnte und, noch wichtiger, noch entscheidender, dass ich darin Arbeiten von mir und von anderen installieren konnte. ... Ich verbrachte eine Menge Zeit damit, die Kunstwerke zu platzieren, und eine Menge Zeit, in Übereinstimmung damit die Renovierung zu planen. Alles sollte von Anfang an gründlich überlegt und dauerhaft sein, was es, verschiedenen Leuten zum Trotz, immer noch ist.“[2]

While he was never able to legally use the title "architect" in Texas due to state licensing laws, it was clear to all that his work with buildings and construction was addressing architectural concerns, and at a level of quality conceptually far more advanced than most licensed practitioners. Judd's "tools" in this endeavor were his ideas; especially his sensitivity to place and his sense of use and appropriateness. His weakness—architecturally speaking—was his lack of understanding (or perhaps concern) for those aspects of architectural composition and logic which result from weather and weathering; the need to keep water out of an enclosed structure or to protect it from deterioration by careful detailing. Form, for Judd, was determined by other factors. It is in fact this disregard or lack of understanding—including aspects of literal architectural structure—which contributes to some of the ongoing issues with conservation and maintenance of his work.

Judd's appropriation and repurposing of extant Marfa structures speak to his regard for pragmatic and respectful (if not expedient) occupation and his lack of desire for acts of willful architectural "design". His actions were considered and considerate—reusing elements where he determined their appropriateness, but primarily removal of poorly conceived work and, crucially, the clarification of structure, proportion, space and form. His efforts were remarkable towards the establishment of space and work as "fact". Speaking of 101 Spring Street Judd said "... any changes must be compatible. My requirements were that the building be useful for living and working and importantly, more definitely, be a space in which to install work of mine and others ... I spent a great deal of time placing the art and a great deal designing the renovation in accordance. Everything from the first was intended to be thoroughly considered and to be permanent, as, despite several, it still is."[2]

The act of occupancy "without associations" or referential precedent was in keeping with his expressed intentions philosophically. This included a profound respect for the givens of circumstance and the reciprocity of new and old. He was not prone to confuse the two and held well-documented disdain for new materials or products which attempted to refer to other

Der Akt der Aneignung „ohne Assoziationen“ oder referenzielles Vorbild geht in philosophischer Hinsicht konform mit seinen geäußerten Absichten. Dazu gehörte ein tiefer Respekt vor den Gegebenheiten und die Reziprozität von Alt und Neu. Er neigte nicht dazu, die beiden zu vermischen, und hatte eine gut dokumentierte Abscheu vor neuen Materialien oder Produkten, die anderen Materialien ähneln, sich völlig gegensätzlich verhalten, eine Nachbildung eines anderen Materials oder einer anderen Sprache sind.

Man könnte sagen, die Ethik des Erschaffens und Bauens basiert auf der pfleglichen und verantwortungsvollen Nutzung der zur Verfügung stehenden Materialien – wahre Ökonomie. Wahrscheinlich wurde Judd stark von den Werten beeinflusst, die seinen Vater bei der Holzverarbeitung leiteten. Die Wiederverwendung von Materialien, oder in diesem Fall von Bauwerken, die weiterhin einen Zweck erfüllen können, steht im Einklang mit dieser Ethik des angemessenen Vorgehens. Wenn Judd verlassene Gebäude kaufte, dann nicht in dem Bestreben, seinen Besitz zu mehren, sondern es ging ihm vielmehr darum, die Bauten, die seiner Meinung nach erhaltenswert waren, davor zu bewahren, durch Nichtbeachtung zu verrotten, auch wenn er nicht sofort eine Verwendung für sie hatte.

Nahezu unbekannt war und ist sein Stolz darauf, niemals unberührtes Land bebaut zu haben („I've never built anything on new land")[3]. Das wäre ihm ein Gräuel gewesen, selbst in einer Kultur, in der alles auf Entwicklung und Landnutzung ausgerichtet ist. Seine diesbezügliche Selbstbeschränkung hatte keine rein künstlerischen Gründe, sondern war ein ethischer und moralischer Akt. Judds Hochachtung vor der Landschaft ist gut dokumentiert, auch wenn anfangs nur schwer erkennbar ist, auf welche besondere Weise sie sich manifestiert. Als er von der Spring Street 101 nach Marfa umzog, brachte er beispielsweise seine Kakteensammlung mit. Und dass er die 165 Sotol-Pflanzen, die rasterförmig zwischen dem Chamberlain-Gebäude und den Eisenbahngleisen wachsen, ganz bewusst dort anpflanzte, fiele den Besuchern wohl kaum auf, wenn sie nicht explizit darauf aufmerksam gemacht würden. Darum ist der in diesem Buch (S. 106) dargestellte Übersichtsplan, auf dem die Pflanzen eingezeichnet sind, auch so wichtig für das Verständnis dieser Maß-

materials or behave in counterfeit manner or in replication of another material or language.

The ethics of making or construction might be said to be rooted in care and stewardship of materials at hand—true economy—and it is likely that the artist was influenced greatly by his father's woodworking values. Reuse of materials, or in this case structures which could still serve a purpose, would be very much in keeping with this ethic of appropriate action. Judd was not acquiring extant buildings as someone attempting to simply expand his holdings, but rather in many instances to keep something from being destroyed by local disregard for structures that he felt deserved to exist whether he had an immediate purpose for it or not.

In addition, his pride in not touching virgin soil ("I've never built anything on new land")[3] was, and is, virtually unheard of, even anathema, in a culture predicated upon "development" and "land use". His restraint was an ethical and moral action more than strictly "artistic". His deep regard for the landscape is well documented even if the specific manifestations might be difficult to see at first. When Judd, for example, moved to Marfa he brought his collection of cacti from 101 Spring Street with him. His deliberate planting of a low grid of 165 sotol alongside the Chamberlain building and the railroad track is almost invisible to visitors for whom such an arrangement would mean very little if not pointed out. So that the site plan showing them in this book (p. 106) is quite important to the understanding of this act. Likewise, Judd's alignment of the 15 concrete works along a true north-south cardinal axis or his works with dual or paired horizontal edges—one to "level" and the second to the site slope—speak as well to this engagement with the landscape and with circumstance or existing conditions.

There is much evidence of his belief in a tight "urban" density in the open landscape to minimize footprint and therefore damage to place; the reduction of architectural massing to the compact and the essential. The ranch houses documented here are perfect examples of such prudent and efficient use of materials available, in opposition to the typical and ubiquitous spreading of structures around an open site in west Texas. Judd wrote "This has two small houses which I've thought a lot about, but

nahme. Ebenso sind Judds Anordnung von 15 Werken aus Beton entlang einer Nord-Süd-Hauptachse oder seine Arbeiten mit doppelt oder paarweise angeordneten horizontalen Kanten – eine waagerecht, die zweite parallel zum Gelände – ein Beleg für seine Interaktion mit der Landschaft und der Lage beziehungsweise den vorhandenen Gegebenheiten.

Es gibt zahlreiche Belege für Judds Bestreben, eine städtische Dichte innerhalb der offenen Landschaft zu schaffen, um dadurch den Fußabdruck und somit die Schädigung eines Ortes zu minimieren; er reduzierte die architektonische Masse auf das Kompakte und Wesentliche. Die hier dokumentierten Ranchhäuser sind perfekte Beispiele für diese umsichtige und effiziente Nutzung der verfügbaren Materialien, ganz im Gegensatz zu dem in Westtexas typischen und allgegenwärtigen Vorgehen, einzelne Bauten großflächig um einen offenen Platz zu arrangieren. Judd schrieb: „Zu dieser Ranch gehören zwei kleine Häuser, über die ich viel nachgedacht, mit denen ich aber nicht viel gemacht habe, da ich das Land um sie herum nicht zerstören will. Hier – überall – ist die Zerstörung von unbebautem Land eine Brutalität."[4]

Die Gebäude des ehemaligen Forts D. A. Russell waren auf diese typische Art lose gruppiert, aber Judd wollte diese willkürliche Anordnung nicht noch verschlimmern. Er hatte beispielsweise vor, eines Tages zehn neue Gewölbekonstruktionen aus Beton auf die vorhandenen Betonplatten südwestlich der Arena zu setzen, um kein weiteres Land bebauen zu müssen. In Judds Art der Raumnutzung, seiner funktionalen Aufteilung von Leben und Arbeit, finden sich interessante Parallelen zum St. Galler Klosterplan und dessen klösterlicher und landschaftsplanerischer Organisation und ebenfalls zum spanischen *Zócalo*, dem traditionellen zentralen Platz einer Stadt, der so typisch für New Mexico und diese Region ist. Es sind Räume zum Leben und zum Arbeiten.

Wenn Proportion die Beziehung zwischen zweidimensionalen Dingen beschreibt, offenbart sich das schwierigere Ganze in der „Dimension" eines Werks, in der Dreidimensionalität, der Relation zwischen Objekten und Volumenkörpern im realen Raum. Die Größenordnung ist vermutlich der am schwersten zu begreifende und zu dokumentierende Aspekt. Sie kann sehr subjektiv sein, aber Judd lag dieses Gespür im Blut. Richard

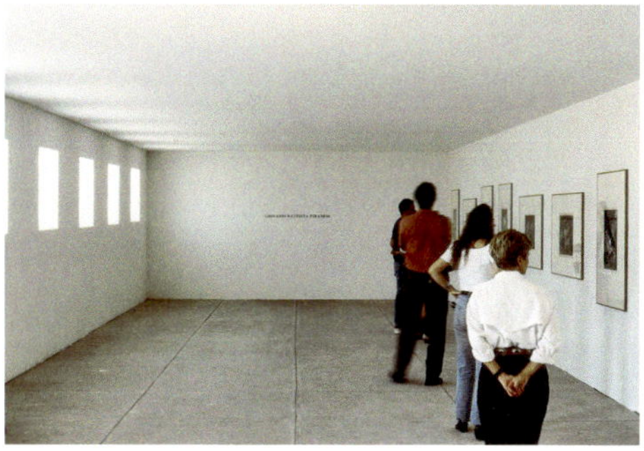

FIG. / ABB. 02

"Giovanni Battista Piranesi" Chinati Special Exhibition, October 1991, The Chinati Foundation

„Giovanni Battista Piranesi" Chinati Sonderausstellung, Oktober 1991, The Chinati Foundation

done little about, since I hate to damage the land around them. Here, everywhere, the destruction of new land is a brutality."[4]

The structures of the original Fort D. A. Russell were sited in this loose aggregation, but his responses were to not exacerbate this casual placement. He hoped one day to place ten new vaulted concrete structures on the existing concrete slabs southwest of the arena in order to not use new site for example. There are interesting alignments in Judd's use of various spaces, his functional live/work distributions by idea, with the Plan of St. Gall and it's monastic and landscaping organization and with the traditional Spanish courtyard or *zocalo* typologies typical to New Mexico and the region. The spaces of life and work.

Finally, if proportion is the relationship between two-dimensional number, the more difficult whole is manifest in the "scale" of work; the three-dimensional relationships. The relationship in actual space between objects and volumes. Scale is perhaps the most difficult set of aspects to understand and to document. It can be very much subjective, but Judd had an innate sense of this quality. Richard Shiff has written extensively and in rich detail on the artist's sketches and notes describing a works relationship to the wall or floor, and the same is true proportionally to the landscape.

If "posture" is understood as dealing with internal concerns, and "gesture" as dealing with external concerns, then it might be said that Donald Judd's cognitive sensibility and regard for an intuitive balance between the two—as with his stated concern for the "whole" of thought and feeling as one thing and not two—held posture and gesture in an elegant "proportion of concerns". A unique and profound sensibility brought to "life" by his work in place.

Shiff, der sich umfassend und detailliert mit den Skizzen und Notizen des Künstlers beschäftigt hat, schreibt von einer Beziehung der Werke zur Wand oder zum Boden, und dasselbe gilt auch im größeren Maßstab für die Landschaft.

Wenn die „Haltung“ als Ausdruck innerer Belange gilt und die „Geste“ als Reaktion auf äußere Belange, dann könnte man sagen, dass Donald Judd in der Lage war, durch seine kognitive Sensibilität und sein Bestreben nach einer intuitiven Balance dieser beiden Bereiche eine Proportion aller Belange zwischen Haltung und Geste zu wahren – was sich in seiner Auffassung zeigt, dass Gedanken und Gefühle eine Gesamtheit bilden. Daraus spricht eine einzigartige und tiefgreifende Sensibilität, die durch sein Wirken zum Leben erweckt wurde.

1 Vincent van Gogh, Brief an Anthon van Rappard (21. März 1883). *The Complete Letters of Vincent van Gogh.* New York Graphic Society, 1958. Über das Schreiben von George Eliot (Mary Ann Evans) in: *Felix Holt, The Radical (1866).*

2 „101 Spring Street, 1989“, in: *Donald Judd. Architektur,* Marianne Stockebrand, Herausgeberin. Münster, 1989. S. 19/17.

3 “Ayala de Chinati, 1989”, in: *Donald Judd. Architektur,* Marianne Stockebrand, Herausgeberin. Münster, 1989. S. 61/55.

4 Ebd., S. 60/55.

1 Vincent van Gogh, letter to Anthon van Rappard (March 21, 1883). *The Complete Letters of Vincent van Gogh.* New York Graphic Society, 1958. Regarding the writing of George Eliot (Mary Ann Evans) in: *Felix Holt The Radical (1866).*

2 “101 Spring Street, 1989”, *Donald Judd Architektur,* Marianne Stockebrand, editor. Munster, 1989. pp. 18–19. Reprinted in *Donald Judd Writings,* ed. Flavin Judd and Caitlin Murray (New York: Judd Foundation/David Zwirner Books, 2016), 586.

3 “Ayala de Chinati, 1989”, *Donald Judd Architektur,* Marianne Stockebrand, editor. Munster, 1989. p. 60. Reprinted in *Donald Judd Writings,* 593.

4 *Donald Judd Architektur,* p. 61; Reprinted in *Donald Judd Writings,* 593.

EINFÜHRUNG: DONALD JUDDS ARCHITEKTUR IN MARFA, TEXAS

Als Künstler des 20. Jahrhunderts hat sich Donald Judd einen Namen gemacht. Weniger bekannt dagegen sind seine Schriften über Architektur sowie der Umfang architektonischer Projekte, die er im Laufe seines Lebens geplant und ausgeführt hat. Heute, 40 Jahre nach dem Beginn seiner Tätigkeit in Marfa, Texas, und mehr als 25 Jahre nach seinem Tod, kommen jährlich Besucher in wachsender Zahl nach Marfa, um sein Gesamtkunstwerk zu sehen – die Einheit seiner Kunst- und Bauwerke und die westtexanische Wüstenlandschaft.

Judd lernte Westtexas im Dezember 1946 kennen, als er im Auftrag der US-Armee zusammen mit vier weiteren Soldaten im Bus das Gebiet durchquerte.

Aus Van Horn, Texas, 114 Kilometer nordwestlich von Marfa, wo die Gruppe am 17. Dezember einen Halt einlegte, schickte Judd ein Telegramm an seine Mutter: „LIEBE MAMA VAN HORN TEXAS. BEVÖLKERUNG 1260. HÜBSCHE STADT SCHÖNE GEGEND BERGE GRUSS DON.“[1] Nachdem er verschiedene Orte im Südwesten als künftigen Wohnsitz in Erwägung gezogen hatte, brach er 1971 von New York City nach Marfa auf. Zunächst wohnte er zur Miete, bevor er 1973 das Anwesen kaufte, das zu seinem texanischen Domizil wurde. Von 1972 bis zu seinem Tod im Jahre 1994 plante und realisierte Judd in Marfa ein bedeutendes Ensemble architektonischer Arbeiten.

Heute haben es sich die beiden Stiftungen Chinati Foundation und Judd Foundation[2] zur Aufgabe gemacht, Judds Hinterlassenschaft zu pflegen und seine Ideen und die Erinnerung an ihn lebendig zu halten. Ein Lageplan von Marfa (s. S. 12–13) enthält ein Verzeichnis der von Judd veränderten Gebäude mit Angabe von Lage und Namen. Neben dem Namen ist in Klammern die für das Gebäude zuständige Stiftung genannt. Die Chinati Foundation hat ihren Sitz im Süden von Marfa, westlich des Highway 67, an der Cavalry Row 1. Die Judd Foundation befindet sich im Zentrum von Marfa an der South Highland Avenue 104 und unterhält außerdem noch ein Büro in New York City. Beide Stiftungen bieten regelmäßig geführte Besichtigungen für Besucher an.

Auf den folgenden Seiten ist in chronologischer Folge eine Auswahl von Judds architektonischem Werk in Marfa und in den nahe gelegenen Chinati Mountains dargestellt. Die Auswahl wur-

INTRODUCTION: DONALD JUDD'S ARCHITECTURE IN MARFA, TEXAS

Donald Judd is well known as a twentieth-century artist, but fewer people are aware of his writing on architecture and how much architectural work he planned and realized during his lifetime. Now, more than forty years after Judd began his work in Marfa, Texas, and over twenty-five years after his death, a growing number of visitors come to Marfa each year to view his *Gesamtkunstwerk*, or unified work of art, architecture, and the landscape of the West Texan desert.

Judd first came through West Texas by bus in December of 1946, traveling with four other soldiers on a U.S. Army assignment. The group stopped at Van Horn, Texas, 74 miles northwest of Marfa, on December 17th. Judd sent a telegram to his mother: "DEAR MOM VAN HORN TEXAS. 1260 POPULATION. NICE TOWN BEAUTIFUL COUNTRY MOUNTAINS LOVE DON."[1] In 1971, after considering various locations in the Southwest in which to settle down, Judd left New York City for Marfa. He initially rented, and in 1973 bought the property that became Texas his residence. From 1972 until his death in 1994, Judd planned and realized a significant body of architectural work in Marfa.

Today, The Chinati Foundation and Judd Foundation[2] work to preserve Judd's achievements and keep his ideas and memory alive. On pages 12–13 in this book, a site plan of Marfa, with an index of the buildings Judd altered, identifies each building's location and name. The foundation in charge of each building is indicated in parentheses next to the name. The Chinati Foundation is located at the southern end of Marfa, west of Highway 67, at 1 Cavalry. Judd Foundation is situated in the center of Marfa on 104 South Highland Avenue Judd Foundation also maintains an office in New York City. Both foundations offer guided tours to visitors on a regular basis.

The following pages present, in chronological order, a selection of Judd's architectural work in Marfa and in the nearby Chinati Mountains. The choice of works was made by the author and represents Judd's most significant architectural achievements in Marfa and the Chinati Mountains. Judd's architectural projects are presented in nine chapters. The book begins with Judd's residence, the Block (named La Mansana de Chinati), followed by the Artillery Sheds, the Arena, the Chamberlain Building, the Architecture Studio, the Whyte Building,

de vom Verfasser getroffen und umfasst Judds bedeutendste architektonische Leistungen in der Stadt Marfa und in den Chinati Mountains. Die Projekte werden in neun Kapiteln vorgestellt. Den Anfang macht Judds privater Wohnsitz, der Block (genannt: La Mansana de Chinati). Es folgen die *Artillery Sheds*, ehemalige Lagerhallen der Artillerie, die Arena, das Chamberlain-Gebäude, das Architekturstudio, das Whyte-Gebäude, die drei Ranchs Casa Morales, Casa Perez und Las Casas etwa 95 Kilometer südwestlich von Marfa, die Judd nach dem Kauf zusammenlegte und in Ayala de Chinati umbenannte, sowie abschließend ein chronologisches Verzeichnis von Judds architektonischen Werken. Die beigefügten Pläne, Schnitte und Ansichten zeigen die Gebäude, bezogen auf ihren Inhalt und Kontext. Eingeschlossen sind kurze Beschreibungen. Fallweise wird, sofern Dokumentationen verfügbar sind, anhand von Schwarz-Weiß-Fotografien der ursprüngliche Zustand – der Renovationsprozess eines Gebäudes – veranschaulicht. In diesem Buch ist das architektonische Werk Judds aus der Perspektive des Architekten dargestellt und wird mit Hilfe von Zeichnungen analysiert. Die Zeichnungen, welche Grundrisse, Schnitte und Ansichten umfassen, geben die Proportionen und Strukturen der Gebäude, Kunstwerke und Möbel in kontextueller Darstellung wieder. Für das Verständnis von Judds holistischer Arbeitsweise in Marfa ist dieser kontextbezogene Ansatz nach Ansicht des Verfassers von grundlegender Bedeutung.

Judds Kunstwerke sind, beginnend in den frühen 1960er-Jahren, in ihrer Mehrzahl ohne Titel. Damit sollte verhindert werden, dass die Betrachtenden sich auf eine bestimmte Deutung festlegen. Architektonische Zeichnungen lassen sich auf vielfältige Weise lesen – etwa aus der Sicht eines Stadtplaners, eines Architekten, eines Innenausstatters, eines Ingenieurs, eines Landschaftsarchitekten oder eines Künstlers. Der Verfasser hofft, mit Hilfe der Zeichnungen einen umfassenden Blick auf Judds Werk zu ermöglichen. Den Lesenden ist überlassen, wie sie die Zeichnungen interpretieren. Judd hat die Aufstellung der Kunstwerke in Marfa auf Dauer geplant. Angesichts dieser Absicht scheint es darum nicht mehr als angemessen, die Zeichnungen als ein Mittel zu präsentieren, Judds Kunstwerke, Möbel und Architektur als Ganzes zu lesen. Raum lässt sich zwar am bes-

Casa Morales, Casa Perez and Las Casas, three ranches which Judd consolidated upon acquirement and collectively named Ayala de Chinati. They are located approximately between forty and sixty miles southwest of Marfa. At the end of the book is a chronological index of Judd's architectural works. The accompanying plans, sections, and elevations show the relationship of the buildings to their content and context. Brief descriptions are included, and in some cases, if documentation is available, the "before" condition—the renovation process of a building—is illustrated through black and white photographs. This book looks at Judd's architectural work in Marfa from an architect's perspective and analyzes it through drawings. The drawings, which include plans, elevations, and sections, provide a contextual depiction of the proportions and structures of the buildings, artwork, and furnishings. In the author's view, this contextual approach is fundamental to understanding Judd's holistic work methods in Marfa.

Most of Judd's artworks, beginning in the early 1960s, are untitled in order to forestall a specific interpretation by the viewer. Architectural drawings can be read in many ways—for example, from the perspective of an urban planner, an architect, an interior designer, an engineer, a landscape architect, or an artist. With the aid of the drawings, the author hopes to offer a comprehensive look at Judd's work. How the drawings are interpreted is up to the reader. Judd intended the artwork installed in Marfa to be permanent. With this in mind, it seems only appropriate to present the drawings as a means to read Judd's artworks, furnishings, and architecture as a whole.While space is best explored and understood on location, the second-best way to understand and comprehend the complexity of Judd's work is by studying scale drawings accompanied by photographs.

The Roman architect Vitruvius, theoretician and author of *Ten Books on Architecture*, argued that good architecture must possess commodity, firmness, and delight. Those dilapidated, ordinary, military structures and industrial buildings in Marfa answer Vitruvius's call for commodity and firmness. However, Donald Judd added the delight—perhaps the most difficult task for an architect to achieve.

ten vor Ort erkunden und verstehen, doch der zweitbeste Weg, die Komplexität von Judds Werk zu verstehen und zu begreifen, ist das Studium maßstabgerechter Zeichnungen, begleitet von Fotografien.

Der römische Architekt Vitruv, Theoretiker und Verfasser der *Zehn Bücher über Architektur*, legte dar, dass gute Architektur sich durch Zweckmäßigkeit, Festigkeit und Schönheit auszeichnen müsse. Die zerfallenen, kommunen Militär- und Industriegebäude in Marfa entsprechen Vitruvs Forderung nach Zweckmäßigkeit und Festigkeit. Donald Judd ergänzte die Schönheit – für einen Architekten vielleicht die schwierigste Aufgabe.

Etwa 95 Kilometer von der mexikanischen Grenze entfernt liegt Marfa in der Chihuahua-Wüste am Südrand der westtexanischen Davis Mountains und gehört in den militärhistorischen Kontext von Fort Davis. Ihren Ursprung nahm die Stadt als Wasserdepot für die Eisenbahnverbindung Galveston – Harrisburg – San Antonio, und der Legende zufolge gab ihr die Frau des Chefingenieurs der Eisenbahngesellschaft 1882 den Namen einer Figur aus Dostoevskijs *Die Brüder Karamazov*.[3] Im August 1942 hatte Marfa eine Einwohnerzahl von 4931;[4] heute leben weniger als 2000 Menschen in dieser ehemaligen Stadt von Rinderzüchtern, einer Stadt, die mit dem wirtschaftlichen Niedergang kämpfte und durch die lebendige Kunst und Architektur Donald Judds transformiert und revitalisiert wurde. Als Judd in Marfa ankam, waren praktisch alle Gebäude, die er selbst oder durch die Dia Art Foundation erwarb, erneuerungsbedürftig. Über das Fort D.A. Russell schreibt Judd:

> Fort Russell war größtenteils eine Ruine. Abgesehen von den beiden Artillerie-Hallen und später der Arena war ich dagegen, es zu kaufen. Es war ein Armee-Stützpunkt gewesen, was nicht so gut ist. Die meisten Gebäude hatten keine Dächer mehr, überall lag Schutt herum, und das Land war verwüstet. Aus einigen der Baracken hatte man kitschige Wohnungen mit dazu passenden Gärten gemacht. Ein Militärgebiet, verschönert mit einer Konsumkitsch-Landschaft: Das ist schwer zu schlagen. Wenigstens waren die Artillerie-Hallen aus Beton und solide, wenn auch undicht.[5]

Located in the Chihuahuan desert at the southern end of the Davis Mountains in West Texas, approximately 60 miles from the Mexican border, Marfa is located in the historic military context of Fort Davis. Marfa originated as a water stop on the Galveston, Harrisburg, and San Antonio Railroad, and as the legend goes, was named in 1882 by the wife of the railroad's chief engineer for a character in Fyodor Dostoyevsky's *The Brothers Karamazov*.[3] In August of 1942, Marfa's population was 4,931,[4] but today there are fewer than 2,000 people living in this former cattle town, a town struggling with a declining economy that was transformed and revitalized by the living art and architecture of Donald Judd. When Judd arrived in Marfa, practically all of the buildings which he acquired himself or through the Dia Art Foundation were in need of repair. Judd said of Fort D.A. Russell:

> Most of Fort Russell was a ruin. Other than the two artillery sheds and later the Arena, I was against buying it. It had been an army base, which is not so good. Most buildings were without roofs, there was trash everywhere and the land was damaged. Some of the barracks had been turned into kitsch apartments with compatible landscaping. Military landscape overlain with a landscape of consumer kitsch is hard to defeat. At any rate the artillery sheds were concrete and solid, although they leaked.[5]

Judd describes a damaged landscape, a landscape littered with increasingly incompatible structures. Judd may have felt dubious about purchasing the site, but he was nevertheless undaunted in his vision for a landscape that could be rewoven—restored by his art and architecture.

By most modern standards, Marfa is in a remote location. The closest major airports are in El Paso to the northwest, or Midland/Odessa to the northeast. From either of these airports it is a three-hour car drive through the rugged west Texas landscape to Marfa. In a way, the three-hour trip to Marfa prepares the visitor for the experience of Judd's work. Visitors are confronted with the enormous spaces of the rugged southwestern landscape. Part of the Marfa experience is the journey to get there. Visitors arriving in Marfa and at The Chinati and Judd Foundations

* „Denn wenn der Staat, nach einem Grundsatze der Philosophen, ein großes Haus ist, und ein Haus hinwiederum ein kleiner Staat, warum sollte man da nicht die Glieder dieser selbst als kleine Wohnungen bezeichnen? Wie z. B. das Atrium, den offenen Säulengang, das Speisezimmer, die Portikus und dergleichen." Leon B. Alberti, *Zehn Bücher über die Baukunst*, Darmstadt 1975. (*De re aedificatoria,* 1443–1452, gedr. 1485), aus dem Lateinischen von Max Theuer, reprograf. Nachdruck der 1. Aufl. Wien u. Leipzig 1912, Darmstadt 1975.

Judd beschreibt eine beschädigte Landschaft, eine Landschaft, übersät mit zunehmend unvereinbaren baulichen Strukturen. Er mag gezögert haben, das Gelände zu kaufen, doch sein Wunschbild einer Landschaft, die neu verwoben werden konnte – wiederhergestellt durch seine Kunst und Architektur, blieb unerschüttert.

Gemessen an modernen Reisestandards ist Marfa abgelegen. Die nächsten größeren Flugplätze liegen in El Paso im Nordwesten und Midland/Odessa im Nordosten. Von beiden Flugplätzen aus dauert die Autofahrt durch die raue westtexanische Landschaft nach Marfa nicht weniger als drei Stunden. In gewisser Weise sind diese drei Autostunden eine Vorbereitung auf das Erlebnis von Judds Werk. Die Besucher finden sich mit den unermesslich weiten Räumen der rauen Landschaft des Südwestens konfrontiert. Zum Erleben von Marfa gehört die Fahrt dorthin. Wer Marfa und die Chinati und die Judd Foundation heute besucht, entdeckt eine Stadt und landschaftliche Umgebung, die durch Vision und Werk von Donald Judd zugleich erhalten, erneuert und umgestaltet wurden, eine Landschaft, die für Künstler, Architekten und alle, die sich vom genius loci berühren lassen, weiterhin eine dynamische Inspiration darstellt.

In seinem Buch *After the City* schildert Lars Lerup, einst Dekan der School of Architecture an der Rice University in Houston, seine Erfahrungen mit Judd und Marfa. „Judds Marfa ist nicht nur von packender Schönheit", schreibt er, „es gibt daraus auch vieles zu lernen."[6] Wie der Buchtitel andeutet, stehen für Lerup urbanistische Aspekte im Vordergrund. Er zitiert und kommentiert ein Diktum von Leon Battista Alberti (1404–1472)*:

> Das Haus ist eine kleine Stadt, und die Stadt ist ein großes Haus, die Kunst ist eine kleine Stadt und ebenso das Mobiliar. Der Spruch könnte trotz seiner Vereinfachungen im Original erneut überzeugen, denn die zusätzlichen und parallelen Reflexionen machen andere, komplexere Berechnungen möglich.[7]

Jedes größere Museum für die Kunst des 20. Jahrhunderts hat mit aller Wahrscheinlichkeit ein Werk von Donald Judd in seiner Sammlung. Im *Museum of Modern Art* in Fort Worth ist ein Beispiel aus Judds vertikalen Arbeiten, den so genannten Stacks, zu sehen. Vergleicht man die Positionierung dieses Werks in Fort

* "If (as the philosophers maintain) the city is like some large house, and the house is in turn like some small city, cannot the various parts of the house—atria, *xysti,* dining rooms, porticoes, and so on—be considered miniature buildings?" Leon B. Alberti. *On the Art of Building in Ten Books.* (Translation of *De re aedificatoria* by Joseph Rykwert, Neil Leach, and Robert Tavernor), 5th edition (Cambridge, Mass. 1994).

today discover a town and surrounding landscape that are simultaneously preserved, renewed, and transformed by the vision and work of Donald Judd—a landscape that continues to be a dynamic inspiration to artists, architects, and anyone who can perceive the genius of place.

Lars Lerup, former Dean of the School of Architecture at Rice University in Houston, describes, in his book *After the City*, his own experience with Judd and Marfa. "Aside from being hauntingly beautiful," he writes, "Judd's Marfa holds many lessons."[6] As his book title suggests, Lerup's focus is an urban one, quoting and expanding on Leon Battista Alberti's (1404–1472) dictum:

> The house is a small town, and the town is a large house, the art is a small town and so is the furniture. The dictum may again ring true despite its original simplifications, because the additional and parallel reflections make other more complex computations possible.[7]

Any major museum showing twentieth-century art most likely has a work by Donald Judd in its collection. At the Museum of Modern Art in Fort Worth, one can see an example of Judd's vertical works, the so-called stacks. Comparing this work's placement in Fort Worth with the installation of work at La Mansana de Chinati, Judd's quarters in Marfa, one can understand what the artist was referring to when he said, "It takes a great deal of time and thought to install work carefully."[8] In Marfa, Judd was in control of the artwork, its placement, and the location. In short, he was in control of all the factors he considered paramount when placing an artwork or establishing spaces in which to live. The visitor to Marfa experiences not just Judd's works but those of his fellow artists in situations the artists themselves chose and considered appropriate.

In his assertive and opinionated essays, Judd criticized architects for designing museums for the sake of the museum itself, exploring formal and spatial interests rather than designing a building for the artwork it was to house. Judd's idea of placing artwork in abandoned industrial buildings was taken up by Michael Govan, president and director of Dia Art Foundation between 1994–2006 who was instrumental that Dia:Beacon became a reality.

Worth mit der Werkinstallation in der Mansana de Chinati, Judds Wohnsitz in Marfa, dann wird deutlich, wovon der Künstler spricht, wenn er sagt: „Kunstwerke sorgfältig zu installieren erfordert viel Zeit und Überlegung.“[8] In Marfa bestimmte Judd selbst über die Kunstwerke, die Aufstellung und den Ort der Aufstellung – kurz, über alle Faktoren, die er für essenziell hielt, wenn er ein Kunstwerk ausstellte oder Wohnräume einrichtete. Der Besucher von Marfa erlebt nicht nur Judds eigene Werke, sondern auch die anderer Künstler in situativen Kontexten, die von den Künstlern selbst ausgewählt und als adäquat betrachtet wurden.

In seinen überaus dezidiert und dogmatisch formulierten Essays übt Judd Kritik an den Architekten. Er wirft ihnen vor, unter Verfolgung formaler und räumlicher Interessen Museen um des Museumsbaus selbst zu entwerfen, statt ein Gebäude mit Blick auf die Kunst zu konzipieren, die sie aufnehmen soll. Judds Idee, Kunst in ausgedienten Industriegebäuden auszustellen, wurde von Michael Govan aufgegriffen, der zwischen 1994 und 2006 Präsident und Direktor der Dia Art Foundation war und damit maßgeblich dafür verantwortlich, dass das Dia:Beacon realisiert wurde.

Die Dia Foundation ließ eine große Fabrikanlage in Beacon, New York, bekannt als Nabisco-Gebäude, in ein Museum umbauen, um darin ihre permanente Sammlung unterzubringen. Umbenannt in Dia:Beacon, stellt das Museum großdimensionierte Kunstwerke einer Reihe bekannter Künstler von Beuys bis Warhol aus. Die ursprüngliche Fabrik stammt aus dem Jahr 1929. Der Künstler Robert Irwin hat sie zusammen mit dem Architekturbüro *OpenOffice arts+architecture* collaborative renoviert, indem er das bestehende Fabrikgebäude durch minimale architektonische Eingriffe modernisierte, ein Ansatz, der sich von den gängigen Ideen für neues Museumsdesign unterschied. 2003, als das Dia:Beacon eröffnet wurde, schrieb Michael Kimmelman von der *New York Times*:

> Vor seinem Tod im Jahr 1994 beklagte sich Donald Judd, seine Skulpturen seien in den meisten Museen mit anderen Kunstwerken zusammengepfercht, und den Objekten werde damit versagt, was er als die ihnen zustehende Unabhängigkeit und Integrität erachtete. „So viel Geld im Namen der Kunst für die Architektur auszugeben, viel mehr als für die

Dia chose a large factory complex known as the Nabisco building in Beacon, New York for conversion into a museum to house its permanent collection. Renamed Dia:Beacon, the museum exhibits large-scale artworks by a number of artists ranging from Beuys to Warhol. The existing factory complex was built in 1929. The artist Robert Irwin, working with the OpenOffice arts+architecture collaborative, renovated it as Dia:Beacon by modernizing the existing factory building with minimal architectural intervention. This was a different approach from popular ideas for new museum design. In 2003, when Dia: Beacon opened to the public, The *New York Times'* Michael Kimmelman wrote:

> **Before he died in 1994, Donald Judd complained that his sculptures were crammed in with other art in most museums and that the objects were denied what he considered their rightful independence and integrity. "So much money spent on architecture in the name of art, much more than goes to art, is wrong," he barked about new museums. "Even if the architecture were good, but it's bad." Dia:Beacon was built to let people see art the way Judd would have wanted.[9]**

Museum patrons often seek fame, notoriety, and increased numbers of visitors by hiring "name" architects to design new museum spaces. The best-known example is probably Frank O. Gehry's design for the Guggenheim Museum in Bilbao, Spain, which opened to the public in 1997. In 2003, Dia:Beacon offered a refreshing alternative to Guggenheim Bilbao, at roughly one third of the cost per square foot. Judd inspired the thinking behind Dia:Beacon with his practice in West Texas. He serves as an inspiration to current designers such as OpenOffice arts+architecture. In his review of Dia:Beacon for *Architectural Record*, James S. Russell first quotes Michael Govan, then concludes in his own words:

> **Dia does not position itself as a model for other institutions, Govan says. It only strives to be true to the specific concerns of a specific group of artists. But the power of the result can't be denied. It could alter the course of museum design.[10]**

> Kunst verwendet wird, ist falsch," wetterte er über neue Museen. „Selbst wenn die Architektur gut wäre, aber sie ist schlecht."
> Das Dia:Beacon wurde gebaut, damit die Besucher Kunst so sehen können, wie Judd es gewünscht hätte.[9]

Die Bauherren von Museen sind oft auf Ruhm, auch dubiosen Ruhm, und auf Steigerung der Besucherzahlen aus, und sie beauftragen deshalb Stars der Architekturszene mit der Gestaltung neuer Museumsräume. Das bekannteste Beispiel ist wohl Frank O. Gehrys Entwurf des Guggenheim-Museums in Bilbao, das 1997 eröffnet wurde. 2003 bot Dia:Beacon zu etwa dreimal tieferen Kosten pro Quadratmeter eine erfrischende Alternative zum Guggenheim Bilbao an. Mit seinem Vorgehen in Westtexas beflügelte Judd das Denken, aus dem Dia:Beacon hervorging. Er ist eine Inspirationsquelle für gegenwärtige Designer wie Open-Office arts+architecture. In seiner Besprechung von Dia:Beacon für den *Architectural Record* zitiert James S. Russell zunächst Michael Govan und zieht dann den Schluss:

> Dia sieht sich nicht als Modell für andere Institute, sagt Govan. Es ist lediglich bemüht, den besonderen Interessen einer besonderen Gruppe von Künstlern zu entsprechen. Aber die Wirkung des Resultats lässt sich nicht leugnen. Sie könnte den Trend des Museumdesigns revidieren.[10]

Konzepte adaptiver Wiederverwendung sind neuerdings populär geworden; Architekturprofessoren verwenden sie in ihren Studioprojekten, damit die Studierenden lernen können, wie ausgediente bestehende Strukturen revitalisiert, reorganisiert und umgestaltet werden können. In den 1980er-Jahren war es üblich, die Theorie und Praxis der Renovierungsmethode des italienischen Architekten Carlo Scarpa zu vermitteln. In derselben Zeit kamen auch Judds Vorstellungen von baulicher Umgestaltung zur Reife. Wie in seiner Kunst folgte Judd eigenen Ideen, als er in den vormals militärischen und industriellen Bauten neue Räume schuf. Darüber hinaus zeigte er sich besorgt um die Landschaft: um ihren Schutz und ihre Erhaltung angesichts schädlicher Nutzung durch unsensible Grundbesitzer. Auf mancherlei Weise hat Judd große Teile von Marfa und Ayala de Chinati, der drei Ranchhäuser südwestlich von Marfa in den Chinati Mountains, davor bewahrt, liquidiert oder ohne Rücksicht auf Straßen, Vegetation

Adaptive-reuse projects have become popular of late, employed by architecture professors in their studio projects so that students can learn how to revitalize, reorganize, and redesign defunct existing structures. In the 1980s it was popular to teach and present the renovation methods of the Italian architect Carlo Scarpa. During the same time, Judd's own ideas about renovation began to flourish. As with his art, Judd worked from his own ideas, creating new spaces in the former military and industrial buildings. Moreover, Judd was concerned about the landscape: how to protect and preserve it from the harmful actions of insensitive landlords. In many ways, Judd protected large parts of the city of Marfa and the Ayala de Chinati, the ranch southwest of Marfa in the Chinati Mountains, from being abandoned or recklessly damaged without concern for the roads, vegetation, and landscape. Judd paid attention to the environment comprised of buildings and landscape before it became *en vogue* among architects to talk about ecological architecture. On the occasion of the opening of The Chinati Foundation in Marfa in 1987, Judd wrote:

> **Art and Architecture—all the arts—do not have to exist in isolation, as they do now. This fault is very much a key to the present society. Architecture is nearly gone, but it, art, all of the arts, in fact all parts of the society, have to be rejoined, and joined more than they have ever been. This would be democratic in a good sense, unlike the present increasing fragmentation into separate but equal categories, equal within the arts, but inferior to the powerful bureaucracies.[11]**

With the founding of The Chinati Foundation, Judd declared his ideas about art and architecture and endowed those ideas with a palpable future through all the buildings he adapted, renovated, designed, and constructed in Marfa. He was 59 when he wrote the above passage. What he could not know was that he had only six more years to live.

und Landschaft skrupellos verschandelt zu werden. Judd schenkte der Umgebung aus Bauten und Landschaft Beachtung, noch bevor es unter Architekten zum guten Ton gehörte, über ökologische Architektur zu sprechen. Aus Anlass der Gründung der Chinati Foundation in Marfa im Jahr 1987 schrieb Judd:

> Kunst und Architektur – alle Künste – dürfen nicht isoliert voneinander existieren, so wie sie es zur Zeit tun. Dieser Fehler ist ein ganz wesentlicher Schlüssel zur heutigen Gesellschaft. Die Architektur ist fast völlig verschwunden, aber sie, die Kunst, alle Künste, eigentlich alle Teile der Gesellschaft, müssen wiedervereint werden, und zwar stärker vereint als sie es jemals waren. [11]

Mit der Gründung der Chinati Foundation hielt Judd seine Vorstellungen von Kunst und Architektur in programmatischer Form fest und gab ihnen in allen Gebäuden, die er in Marfa umbaute, erneuerte, entwarf und erbaute, eine sinnlich fassbare Zukunft. Als er die zitierte Passage schrieb, war er 59 Jahre alt. Er konnte nicht wissen, dass er nur noch sechs Jahre zu leben hatte.

Der italienische Barockkünstler Gian Lorenzo Bernini nahm die großen Projekte seines architektonischen Schaffens im Alter von 60 Jahren in Angriff. Bernini hatte das Glück, seine Arbeit zwei weitere Jahrzehnte fortführen und seine bedeutenden Leistungen als Architekt abschließen zu können – er starb mit 82 Jahren. Laut James S. Ackerman, einem der führenden Kunst- und Architekturhistoriker, zählte Bernini zu den wenigen Bildhauern der Vormoderne, die Judds Wertschätzung genossen. [12] Mit Berninis Werk war Judd als Student der Columbia University vertraut geworden, wo er den Master-Studiengang in Kunstgeschichte belegte und bei dem Berninispezialisten Rudolf Wittkower studierte. Wittkowers grundlegendes Werk *Architectural Principles in the Age of Humanism*, das 1949 erstmals erschien und bis heute nachgedruckt wird, hat die Ausbildung zahlreicher Kunst- und Architekturstudierender geprägt. Wichtig ist, sich klarzumachen, dass sich Wittkowers Einfluss auf die Ausbildung in Kunstgeschichte wie auch Architektur erstreckte. Nach dem Studium der Malerei und einem Abschluss als Bachelor of Science in Philosophie an der Columbia-Universität kehrte Judd zehn [13] Jahre nach Studienbeginn an seine Universität zurück,

The Italian Baroque artist Gianlorenzo Bernini began his major projects as an architect at the age of 60. Bernini was fortunate to have more than two decades—he lived to the age of 82—to accomplish his major contributions as an architect. Bernini, according to James S. Ackerman, a leading historian of art and architecture, was one of the few pre-modern sculptors Judd respected. [12] Judd became very familiar with Bernini's work while a student at Columbia University, pursuing a master's degree in art history and studying with the Bernini scholar Rudolf Wittkower, whose seminal work, *Architectural Principals in the Age of Humanism*, first published in 1949 and still in print today, shaped the education of many art and architecture students. It is important to recognize that Wittkower influenced both art history and architecture education. After studying painting and receiving his bachelor of science in philosophy from Columbia, Judd returned to the university ten [13] years later to pursue his master's in art history. Judd was very interested in the history of art, and his time at Columbia prepared him well for his groundbreaking work in the early 1960s. Baroque and Minimalism are rarely mentioned in the same sentence; however, both Bernini and Judd revolutionized the way their work was placed in the space and how it was lit by natural light. In his writings on Bernini, Wittkower points out the holistic relationship of Bernini's architecture and sculpture:

> **Bernini's figures not only move freely in depth but seem to belong to the same space in which the beholder lives. Differing from Renaissance statuary, his figures need the continuum of space surrounding them and without it they would lose their *raison d'être*. [14]**

A similar observation can be made about Judd, who made it clear that the work placed in various spaces in Marfa belonged there. Without the art, furniture, and objects Judd collected, the spaces in Marfa would lose their *raison d'être* as well.

The idea that art and architecture should complement each other is not new. In the Renaissance, architecture had been seen as the art that champions all the others. Michelangelo is the shining example of that idea, having succeeded in the disciplines of painting and sculpture before his ultimate architectural

um das Master-Studium in Kunstgeschichte aufzunehmen. Für die Geschichte der Kunst hatte Judd großes Interesse, und seine Zeit an der Columbia University war eine gute Vorbereitung auf seine bahnbrechenden Arbeiten der frühen 1960er-Jahre. Barock und Minimalismus werden normalerweise kaum in einem Satz genannt, doch sowohl Judd wie Bernini haben die Positionierung ihrer Werke im Raum und die Art ihrer Beleuchtung durch natürliches Licht revolutioniert. In seinen Schriften über Bernini weist Wittkower auf die ganzheitliche Beziehung zwischen Berninis Architektur und seinen Skulpturen hin:

> Berninis Figuren zeigen nicht nur ungezwungen ausgreifende Bewegungen, sondern scheinen auch demselben Raum anzugehören, in dem der Betrachter lebt. Im Unterschied zu den Statuen der Renaissance brauchen seine Figuren das sie umgebende Raumkontinuum; ohne dasselbe würden sie ihre *raison d'être* verlieren.[14]

Ähnliches ließe sich von Judd sagen, der klarstellte, dass die Arbeiten, die an den verschiedenen Orten in Marfa ihren Platz bekamen, dorthin gehören. Ohne die Kunstwerke, die Möbel und Objekte, die Judd gesammelt hat, würden auch die Räume in Marfa ihre *raison d'être* verlieren.

Die Vorstellung, dass Kunst und Architektur sich ergänzen sollten, ist nicht neu. In der Renaissance hatte die Architektur als diejenige Kunst gegolten, die alle anderen trägt und stärkt. Das leuchtende Beispiel für diese Idee ist Michelangelo, der auf den Gebieten der Malerei und Skulptur brillierte, bevor er sein architektonisches Meisterwerk, die Planung des Peters-Doms in Rom, ausführte. Die Idee der Integration der Künste hielt sich bis weit ins 20. Jahrhundert hinein und fand ihre Fürsprecher in Architekten wie Le Corbusier, dessen Vorstellung vom „universellen Design“ in seinen urbanistischen Konzepten ebenso Ausdruck fand wie in seinen Bauten, den Möbelentwürfen und seiner Malerei.

Walter Gropius, Begründer das Bauhauses, der einflussreichsten Kunstschule im 20. Jahrhundert, setzte sich im Bauhaus-Manifest von 1919 für die Wiedervereinigung von Kunst und Handwerk ein. Das Manifest beginnt mit den Worten:

accomplishment of planning St. Peter's Basilica in Rome. The idea of the integrated arts continued well into the twentieth century, advocated by architects such as Le Corbusier, whose ideas of "total design" were expressed in his urban design, architecture, and furniture design, as well as his paintings. Walter Gropius, founder of the Bauhaus, the twentieth century's most influential design school, argued for a reuniting of the arts and crafts in the Bauhaus manifesto of 1919. The manifesto begins:

> **The ultimate aim of all visual arts is the complete building! To embellish buildings was once the noblest function of the fine arts; they were the indispensable components of great architecture. Today the arts exist in isolation, from which they can be rescued only through the conscious, co-operative effort of all craftsmen. Architects, painters, and sculptors must recognize anew and learn to grasp the composite character of a building both as an entity and in its separate parts. Only then will their work be imbued with the architectonic spirit which it has lost as "salon art".[15]**

Judd's statement for the opening of The Chinati Foundation and Gropius' statement for the Bauhaus manifesto bear clear similarities—they both espouse the idea of reuniting art and architecture. Donald Judd could not call himself an architect in the state of Texas yet architecture is what he achieved in his work in Marfa.

While the Bauhaus called for a reunion of the arts, it placed architecture at the pinnacle of what was taught at the school, continuing the Renaissance tradition. The first director of the Bauhaus in Dessau was an architect, Gropius, as was the last director, Ludwig Mies van der Rohe, leaving no doubt as to who was granted the authority to oversee the school's future.

Following the lead of the Bauhaus, architecture schools around the world have championed the idea of the integrated arts in history classes and design studios. The idea has been established in the mind of many architects that they should be, as Vitruvius intended, versatile in various fields.

Das Endziel aller bildnerischen Tätigkeit ist der Bau! Ihn zu schmücken war einst die vornehmste Aufgabe der bildenden Künste, sie waren unablösliche Bestandteile der großen Baukunst. Heute stehen sie in selbstgenügsamer Eigenheit, aus der sie erst wieder erlöst werden können durch bewusstes Mit- und Ineinanderwirken aller Werkleute untereinander. Architekten, Maler und Bildhauer müssen die vielgliedrige Gestalt des Baues in seiner Gesamtheit und in seinen Teilen wieder kennen und begreifen lernen, dann werden sich von selbst ihre Werke wieder mit architektonischem Geiste füllen, den sie in der Salonkunst verloren.[15]

Judds Erklärung zur Eröffnung der Chinati Foundation und Gropius' Erklärung im Bauhaus-Manifest zeigen eine deutliche Verwandtschaft: beide treten dafür ein, Kunst und Architektur wieder zusammenzuführen. Donald Judd durfte sich in Texas nicht als Architekt bezeichnen, doch was aus seinem Werk in Marfa hervorging, war Architektur.

Das Bauhaus rief zwar nach einer Wiedervereinigung der Künste, räumte aber der Architektur im Lehrplan den Vorrang ein und setzte damit die Renaissance-Tradition fort. Sowohl der erste Direktor des Bauhauses, Walter Gropius, als auch der letzte, Ludwig Mies van der Rohe, waren Architekten, und es bestand kein Zweifel daran, wer die Autorität besaß, über die Zukunft der Schule zu bestimmen.

Architekturfakultäten in aller Welt setzen sich, dem Beispiel des Bauhauses folgend, in den historischen Fächern und in Entwurfsstudios für die Idee der integrierten Künste ein. Im Denken zahlreicher Architekten ist die Vorstellung, dass man Vitruvs Forderung gemäß auf verschiedenen Gebieten kompetent sein müsse, zu einer Selbstverständlichkeit geworden.

War Donald Judd ein Architekt? Amtlich eingetragen als solcher war er nicht, und er besaß auch keinen Abschluss im Fach Architektur. Doch er hatte eine exzellente akademische Ausbildung, war ein leidenschaftlicher Leser und mit der Baukunst sehr vertraut. Judd war einer der seltenen, begabten Menschen, die ein Thema gleichzeitig unter mehreren Gesichtspunkten betrachten können. Er vertrat den Standpunkt des Künstlers, dessen

Was Donald Judd an architect? He was not registered as one, nor did he have a degree in architecture. However, Judd, with his excellent academic background, was an avid reader and very familiar with architecture. Judd was one of those rare, gifted individuals who can hold multiple viewpoints on a topic at the same time. He could take the position of the artist who is concerned about the artwork, but he could just as easily take the position of the architect who places a work of art in a specific location and context. Architects are accustomed to the idea that the architect designs the place for the artwork, therefore assuming control of the environment. Implicit in that assumption is the notion that architects know what they're doing. Judd reversed that notion. He criticized leading contemporary architects of the Postmodern and Deconstructive period from the 1980s. The architectural elite was not used to hearing blunt criticism from an artist who was not a formally trained licensed architect. Even though the title "architect" is protected in the United States, the licensing of architects is relatively new. Architectural success, however, is not guaranteed with licensing or academic schooling; Judd certainly knew this.

In the United States, the title "architect" is reserved for those who earn it through academic schooling and practice, as proven by an exam. The question of whether or not Judd wanted to become an architect was perhaps best answered by Judd himself in his 1987 essay "Art and Architecture":

> **While I was in the army in '47, helping to occupy Korea, before going to college, my assignment to myself was to decide between being an architect or an artist, which to me was being a painter. Art was the most likely in the balance, but the decisive weight was that in architecture it was necessary to deal with the clients and the public. This seemed impossible to me, as did the business of a firm.[16]**

Interesse den Kunstwerken gilt, konnte aber ebenso leicht die Position des Architekten einnehmen, der einem Kunstwerk einen bestimmten Platz in einem bestimmten Kontext zuweist. Architekten sind an die Vorstellung gewöhnt, dass der Architekt den Platz für das Kunstwerk konzipiert, und gewinnen damit Einfluss auf die Umwelt. Stillschweigend vorausgesetzt ist dabei die Auffassung, die Architekten wüssten, was sie tun. Judd wies diese Annahme zurück. Er ging mit führenden zeitgenössischen Architekten der Postmoderne und des Dekonstruktivismus aus den 1980er-Jahren kritisch ins Gericht. Kritik aus dem Mund eines Künstlers, dem Fachausbildung und Zulassung als amtlich zugelassener Architekt fehlten, war für die Architektenelite neu. Die Berufsbezeichnung „Architekt" ist in den Vereinigten Staaten zwar geschützt, die amtliche Zulassung aber jüngeren Datums. Den architektonischen Erfolg allerdings garantieren weder die Zulassung noch die akademische Schulung, und das war Judd zweifellos bewusst.

In den Vereinigten Staaten ist der Titel „Architekt" denen vorbehalten, die ihn sich durch akademische Ausbildung und Praxis samt Examensnachweis verdient haben. Die Frage, ob Judd Architekt werden wollte, hat er 1987 in seinem Aufsatz „Art and Architecture" selbst am besten beantwortet:

> Als ich 1947 im Militär war und half, Korea zu besetzen, bevor ich aufs College ging, stellte ich mir selbst die Aufgabe, mich zu entscheiden zwischen einem Leben als Architekt oder als Künstler, was für mich hieß, Maler zu sein. Kunst kam für mich am ehesten in Frage, aber den Ausschlag gab, dass es für einen Architekten notwendig ist, mit Auftraggebern und mit der Öffentlichkeit umzugehen. Das schien für mich unmöglich, wie auch das Betreiben einer Firma es war.[16]

Judd erwog also, die Architektenlaufbahn einzuschlagen, doch seine Entscheidung, Maler zu werden, hatte weniger damit zu tun, dass er zwischen den beiden Berufen einen fundamentalen Unterschied ausgemacht hätte, als vielmehr mit der Vorstellung von schöpferischer Autonomie. Judd brachte ein neues Verständnis und eine neue Dimension der Erfahrung in die Bildhauerkunst ein, und beide Momente prägen auch sein Bauen: die

Judd considered taking the route to become a professional architect, but his choice to become a painter had less to do with any fundamental difference that he perceived between art and architecture than it did with the notion of creative autonomy. Judd brought a new understanding and quality of experience to the art of sculpting, and he brought that same understanding and experience to his architecture, namely the opening of interior space within a container so that it can be perceived fully from the exterior. Although some art historians categorize Judd as a sculptor, Judd himself rejected the category, calling his three-dimensional art "works." Architecture is space, its boundaries defined by the architect, and Judd thought of sculpture much as an architect would—in terms of boundaries set by space and light. Judd explored his notions of space not in the traditional sense of "sculpture" but in "pieces" or "works." His use of these terms is significant, for it reveals how much Judd was thinking as the architect that he most certainly was.

In "Specific Objects" (1965), one of his defining essays about his view of space, Judd wrote: "The thing as a whole, its quality as a whole, is what is interesting."[17] By "whole" Judd referred to a thing that has holistic qualities, echoing, if not directly referring to, a concept of space rooted in the Renaissance. Andrea Palladio, perhaps the most influential architect of all time, wrote in *The Four Books on Architecture*:

> Beauty will result from the form and correspondence of the whole, with respect to the several parts, of the parts with each other, and of these again to the whole; that the structure may appear an entire and complete body, wherein each member agrees with the other, and all necessary to compose what you intend to form.[18]

Judd made what Lars Lerup called those "complex computations"[19] in his work at Marfa. The interrelated unity of Judd's holistic approach to design is, in part, the result of his work process. Around the time that he wrote "Specific Objects," Judd began commissioning the production of his pieces from small specialty metal shops such as Bernstein Bros. in New York. Over the years Judd collaborated with various national and international specialty shops. Considering the development of Judd's

Öffnung von Innenraum in einem Behälter, so dass er von außen her voll sichtbar wird. Einige Kunsthistoriker nennen ihn zwar einen Bildhauer, doch Judd wies diese Kategorie zurück und bezeichnete seine dreidimensionale Kunst als „Werke“. Architektur ist Raum, dessen Grenzen der Architekt definiert, und Judd verstand Skulptur durchaus im architektonischen Sinn – als Grenze, gesetzt durch Raum und Licht. Seine Raumvorstellungen erkundete Judd nicht im herkömmlichen Sinne der „Skulptur“, sondern in „Stücken“ oder „Werken“. Sein Gebrauch dieser Begriffe ist bezeichnend, macht er doch kenntlich, wie ausgeprägt Judd als der Architekt dachte, der er unzweifelhaft war.

In „Spezifische Objekte“ (1965), einem von Judds Schlüsselessays über seine Raumauffassung, findet sich der Satz: „Das Ding als Ganzes ist das Interessante.“ [17] Unter das „Ganze“ versteht Judd ein Ding mit ganzheitlichen Eigenschaften und bezieht sich damit, bewusst oder unbewusst, auf einen Raumbegriff der Renaissance. Andrea Palladio, der vielleicht einflussreichste Architekt überhaupt, schreibt in seinem Werk *Die vier Bücher zur Architektur*:

> Schönheit entspringt der schönen Form und der Entsprechung des Ganzen mit den Einzelteilen, wie der Entsprechung der Teile untereinander und dieser wieder zum Ganzen, so dass das Gebäude wie ein einheitlicher und vollkommener Körper erscheint. Entspricht doch ein Teil dem anderen und sind doch alle Teile unabdingbar notwendig, um das zu erreichen, was man gewollt hat. [18]

Judds in Marfa entstandene Arbeiten sind Ausweis dessen, was Lars Lerup die „komplexen Berechnungen“ [19] nennt. Die intern vernetzte Einheit von Judds holistischem Designansatz ist zum Teil das Ergebnis seines Arbeitsprozesses. Etwa seit der Zeit, als der Aufsatz „Spezifische Objekte“ entstand, ließ Judd seine Stücke von kleinen spezialisierten Metallbetrieben wie Bernstein Bros. in New York herstellen. Im Lauf der Jahre arbeitete Judd dann mit verschiedenen in- und ausländischen Fachwerkstätten zusammen. Ein Blick auf die Entwicklung der Arbeiten Judds von den frühen bis zu den späten Stücken macht deutlich, wie die Objekte zunehmend präziser und ausgefeilter wurden. Sein

work, from the early to late pieces, one can see how increasingly precise and refined the pieces became. His work process, then, was similar to the working methods of architects. Architects, designers, and industrial designers search for the best contractor, builder, craftsmen, or manufacturing company to produce their designs. The designer builds a relationship with a manufacturer for years and improves, over time, the craftsmanship of the work.

In her essay "Donald Judd" in the catalogue raisonné published on the occasion of the 1975 exhibition of Judd's work in the National Gallery of Canada in Ottawa, Roberta Smith described Judd's work process when he moved from two-dimensional painting to the three-dimensional freestanding pieces: "The decisions take place before the objects are made. His work is not additive; it is not made or perceived that way." [20] For the architect, the only chance to assure that his architectural vision persists is to test creative ideas *before* the construction process begins. Afterthoughts arising while a building is under construction usually entail additional costs not welcomed by clients and contractors. Judd's planning process for a particular piece was finished when he sent it to a fabricator. When a work was physically completed by the shop workers, Judd would always inspect the final result and either approve or reject it if it did not fulfill his high quality standards. But he did not stop there. Increasingly, he became concerned about how and where his works were ultimately placed. Judd himself recalls in a 1971 interview with John Coplans the time when he made the first freestanding pieces:

> **I was surprised, when I made those first two free-standing pieces, to have something set out into the middle of the room. It puzzled me. On the one hand, I didn't quite know what to make of it, and on the other, they suddenly seemed to have an enormous number of possibilities. It looked at that point, and from then on, as though I could do anything. Anyway, I certainly didn't think I was making sculpture.** [21]

Arbeitsprozess ist also mit der Arbeitsmethode von Architekten zu vergleichen. Architekten, Designer und Industriedesigner suchen für die Ausführung ihrer Entwürfe nach dem besten Generalunternehmer, Bauunternehmer, den besten Handwerkern oder Herstellern. Der Designer baut mit dem Hersteller über die Jahre eine Beziehung auf und verbessert mit der Zeit die handwerkliche Qualität der Arbeit.

Im Catalogue Raisonné der Ausstellung von Judds Werken, die 1975 in der kanadischen Nationalgalerie in Ottawa stattfand, beschreibt Roberta Smith in ihrem Aufsatz „Donald Judd" den Arbeitsprozess des Künstlers beim Wechsel von der zweidimensionalen Malerei zu den dreidimensionalen frei stehenden Stücken: „Die Entscheidungen fallen, bevor die Objekte entstehen. Sein Schaffen ist nicht additiv; weder entsteht es so, noch wird es so wahrgenommen."[20] Kreative Ideen zu überprüfen, bevor die Bauarbeiten beginnen, ist für den Architekten die einzige Möglichkeit sicherzustellen, dass seine architektonischen Vorstellungen erhalten bleiben. Nachträgliche Bedenken, wenn der Bau eines Gebäudes schon im Gang ist, bringen im Allgemeinen zusätzliche Kosten mit sich, die Bauherren und Generalunternehmer wenig schätzen. Judds Planungsprozess für ein bestimmtes Stück war beendet, wenn er es an einen Hersteller schickte. War eine Arbeit dann in der Werkstatt fertiggestellt, unterzog Judd das endgültige Resultat immer einer genauen Überprüfung und befand es für gut oder verwarf es, wenn es seinem hohen Qualitätsmaßstab nicht genügte. Doch er ging noch weiter. Immer mehr lag ihm die Frage am Herzen, wie und wo seine Arbeiten schließlich ihren Platz finden würden. In einem Interview mit John Coplans erinnert sich Judd 1971 an die Zeit, als seine ersten frei stehenden Stücke entstanden:

> Als ich diese ersten zwei frei stehenden Stücke machte, war ich überrascht, etwas in die Mitte des Zimmers gestellt zu haben. Ein verblüffender Eindruck. Einerseits war ich nicht sicher, was davon zu halten sei, andererseits schienen sie plötzlich eine Unmenge von Möglichkeiten zu besitzen. In diesem Moment und von da an sah es so aus, als könnte ich machen, was ich nur wollte. Jedenfalls aber hatte ich nicht die Vorstellung Skulpturen zu machen.[21]

Judd's untitled 100 mill-aluminum pieces in Marfa confirm that statement. He limited the work to 100 because it was the number of pieces he could accommodate in the two sheds, but he could have continued to produce more variations, or, as he said, an "enormous number of possibilities." In Marfa, Judd's architectural work grew at a rapid pace—evidence that his careful thinking allowed him to realize his plans. Unlike most architecture, a traditional piece of artwork is usually easily removed, so the true test for architecture comes after the building is realized.

Judd's work process was put on view in 1976 at an exhibition at the Kunsthalle in Bern, Switzerland, and a parallel exhibition of drawings at the Kunstmuseum in Basel. Judd traveled to Switzerland to examine the exhibition space in Bern and then made his proposal. The Kunsthalle director, Johannes Gachnang, who described Judd's work in a glowing critique, produced a small black and white exhibition catalogue with an introduction:

> **This book is a document of the 5 sculptures made by Donald Judd for his exhibition in the 5 rooms of Kunsthalle Bern. After a first visit of the place in summer of 1975 and an examination of the ground plan he made 5 sketches for 5 individual sculptures relating to the rooms. They are Finnish birch plywood ¾ inches thick, each 48 inches high with a distance always of 60 inches from the walls. The 5 works were fabricated by two men of Mr. Heinz Geiser's carpenter shop in Bern and are exhibited at the Kunsthalle Bern from April 14 to May 30; after the exhibition they will be removed and dismantled.**
>
> **Each of these 5 sculptures can be looked at separately from the others and together they relate, widely and openly. In connection with his work Donald Judd is a *sovereign architect* [emphasis mine] of our time, able to handle volume and hollow space.[22]**

The exhibition catalogue shows a floor plan of the museum with Donald Judd's five floor pieces (Fig. 01). In addition, the catalogue includes photographs of the finished Judd pieces and construction photographs (Fig. 02) showing the carpenters assembling the pieces on site. By visiting the exhibition space first,

Judds in Marfa ausgestellte 100 Objekte ohne Titel aus Walzaluminium können als Bestätigung dieser Feststellung gelten. Er begrenzte die Stückzahl auf 100, weil es die Anzahl war, die er in den beiden Hallen unterbringen konnte, aber er hätte weitere Variationen schaffen können, oder wie er sagte, „eine Unmenge von Möglichkeiten". In Marfa nahm Judds architektonisches Werk rasch an Umfang zu – ein Beweis dafür, dass ihm seine sorgfältige Denkarbeit erlaubte, seine Pläne zu realisieren. Ein Kunstwerk herkömmlicher Art lässt sich anders als die meiste Architektur leicht von seinem Platz entfernen, daher zeichnet sich der eigentliche Test für ein Bauwerk erst mit der Fertigstellung des Gebäudes ab.

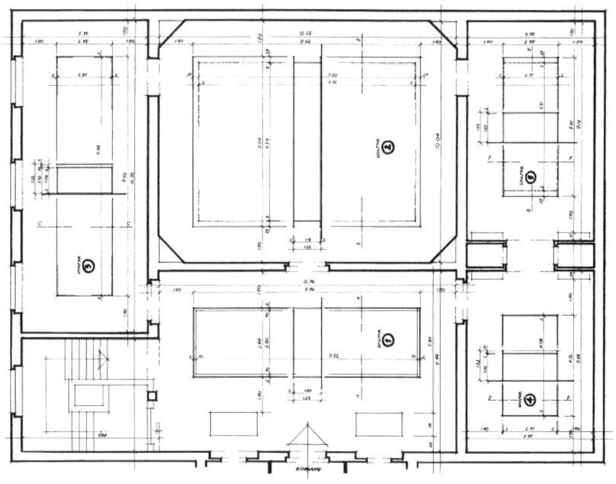

FIG./ABB. 01

Floor plan Kunsthalle, Bern[23]

Ausführungsplan – Erdgeschoss, Kunsthalle Bern[23]

In einer Ausstellung der Kunsthalle Bern von 1976 und einer Parallelausstellung von Zeichnungen Judds im Kunstmuseum Basel wurde Judds Schaffensprozess dokumentiert. Judd reiste in die Schweiz, um den Ausstellungsraum in Bern zu prüfen, und machte dann seine Vorschläge. Johannes Gachnang, der damalige Direktor der Kunsthalle Bern, der Judds Werk eine enthusiastische Kritik widmete, gab einen kleinen, in Schwarz-Weiß gehaltenen Katalog mit Einführung heraus:

> Dieses Buch dokumentiert 5 Skulpturen, die von Donald Judd für die 5 Räume des Erdgeschosses der Kunsthalle Bern geschaffen wurden. Nach einer ersten Besichtigung der Örtlichkeiten im Sommer 1975, der Einsichtnahme der Grundrisspläne der Kunsthalle und 5 Ideenskizzen des Künstlers entstanden 5 unterschiedliche, raumbezogene Skulpturen, gefertigt aus 19 mm starken finnischen Sperrholzplatten (Birke), jede mit einer Höhe von 122 cm und einem allseitigen Abstand von 150 cm von den Wänden. Aufgebaut wurden die 5 Arbeiten von zwei Mitarbeitern der Schreinerei Heinz Geiser, Ostermundigen/Bern, und sie sind in der Kunsthalle Bern vom 14. April bis 30. Mai 1976 zu sehen; nach der Ausstellung werden sie ihrer Funktion enthoben und abgebaut.
>
> Jede einzelne dieser 5 Skulpturen kann unabhängig von der andern als Ganzes für sich und im Raum gesehen werden, und alle zusammen ergeben eine neue, in sich geschlossene Ganzheit, weit und offen. Im Umgang und in seiner Arbeit

Judd was not unlike an architect who goes to the site, evaluates it, and then responds with a design. Then a contractor builds the building from the plans of the architect. The architect oversees the work, but he is removed from the actual building process. Robin Evans describes the architect's role best in his essay "Architectural Projections:" "Architects do not make buildings, they make drawings of buildings."[25] The exhibition in Basel, "Donald Judd Drawings/Zeichnungen from 1956–1976," displayed Judd's drawings, which communicate with great legibility, sometimes accompanied with measurements and indications of materials. Many of the drawings were done freehand, not unlike the drawings architects produce to communicate their ideas.

Not only can Judd's work process be compared to that of an architect, there is of course the spatial aspect, "the thing as a whole" as Judd described it in "Specific Objects." In this essay he compares the Badia di Fiesole near Florence to Leon Battista Alberti's Palazzo Rucellai, arguing that the spatial quality of the Badia surpasses the representational character of Alberti's Palazzo Rucellai, typically introduced to architecture students in their history classes because of the compositional quality of the facade. To Judd, the interior space is more interesting than the facade:

> **The difference between the new work and earlier painting and present sculpture is like that between one of Brunelleschi's windows in the Badia di Fiesole and the**

mit Volumen und Hohlraum erweist sich Donald Judd als *souveräner Architekt* dieser Zeit. [Kursiv vom Verf.][22]

Der Ausstellungskatalog zeigt einen Geschossgrundriss des Museums mit Donald Judds fünf Geschossobjekten (Abb. 01). Weiter umfasst der Katalog Fotografien der fertiggestellten Objekte Judds und Konstruktionsfotos (Abb. 02), die zeigen, wie die Schreiner die Stücke vor Ort zusammenbauen. Mit seiner vorgängigen Besichtigung des Ausstellungsraums verhielt sich Judd ähnlich wie der Architekt, der zum Bauplatz geht, ihn begutachtet und dann mit einem Entwurf reagiert. Danach errichtet der Bauunternehmer das Gebäude nach den Plänen des Architekten. Der Architekt beaufsichtigt die Arbeiten, bleibt aber von der eigentlichen Bautätigkeit ausgeschlossen. Am zutreffendsten ist die Rolle des Architekten in Robin Evans' Aufsatz „Architectural Projections" beschrieben: „Architekten machen keine Gebäude, sie machen Zeichnungen von Gebäuden."[25] Die Basler Ausstellung „Donald Judd, Zeichnungen/Drawings 1956–1976" stellte Judds Zeichnungen aus, sprechende, gut lesbare Dokumente, manchmal begleitet von Maßangaben und Hinweisen auf die Materialien. Häufig sind es Freihandzeichnungen, nicht unähnlich den Zeichnungen, in denen Architekten ihre Ideen darstellen.

Judds Arbeitsprozess lässt sich nicht nur mit dem der Architekten vergleichen; da ist außerdem natürlich noch der räumliche Aspekt, „das Ding als Ganzes", wie Judd es in „Specific Objects" beschreibt. Er vergleicht in diesem Aufsatz die Badia di Fiesole in der Nähe von Florenz mit Leon Battista Albertis Palazzo Rucellai und kommt zu dem Schluss, die Raumqualität der Badia sei dem Darstellungscharakter von Albertis Palazzo Rucellai überlegen, der den Studierenden im Fach Architekturgeschichte gewöhnlich als Beispiel für eine kunstgerechte Fassadengliederung vorgeführt wird. Für Judd ist der Innenraum interessanter als die Fassade:

> Der Unterschied zwischen den neuen Arbeiten und älterer Malerei wie zeitgenössischer Bildhauerei ist ähnlich dem, der zwischen einem Fenster von Brunelleschi in der Badia di Fiesole und der Fassade des Palazzo Rucellai besteht; diese ist als Ganzes nur ein unentwickeltes Rechteck und hauptsächlich eine Sammlung von sehr geordneten Teilen.[26]

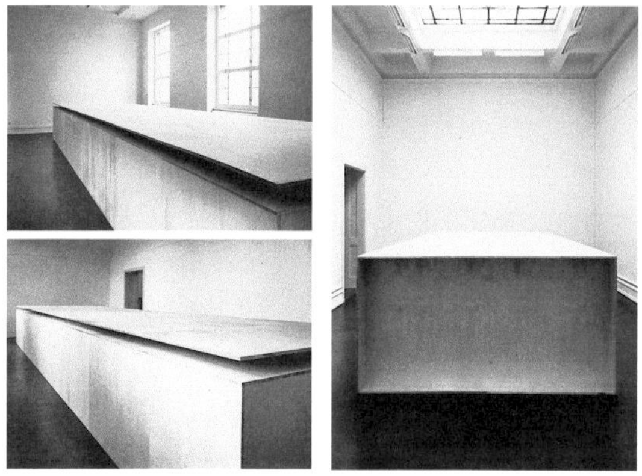

FIG./ABB. 02

Installation view, Donald Judd: Skulpturen, Kunsthalle Bern,[24] Switzerland, April 14-May 30, 1976.

Installation, Donald Judd: Skulpturen, Kunsthalle Bern,[24] Schweiz, 14. April–30. Mai 1976

> facade of the Palazzo Rucellai, which is only an undeveloped rectangle as a whole and is mainly a collection of highly ordered parts.[26]

Judd was prescient in his critique, for today one of the most respected Brunelleschi scholars, Howard Saalman, strongly doubts that Brunelleschi is the architect of the Badia, the first building of the Italian Renaissance covered with masonry barrel vaults. In subsequent studies Saalman attempts to demonstrate that the Badia's design should be credited to Alberti.[27] More interesting is that Judd, when he wrote his fundamental essay, was interested in the spatial quality of the building interior, not in the compositional aspect of the facade.

In 1968, Judd purchased a cast-iron building on 101 Spring Street in SoHo, New York, designed by architect Nicholas Whyte, which he subsequently renovated and installed with his own art work and the work of his friends. This cast-iron building set the precedent for Judd's architectural renovations. This is how Judd described his work on 101 Spring Street:

> These ideas were precedents for some small pieces and then for 100 mill aluminum pieces in The Chinati Foundation. The renovation of the building and the permanent purpose of the building are precedents for the larger spaces in my place in Texas, La Mansana de Chinati, for The Chinati Foundation, and will be for Ayala de Chinati.[28]

Judd's architectural work in Marfa suggests that by this stage his thinking had developed past the ideas expressed when he began renovating 101 Spring Street. In Marfa, Judd was able to

Judds Kritik erwies sich als hellsichtig. Heute macht Howard Saalman, einer der angesehensten Brunelleschi-Spezialisten, starke Zweifel geltend, ob Brunelleschi der Architekt der Badia gewesen sei, dem ersten Gebäude der italienischen Renaissance, das mit gemauerten Tonnengewölben gedeckt ist. In seinen Studien versucht Saalman zu belegen, dass der Entwurf der Badia Alberti zuzuschreiben sei.[27] Bemerkenswerter ist, dass sich Judd bei der Abfassung seines grundlegenden Aufsatzes für die räumliche Qualität des Gebäudeinneren interessierte und nicht für die Gestaltung der Fassade.

1969 kaufte Judd ein gusseisernes Haus an der Spring Street 101 im New Yorker Stadtteil SoHo, entworfen vom Architekten Nicholas Whyte, das er laufend erneuerte und mit eigenen Kunstwerken und Arbeiten seiner Freunde ausstattete. Dieses Gusseisen-Gebäude kann als Vorläufer aller späteren baulichen Bereinigungen Judds gelten. Judd schildert seine Arbeit in der Spring Street 101 wie folgt:

> Diese Ideen waren die ersten Vorläufer einiger kleiner Arbeiten und dann der 100 Arbeiten aus gewalztem Aluminium in der Chinati Foundation. Die Renovierung des Gebäudes und seine bleibende Bestimmung sind Vorbild für die größeren Räume in meinem Haus in Texas, der La Mansana de Chinati, für die Chinati Foundation und werden es für die Ayala de Chinati sein.[28]

Judds architektonisches Werk in Marfa macht deutlich, dass sein Denken in jener Phase die Ideen, die seiner Erneuerung des Spring-Street-Gebäudes zugrunde liegen, hinter sich gelassen hatte. In Marfa war Judd fähig, seine architektonischen Vorstellungen über die Grundfläche eines bestehenden Gebäudes hinauszuführen. In La Mansana de Chinati hat er den existenten urbanen Status des Gebäudes im Rahmen von Marfa redefiniert. Judd plante und errichtete innerhalb von La Mansana auch neue Gebäude und Anlagen. Eine ähnliche Beobachtung lässt sich auf dem Gelände des ehemaligen Fort D.A. Russell machen, aus dem die Chinati Foudation wurde, und ebenso in Ayala de Chinati, dem Ensemble von Judds drei Farmen. An diesen Standorten plante und erstellte Judd neue Gebäude. Darüber hinaus wurden neben den neuen Strukturen auch Landschaft und Möblierung des

expand his architectural ideas beyond the footprint of an existing building. At La Mansana de Chinati, he redefined the buildings' existing urban condition within the town of Marfa. Judd also planned and built new buildings and structures within the La Mansana. A similar observation can be made at the grounds of former Fort D.A. Russell, which became The Chinati Foundation, and at Ayala de Chinati, Judd's three ranches. Judd planned and built new structures on these sites. Furthermore, the landscape and outdoor furnishings became an integral part of the design, as did the new structures. Judd carefully wove them within the pattern of existing buildings and the site. Exterior spaces surrounding the buildings and structures both old and new became as important as the volume of the buildings themselves, not unlike the spaces between his stacks, the vertical artworks Judd became so well known for. Also, Judd's building at 101 Spring Street had architectural qualities *before* Judd's interventions, thanks to the original design of architect Nicholas Whyte. The elegant cast-iron structure and the large generous windows are the building's defining architectural qualities. The situation in Marfa was very different. With the exception of the Architecture Studio, originally the Marfa National Bank building, most of the buildings that Judd renovated in Marfa had little architectural quality before Judd's intervention. The Chamberlain Building, a former warehouse and office building for the Marfa Wool & Mohair Company, exemplifies Judd's planning process: the building was developed from a utilitarian storage and office building to become a successful exhibition space for John Chamberlain's art. A feat few architects would have been able to imagine.

Judd condemned the commercial approach of the late twentieth-century museum boom with the authority of one of his generation's most respected and established artists. In his frequent essays and interviews on art and architecture, he strongly criticized such leading architects as Peter Eisenman, Hans Hollein, and Frank Gehry. In the catalogue entry for his 1991 Vienna exhibition, Judd condemned the designs for art museums by Hollein and Gehry:

Außenraums zum integralen Teil des Entwurfs. Judd verwob sie behutsam mit dem Muster der bestehenden Bauten und dem Gelände. Die Außenräume, welche die alten wie auch neuen Gebäude und Anlagen umgeben, wurden so wichtig wie die Baukörper selbst, vergleichbar den Räumen zwischen seinen Stacks, den vertikalen Kunstwerken, die sich vor allem mit seinem Namen verbinden. Gleichermaßen besaß das Haus in der Spring Street 101 dank dem Originalentwurf des Architekten Nicholas Whyte schon vor Judds Eingriffen bauliche Qualitäten. Sie sind wesentlich gegeben durch das elegante Skelett aus Gusseisen und die großzügigen hohen Fenster. Die Situation in Marfa war eine völlig andere. Mit Ausnahme des Architekturstudios, ursprünglich das Gebäude der Nationalbank Marfa, besaßen die von Judd in Marfa erneuerten Gebäude *vor* Judds Eingriffen nur wenig architektonische Qualität. Das Chamberlain-Gebäude, ein ehemaliges Lagerhaus und Bürogebäude für die Marfa Wool & Mohair Company, veranschaulicht Judds Planungsprozess: die industriell genutzte Zweckarchitektur eines Speicher- und Bürokomplexes wurde zu einem erfolgreichen Ausstellungsraum für die Kunst von John Chamberlain entwickelt. Ein Bravourstück, das sich wohl nur die wenigsten Architekten hätten einfallen lassen.

Mit der Autorität eines der meist geachteten und anerkannten Künstler seiner Generation stellte Judd den kommerziell orientierten Museumsboom des späten 20. Jahrhunderts an den Pranger. In seinen zahlreichen Aufsätzen und Interviews zu den Themen Kunst und Architektur ging er mit führenden Architekten wie Peter Eisenman, Hans Hollein und Frank Gehry scharf ins Gericht. In einem Beitrag zum Katalog seiner Wiener Ausstellung von 1991 verurteilte er die Museumsentwürfe von Hollein und Gehry:

> Das Kunstmuseum wird hochgradig sinnlos, eine Scheinarchitektur für Scheinkunstwerke, das Allerheiligste einer Scheingesellschaft. Das ist natürlich Hans Holleins Stärke. Er und das New Yorker Guggenheim Museum planen ein negatives und gefälschtes Guggenheim für Salzburg, ein Loch im Boden. Was sollen die Öffentlichkeit und die Studenten von Frank Gehrys entsetzlichem Entwurf für das Vitra Design Museum halten? Diese Bauwerke machen einen

> The art museum becomes exquisitely pointless, a fake for fakes, a double fake, the inner sanctum of a fake society. Of course Hans Hollein is good at this. He and the Guggenheim Museum of New York plan a negative and fake Guggenheim for Salzburg, a hole in the ground. What is the public and what are students supposed to think of the horrifying design of Frank Gehry's museum of design for Vitra? These buildings make a joke of architecture, of art, of culture of the community, and of the whole society.[29]

An architect who shared Judd's sculptural sense of architecture was Rudolph M. Schindler (1887–1953), the Austrian-born, Los Angeles-based architect and student of Frank Lloyd Wright. Schindler called his architectural philosophy "Space Architecture," which he, as a modernist, believed would change how architects think about design. Schindler and Gehry had opposite approaches to architecture. Schindler designed his buildings from the inside out, and this method made him different from many of his contemporaries. As Schindler said:

> The architect of the past saw the building as a mass of structural material which he carved. His medium of expression was the same as the sculptor's mass form. The architect of our time is discovering a new medium: space. The house of the future is a symphony of "space forms"—each room a necessary and unavoidable part of the whole. Structural materials, walls, ceilings, floors, are only the means to an end: the definition of space forms. They lose their individual importance and are simplified to the utmost—a simple weave of a few materials articulates space into the rooms.[30]

Judd owned several pieces of Schindler furniture and appreciated Schindler's ideas and interest in space architecture. In one small building Judd modified in Marfa, his own early paintings are placed in harmony with Schindler's furniture. Judd also collected furniture by Alvar Aalto, Gerrit Rietveld, Ludwig Mies van der Rohe, as well as Arts and Crafts pieces, especially the furniture of Gustav Stickley. Judd's own furniture design has been well recognized and documented; it continues the Arts and Crafts and Modernist traditions, seeking a unity in design and linking

> Witz aus der Architektur, aus der Kunst, aus dem Gemeinwesen und der gesamten Gesellschaft.[29]

Ein Architekt, der Judds skulpturale Auffassung von Architektur teilte, war Rudolph M. Schindler (1887–1953), der in Österreich geborene und in Los Angeles lebende Architekt und Schüler von Frank Lloyd Wright. Schindler bezeichnete seine Architekturphilosophie als „Raumarchitektur", ein Konzept, das, wie er als Modernist glaubte, die Vorstellung der Architekten vom baulichen Entwurf verändern würde. Die methodischen Ansätze Schindlers und Gehrys sind grundverschieden. Schindler entwarf seine Gebäude aus dem Inneren heraus, ein Vorgehen, in dem er sich von vielen seiner Zeitgenossen unterschied. Schindler sagt:

> Der Architekt der Vergangenheit betrachtete das Gebäude als eine Masse baulichen Materials, das er zurechtmeißelte. Sein Ausdrucksmedium war das des Bildhauers – das Formen von Masse. Der Architekt unserer Zeit ist dabei, ein neues Medium zu entdecken: den Raum. Das Haus der Zukunft ist eine Symphonie von „Raumformen" – jedes Zimmer ein notwendiger und unvermeidlicher Teil des Ganzen. Baustoffe, Wände, Decken, Böden sind nur die Mittel zum Zweck: der Definition von Raumformen. Sie verlieren ihre individuelle Bedeutung und werden aufs äußerste vereinfacht – einfaches Verweben weniger Materialien artikuliert den Raum in die Zimmer.[30]

Judd besaß verschiedene Möbelstücke Schindlers und schätzte seine Ideen und sein Interesse für die Raumarchitektur. In einem von Judd umgebauten kleinen Haus in Marfa bilden seine eigenen frühen Bilder eine harmonische Einheit mit Schindlers Möbeln. Judd sammelte auch Möbel von Alvar Aalto, Gerrit Rietveld und Ludwig Mies van der Rohe ebenso wie Stücke der Arts-and-Crafts-Bewegung, besonders aus der Werkstatt von Gustav Stickley. Judds eigene Möbelentwürfe sind anerkannt und gut dokumentiert. In Fortführung der Tradition der Arts-and-Crafts-Konzepte und der Modernisten streben sie nach Einheit der Gestaltung und verbinden Architektur, Mobiliar und die dekorativen und praktischen Künste. Bei seiner Suche nach einem räumlichen Kontinuum vertiefte Judd seine architektonischen Vorstellungen vom Raum durch seine Möbelentwürfe.

architecture, furniture, and the decorative and practical arts. In his search for a spatial continuum, Judd furthered his architectural ideas about space through his furniture design.

Just as unity in design was a Modernist principle, so was proportion, that most basic component of all Classical design. The leaders of early twentieth-century Modernism claimed to break with the past, yet the work of Mies van der Rohe[31] and Le Corbusier,[32] as recent research shows, is much more related to classical architecture than the originators wanted us to believe. For example, Corbusier's proportioning system, the Modulor, shows a concern for proportions very much in keeping with the traditions of antiquity and the Renaissance. For Judd, proportions were also significant:

> **Proportion is very important to us, both in our minds and lives and as objectified visually, since it is thought and feeling undivided, since it is unity and harmony, easy or difficult, and often peace and quiet. Proportion is specific and identifiable in art and architecture and creates our space and time. Proportion and in fact all intelligence in art is instantly understood, at least by some. It's a myth that difficult art is difficult.[33]**

Judd respected the work of several twentieth-century architects. At the first superficial glance, Judd's work can be regarded in that Modernist tradition. However, if we compare the Modernists and Judd, we quickly see that the Modernists were not concerned with the renovation of existing structures. The Modernist idea involved a profound break with the past, and the Modernist architect did not want to compromise a design by using historic structures that would compete with Modern additions. Especially in North America, where the typical building substance does not have as long a history as in Europe, there has usually been only one solution—tear down and make room for the new. A prominent, well-recognized exception to this is the addition to Yale's University Art Gallery (1951–1953) in New Haven, Connecticut by Louis I. Kahn (Fig. 03). A quick look at the facade's exterior clearly reveals Kahn's intention of contrasting the building with the neo-Gothic context of the university. During the same time in Europe, the still relatively unknown

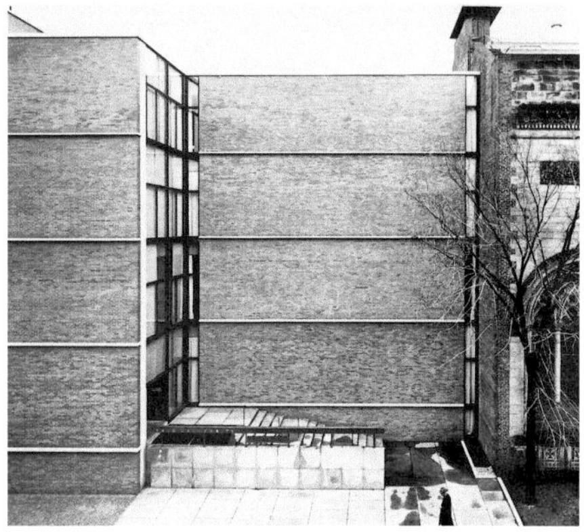

FIG./ABB. 03.

Entrance Yale Art Gallery Addition, New Haven, CT[34]

Eingang zum Anbau der Yale-Kunstgalerie, New Haven, CT[34]

Nicht nur die Einheit der Gestaltung war ein Prinzip der künstlerischen Moderne, sondern auch die Proportion, das fundamentale Element klassischer Gestaltung schlechthin. Die führenden Vertreter der Moderne des frühen 20. Jahrhunderts behaupteten mit der Vergangenheit zu brechen, doch das Werk Mies van der Rohes[31] und Le Corbusiers[32] ist, wie jüngere Untersuchungen zeigen, der klassischen Architektur stärker verbunden, als seine Schöpfer vorgaben. Le Corbusiers Maßsystem zum Beispiel, der Modulor, beruht auf einem Interesse an Proportionen, das durchaus in Einklang steht mit den Konventionen der Antike und der Renaissance. Auch für Judd hatten Proportionen ihre Bedeutung:

> Proportion ist für uns sehr wichtig, sowohl in unserem Denken und Leben als auch visuell umgesetzt, denn in ihr sind Denken und Fühlen nicht voneinander getrennt, sie ist Einheit und Harmonie, einfach oder schwierig und oft Frieden und Ruhe. In der Kunst und in der Architektur ist Proportion spezifisch und identifizierbar, sie schafft unsere Zeit und unseren Raum. Proportion und eigentlich jede Intelligenz in der Kunst wird augenblicklich verstanden, zumindest von einigen. Es ist ein Mythos, dass schwierige Kunst schwierig sei.[33]

Dem Werk einiger Architekten des 20. Jahrhunderts brachte Judd durchaus Respekt entgegen. Oberflächlich betrachtet lassen sich Judds Arbeiten in diese Tradition der Moderne einreihen. Ein Vergleich Judds mit den Modernisten zeigt jedoch schnell, dass es diesen nicht um die Erneuerung bestehender Strukturen ging. Zur Idee der Moderne gehörte ein radikaler Bruch mit der Vergangenheit, und ein Architekt, der dieser Idee verpflichtet war, wollte seinen Entwurf nicht dadurch kompromittieren, dass er historische Strukturen benutzte, die mit modernen Ergänzungen in Konkurrenz treten würden. Besonders in Nordamerika, wo die typische Bausubstanz keine so lange Geschichte hat wie in Europa, gab es in der Regel nur eine Lösung: abreißen und Raum für Neues schaffen. Eine prominente und allgemein anerkannte Ausnahme ist der von Louis I. Kahn gestaltete Anbau der Kunstgalerie der Yale University in New Haven, Connecticut (1951–1953). (Abb. 03) Beim ersten Blick auf die

German architect Hans Dollgast (1891–1974) reconstructed and expanded the Bavarian Alte Pinakothek (constructed 1826–1836, reconstruction 1952–1957) in Munich (Fig. 04), which was damaged during World War II. His method of restoring the building was to use different materials and finishes but retain the same proportions of the arches by the original architect Leo von Klenze (1784–1864). Carlo Scarpa (1906–1978) developed his method of renovation and additions to historic buildings with the renovation of the Museo di Castelvecchio (1958–1964) in Verona.

These examples, while very different, share one common idea—old and new are clearly marked. Each of them added to an existing building, making it clear to the visitor where the historical building stops and where the new begins. Scarpa's ability to reveal old and new—through gaps, joints, and changes in material—became very influential, as architects began to emphasize, in their building projects, that which already exists and that which is new.

Judd, however, was *not* concerned with the idea of distinguishing the existing building from his own additions; in fact, in most cases he altered the existing building. Judd was concerned with the *whole*, which means the building and its context. He was not interested in a dialogue between old and new; his dialogue was about the building, the art, and the urban or landscape context. A museum designed for the sake of architecture ignores the artwork, which should be the main reason for the building's existence. The examples of Kahn, Dollgast, and Scarpa are widely presented and taught at architecture schools in Europe and

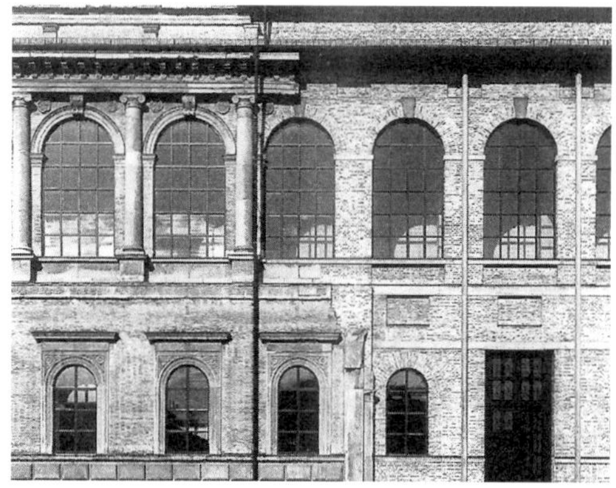

FIG./ABB. 04.

Elevation Alte Pinakothek, Munich[35]
Ansicht Alte Pinakothek, München[35]

Außenfassade wird klar, dass Kahn beabsichtigte, das Gebäude zum neugotischen Kontext der Universität in Kontrast zu setzen. Gleichzeitig leitete in Europa der noch wenig bekannte Architekt Hans Döllgast (1891–1974) den Wiederaufbau und Umbau der Alten Pinakothek in München (erbaut 1826–1836, Wiederaufbau 1952–1957) (Abb. 04), die während des Zweiten Weltkriegs stark beschädigt worden war. Döllgast benutzte zur Restaurierung des Bauwerks unterschiedliche Materialien und Anstriche, behielt aber die Proportionen bei, die der Erbauer des Museums, Leo von Klenze (1784–1864), den Gewölben gegeben hatte. Carlo Scarpa (1906–1978) entwickelte seine Methode der Renovierung und Erweiterung historischer Gebäude bei der Erneuerung des Museo di Castelvecchio (1958–1964) in Verona.

Die genannten Beispiele sind höchst unterschiedlich, und dennoch ist ihnen etwas gemeinsam: die Vorstellung, Altes und Neues deutlich zu markieren. In jedem Fall wurde ein bestehendes Gebäude so erweitert, dass für die Betrachtenden klar zu Tage tritt, wo das historische Gebäude endet und wo das Neue beginnt. Scarpas Fähigkeit, Altes und Neues kenntlich zu machen – durch Spalten, Fugen und Wechsel des Materials – gewann an Einfluss, als immer mehr Architekten dazu übergingen, in ihren Bauprojekten Bestehendes und Neues zu betonen.

Judd ging es allerdings *nicht* darum, das bestehende Gebäude von seinen eigenen Ergänzungen zu unterscheiden; in den meisten Fällen wurde das bestehende Bauwerk sogar verändert. Ihm ging es um das *Ganze*, das heißt um das Gebäude und seinen Kontext. Ein Dialog zwischen Alt und Neu interessierte ihn nicht; sein Gespräch verlief zwischen dem Gebäude, der Kunst und dem urbanen oder landschaftlichen Kontext. Ein Museum, das um der Architektur willen gebaut wird, ignoriert die Kunst, die der Hauptgrund für die Existenz des Gebäudes sein sollte. An den Architekturfakultäten in Europa und Amerika sind die Beispiele von Kahn, Döllgast und Scarpa im Lehrstoff prominent vertreten. Für Judd hat ein Museumsbau seine Berechtigung in erster Linie darin, Kunst aufzunehmen – und, wenn möglich, zu ergänzen, keinesfalls aber, sie zu konkurrenzieren oder ihr den Rang abzulaufen. Darum lehnte er die meisten Museen des 20. Jahrhunderts und ihre Erbauer ab. Seiner Auffassung nach waren viele führende Architekten mehr um ihre

America. Judd understood that a museum building existed first and foremost in order to shelter art—and, if possible, to complement the art, but never to compete with or overpower the art. Thus he vigorously rejected most late twentieth-century museums and their designers. To his way of thinking, many leading architects were more concerned with their own aesthetic expression, and with promoting their own reputation, than with creating a good space for art.

The buildings in Marfa, before Judd acquired them, were mostly military, industrial or commercial structures. The straightforward geometry of those buildings was agreeable to Judd's design philosophy—a philosophy that might have originated during Judd's service as a military engineer in 1946 and 1947.[36] Thomas Kellein, author of *The Whole Space. The Early work of Donald Judd*, proposes such a connection in his book, *Donald Judd. Early Work 1955–1968*:

> **Viewing the extent and nature of the building activities at Marfa in light of Judd's biography, one cannot help registering that even before he decided to work as an artist, he had already been involved in engineering projects where he created enclosed areas and walk-in spaces. According to an *Army of the United States Separation Qualification Record*, during his military service Judd, together with three other U.S. army personnel and fifty Koreans, erected "frames and pre-fabricated buildings"—just as he was to do again at his Mansana de Chinati thirty years later.[37]**

ästhetischen Ausdrucksmöglichkeiten und ihre Reputation bemüht als darum, guten Raum für Kunst zu schaffen.

Die meisten Gebäude in Marfa, die Judd erwarb, hatten militärischen, industriellen oder kommerziellen Zwecken gedient. Die einfache Geometrie dieser Bauten kam Judds Entwurfsphilosophie entgegen – eine Philosophie, deren Ursprung in den Jahren 1946/47 liegen könnte, in denen Judd während seines Militärdienstes auch als Bauingenieur im Einsatz war.[36] Thomas Kellein, Verfasser von *Donald Judd: Der ganze Raum. Das Frühwerk 1955–1968*, bringt eine solche Verbindung in seinem Werk *Donald Judd. Das Frühwerk 1955–1968* zur Sprache:

> Wenn man Umfang und Art seiner abschließenden baulichen Tätigkeit in Marfa vor dem Hintergrund von Judds Biografie betrachtet, fällt auf, dass er noch vor der Entscheidung zur eigenen künstlerischen Tätigkeit eine Bauingenieursaufgabe übernommen hatte, mit der er Einfriedungen und begehbare Räume schuf. Laut einem *Army of the United States Separation Qualification Record* richtete er mit drei anderen US-Soldaten und fünfzig Koreanern während seines Militärdienstes – wie dreißig Jahre später um seine Mansana de Chinati – Ziegelsteinrahmen und vorfabrizierte Gebäude auf.[37]

Kellein wirft Licht auf Judds Laufbahn, wenn er berichtet, dass „Bauen" von früh an zu Judds Tätigkeiten gehörte. Doch Kelleins Annahme, Judd habe „Ziegelsteinrahmen und vorfabrizierte Gebäude" errichtet „wie dreißig Jahre später um seine Mansana de Chinati" ist irreführend. Die zwei ehemaligen Flugzeughangars der Armee, eine Konstruktion aus vorfabrizierten Eisenpfeilern und -trägern, standen schon auf dem Gelände, als Judd den Besitz erwarb. Judd wählte als Materialien für seine neu entworfenen und errichteten Gebäude Lehmziegel, Beton und Holz. Ein konventionelles architektonisches Verfahren lehnte er ab, weil er überzeugt war, in dem traditionellen Kontext von Bauherr und Öffentlichkeit nicht arbeiten zu können.[38] Sein Berufsleben war jedoch meist von eingehenden Überlegungen zu Bauten und Architektur begleitet.

Judd war bemüht, seinen Gebäuden eine Einheit und Erhabenheit zu geben, die durch Raum erfahrbar wird. Das erreichte

Kellein sheds light on Judd's career, revealing that from early on he was involved in "building." However, Kellein's suggestion that Judd erected "frames and prefabricated buildings"—just as he was to do again at his La Mansana de Chinati thirty years later" is misleading. The two former military aircraft hangars, a structural system made of prefabricated steel columns and trusses, existed at the site when Judd acquired the property. Judd's materials of choice for his newly designed and built structures at La Mansana de Chinati were adobe, concrete, and wood. Judd rejected a conventional architecture practice because he felt he could not work within the traditional realm of the client and the public.[38] Throughout most of his career, however, he carefully thought about buildings and architecture.

Judd was interested in giving his buildings a unity and grandeur experienced through space. He achieved this by closing openings, making new ones, and adding skylights. The effect, seen at the Arena, the Artillery Sheds, and the Chamberlain Building, is powerful and dramatic. It is not obvious to the viewer what exactly was added or subtracted. Here again, unlike Scarpa and others, Judd did not intend to express the difference between old and new through architectural detailing; rather he wanted the visitor to focus on the entire experience. Just as he intended his artworks to be experienced as exterior expressions of the interior, Judd employed similar principles in his architecture. One can simultaneously perceive exterior and interior spatial relations in the Artillery Sheds, the Arena, and the Chamberlain Building.

Architecture must be experienced in person to be understood and appreciated. One cannot see space; one can only see its boundaries, its limits. Similarly, music affects us most intensely as three-dimensional experience—the sight, sound, and the very presence of the performer(s) and audience create an integrated experience for the senses. The complex unity of Judd's spaces can be compared to a musical performance. Similar to music, space surrounds the entire body. It is important in architectural education that students be constantly reminded of this aspect of the three-dimensional experience. A palpable sensitivity to space is essential to anyone who designs for a living. The three-dimensional experience cannot be reduced

er durch das Schließen von Öffnungen, das Einfügen neuer Öffnungen und den Einbau von Oberlichtern – Eingriffe von starker und dramatischer Wirkung, wie sie in der Arena, den Artillerie-Hallen und im Chamberlain-Gebäude zu spüren sind. Was genau ergänzt oder entfernt wurde, springt nicht ins Auge. Auch hier hatte Judd im Unterschied zu Scarpa und anderen nicht die Absicht, durch bauliche Details die Differenz zwischen Alt und Neu auszudrücken; er wünschte vielmehr, dass sich die Betrachtenden auf das Erfahrungsganze konzentrierten. Ebenso wie er seine Kunstwerke als äußeren Ausdruck des Inneren erlebt wissen wollte, verwendete er ähnliche Prinzipien in seiner Architektur. In den Artillerie-Hallen, der Arena und im Chamberlain-Gebäude lassen sich gleichzeitig äußere und innere Raumbeziehungen wahrnehmen.

Architektur kann nur durch persönliche Erfahrung verstanden und geschätzt werden. Raum kann man nicht sehen; sichtbar sind nur die Scheidelinien, die Grenzen. Auch Musik berührt uns am intensivsten als dreidimensionales Erlebnis – das Gesehene und das Gehörte zusammen mit der rein körperlichen Gegenwart von Musikern und Publikum verbinden sich zu einer einheitlichen Sinneserfahrung. Die komplexe Einheitlichkeit von Judds Räumen lässt sich mit einer musikalischen Aufführung vergleichen. Wie die Musik umfängt der Raum den ganzen Körper. Es ist wichtig, die Architekturstudenten während der Ausbildung beständig an diesen Aspekt der dreidimensionalen Erfahrung zu erinnern. Ein ausgeprägtes Raumempfinden ist die wesentliche Voraussetzung für jeden, der als Architekt arbeiten will. Die dreidimensionale Erfahrung lässt sich nicht auf die Zweidimensionalität von Film oder Fotografie reduzieren, und darum ist für Studierende ein Besuch in Marfa unerlässlich, um ein Verständnis dafür zu entwickeln, wie Donald Judd architektonischen Raum geschaffen hat. Dann würden sie vielleicht der folgenden Aussage des italienischen Architekten und Kritikers Bruno Zevi zustimmen:

> (...) Auch wenn die anderen Künste ihren Beitrag zur Architektur leisten – es ist der *innere* Raum, der Raum, der uns umgibt und einschließt, der die Grundlage für unsere Beurteilung eines Gebäudes darstellt, der das Ja oder Nein der ästhetischen Entscheidung bestimmt. Alles Übrige ist wich-

to two-dimensional photography or film, and for this reason, it is imperative that students of design visit Marfa to develop an understanding of how Donald Judd created architectural space. Then, perhaps, students of architecture would agree with the proposition of the Italian architect and critic Bruno Zevi:

> ... even if the other arts contribute to architecture, it is *interior space*, the space which surrounds and includes us, which is the basis for our judgment of a building, which determines the "yea" or "nay" of esthetic pronouncement of architecture. All the rest is important or perhaps we should say *can* be important, but always in a subordinate relation to the spatial idea. Whenever critics and historians lose sight of this hierarchy, they create confusion and accentuate the present disorientation in architecture.
>
> That space-void should be the protagonist of architecture is after all natural. Architecture is not art alone, it is not merely a reflection of conceptions of life or a portrait of a system of living. Architecture is environment, the stage on which our lives unfold.[39]

This "environment," this "stage" is what Judd achieved in Marfa. Like the work of a Renaissance master most interested in the holistic, spatial experience of architecture, Judd's altered buildings in Marfa speak for themselves as architecture. After about two decades, when Judd publicly criticized leading contemporary architects, his work presents itself as remarkably fresh and timeless. Judd's architectural ideas are not based on any attention-seeking invention of new forms. His architecture is based on the classic principle of proportion and a concern for space. In many ways his ideas for adaptive-reuse of old structures in remote locations can serve as an inspiration for architects today. His ability to reorchestrate the raw space of a military building, a warehouse, or a ranch, employing a minimum of change to create a maximum result, stands unparalleled. Judd understood a building's context as well as its limitations. Rural America builds very much from a traditional understanding of architecture. Contemporary architectural education tends to promote ideas in a new medium, finding forms and spaces with the use of the computer. Although computer-aided design has its place,

> tig, oder vielleicht sollten wir sagen, kann wichtig sein, doch immer auf einer Ebene, die der Raumidee untergeordnet ist. Wenn Kritiker und Historiker diese Hierarchie aus dem Blick verlieren, stiften sie Verwirrung und akzentuieren die Desorientierung, die für die heutige Architektur kennzeichnend ist.
> Dass Raum-Leere in der Architektur die Hauptrolle spielt, ist nur natürlich. Architektur ist nicht nur Kunst, nicht nur ein Reflex von Lebensauffassungen oder das Bild eines Lebenssystems. Architektur ist Umwelt, die Bühne, auf der sich unser Leben entfaltet.[39]

Diese „Umwelt", diese „Bühne" hat Judd in Marfa geschaffen. Wie das Werk eines Meisters der Renaissance, dessen höchstes Interesse der ganzheitlichen, räumlichen Erfahrung von Architektur galt, sprechen Judds veränderte Bauten in Marfa als Architektur für sich selbst. Heute, etwa zwei Jahrzehnte nach Judds öffentlicher Kritik an führenden Architekten der Gegenwart, präsentiert sich Judds Werk in bemerkenswert zeitloser Frische. Judds bauliche Ideen beruhen nicht auf einer Aufmerksamkeit heischenden Erfindung neuer Formen. Grundlage seiner Architektur sind die klassischen Prinzipien der Proportion und das intensive Interesse am Raum. Heutigen Architekten können seine Ideen einer adaptiven Wiederverwendung alter Bauten in abgelegenen Gebieten auf vielfältige Art als Quelle der Inspiration dienen. Seine Fähigkeit, den kruden Raum eines Militärgebäudes, eines Lagerhauses oder einer Ranch zu reorchestrieren und dabei mit einem Minimum an Veränderung ein maximales Resultat zu bewirken, ist beispiellos. Judd verstand den Kontext eines Gebäudes ebenso wie seine Begrenzungen. Die Bauweise des ländlichen Amerika wird weitgehend von einem traditionellen Architekturverständnis bestimmt. Die heutige Architektenausbildung benutzt als Ideenschmiede im Allgemeinen die neuen Medien und erfindet Formen und Räume mit Hilfe des Computers. Computergestütztes Entwerfen hat seine Berechtigung, doch Judds architektonisches Werk ist zeitlos, weil es nicht aus der Absicht entstand, eine neue Form zu suchen oder mit der letzten Stilrichtung zu konkurrieren. Judds Baukunst arbeitet mit der Realität des ländlichen Amerika und lässt sich nicht

Judd's architectural work is timeless because it isn't about seeking a new form or trying to compete with the latest style. Judd's architecture works with the reality of rural America, and cannot fit within the traditional category of a style, because it is *not* a style; it is a philosophy of building. Artists, architects, landscape architects, and interior designers come to see Donald Judd's work in Marfa. In this regard, he succeeded in reuniting art and architecture, because his work attracts people across the design spectrum. Visitors may all see his work differently, but they leave Marfa enriched and inspired.

In the end, the question of whether Donald Judd was an architect is perhaps not important. It is more important that art and architecture relate to each other, and that art and architecture, artist and architect, can find common ground and share ideas, just as Judd intended in his statement marking the opening of the The Chinati Foundation.

1 Serota, Nicholas (ed.). *Donald Judd* (D.A.P./Distributed Art Publishers, Inc.) on the occasion of the exhibition at Tate Modern, London. 5 February–25 April 2004, p. 246
2 The Judd Foundation was formed in 1996.
3 Thompson, Cecilia. *History of Marfa and Presidio County, Texas 1535–1946 Volume One, 1535–1900*, First Edition, (Nortex Press A Division of Eakin Publications, Inc., Austin, Texas, 1985), p. 188
4 Thompson, Cecilia. *History of Marfa and Presidio County, Texas 1535–1946 Volume Two, 1901–1946* First Edition, (Nortex Press A Division of Eakin Publications, Inc., Austin, Texas, 1985), p. 489
5 *Donald Judd. Architektur*, 3rd edition, (Ostfildern near Stuttgart: Cantz, 1992), p. 72.
6 Lerup, Lars. *After the City* (MIT Press, 2000), p. 80
7 Lerup, Lars. *After the City* (MIT Press, 2000), p. 82

in der überlieferten Kategorie eines Stils fassen, weil sie kein Stil *ist*. Sie ist eine Philosophie des Bauens. Künstler, Architekten, Landschaftsarchitekten und Innenraumgestalter kommen nach Marfa, um Judds Arbeiten zu sehen. In dieser Hinsicht kann sein Versuch der Wiedervereinigung von Kunst und Architektur als erfolgreich gelten, zieht sein Werk doch Vertreter des gesamten Gestaltungsspektrums an. Jeder Besucher sieht seine Arbeiten vielleicht anders, aber alle verlassen Marfa bereichert und inspiriert.

Die Frage, ob Donald Judd ein Architekt war, ist letzten Endes vielleicht bedeutungslos. Entscheidender ist, dass Kunst und Architektur sich aufeinander beziehen, dass Kunst und Architektur, Künstler und Architekt zu einer gemeinsamen Basis und zu gemeinsamen Ideen finden, so wie es Judd in seiner Erklärung zur Eröffnung der Chinati Foundation als Absicht geäußert hat.

1 Nicholas Serota (Hg.), *Donald Judd*, S. 246 (erschienen anlässlich der Ausstellung in der Tate Modern, London, vom 5. Februar – 25. April 2004).

2 Die *Judd Foundation* wurde 1996 gegründet.

3 Cecilia Thompson, *History of Marfa and Presidio County, Texas 1535–1946*, Bd. 1, 1535–1900, 1. Aufl., Austin, Texas, 1985, S. 188.

4 Dies., *History of Marfa and Presidio County, Texas 1535–1946*, *Bd. 2, 1901–1946*, 1. Aufl., Austin, Texas, 1985, S. 489.

5 *Donald Judd. Architektur*, Münster 1989, S. 68 (Publikation anlässlich der Ausstellung „Donald Judd – Architektur" im Westfälischen Kunstverein Münster, 16. April bis 4. Juni 1989).

6 Lars Lerup, *After the City*, Boston, MA, 2000, S. 80.

7 A.a.O., S. 82.

8 Donald Judd. *The Chinati Foundation.* Herausgegeben von The Chinati Foundation, Bodmer + Weber, Zürich, Schweiz, 1987, S. 5

9 Michael Kimmelman in *The New York Times Magazine*, 6. April 2003, Teil 6, S. 32,

10 *Architectural Record*, Oktober 2003, Bd. 191, S. 109.

11 *Donald Judd, Architektur*, Münster 1989, S. 64.

12 James S. Ackerman, *On Sculpture in the Context of Architecture*, Marfa 2000, S. 26.

13 Serota Nicholas, Hrsg. *Donald Judd* D.A.P. / Distributed Art Publishers, Inc. anlässlich der Ausstellung in der Tate Modern, London. 5. Februar–25. April 2004. S. 246

14 Rudolf Wittkower, *Art and Architecture in Italy 1600–1750, II. High Baroque*, New Haven, CT, 1999, S. 11.

15 Walter Gropius, Bauhaus-Manifest Flugblatt 1918. www.kunstdirekt.net/kunstzitate/bildendekunst/manifeste/bauhaus_1919

16 Donald Judd, *Architektur*, Münster 1989, S. 167.

17 Donald Judd, Specific Objects/Spezifische Objekte (1964), in: Thomas Kellein, *Donald Judd 1955–1968*, Bielefeld 2002, S. 94 (Publikation zur Ausstellung „Donald Judd, Das Frühwerk 1955–1968“ vom 5. Mai bis 21. Juli 2002 in der Kunsthalle Bielefeld).

18 Andrea Palladio, *Die vier Bücher zur Architektur*, Zürich und München 1983, S. 20.

19 Lars Lerup (*After the City*) wurde auf S. 28 wie folgt zitiert: „Das Haus ist eine kleine Stadt, und die Stadt ist ein großes Haus, die Kunst ist eine kleine Stadt und ebenso das Mobiliar. Der Spruch könnte trotz seiner Vereinfachungen im Original erneut überzeugen, denn die zusätzlichen und parallelen Reflexionen machen andere, komplexere Berechnungen möglich.“

20 Roberta Smith, „Donald Judd“, in: Brydon Smith (Hg.), *Donald Judd. A Catalogue of the Exhibition at the National Gallery of Canada, 14 May – 6 July 1975, Catalogue Raisonné of Paintings, Objects and Wood-Blocks*, Ottawa 1975, S. 22.

21 John Coplans, „An Interview with Don Judd“, in: *Artforum*, Bd. IX, Nr. 10, Juni 1971, New York 1971, S. 43.

22 Johannes Gachnang, in: *Donald Judd: Skulpturen, Kunsthalle Bern 14.4. – 30.5. 1976*. Ausstellungskatalog, S. 7.

23 A. a. O., S. 5.

24 A. a. O., S. 17.

25 Robin Evans, *Architecture and its Image: Four Centuries of Architectural Representation: Works from the Collection of the Canadian Center for Architecture*, hg. v. Eve Blau und Edward Kaufman, Cambridge, MA, und London 1989, S. 21.

26 Donald Judd, „Specific Objects/Spezifische Objekte“ (1964), in: Thomas Kellein, a.a.O., S. 95.

27 Howard Saalman, Filippo Brunelleschi, *The Buildings*, Pennsylvania State University Press 1993, S. 371.

28 *Judd, Donald, Architektur*, Münster 1989, S. 17.

29 Peter Noever (Hg.), *Donald Judd – Architecture Architektur*, Ostfildern-Ruit 2003, S. 22.

30 Rudoph M. Schindler, „Furniture and the Modern House: A Theory of Interior Design – Space Architecture“, in: *Architect and Engineer*, San Francisco, Bd. 123, Dezember 1935, S. 22–25. Neu veröfftl. in: *R.M. Schindler, Architect: 1887–1953*, New York 1988, S. 53.

31 Fritz Neumeyer, *Mies van der Rohe. Das kunstlose Wort*, Berlin 1986.

8 Judd, Donald. *The Chinati Foundation*. published by The Chinati Foundation, Bodmer + Weber, Zuerich, Switzerland, 1987, p. 5

9 Kimmelman, Michael. *The New York Times Magazine*, (April 6 2003/ Section 6), p. 32.

10 *Architectural Record* (October 2003. Volume 191), p. 109

11 *Donald Judd. Architektur*, 3rd edition (Ostfildern near Stuttgart: Cantz, 1992), p. 67.

12 Ackerman, James S. *On Sculpture in the Context of Architecture, Art and Architecture* (The Chinati Foundation/La Fundación Chinati Marfa Texas: The Chinati Foundation 2000), p. 16.

13 Serota Nicholas, Ed. *Donald Judd* D.A.P. / Distributed Art Publishers, Inc. on the occasion of the exhibition at Tate Modern, London. 5 February–25 April 2004. p. 246

14 Wittkower, Rudolf. *Art and Architecture in Italy 1600–1750 II. High Baroque*, Yale University Press Pelican History of Art (New Haven, CT 1999), p. 11.

15 Gropius, Walter. *Bauhaus Manifesto 1919. Programs and Manifestoes on 20th-Century Architecture*, edited by Conrads, Ulrich (MIT Press Cambridge, MA), p. 49.

16 *Donald Judd. Architektur*, 3rd edition (Ostfildern near Stuttgart: Cantz, 1992), p. 195.

17 Judd, Donald. *Complete Writings 1959–1975*, Gallery Reviews Book reviews Articles letters to the Editor Reports Statements Complaints. Specific Objects. (New York University Press, New York: The Press of Nova Scotia College of Art and Design, Halifax, 1975), p. 187.

18 Palladio, Andrea. *The Four Books of Architecture* (Dover Publications, Inc., New York, 1965), p. 1.

19 The author quoted Lars Lerup from his book *After the City* earlier in this book the following: “The house is a small town, and the town is a large house, the art is a small town and so is the furniture. The dictum may again ring true despite its original simplifications, because the additional and parallel reflections make other more complex computations possible.”

20 Smith, Roberta. “Donald Judd”, in Brydon Smith ed., *Donald Judd. A Catalogue of the Exhibition at the National Gallery of Canada, 14 May – 6 July 1975, Catalogue Raisonné of Paintings, Objects and Wood-Blocks* (Ottawa, Canada, 1975), p. 22.

21 Coplans, John. “An Interview with Donald Judd”, *Artforum Vol. IX, Number 10*, June 1971 (Publisher Charles Cowles, 667 Madison Avenue, New York N.Y. 1971), p. 43.

22 Gachnang, Johannes. *Donald Judd*, and Kunsthalle Bern, *Donald Judd Skulpturen* (Bern, Switzerland: Staempfli+Cie AG, 1976), p. 7.

23 Gachnang, Johannes. *Donald Judd*, and Kunsthalle Bern, *Donald Judd Skulpturen* (Bern, Switzerland: Staempfli+Cie AG, 1976), p. 5.

24 Gachnang, Johannes. *Donald Judd*, and Kunsthalle Bern, *Donald Judd Skulpturen* (Bern, Switzerland: Staempfli+Cie AG, 1976), p. 17.

25 Evans, Robin. *Architecture and its Image: Four Centuries of Architectural Representation: Works from the Collection of the Canadian Center for Architecture*, ed. by Eve Blau and Edward Kaufman (Cambridge, Massachusetts and London, England: MIT Press, 1989), p. 21.

26 Judd, Donald. *Complete Writings 1959–1975,* Gallery Reviews Book reviews Articles letters to the Editor Reports Statements Complaints. Specific Objects. (New York University Press, New York: The Press of Nova Scotia College of Art and Design, Halifax, 1975), p. 187.

32 Sambal Oelek u. Benedikt Loderer, *Jünglingserwachen. Die ersten 38% aus Le Corbusiers Leben*, Zürich 1989.
33 *Donald Judd. Architektur*, Münster 1989, S. 143.
34 Louis I. Kahn, Heinz Ronner u. Sharad Jhavery, *Louis I. Kahn, Complete Work 1935–1974*, Boulder, Co., 1977, S. 58.
35 Architecture d'aujourd'hui, Bd. 331, November/Dezember, S. 60. Fotograf Franz Wimmer.
36 Thomas Kellein, *Donald Judd 1955–1968*, Bielefeld 2002, S. 14 (Publikation zur Ausstellung „Donald Judd, Das Frühwerk 1955–1968" vom 5. Mai bis 21. Juli 2002 in der Kunsthalle Bielefeld).
37 A.a.O., S. 32.
38 Vgl. dazu S. 34: „Kunst kam für mich am ehesten in Frage, aber den Ausschlag gab, dass es für einen Architekten notwendig ist, mit Auftraggebern und mit der Öffentlichkeit umzugehen. Das schien für mich unmöglich, wie auch das Betreiben einer Fabrik es war."
39 Bruno Zevi, *Saper vedere l'architettura. Saggio sull'Interpretazione spaziale dell' architettura*, Turin 1948, S. 32f.

27 Saalman, Howard. *Filippo Brunelleschi: The Buildings* (Barbara Building, Suite C, University Park, PA: Pennsylvania State University Press, 1993), p. 371.
28 *Donald Judd. Architektur,* 3rd edition (Ostfildern near Stuttgart: Cantz, 1992), p. 19.
29 Noever, Peter (ed.). *Donald Judd—Architecture, Architektur* (Ostfildern-Ruit, Hatje Cantz Verlag, 2003), p. 17.
30 Schindler, Rudolph M. "Furniture and the Modern House: A Theory of Interior Design – Space Architecture", in *Architect and Engineer* (San Francisco), vol. 123 December, 1935, pp. 22–25. Republished in *R.M. Schindler, Architect: 1887–1953*, (New York, NY: Rizzoli, 1988), p. 53.
31 Neumeyer, Fritz. *The Artless Word: Mies van der Rohe on the Building Art* (Cambridge, MA: MIT Press), 1991.
32 Oelek, Sambal and Loderer, Benedikt. *Jünglingserwachen* (Zurich, Switzerland: Tagesanzeiger Verlag), 1989.
33 *Donald Judd. Architektur,* 3rd edition (Ostfildern near Stuttgart: Cantz, 1992), p. 177.
34 Ronner, Heinz and Jhaveri, Sharad. *Louis I. Kahn. Complete Work 1935–1974* (Boulder, CO: Westview Press, 1977), p. 58.
35 *Architecture d'aujourd'hui, Vol. Nov.–Dec.*, 331 p. 60. Photograph Franz Wimmer.
36 Kellein, Thomas. *Donald Judd. Early Work 1955–1968* (New York, NY: Distributed Art Publishers, Inc., 2002), p. 14.
37 Kellein, Thomas. *Donald Judd. Early Work 1955–1968* (New York, NY: Distributed Art Publishers, Inc., 2002), p. 32.
38 The author quoted Judd on page 3 in this essay: "Art was the most likely in the balance, but the decisive weight was that in architecture it was necessary to deal with the clients and the public. This seemed impossible to me, as did the business of a firm."
39 Zevi, Bruno. *Architecture as Space, How to look at Architecture. Architecture—The Unknown* (New York, NY: Horizon Press, 1957), p. 32.

LA MANSANA DE CHINATI / THE BLOCK

Seine zweite architektonische Intervention in Marfa realisierte Donald Judd auf seinem Anwesen La Mansana de Chinati, von ihm auch der Block genannt. Vorhergegangen war die Instandsetzung eines kleinen Hauses am Stadtrand, das ihm während der Arbeiten am Block als Wohnsitz diente.

1973 kaufte er das erste von drei Gebäuden, aus denen der heutige Block entstand, im darauf folgenden Jahr erwarb er die übrigen zwei. Die Renovierung nahm mehrere Jahre in Anspruch, so dass Judd zusammen mit seiner Familie erst 1979 umziehen konnte.[1] Heute umfasst die Anlage aus Arbeits- und Wohnbereichen neun frei stehende Objekte, darunter ein kleines Badehaus, ein Büro, eine Pergola, eine Kombination aus Treibhaus, Hundezwinger und Hühnerstall sowie ein Wasserbecken und einen Grillplatz, die alle neu errichtet wurden. Die beiden Hauptgebäude waren in ihrer ursprünglichen Form von der US-Armee auf einem Militärflugplatz außerhalb von Marfa als Flugzeughangars erstellt worden; später wurden sie zwecks Umnutzung verlegt

Donald Judd undertook his second architectural intervention in Marfa at his residence La Mansana de Chinati, or as he also called it, the Block. Before this he had begun renovating a small house on the edge of the town that served as his home while work on the Block proceeded. In 1973 he acquired the first of three buildings which were to become the Block; the two remaining structures were purchased in the following year. Renovation took several years, so that Judd's family didn't move in until 1979.[1] Today nine freestanding structures comprise the complex of work and living quarters, including a bathhouse, office, pergola, and dog kennel/chicken coop/greenhouse, as well as a pool and a barbecue pit, all newly constructed. The two main original buildings were constructed by the military as airplane hangars on an airstrip outside of Marfa, but salvaged and reconstructed at their current site as warehouses for Fort D. A. Russell, whose main compound would later be transferred into The Chinati Foundation. The third and smaller building is a traditional two-

und dienten, neu aufgebaut, an ihrem gegenwärtigen Standort als Lagerhallen für einen Truppenstützpunkt, das Fort D. A. Russell, dessen Hauptareal später an die Chinati Foundation überging. Das dritte, kleinere Gebäude, ein zweigeschossiger traditioneller Holzrahmenbau, war vordem der Dienstsitz des Quartiermeisters.

Um dem Komplex den Charakter eines privaten und klar definierten Raums zu geben, ließ Judd den Block mit einer Mauer aus Adobe-Ziegeln, den ortsüblichen luftgetrockneten Lehmziegeln, einfrieden, die in der Höhe bis an die Fensterbänder der beiden größeren Gebäude reicht. Zwischen den Gebäuden wurde eine zweite, diesmal u-förmige und nach Norden offene Lehmziegelmauer errichtet, deren leicht geneigte Oberkante auf das nach Nordwesten abfallende Gelände Bezug nimmt. Die zwei Mauern rufen frühere Außenraumwerke Judds in Erinnerung: Ohne Titel, zwei stählerne Rechtecke, die er 1971 für den Park der Familie Pulitzer in Saint Louis entworfen hatte, sowie Ohne Titel aus dem Jahr 1977, zwei konzentrische Ringe aus Beton für ein sanft abfallendes Gelände am Aasee im deutschen Münster. Alle drei Arbeiten folgen demselben formalen Prinzip: bei gleich bleibender Höhe einer der beiden konzentrischen Formen weist die andere parallel zum Abfall des Geländes eine Neigung auf.

Alle übrigen baulichen Anlagen der Mansana de Chinati hat Judd selbst entworfen, so das Wasserbecken, das Treibhaus mit Hundezwinger und Hühnerstall, die mit einem Flachdach gedeckten Baderäumlichkeiten, ein kleines Büro, ein provisorisches Lagerhausgebäude und eine Pergola. Treibhaus und Pergola sind aus Holz hergestellt, für das Badehaus und das Büro wurden Lehmziegel benutzt. Das behelfsmäßige Lagergebäude ist eine Holzrahmenkonstruktion.

Judd plante auch das Landschaftsbild: Eine Reihe von sieben Zierpflaumenbäumen schafft einen langen schmalen Raum zwischen dem östlichen Gebäude und der Hofmauer; 12 Pappeln umgeben das Wasserbecken, und die Pergola, deren äußere Dimensionen denen des Beckens entsprechen, ist mit Weinlaub bedeckt. An die im Osten bzw. Westen gelegenen Gebäude schließen sich im Norden kleinere, mit Kakteen und Sukkulenten bepflanzte Areale an, die von Wegen mit Ziegelsteinpflaster eingefasst sind.

story wood-framed structure that formerly served as the quartermaster's headquarters.

To provide the compound with privacy and turn it into a defined space, Judd constructed an adobe wall around the Block, the height of which reaches up to the clerestory windows of the large buildings. Between the buildings, Judd had another adobe wall built, this one in a U-shape open to the north. The top of this wall has a slight slope that references the slope of the terrain to the northwest. These two walls echo earlier outdoor works by Judd, namely untitled, consisting of two steel rectangles designed in 1971 for the park of Mr. and Mrs. Pulitzer in Saint Louis, and untitled (1977), consisting of two concentric concrete rings for a sloping terrain on Lake Aasee in Muenster, Germany. All three works observe a similar formal principal: one of the concentric forms is level at the top, while the other follows the slope of the land.

Judd designed all the remaining structures at La Mansana de Chinati, including the pool, the greenhouse with dog kennel and the chicken coop, the flat-roofed bathroom facilities, a small office, a temporary storage building, and a pergola. The greenhouse and pergola were built of wood, whereas the bathrooms and office were built of adobe. The temporary storage building is wood-framed. Judd also planned the landscape: a row of seven fruitless plum trees creates a long narrow space between the east building and the courtyard wall; twelve cottonwoods surround the pool; and grapevines cover the pergola, which has the same outer dimensions as the pool. To the north of the east and west buildings are smaller areas planted with cacti and succulents that are defined by walkways laid in brick.

The 12-foot-high adobe wall creates a courtyard measuring 265 by 242 feet, protecting it from noise generated by Highway 90 to the south and the Union Pacific Railroad tracks to the north. An even spread of gravel covers the ground, giving the space a homogenized appearance, linking all parts visually and physically. Outside the courtyard, but attached to it at the southwest corner, lies a much smaller courtyard—the winter garden. Both courtyards are furnished with various examples of Judd's furniture, including tables and benches and a plastered adobe barbecue pit.

Die ca. dreieinhalb Meter (12 ft) hohe Lehmziegelmauer lässt einen Innenhof von ca. 79 × 74 Metern (265 × 242 ft) entstehen und schützt ihn zugleich vor dem Verkehrslärm, der von der südlich angrenzenden Nationalstraße (Highway 90) und den Bahngleisen der Union Pacific Railroad im Norden herüberdringt. Der gleichmäßige Kiesbelag des Bodens schafft eine physische und visuelle Verbindung aller Teile und lässt den Raum homogen erscheinen. Außerhalb des Hofs, ihm in der Südwestecke jedoch angeschlossen, liegt ein zweiter, sehr viel kleinerer Hof – der Wintergarten. Beide Höfe sind mit verschiedenen von Judd entworfenen Möbelstücken eingerichtet – mit Tischen, Bänken und einem verputzen Adobe-Grill.

In den Innenräumen der Gebäude wird eine Sammlung von Kunstwerken gezeigt, die unter anderem Arbeiten von Judd, Dan Flavin und Frank Stella umfasst. Außerdem sind Kunstgegenstände aus der Hand der indianischen Ureinwohner Amerikas ausgestellt. Einen Großteil des Mobiliars hat Judd selbst entworfen, darunter die Bücherregale für zwei Bibliotheken mit etwa 13 000 Werken über verschiedenste Themen, vornehmlich über Kunst, Architektur, Philosophie und Naturwissenschaften. Neben Judds eigenen Entwürfen sind in den Räumen auch zahlreiche Möbelstücke von Gustav Stickley zu finden.

Im Freien ließ Judd zwischen dem zweigeschossigen Bau und dem Ostgebäude ein separates Badehaus errichten und schuf damit eine spannungsvolle Sequenz schmaler Außenräume, die auf der einen Seite zum Innenhof, auf der anderen zur Reihe der Pflaumenbäume führt. Die Außentreppe an der Südfassade des zweigeschossigen Gebäudes wurde durch eine zentral gelegene Innentreppe ersetzt. Im ersten Stock ließ Judd sämtliche Innenwände entfernen, so dass ein einziger großer Raum entstand, der durch die zahlreichen Fenster von vier Seiten her mit Tageslicht durchflutet wird. Im Erdgeschoss richtete Judd die Küche ein und entwarf für den Essbereich einen Tisch und Stühle aus Kiefernholz. An der Ostseite des Hauses trennte er zwei gleich große Schlafzimmer für seine Kinder ab und entwarf einen innerhalb dieser zwei Zimmer gelegenen Vorratsraum, der nur über eine kleine Leiter zu erreichen ist (s. Längsschnitt, zweigeschossiges Gebäude).

Inside the buildings, a collection of artworks is displayed, including works by Judd, Dan Flavin, and Frank Stella. A collection of Native American Indian artifacts is also displayed. Judd designed much of the furniture, such as the bookshelves for the two libraries. They hold a collection of some 13,000 books, which cover a wide range of topics with an emphasis on art, architecture, philosophy, and science. In addition to Judd's own designs, numerous pieces by Gustav Stickley are to be found inside the buildings.

Outside, Judd erected a separate bath structure between the two-story building and the east building, thus creating a dramatic sequence of narrow outdoor spaces leading to the courtyard on one side and to the row of plum trees on the other. Judd removed the exterior staircase on the south facade of the two-story building and replaced it with a central interior staircase. On the second floor he removed all the walls, thus creating one large single room flooded with daylight through multiple windows running around all four sides. Judd designed the kitchen on the first floor and furnished the dining area with table and chairs in pinewood from his own design. On the east side, he separated two equal-sized bedrooms for his children, and within the two rooms, designed a storage space that can only be reached by a small ladder (see longitudinal section, two-story building).

While La Mansana de Chinati was designed to serve as Judd's residence, the process of converting the buildings and installing them with artworks influenced his thought about the way art should be displayed. During Judd's lifetime, La Mansana de Chinati became a living museum, where Judd lived, worked, and studied, and where family and guests always had access to the spaces. In his article "In defense of my work," Judd referred to the insights he gained from creating the installation in these buildings: "The fine installation of early pieces in the National Gallery of Canada was possible because of the early pieces in the south room of the east building in Marfa. This installation took a great deal of thought and revision over two or three years."[2] It was essential for Judd to live with his work, and that of others, which resulted in the mix of artwork, architecture, and furniture on view at the Block.

La Mansana de Chinati wurde von Judd als sein privater Wohnsitz entworfen. Doch der Prozess der Umgestaltung der Bauten und ihrer Einrichtung für die Darbietung von Kunstwerken beeinflussten seine Vorstellungen von der Art und Weise, wie Kunst angemessen zu präsentieren sei. Zu Judds Lebzeiten wurde La Mansana ein lebendes Museum, in dem Judd wohnte, arbeitete und studierte und dessen Räume der Familie wie auch Gästen jederzeit offen standen. In seinem Artikel „In Defense of my Work" („Verteidigung meiner Arbeit") spricht Judd die Erfahrungen an, die er aus der Einrichtung der Gebäude gewonnen hatte: „Die großartige Installierung früher Werke in der kanadischen Nationalgalerie wurde möglich aufgrund der frühen Stücke im Südraum des Ostgebäudes von Marfa, eine Installierung, die zwei oder drei Jahre lang viel Nachdenken und laufende Überarbeitung erforderte."[2] Mit seinen Arbeiten und denen von anderen zu leben war für Judd ein essenzielles Bedürfnis, und es führte zu jener Mischung aus Kunst, Architektur und Mobiliar, die im Block zu sehen ist.

Judds Einteilung von Räumen und deren Funktion wird wahrnehmbar, wenn man sich durch sie hindurch bewegt. La Mansana de Chinati ist als Serie genau orchestrierter Erfahrungen von Innen- und Außenräumen entworfen. Minuziös wurden auch kleinste Details wie der Mechanismus des Eingangstors und der Türöffnung bedacht. Seine Möbelentwürfe plante Judd auf Basis der Standardmasse von Bauholz, wie sie auf den Bauhöfen zur Verfügung standen. Ebenfalls zur Planung gehörte die Beschränkung auf eine begrenzte Auswahl lokaler Baustoffe und Holzarten. Die Lage Marfas in einer abgelegenen Gegend zwang ihn dazu, sich auf Materialien zu konzentrieren, die verfügbar waren und die dennoch seinen architektonischen Vorstellungen entsprachen. Was viele Architekten als Nachteil betrachtet hätten, machte Judd zu einer persönlichen Ausdrucksform, die dazu beitrug, einen zeitlosen und transparenten Raum zu schaffen.

1 Information von Marianne Stockebrand, mitgeteilt in einem Gespräch am 9. Februar 2006.

2 Donald Judd, *Complete Writings 1975–1986*, Eindhoven 1987, S. 163.

Judd's zoning of rooms and their function becomes apparent as one moves through them.

Judd designed La Mansana de Chinati as a series of precisely orchestrated outdoor and indoor spatial experiences. He meticulously considered the smallest details, such as the entry gate and door-opening mechanism. His furniture designs were well planned on the basis of the standard dimensions of lumber available at the yards. Made part of the planning was the limited selection of building materials and lumber types to be found in the area. Marfa's remote location required him to concentrate on those materials that were available and that could still fulfill his architectural vision. What many architects would have regarded as a disadvantage, Judd turned into a personal expression that helped create a timeless and lucid space.

1 Information provided by Marianne Stockebrand, in conversation on February 9, 2006.

2 Judd, Donald. *Complete Writings 1975–1986*, Eindhoven 1987, p. 163

La Mansana de Chinati. West Building, south room, with works by Donald Judd, view to south.

Westgebäude, Südzimmer, mit Arbeiten von Donald Judd, nach Süden.

JUDD FOUNDATION

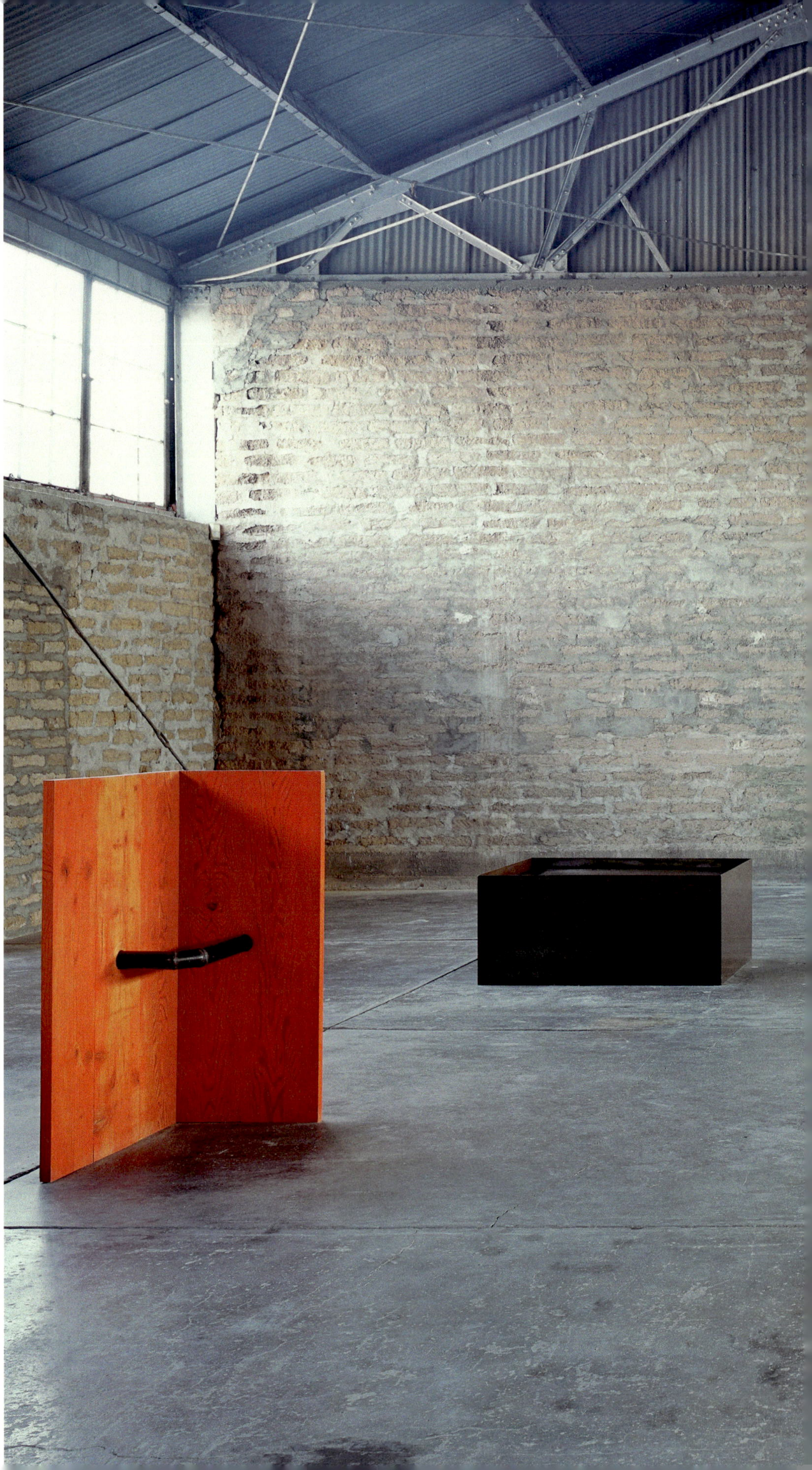

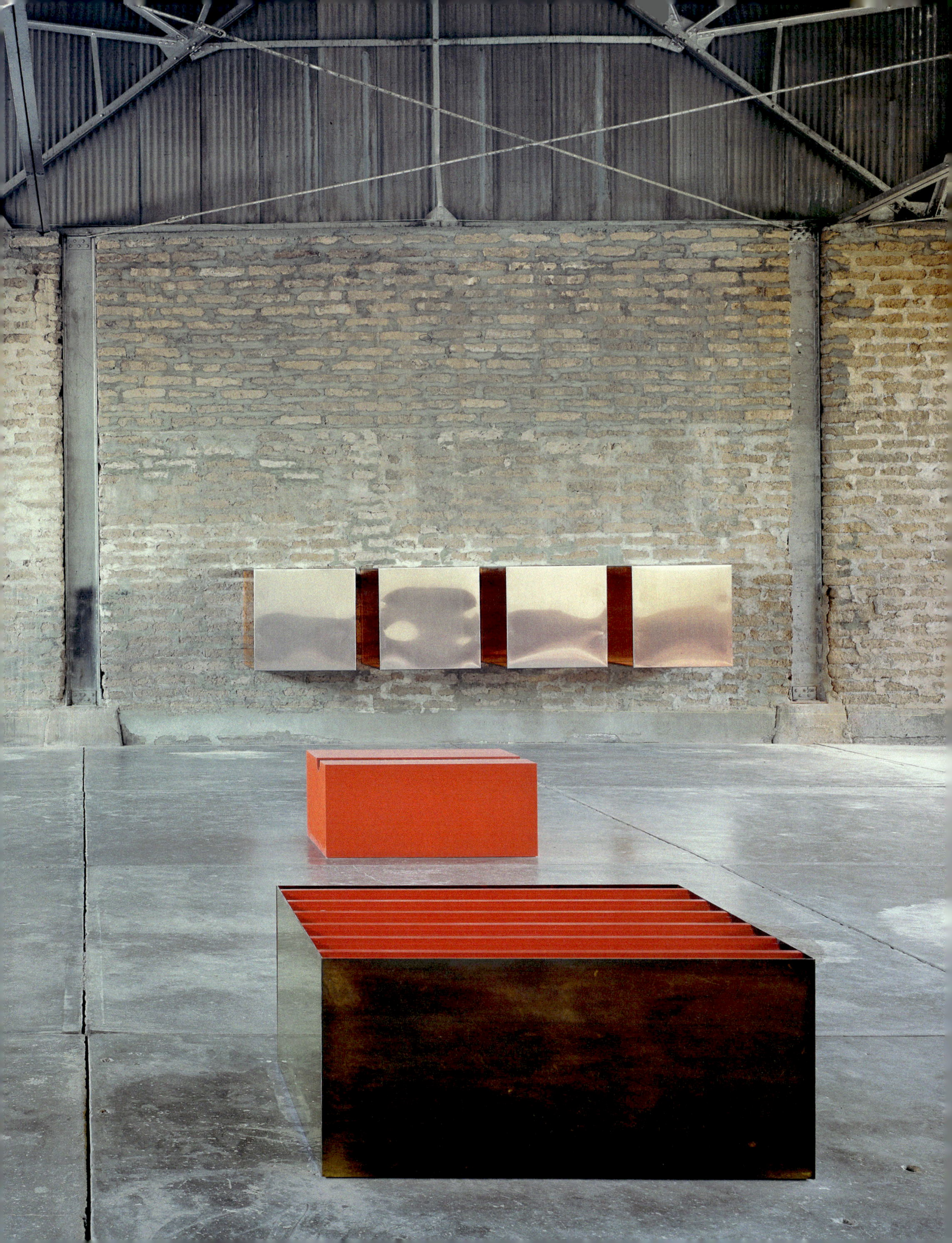

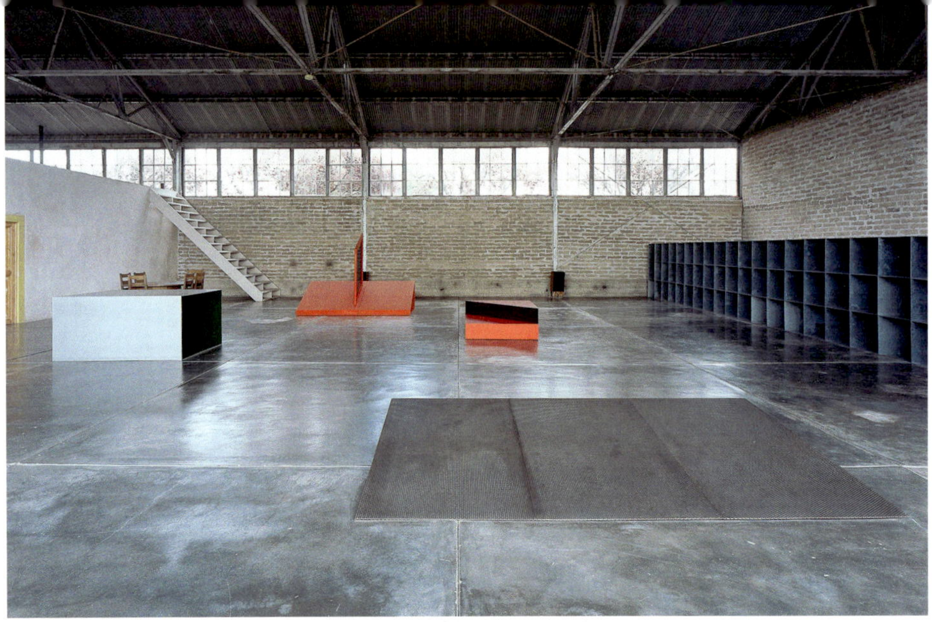

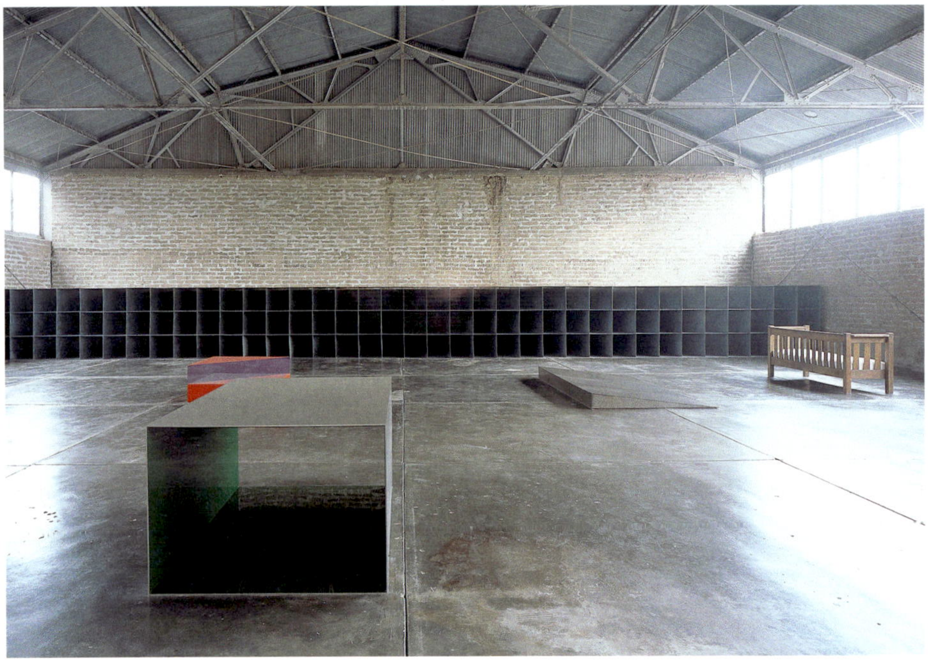

La Mansana de Chinati. East Building, south room with works by Donald Judd and furniture by Gustav Stickley, view to east.

Ostgebäude, Südzimmer, mit Arbeiten von Donald Judd und Möbeln von Gustav Stickley, nach Osten.

La Mansana de Chinati. East Building, south room with works by Donald Judd and bench by Gustav Stickley, view to south.

Ostgebäude, Südzimmer, mit Arbeiten von Donald Judd und Bank von Gustav Stickley, nach Süden.

JUDD FOUNDATION

La Mansana de Chinati. East Building, with works by Donald Judd, view to east.

Ostgebäude, mit Werken von Donald Judd, nach Osten.

La Mansana de Chinati. East Building, with works by Donald Judd, view to west.

Ostgebäude, mit Werken von Donald Judd, nach Westen.

JUDD FOUNDATION

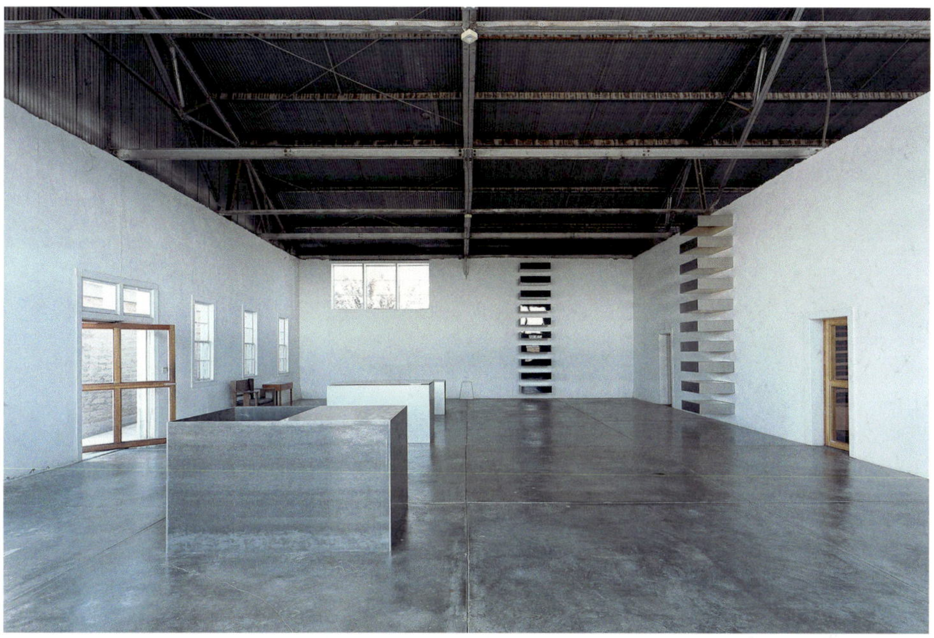

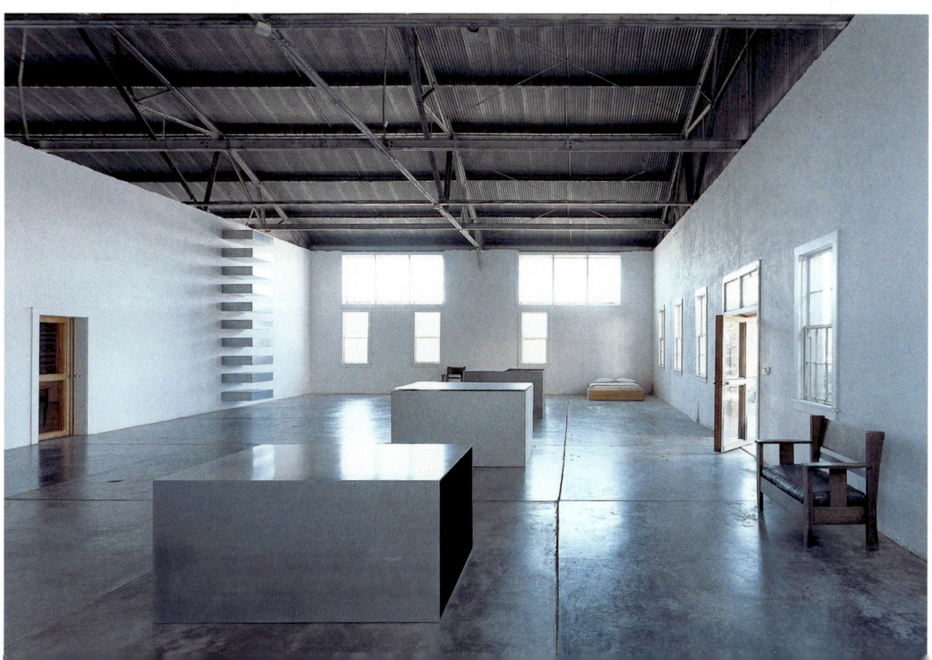

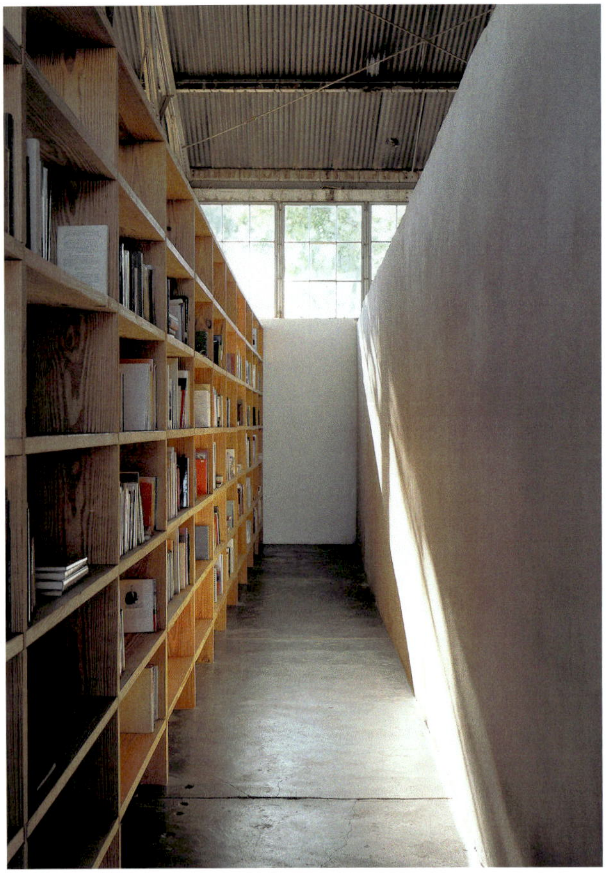

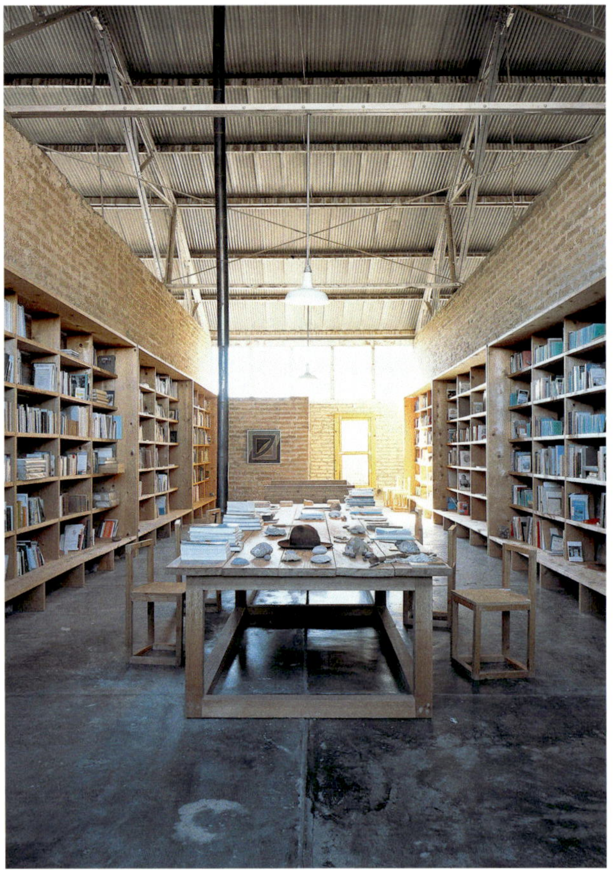

La Mansana de Chinati. West Building, library 1, bookshelves by Donald Judd, view to west.

Westgebäude, Bibliothek 1, Bücherregale von Donald Judd, nach Westen.

La Mansana de Chinati. West Building, library 2 with furniture by Donald Judd and painting by Frank Stella, view to west.

Westgebäude, Bibliothek 2, mit Möbeln von Donald Judd und einem Gemälde von Frank Stella, nach Westen.

JUDD FOUNDATION

La Mansana de Chinati. West Building, library 1 with works by Dan Flavin and Donald Judd, bookshelves by Donald Judd, view to west.

Westgebäude, Bibliothek 1, mit Werken von Dan Flavin und Donald Judd, Bücherregale von Donald Judd, nach Westen.

JUDD FOUNDATION

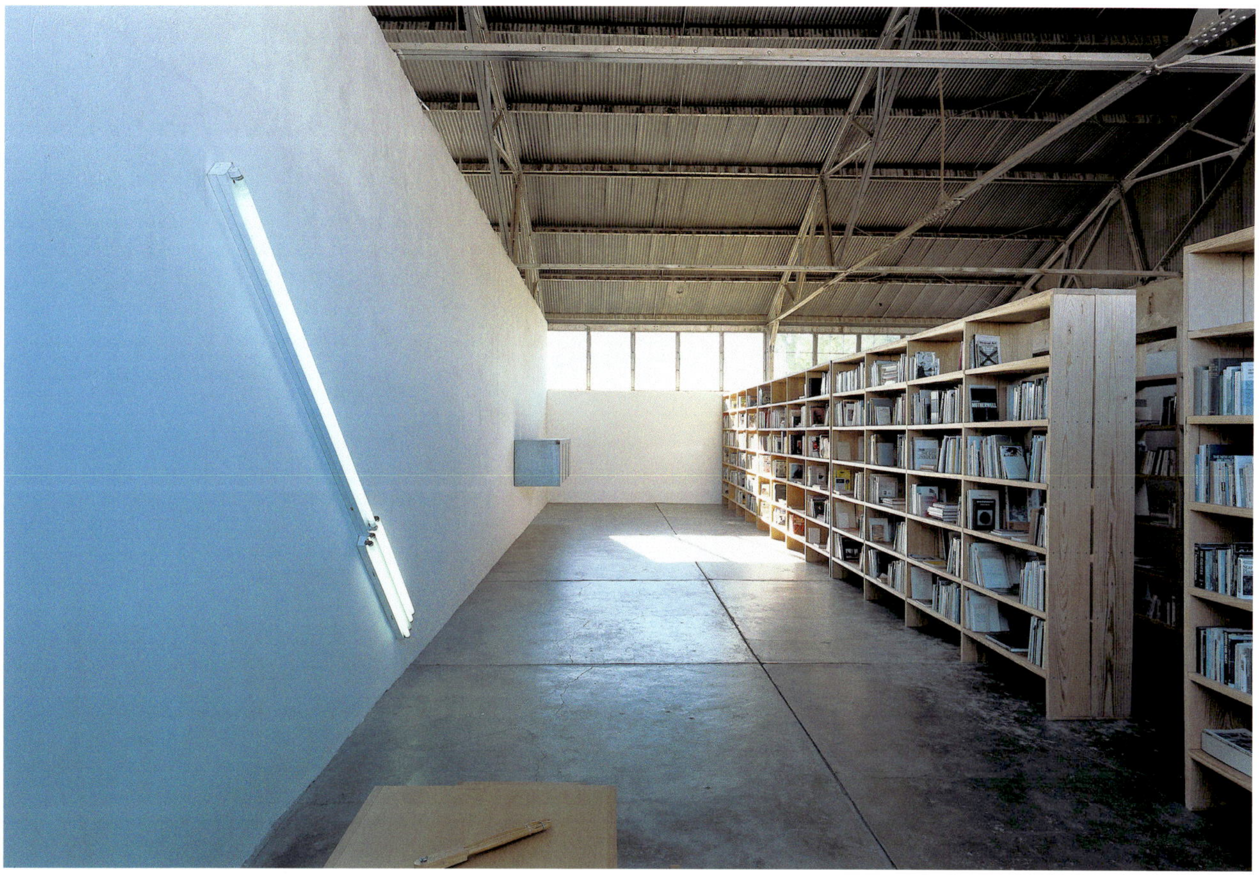

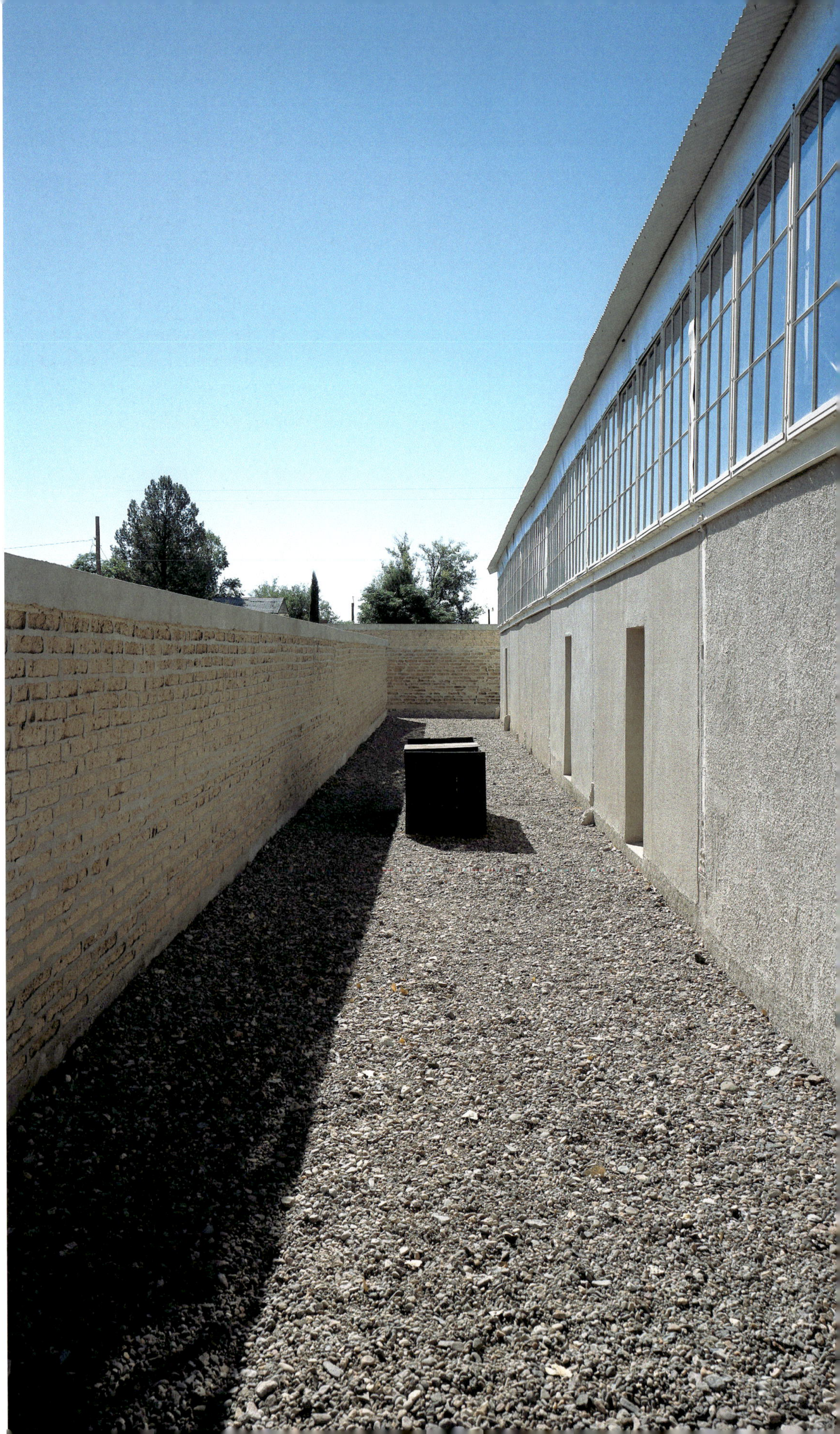

La Mansana de Chinati. Space between U-shaped wall, untitled 1977 and West Building with bench by Donald Judd, view to south.

Raum zwischen u-förmiger Mauer, ohne Titel 1977 und Westgebäude, mit Bank von Donald Judd, nach Süden

JUDD FOUNDATION

La Mansana de Chinati. View of courtyard, view to south.

Innenhof, nach Süden.

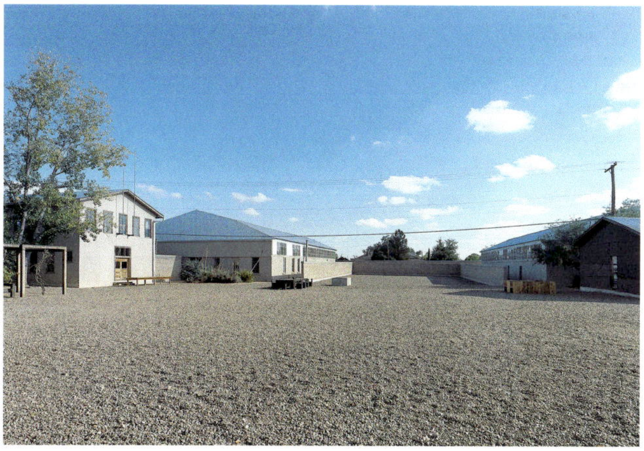

La Mansana de Chinati. View of courtyard pergola, two-story building, bathroom building, East Building, furniture and barbecue pit by Donald Judd, view to east.

Innenhof-Pergola, zweigeschossiges Gebäude, Badehaus, Ostgebäude, Möbel und Grill von Donald Judd, nach Osten.

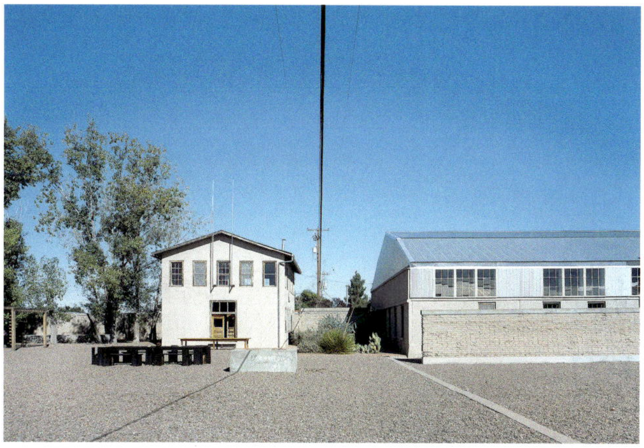

La Mansana de Chinati. View of courtyard with West Building, storage building, chicken coop / dog kennel / greenhouse, furniture and barbecue pit by Donald Judd, view to west.

Innenhof mit Westgebäude, Lagerhausgebäude, Hühnerstall / Hundezwinger / Treibhaus sowie Möbeln und Grill von Donald Judd, nach Westen.

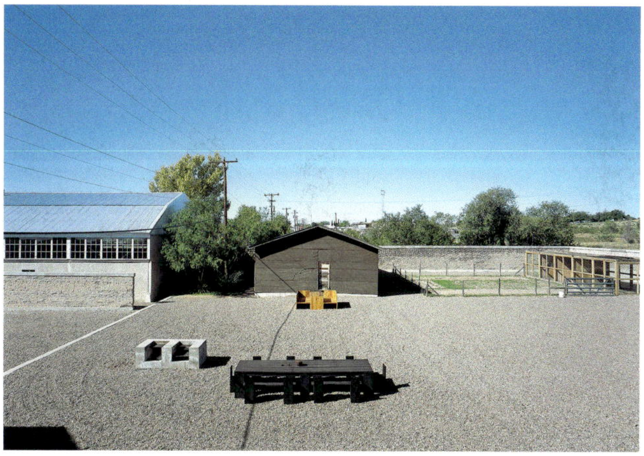

La Mansana de Chinati. East Building before renovation circa 1930, view to southeast.

Ostgebäude vor der Renovierung, ca. 1930, nach Südosten.

JUDD FOUNDATION

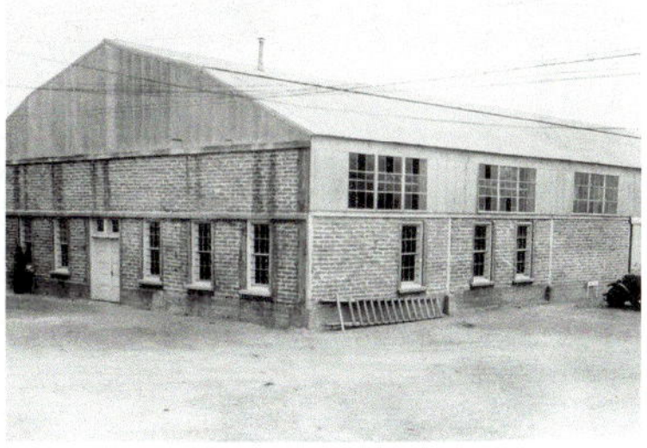

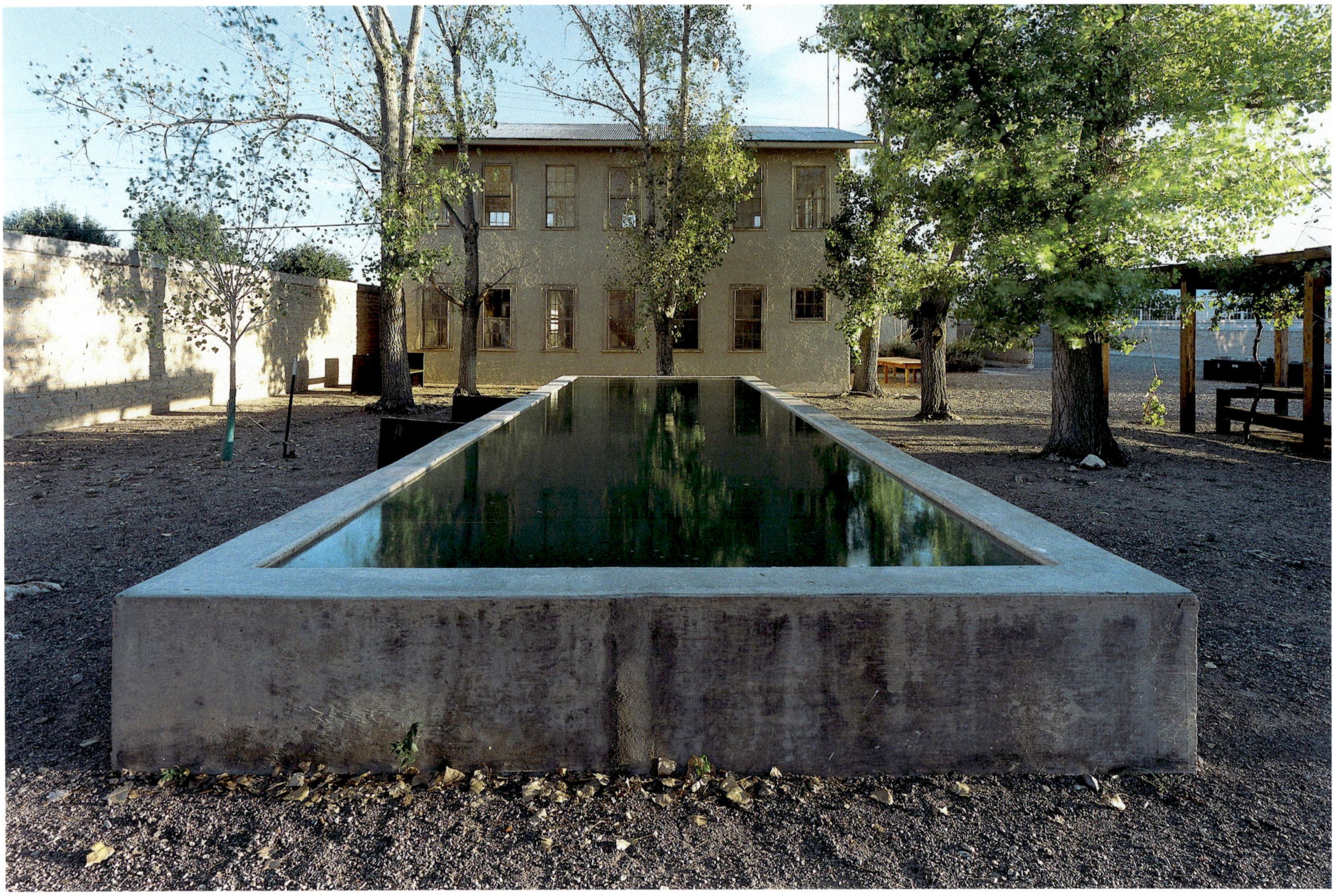

**La Mansana de Chinati.
Pool and two-story building,
view to south.**

Wasserbecken und zweigeschossiges Gebäude,
nach Süden.

JUDD FOUNDATION

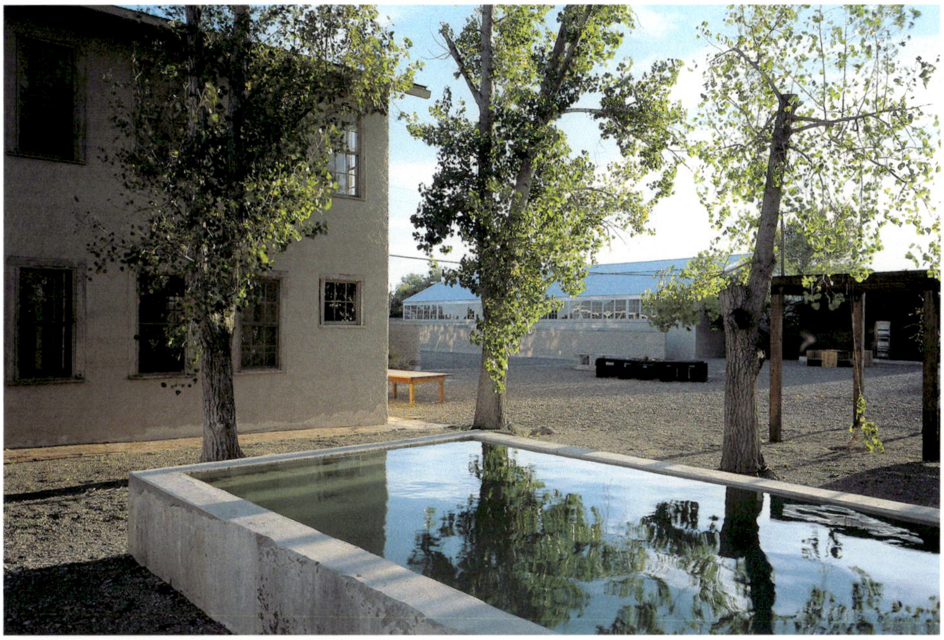

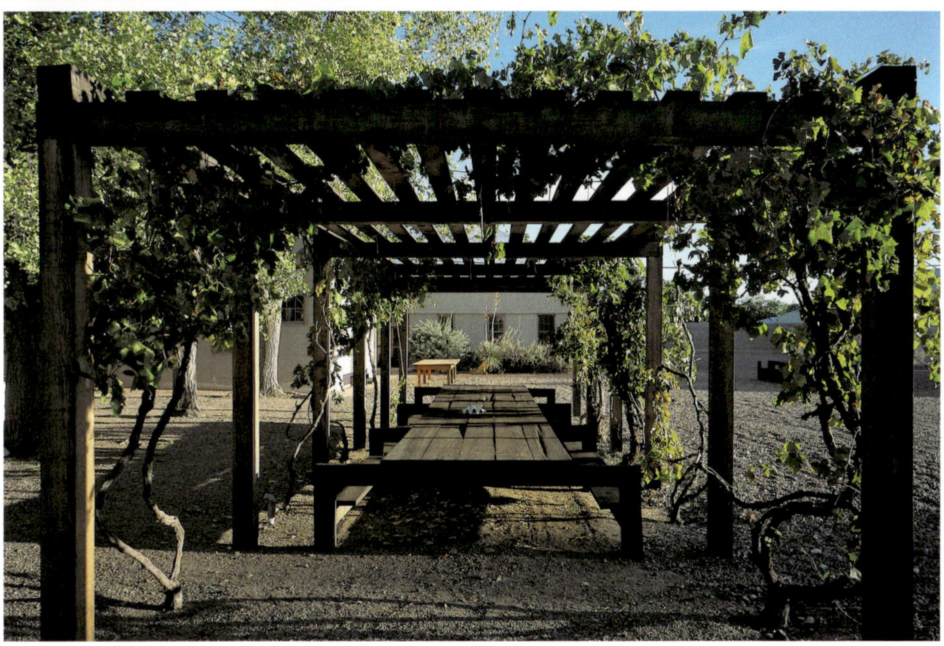

La Mansana de Chinati. View of pool, two-story building and West Building, view to southwest.

Wasserbecken, zweigeschossiges Gebäude und Westgebäude, nach Südwesten.

La Mansana de Chinati. Pergola with bench and table, by Donald Judd, view to south.

Pergola mit Bank und Tisch von Donald Judd, nach Süden.

JUDD FOUNDATION

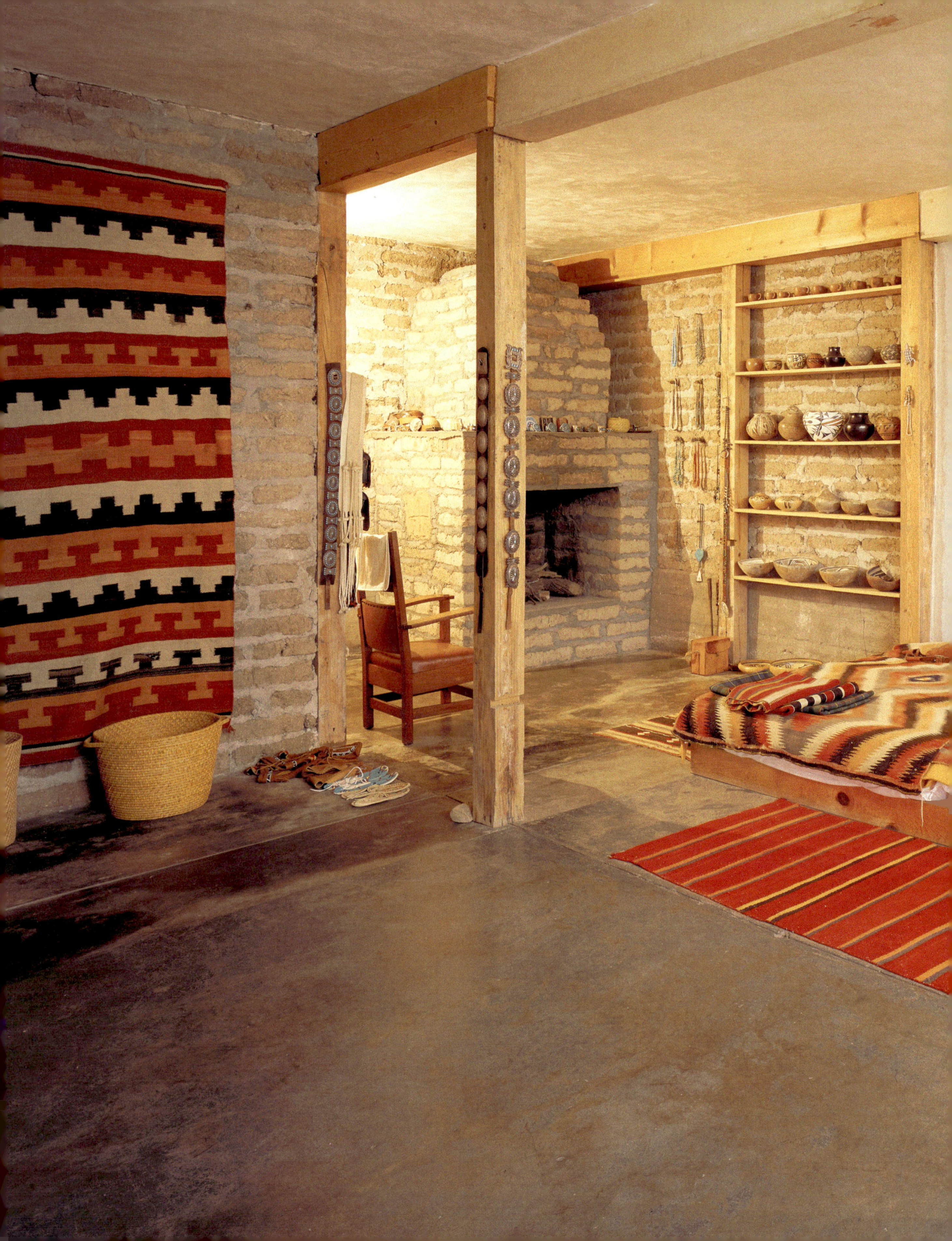

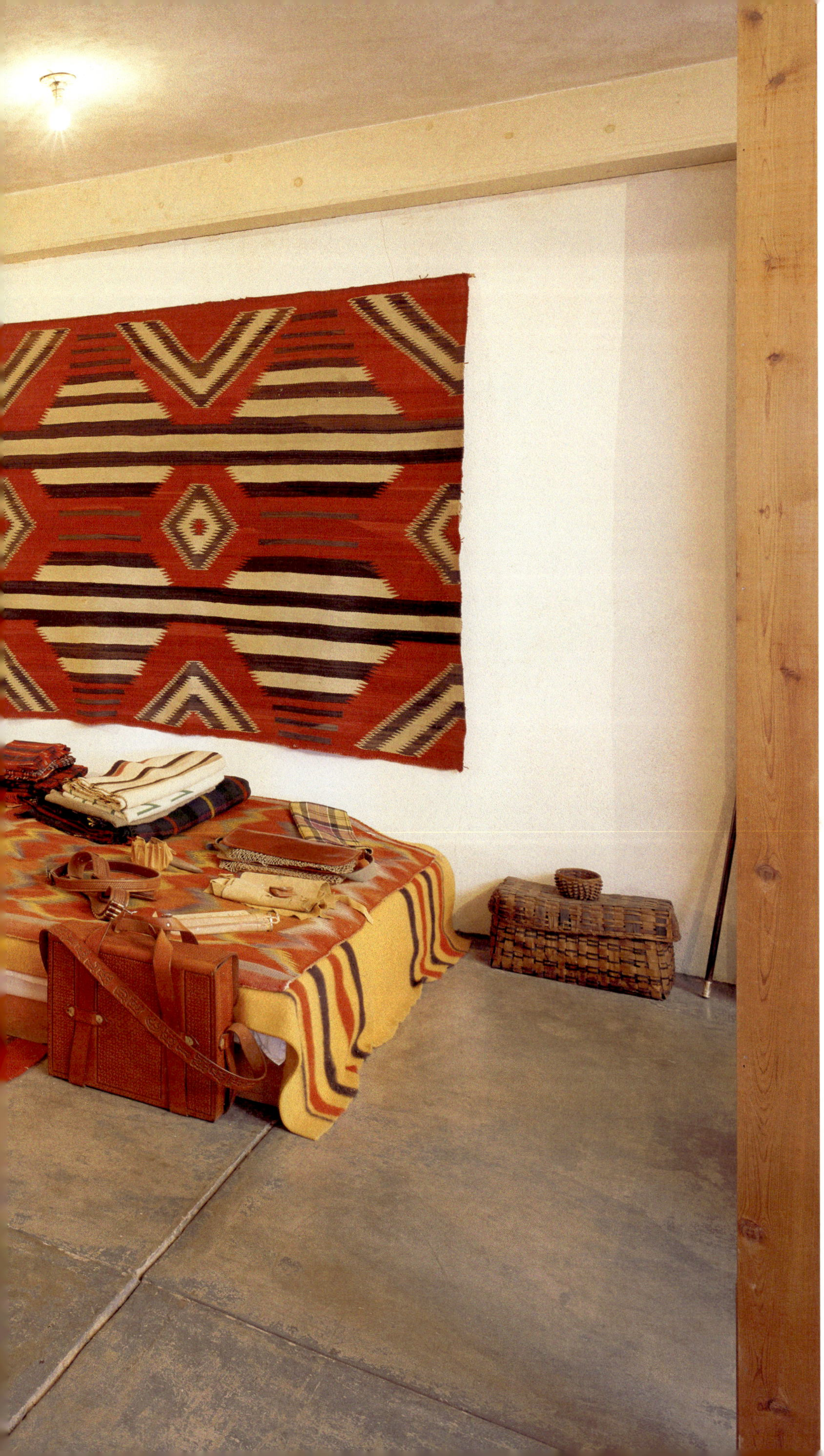

La Mansana de Chinati. Bedroom with native Indian pottery and rugs, view towards northwest.

Schlafzimmer mit indianischen Tonwaren und Teppichen, nach Nordwesten.

JUDD FOUNDATION

| 2 |
| 3 |
| 1 | 6 |

1 **La Mansana de Chinati, situation**
La Mansana de Chinati, Lageplan

2 **Building section A-A**
Gebäudeschnitt A-A

3 **Building section B-B**
Gebäudeschnitt B-B

4 **Building section C-C**
Gebäudeschnitt C-C

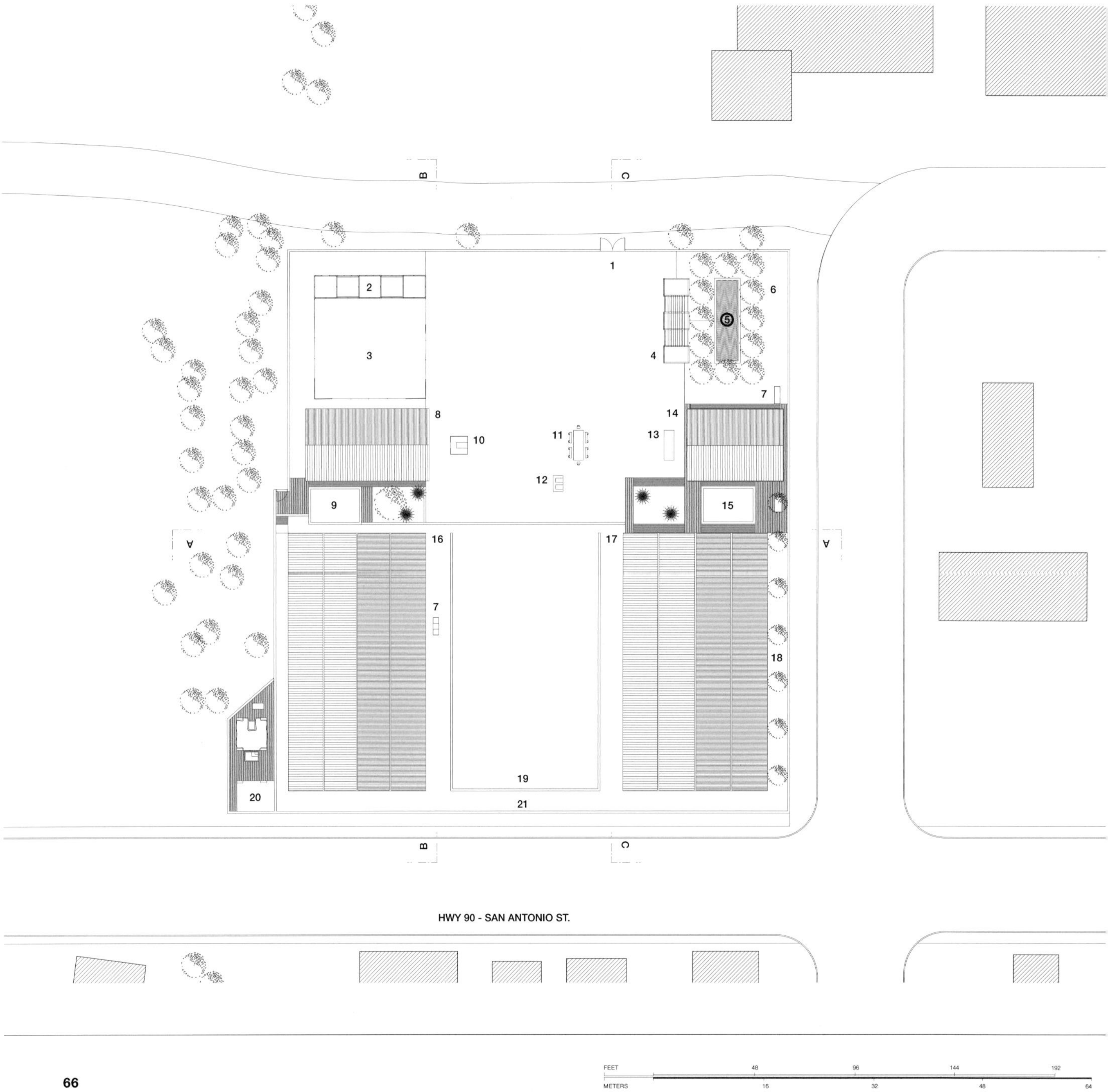

1.1 Entry Gate Eingangstor

1.2 Dog Kennel, Chicken Coop, Greenhouse Hundezwinger, Hühnerstall, Treibhaus

1.3 Vegetable Garden Gemüsegarten

1.4 Pergola Pergola

1.5 Pool Wasserbecken

1.6 Cottonwood Trees Pappeln

1.7 Bench Bank

1.8 Storage Building; unfinished Lagerhausgebäude

1.9 Office Büro

1.10 Bench and Table Bank und Tisch

1.11 Table and Benches Tisch und Bänke

1.12 Barbeque Pit Grill

1.13 Table Tisch

1.14 Two-story Building Zweigeschossiges Gebäude

1.15 Bathroom Building Badehaus

1.16 West Building Westgebäude

1.17 East Building Ostgebäude

1.18 Fruitless Plum Trees Zierpflaumenbäume

1.19 Donald Judd, untitled, 1977 Donald Judd, ohne Titel, 1977

1.20 Wintergarden and Bench Wintergarten und Bank

1.21 Adobe Courtyard Wall Lehmziegelmauer (Hof)

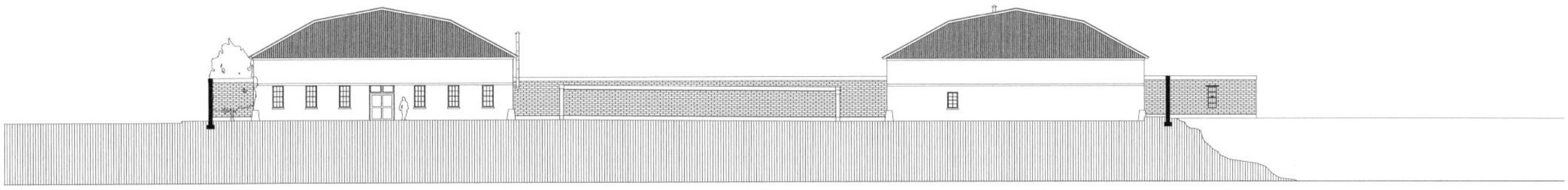

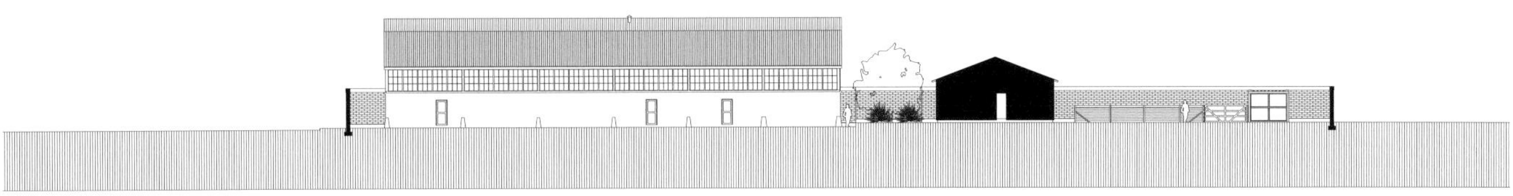

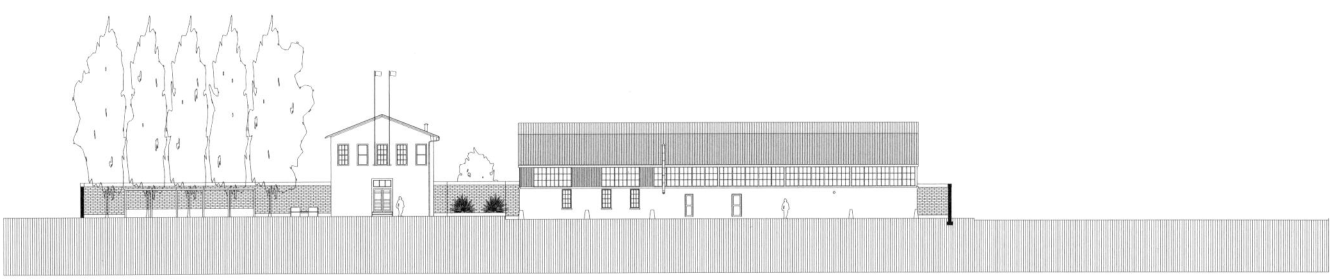

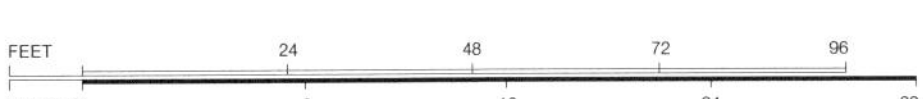

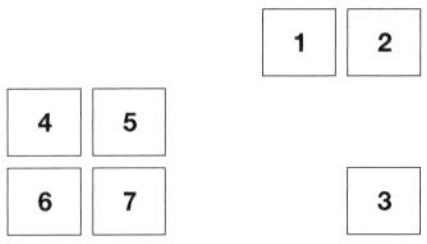

1 **Two-story building, first floor, plan**
Zweigeschossiges Gebäude, Grundriss Erdgeschoss

2 **Second floor, plan,**
Grundriss, Obergeschoss

3 **Section A-A**
Schnitt A-A

4 **West elevation**
Westansicht

5 **East elevation**
Ostansicht

6 **View to north**
Nordansicht

7 **South elevation**
Südansicht

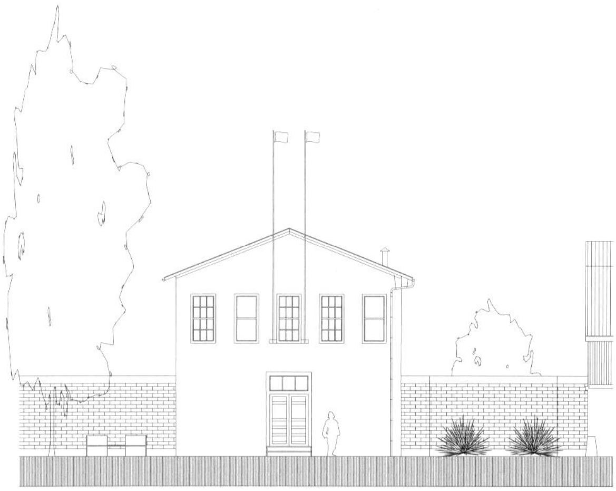

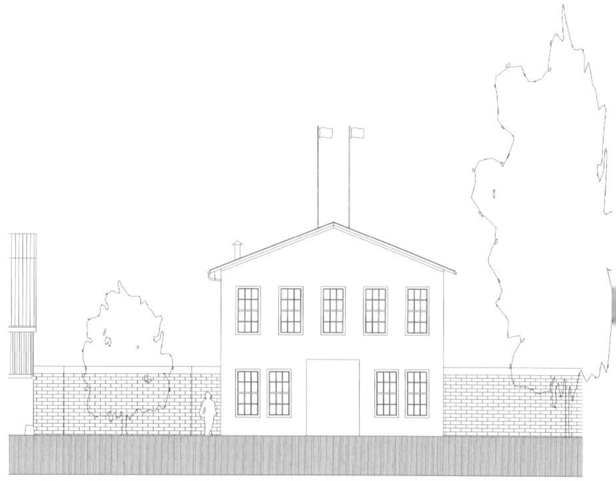

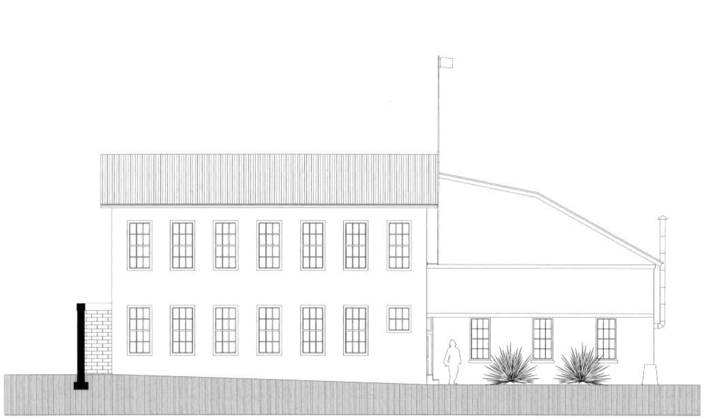

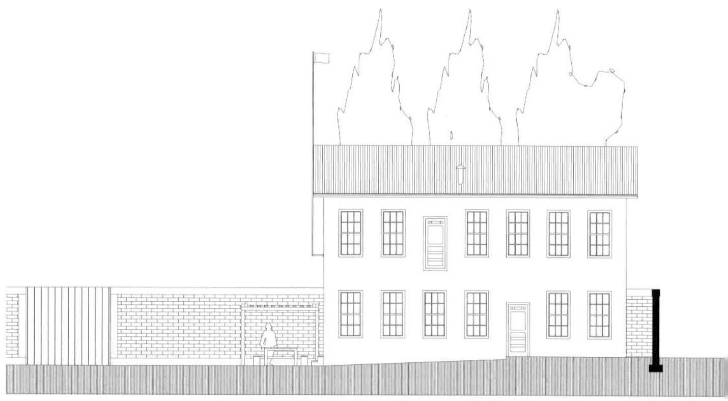

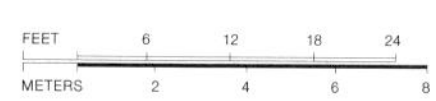

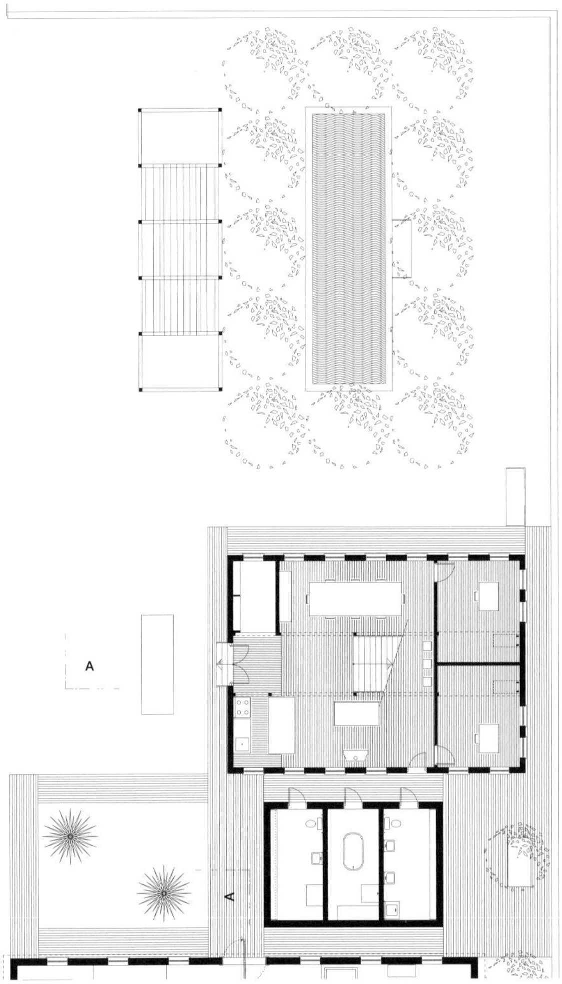
A
A
A

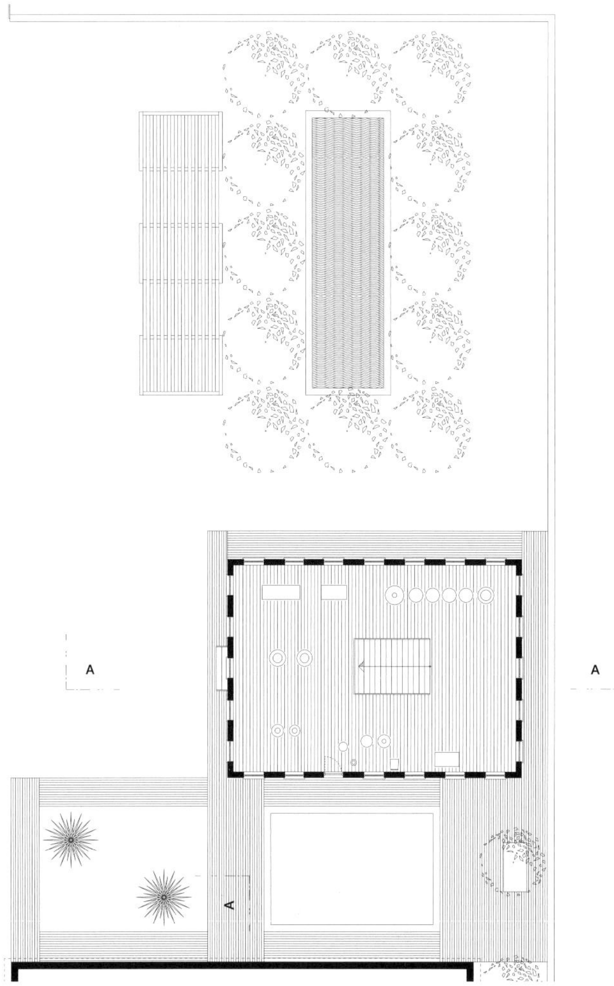
A
A
A

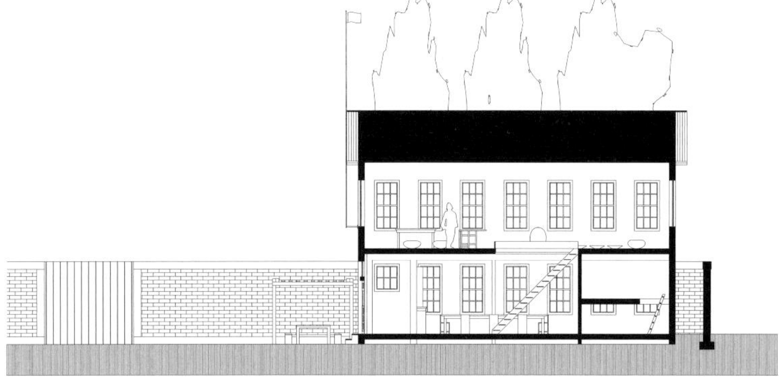

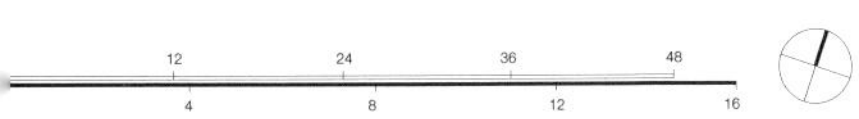
12 24 36 48
4 8 12 16

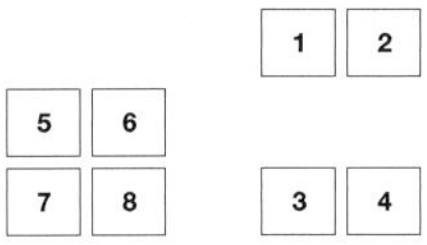

1 **La Mansana de Chinati, West Building, first floor, plan** Westgebäude, Grundriss Erdgeschoss

2 **Second floor, plan** Grundriss Obergeschoss

3 **Building section A-A** Gebäudeschnitt A-A

4 **Building section B-B** Gebäudeschnitt B-B

5 **East elevation** Ostansicht

6 **North elevation** Nordansicht

7 **West elevation** Westansicht

8 **South elevation** Südansicht

A **Storage room** Abstellraum

1.1 **Storage shelves** Abstellregale

B **Map room** Kartenraum

1.2 **Gustav Stickley Chair** Stuhl

1.3 **Stove** Ofen

C **Library 2** Bibliothek 2

1.4 **Donald Judd Table and Chair** Tisch und Stuhl

1.5 **Donald Judd Library Bookshelf, type 1** Bücherregal für Bibliothek, Typ 1

1.6 **Donald Judd, To Susan Buckwalter, 1964** Für Susan Buckwalter, 1964

1.7 **Dan Flavin, Alternate diagonals of March 2, 1964 (to Don Judd), 1964** Alternierende Diagonalen vom 2. März, 1964 (für Don Judd), 1964

1.8 **Donald Judd Table and Chairs and Stool** Tisch und Stühle und Hocker

D **Library 1** Bibliothek 1

1.9 **Donald Judd Library Bookshelf, type 2** Bücherregal für Bibliothek, Typ 2

1.10 **Donald Judd Chairs** Stühle

1.11 **Donald Judd Bed** Bett

1.12 **Stove** Ofen

1.13 **Donald Judd Table and Chairs** Tisch und Stühle

1.14 **Donald Judd Bench** Bank

E **Magazine Room** Zeitschriftenraum

1.15 **Storage Shelves** Abstellregale

F **South Room West Building** Südzimmer Westgebäude

1.16 **Gustav Stickley Bench** Bank

1.17 **Donald Judd, untitled, 1966** Ohne Titel, 1966

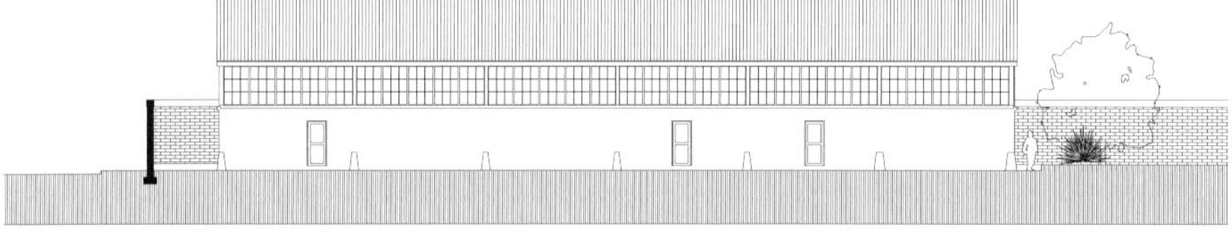

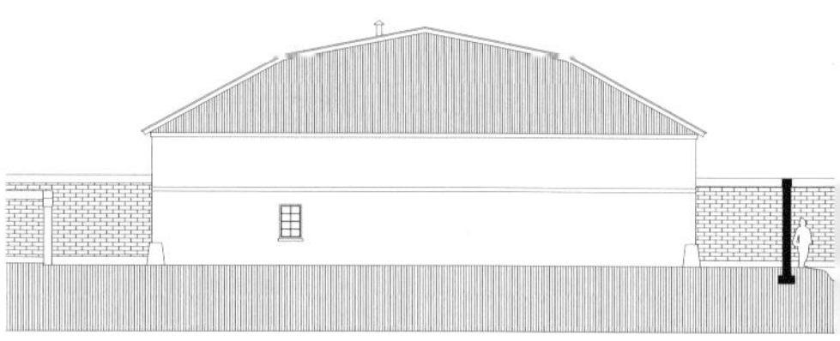

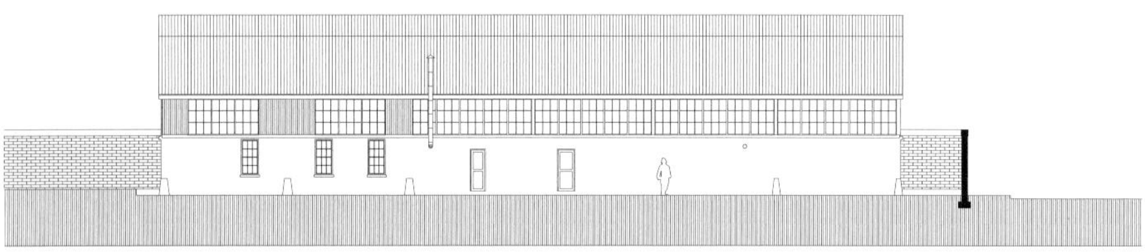

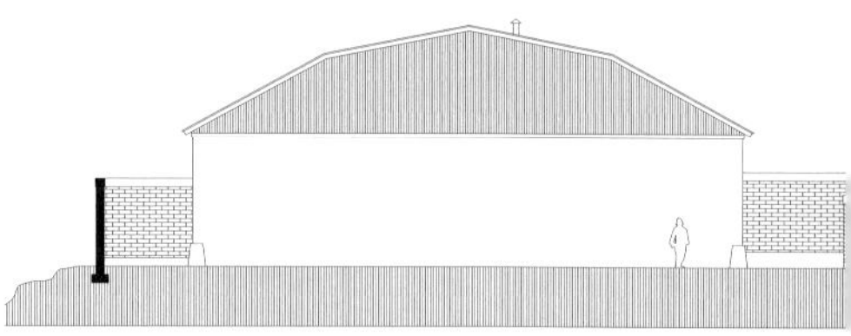

1.18 Donald Judd To Dave Shackman, 1964
Für Dave Shackman, 1964

1.19 Donald Judd, untitled, 1962
Ohne Titel, 1962

1.20 Donald Judd, untitled, 1965
Ohne Titel, 1965

1.21 Donald Judd, Bed Bett

1.22 Donald Judd, untitled, 1962
Ohne Titel, 1962

1.23 Donald Judd, untitled, 1965
Ohne Titel, 1965

1.24 Donald Judd, untitled, 1963
Ohne Titel, 1963

1.25 Donald Judd, untitled, 1965
Ohne Titel, 1965

1.26 Donald Judd, untitled, 1966
Ohne Titel, 1966

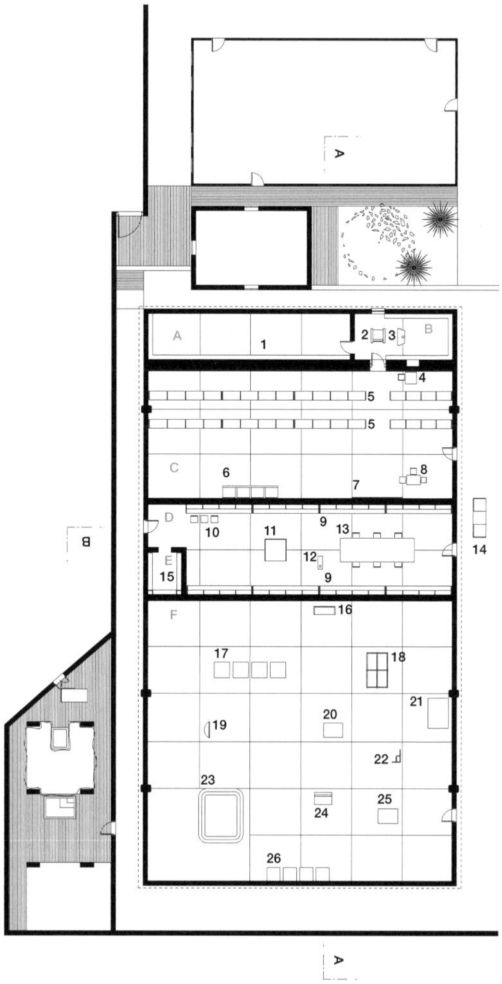

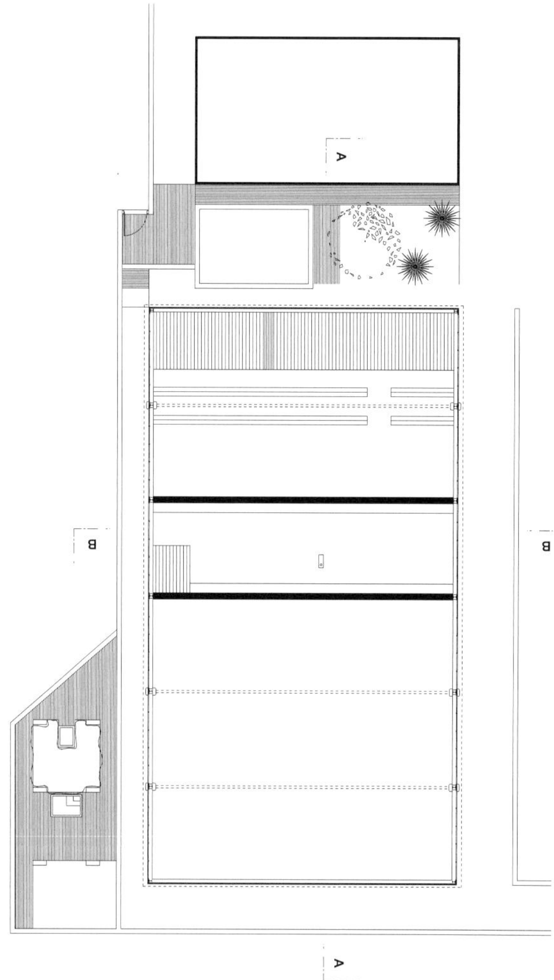

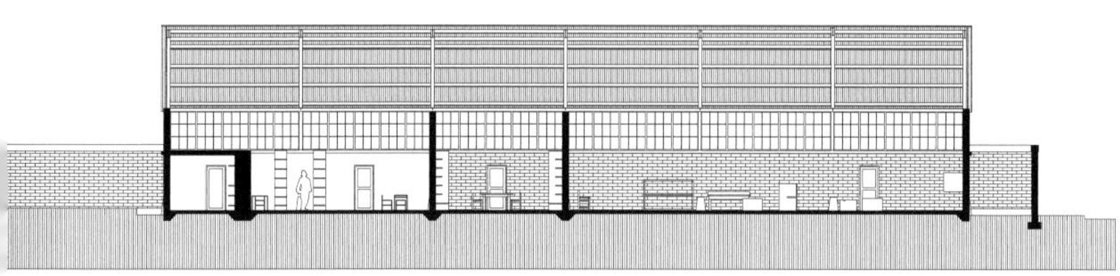

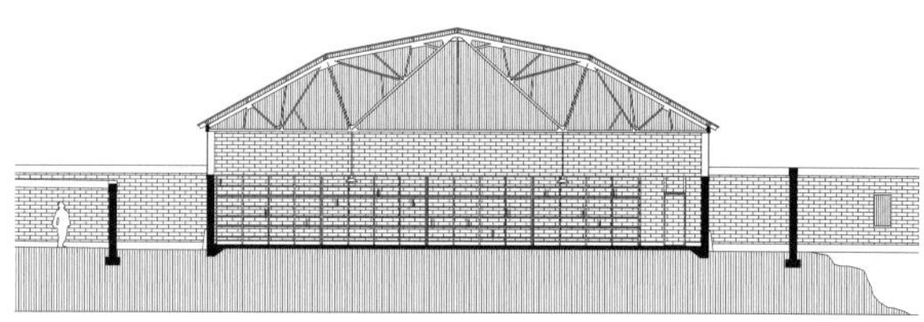

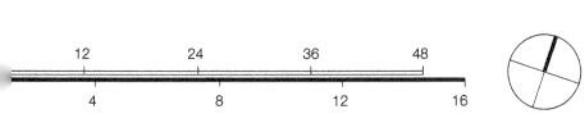

1 **La Mansana de Chinati, East Building, first floor, plan**
La Mansana de Chinati Ostgebäude, Grundriss Erdgeschoss

2 **Second floor, plan**
Grundriss Obergeschoss

3 **Building section A-A**
Gebäudeschnitt A-A

4 **Building section B-B**
Gebäudeschnitt B-B

5 **East elevation**
Ostansicht

6 **North elevation**
Nordansicht

7 **West elevation**
Westansicht

8 **South elevation**
Südansicht

G **Summer Bedroom**
Sommerschlafraum

1.27 **Donald Judd Bed** Bett

1.28 **Gustav Stickley Bench** Bank

1.29 **Chest for Bagpipe**
Truhe für Dudelsack

1.30 **Donald Judd, untitled, 1978**
Ohne Titel, 1978

1.31 **Donald Judd, untitled, 1969**
Ohne Titel, 1969

1.32 **Donald Judd, untitled, 1975**
Ohne Titel, 1975

1.33 **Gustav Stickley Chair** Stuhl

1.34 **Donald Judd, untitled, 1975**
Ohne Titel, 1975

1.35 **Donald Judd, untitled, 1977**
Ohne Titel, 1977

1.36 **Donald Judd, untitled, 1968**
Ohne Titel, 1968

H **Winter Bedroom**
Winterschlafraum

1.37 **Donald Judd Adobe Fireplace**
Kamin aus Lehmziegeln

1.38 **Gustav Stickley Chair** Stuhl

1.39 **Donald Judd Bed** Bett

1.40 **Table and Chair**
Tisch und Stuhl

1.41 **Chaise Longue**
Chaiselongue

J **Dining/Kitchen**
Essküche

1.43 **Gustav Stickley Cabinet** Schrank

1.44 **Gustav Stickley Table and Chairs**
Tisch und Stühle

1.45 **Chair** Stuhl

1.46 **Donald Judd Table** Tisch

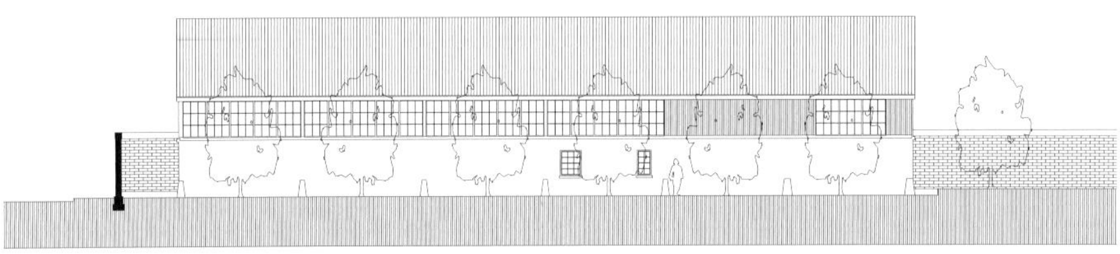

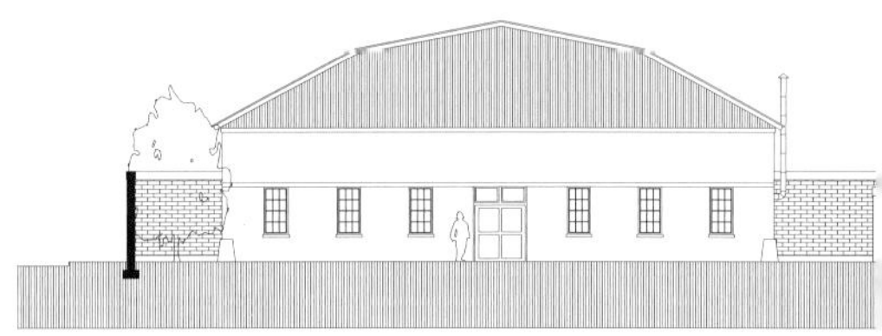

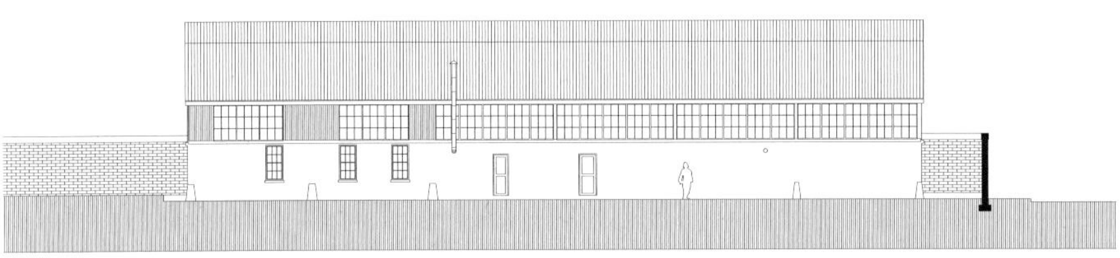

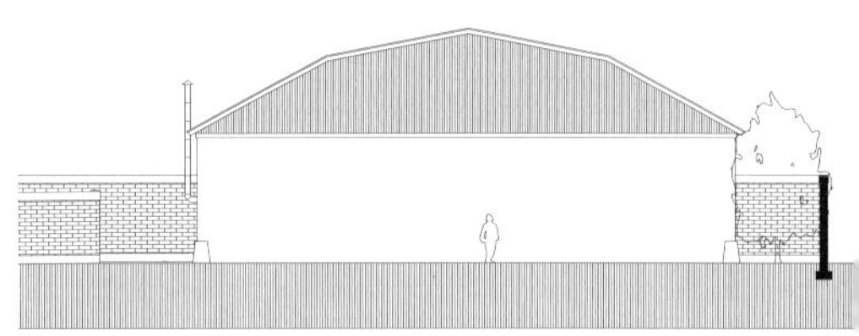

K **South Room**
Südzimmer

1.47 **Gustav Stickley Table and Chairs**
Tisch und Stühle

1.48 **Donald Judd, untitled, 1963**
Ohne Titel, 1963

1.49 **Donald Judd, untitled, 1969**
Ohne Titel, 1969

1.50 **Donald Judd, untitled, 1963**
Ohne Titel, 1963

1.51 **Gustav Stickley Bench** Bank

1.52 **Donald Judd, untitled, 1968**
Ohne Titel, 1968

1.53 **Donald Judd, untitled, 1963**
Ohne Titel, 1963

1.54 **Donald Judd, untitled, 1969**
Ohne Titel, 1969

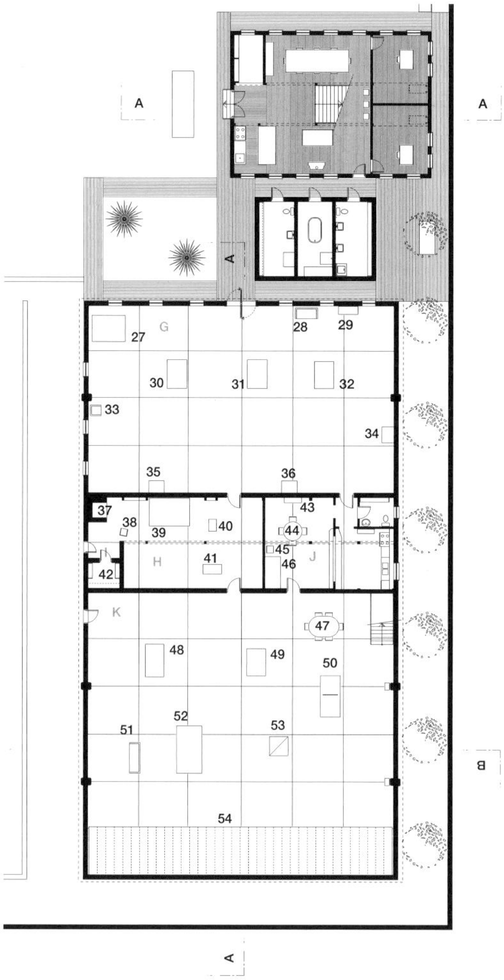

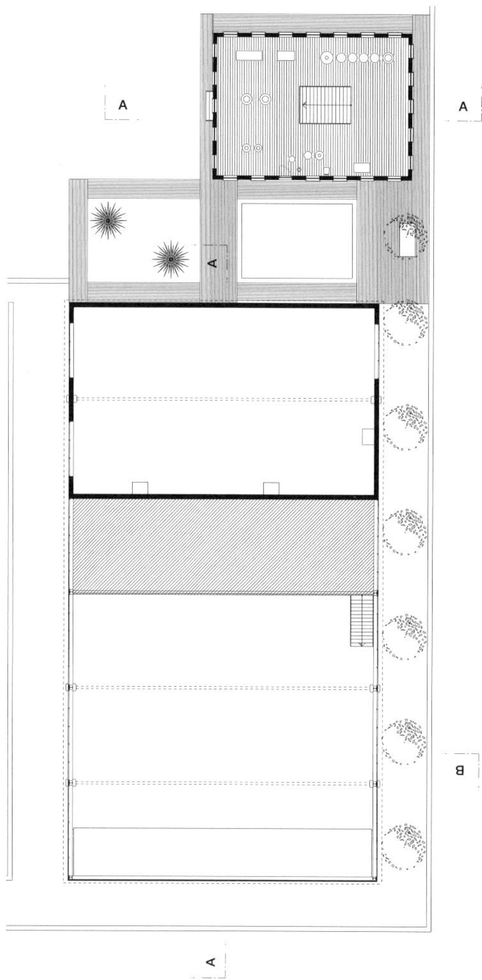

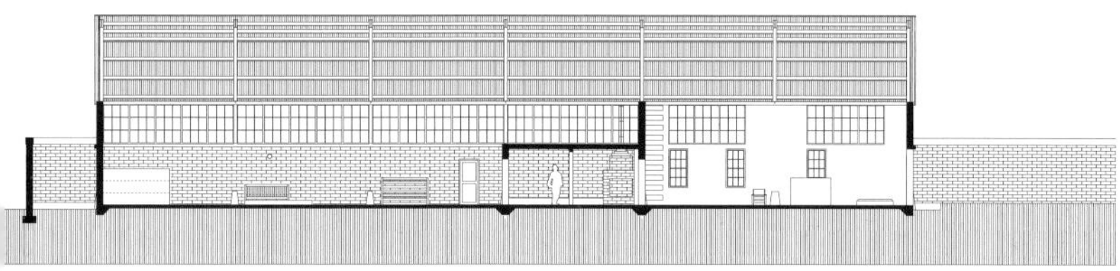

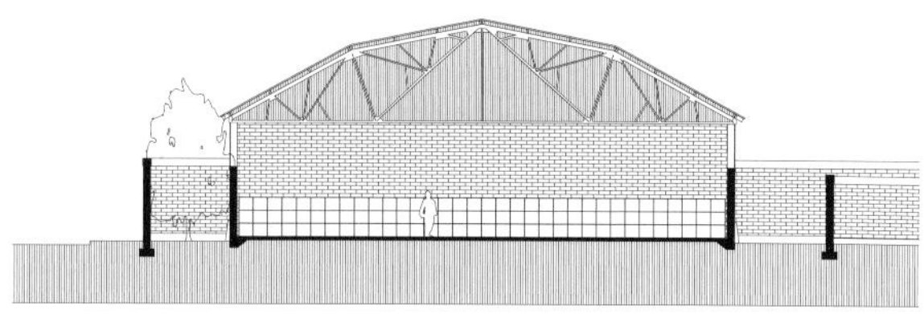

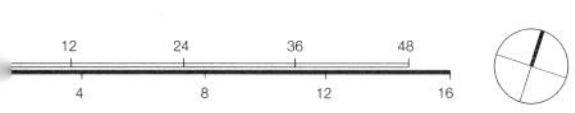

DIE ARTILLERIE-HALLEN

Die zwei vormaligen Geschützunterstände wurden 1979 von Judd erworben und beherbergen 100 seiner Arbeiten ohne Titel aus gewalztem Aluminium (jede im Einheitsmaß von 94 × 129 × 183 cm / 41 × 51 × 72 in), die der Künstler für diese zwei Gebäude entworfen hat. Sie wurden in Blöcken zu maximal 25 Stück in Connecticut hergestellt, nach Marfa transportiert und zwischen 1982 und 1986 dort aufgestellt. Die beiden Hallen liegen auf einem leicht bogenförmigen, von Nordosten nach Südwesten ausgerichteten Landstreifen. Die nordöstlich gelegene Halle 1 (81,70 m × 19,20 m / 286 × 63 ft) enthält 52 Arbeiten; in Halle 2 (72 m × 19,20 m / 269 × 63 ft) sind die restlichen 48 ausgestellt.

Das Äußere der beiden Bauten wurde von Judd drastisch verändert: Auf die ursprünglichen Flachdächer ließ Judd zwei riesige Nissenhütten setzen, flache Tonnengewölbe aus gewelltem Metall, wodurch sich die Gebäudehöhe verdoppelte. Diese Gewölbe verhalfen den Hallen zu einem neuen, monumentalen Erscheinungsbild. Der Plan, die vier halbrunden Enden der Dachstruktur mit Glas zu schließen,[1] wurde aus Kostengründen fallen gelassen.[2]

Die zweite größere Veränderung war der Ersatz der ursprünglichen Industrietore an den Längsseiten des Gebäudes durch gleich große Fenster mit Aluminiumprofilen (Breite 3,66 m / 12 ft). Die Fenster sind viergeteilt; Höhe und Breite stehen im Verhältnis 6:5. Eine Fotografie aus den frühen 1980er-Jahren zeigt einen Prototyp der Fenster mit neunteiliger Gliederung, doch diese kleinere Gitterung wurde verworfen. Bei aller Ähnlichkeit weisen die Hallen jedoch einige Unterschiede auf: Die Tür an der

THE ARTILLERY SHEDS

Purchased in 1979, the two former Artillery Sheds house 100 untitled mill-aluminum works by Donald Judd (each measuring 41 × 51 × 72 inches) conceived by the artist for these two buildings. They were fabricated in groups of twenty-five or fewer in Connecticut, then shipped to Marfa and installed between 1982 and 1986. The two sheds are situated along a slight northeast to southwest arc. The shed to the northeast, shed number one (286 by 63 feet) houses fifty-two works, while shed number two (269 by 63 feet) displays the remaining forty-eight.

Judd dramatically changed the appearance of the two buildings by placing two large Quonset roofs on top of the original flat roofs, doubling their height. These vaults give the sheds a monumental appearance. Judd's original intention was to glaze the four semi-circular ends of the Quonset-huts,[1] but due to a lack of funds,[2] this was not carried out.

The other major architectural change was the replacement of the original industrial garage doors on the long side of the structure by aluminum-framed windows (12 feet wide) of the same size, quartered into a vertical-to-horizontal ratio of 6 to 5. A photograph taken in the early 1980s of a prototype shows a window divided into nine fields, but this smaller division was rejected. Although the two sheds appear very similar, they have a few differences: the door on the northeast facade of shed number one is off center from the longitudinal axis and has three more windows than the remaining three facades. This first facade has seven windows altogether, four to the southeast and three to the northwest of the door. The other three facades show doors

Nordostfassade von Halle 1 ist, bezogen auf die Längsachse, außermittig angeordnet, und die Fassade hat drei Fenster mehr als die übrigen drei Seiten – insgesamt sieben: vier südöstlich und drei nordwestlich der Tür. Bei den drei anderen Fassaden liegt die Tür genau auf der Längsachse, und die Fenster sind symmetrisch angeordnet. An seiner Nordostseite hat jedes Gebäude einen kleineren Raum, eine Art Vorzimmer, das den Besucher auf die sehr viel größeren Räume einstimmt. Jeder dieser kleineren Räume enthält vier Aluminium-Arbeiten; die Größe dieser Zimmer allerdings differiert und damit auch die Anordnung der Objekte. Die zwei großen Hallenräume unterscheiden sich in der Anzahl ihrer Fenster wie auch in der Positionierung kurzer Wände, die quer durch die Räume laufen: zwei Ziegelmauern in Halle 1 deuten nach dem achten Fenster eine leichte Teilung an, während in Halle 2 eine kurze, grau bemalte Wand in die Mitte des sechsten Fensters gesetzt ist.

Die Artillerie-Hallen sind Zeugnis der strikten, durchdachten Detailgenauigkeit in Judds Planungsprozess. Fotografien aus der Zeit der Renovierungsarbeiten illustrieren die Wirkung von Judds Interventionen beim Umbau dieser Sheds für die Aufnahme von Kunst. Sie zeigen die zwei heruntergekommenen ehemaligen Militärbauten, umgeben von einer verwahrlosten Landschaft, in Erwartung ihrer künftigen Bestimmung – der Synthese von Kunst und Architektur in einem erneuerten landschaftlichen Kontext. Wenn der Besucher sich durch die 100 Aluminiumobjekte bewegt, erlebt er den Dialog zwischen Innen- und Außenraum. Doch bedeutsamer ist die Beziehung zwischen den Kunstwerken und dem Raum, dessen Ergänzung sie bilden. Judd benutzte die Proportionen der zwei Artillerie-Hallen, um die Größe, die Zahl und das Arrangement der Kunstwerke festzulegen. So wurden drei Reihen von Objekten aus Walzaluminium in den größeren Räumen jeder Halle aufgestellt. Auf diese Weise entstand ein neues Ganzes, in dem Kunst, Architektur und Landschaft in dem natürlichen Licht konvergieren, das den Innenraum durchströmt und sich spielerisch an Metall, Glas und polierten Betonoberflächen bricht.

1 *Donald Judd. Architektur*, Münster 1989, S. 69.
2 Mitteilung von Marianne Stockebrand in einem Gespräch am 9. Februar 2006.

precisely in line with the longitudinal axis and a symmetrical window arrangement. Each building has on its northeast side a smaller room, like an antechamber, that prepares the visitor for the much larger spaces. Each of these smaller spaces contains four aluminum works, although the sizes of the rooms differ and therefore the positions of the works. The two large principal spaces differ in their number of bays (18 versus 16) as well as in the placement of shorter walls running across the spaces: two brick walls make a slight division in shed number one after the eighth bay, while in shed number two a short wall, painted grey, is placed in the center at the sixth bay.

The Artillery Sheds are evidence of the rigor and thoughtful attention to detail in Judd's planning process. Photographs taken during the renovation process of the Sheds illustrate the effect that Judd's interventions had when he adapted these buildings for art. They show the two well-worn former military buildings standing in a neglected landscape, awaiting their new purpose that would become a synthesis of art and architecture within a restored landscape. While walking around the 100 mill-aluminum works, the visitor experiences the dialogue between interior and exterior space. More significant, however, is the relationship between artworks and the spaces they complement. Judd used the proportions of the two Artillery Sheds to determine the size, number, and arrangement of the artwork, placing three rows of mill-aluminum pieces in the larger spaces of each Shed. Thus Judd created a new whole, where art, architecture, and landscape converge in the natural light that floods the interiors, playfully refracting off the metal, glass, and polished concrete surfaces.

1 *Donald Judd. Architektur*, 3rd ed. (Ostfildern, 1992), p. 29.
2 Information provided by Marianne Stockebrand, in conversation on February 9, 2006.

Artillery Sheds 2 and 1. View to northeast.

Artillerie-Hallen 2 und 1, nach Nordosten.

Artillery Shed with early wooden prototype window. Northwest elevation circa 1979.

Eine Artillerie-Halle mit dem frühen Prototyp des Holzfensters. Nordwest-Ansicht, ca. 1979.

THE CHINATI FOUNDATION

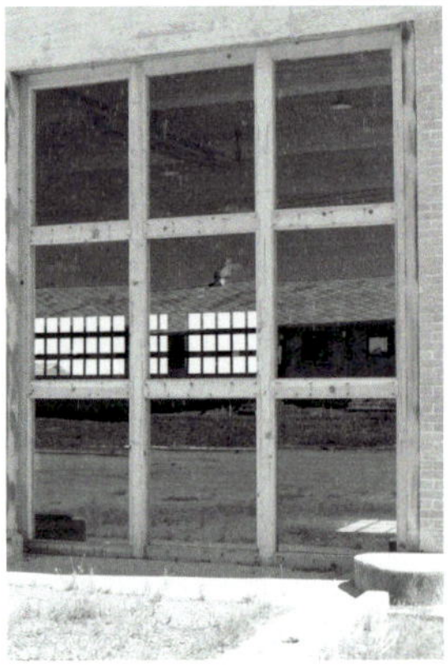

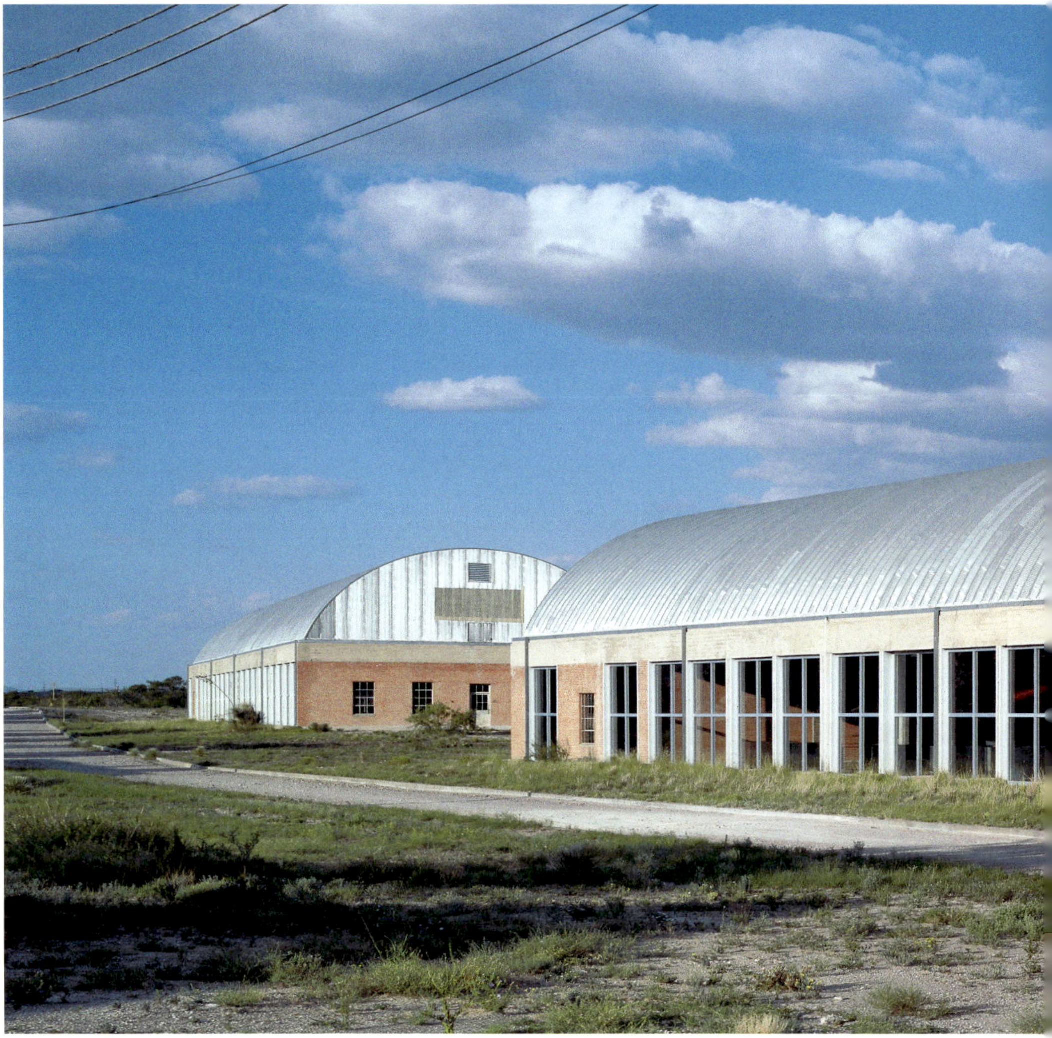

Artillery Shed after removal of original garage doors. Northwest elevation circa 1980.

Eine Artillerie-Halle nach Entfernung der ursprünglichen Garagentore. Nordwest-Ansicht, ca. 1980.

Artillery Shed 2 with Quonset roof under construction circa 1984. View to northeast.

Artillerie-Halle 2, Errichtung des gewölbten Metalldachs, ca. 1984, nach Nordosten.

THE CHINATI FOUNDATION

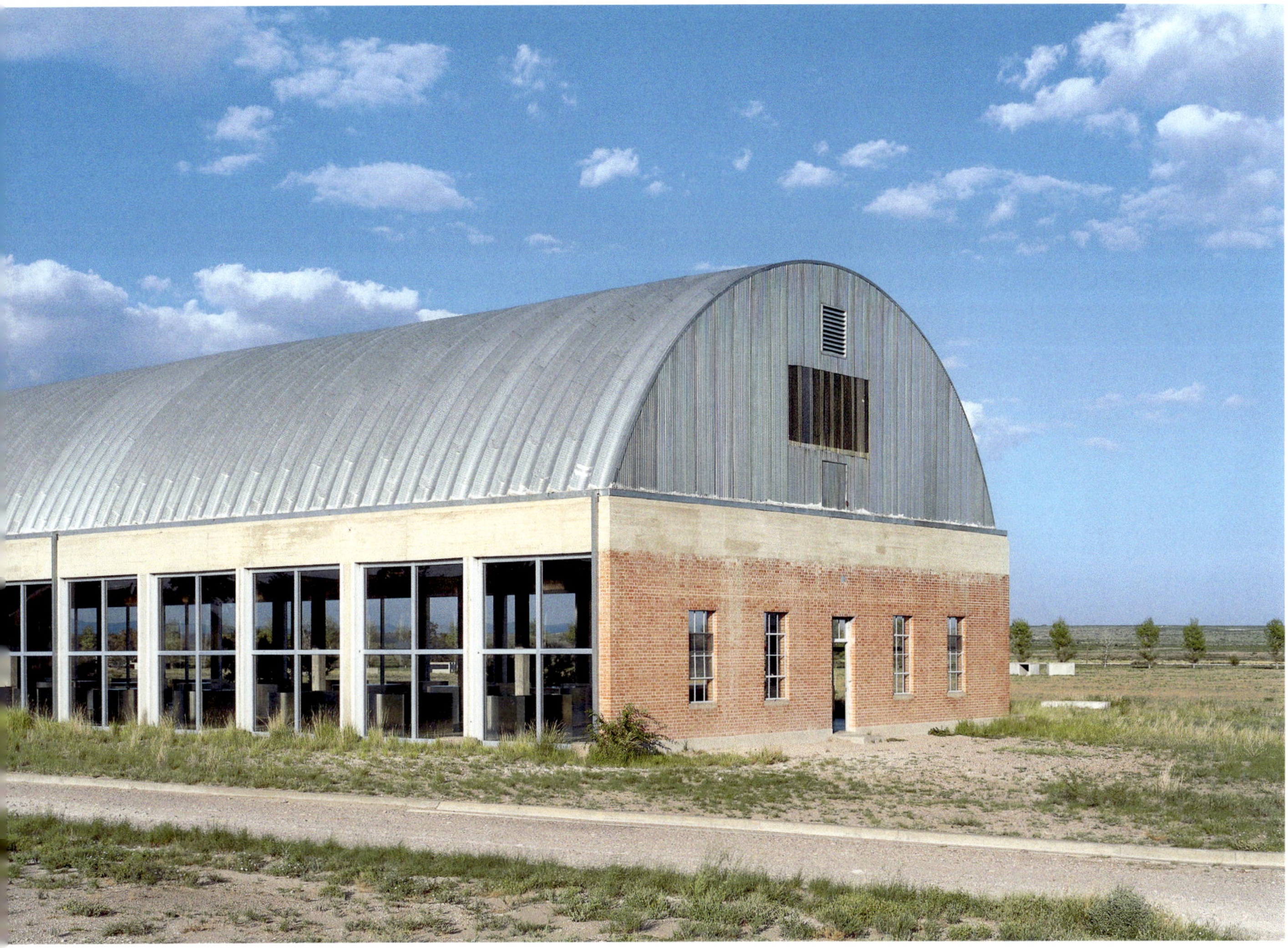

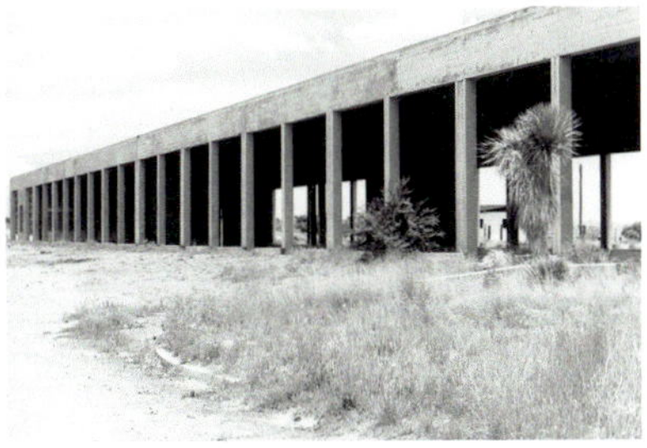

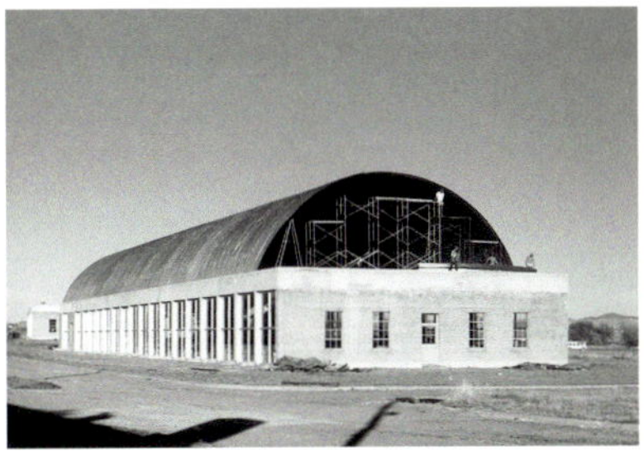

Artillery Shed.
View of northwest elevation.

Artillerie-Halle,
Nordwest-Ansicht.

THE CHINATI FOUNDATION

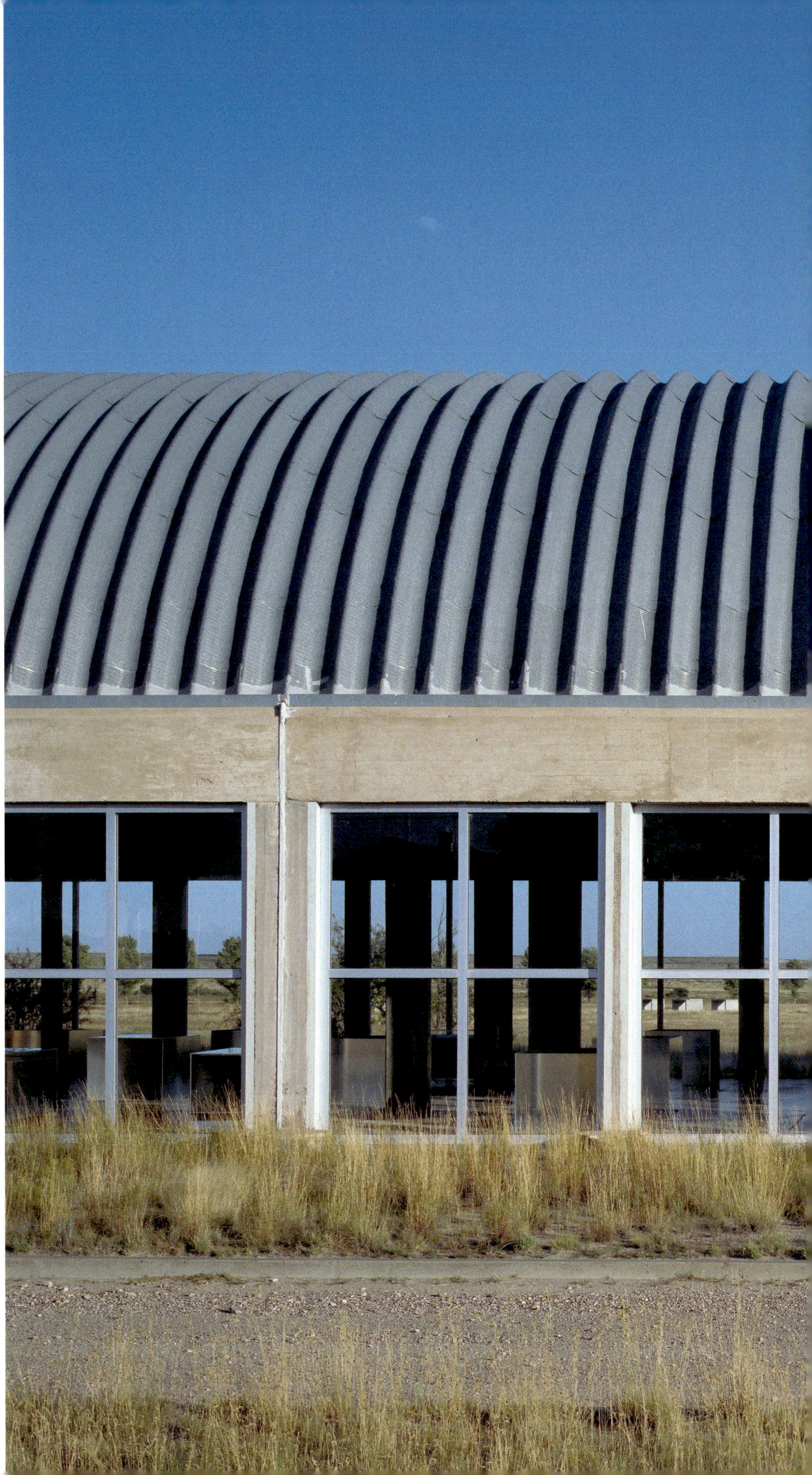

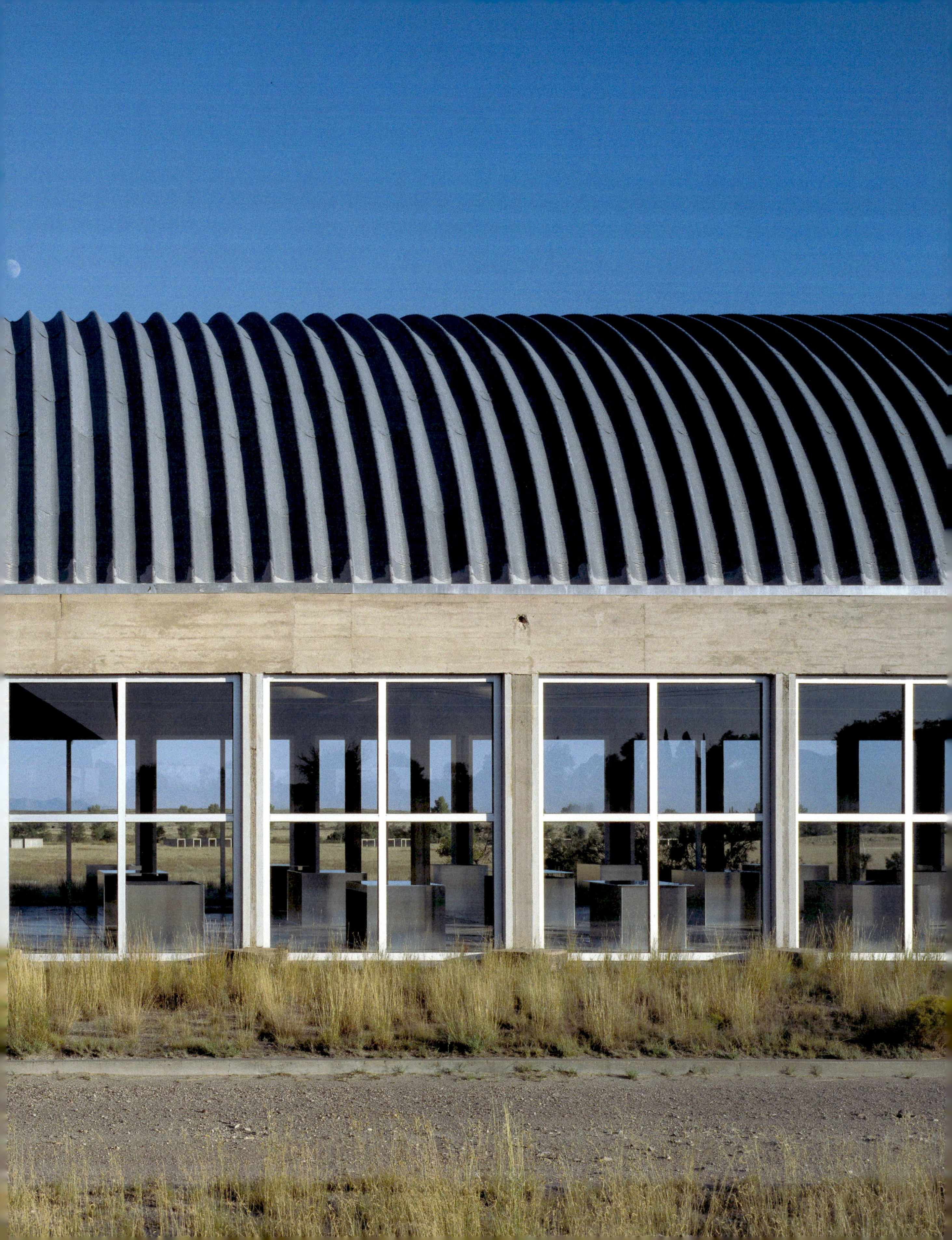

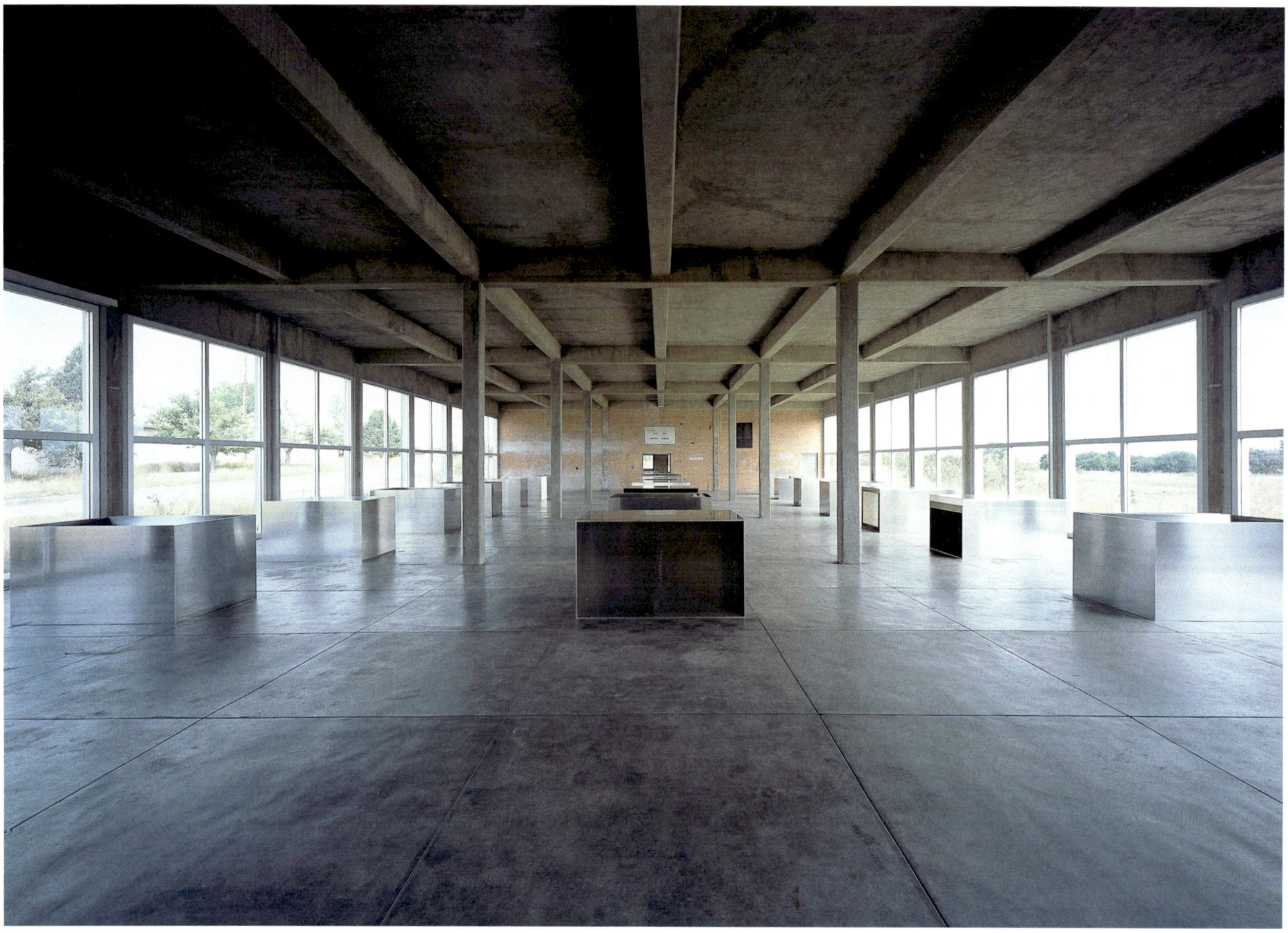

Artillery Shed 1. With 52 of a total of 100 untitled mill-aluminum works by Donald Judd 1982–1986. View to northeast.

Artillerie-Halle 1 mit 52 von insgesamt 100 Arbeiten ohne Titel aus Walzaluminium von Donald Judd, 1982–1986, nach Nordosten.

THE CHINATI FOUNDATION

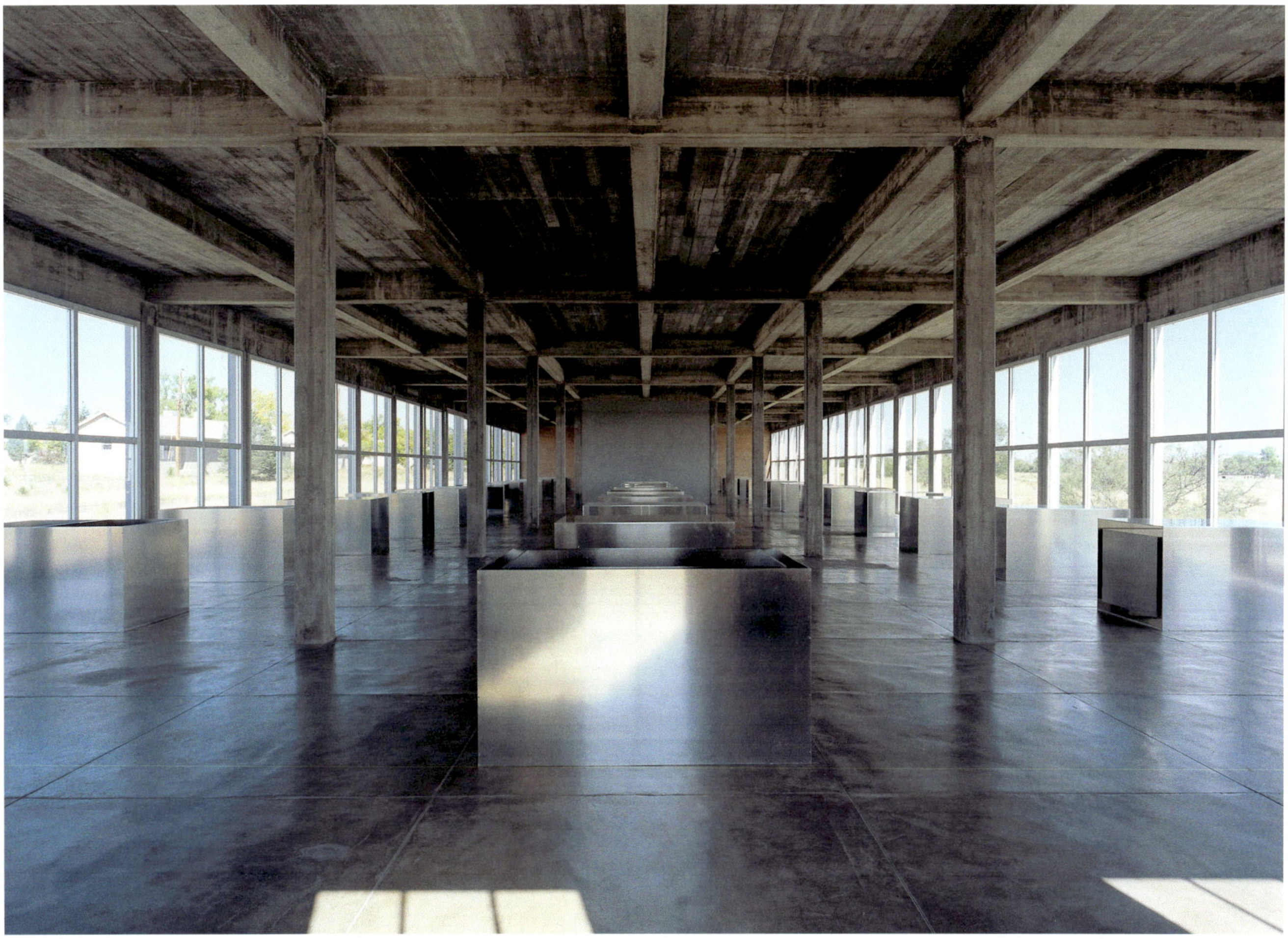

Artillery Shed 2. With 48 of a total of 100 untitled mill-aluminum works by Donald Judd 1982–1986. View to northeast.

Artillerie-Halle 2 mit 48 von insgesamt 100 Arbeiten ohne Titel aus Walzaluminium von Donald Judd, 1982–1986, nach Nordosten.

THE CHINATI FOUNDATION

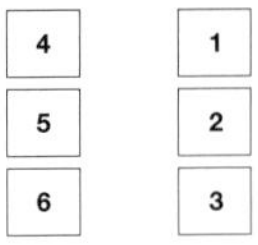

1 **Artillery Shed 1 floor plan**
Artillerie-Halle 1 Grundriss

2 **Northwest elevation**
Nordwestansicht

3 **Southeast elevation**
Südostansicht

4 **Section A-A**
Schnitt A-A

5 **Northeast elevation**
Nordostansicht

6 **Southwest elevation**
Südwestansicht

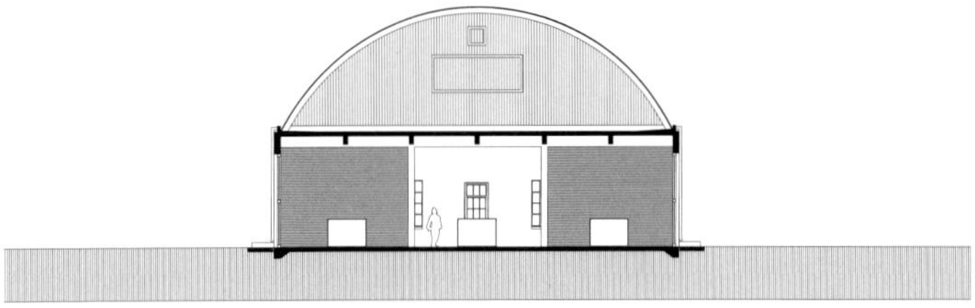

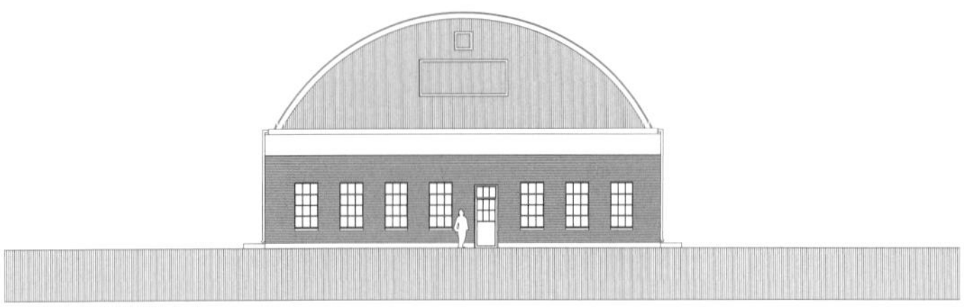

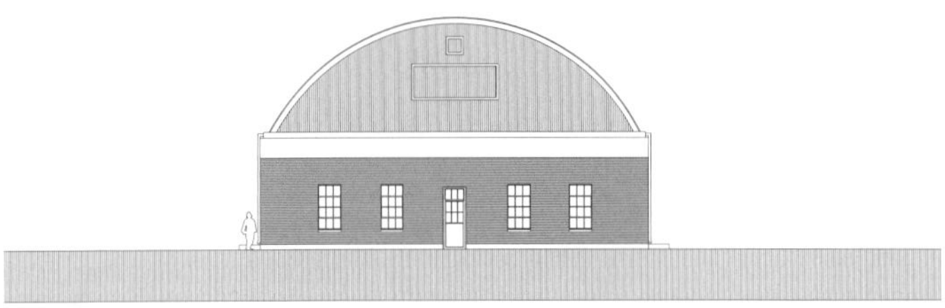

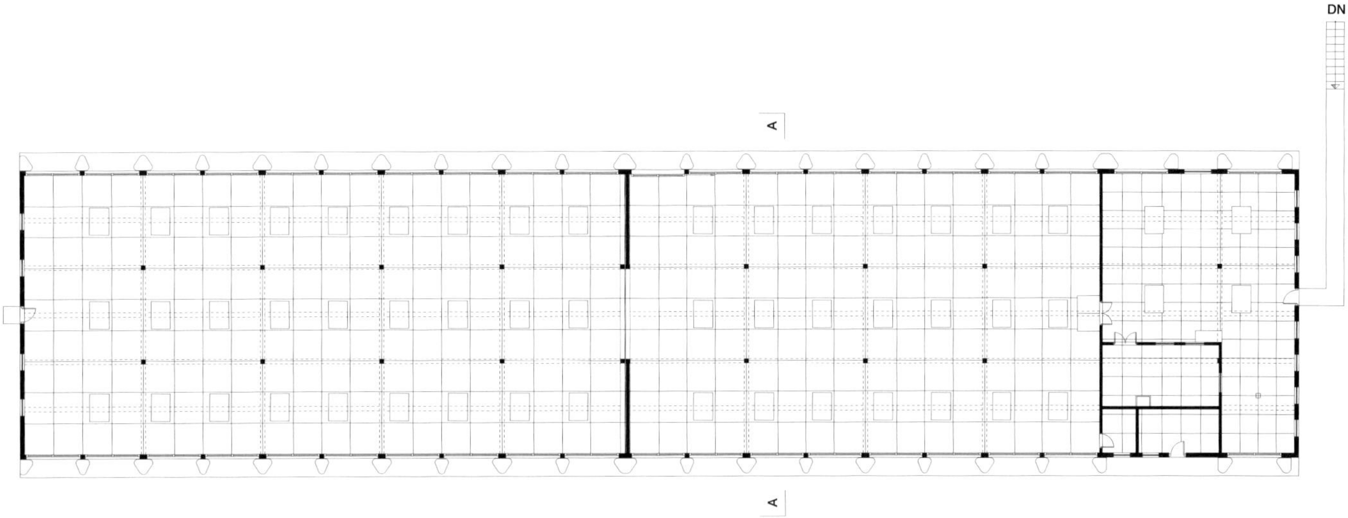
DN
A
A

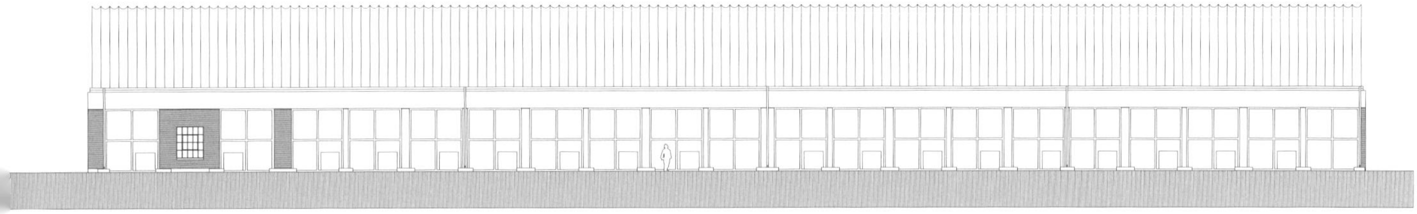

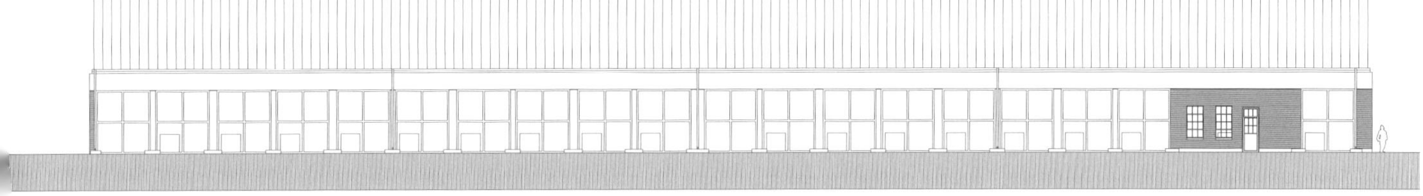

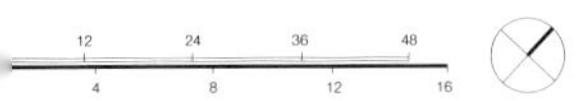
12 24 36 48
4 8 12 16

4	1
5	2
6	3

1 **Artillery Shed 2 floor plan**
Artillerie-Halle 2 Grundriss

2 **Southeast elevation**
Südostansicht

3 **Northwest elevation**
Nordwestansicht

4 **Section A-A**
Schnitt A-A

5 **Northeast elevation**
Nordostansicht

6 **Southwest elevation**
Südwestansicht

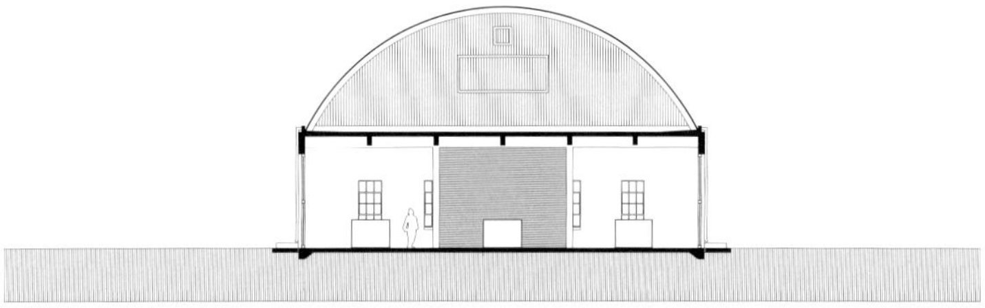

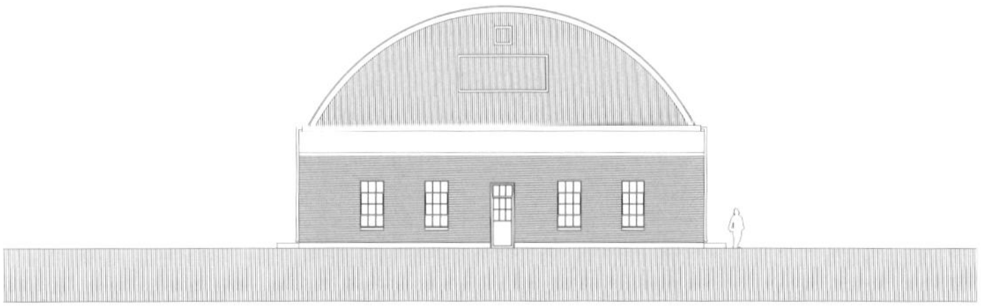

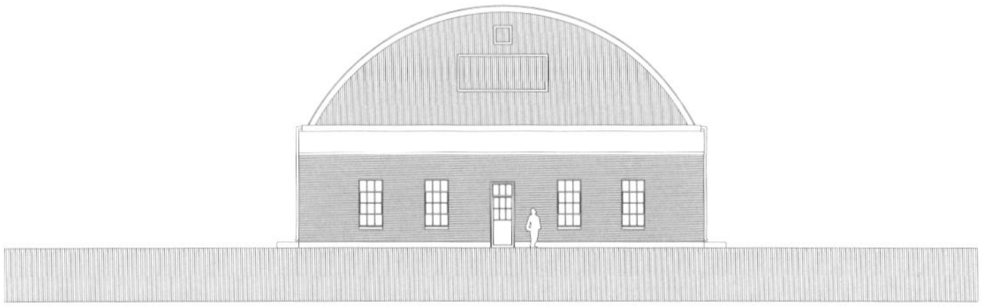

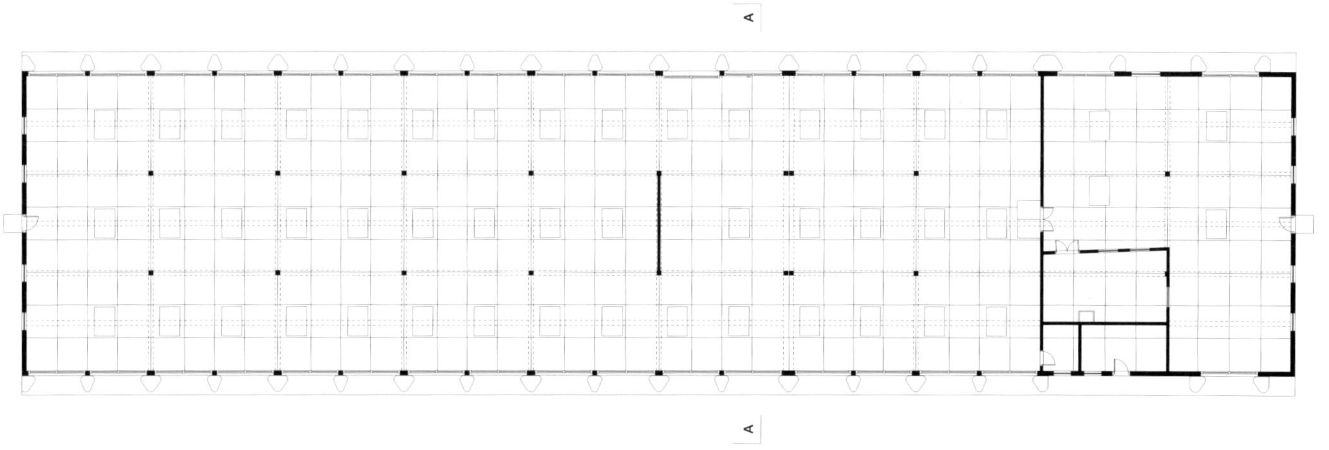
A
A

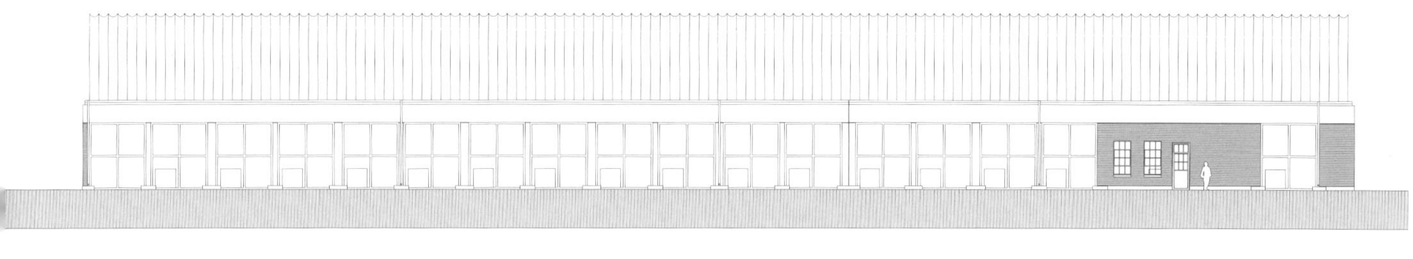

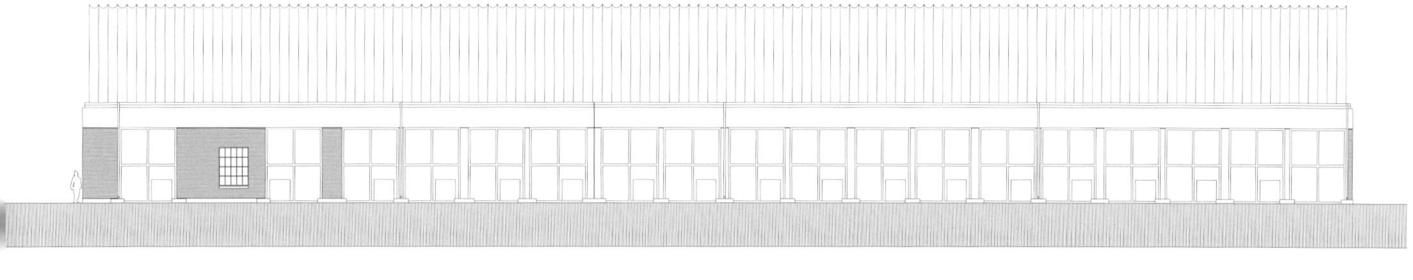

12 24 36 48
4 8 12 16

DIE ARENA

Ursprünglich ein Flugzeughangar, diente die Arena später als Turnhalle für das Fort D. A. Russell und nach der Schließung des Forts als Reithalle. Judd kaufte das Gebäude 1979; die Erneuerungsarbeiten begannen in den frühen 1980er-Jahren. Anders als die übrigen Bauten auf dem Gelände des früheren Armeestützpunktes ist die Arena genau an der Nord-Süd-Achse ausgerichtet.

Fotografien vom Renovierungsprozess zeigen das wüste, mit Schutt übersäte Gelände und den heruntergekommenen Zustand des Gebäudes vor der Instandsetzung. Judds architektonischer Weitblick bekundet sich vor allem in der geschickten Adaptation eines kleinen Betriebs- und Heizungsgebäudes des früheren Hangars, aus dem er ein Außenbad mit Hof und Sonnenterrasse machte – ein Vorgehen, das sein Talent illustriert, den praktischen Nutzen eines bestimmten Gebäudes durch minimale bauliche Veränderungen zu maximieren. Dieses der großen Halle nach Süden vorgelagerte kleinere Nebengebäude enthielt die technischen Einrichtungen für die Beheizung der Arena. Becken

THE ARENA

Originally an airplane hangar, the Arena later served as a gymnasium for Fort D. A. Russell, and after the closing of the fort as an equestrian hall. The building was acquired in 1979; renovations began in the early 1980s. Unlike the other structures on the former army base, the Arena is aligned precisely along the north/south longitudinal axis.

Photographs of the renovation process show the cluttered grounds and the worn-down condition of the structure prior to Judd's alterations. His architectural vision is especially evident in his clever adaptation of a small structure for the original hangar, which he turned into an outdoor pool with sundeck and courtyard—a move that demonstrates his ability to maximize the practical use of a given structure with minimal modifications. Located to the south of the large building, this smaller utilitarian structure housed all of the mechanical equipment used to heat the Arena. Castellated adobe walls plastered on both sides enclose bath and courtyard; they were left in the natural gray cement color while the main building was painted an adobe color.

und Hof sind von beidseitig verputzten, zinnenartig gebauten Adobe-Mauern umschlossen, die in der natürlichen grauen Zementfarbe belassen wurden, während das Hauptgebäude einen lehmfarbigen Anstrich erhielt. Wie in der Mansana de Chinati sind in den Kiesbelag des Hofes aus Ziegelsteinen gepflasterte Wege eingebettet. Für einen Standort in der Südwestecke nahe beim Kücheneingang entwarf Judd einen großen Tisch mit Bänken. Im Westen der Arena wurde außerhalb des Innenhofs und unmittelbar neben einem verputzen, aus Lehmziegeln gemauerten Grill ein zweiter Tisch mit Bänken aufgestellt.

Das Innere der Arena ist von der Ost-, West- und Nordfassade her durch viergeteilte Türen aus Holz und Glas erschlossen, die sich um die vertikale Mittelachse drehen. Ein paar der vorhandenen Öffnungen auf Geländehöhe ließ Judd schließen, um die natürliche Lichtquelle zu konzentrieren, so dass das Tageslicht nur durch die drei Drehtüren und, was entscheidend ist, durch die darüber liegenden Fensterbänder einfällt. Die Wände sind weiß gestrichen. Dieser große Raum ist mit Tischen und Stühlen nach Judds Entwürfen möbliert. Besondere Beachtung schenkte er dem Fußboden. Er beließ die langen Betonbänder, die ursprünglich als Fundament für die Balken des alten Holzfußbodens der Turnhalle gedient hatten, und füllte den Raum zwischen den Bändern mit Kies auf. An beiden Hallenenden wurden neue Betonböden gegossen und mit den bestehenden Bändern schwalbenschwanzförmig verbunden. Die größere Zone dieser neuen Bodenfläche bildet den Essbereich, die kleinere am Nordende den Eingangsbereich. Dort ist eine Skulptur von David Rabinowitch aufgestellt. An der Südseite des Gebäudes liegen mehrere kleine Zimmer – eine Küche mit Speisekammer sowie ein Bad und ein Büro. Eine Holztreppe führt in einen Loft mit einem Bett und einer weiteren Skulptur von David Rabinowitch. Von dort öffnen sich zwei Türen auf ein hölzernes Außendeck mit Blick auf das Schwimmbecken und den Innenhof.

In der Arena fanden Judds jährlich Open-House-Feste statt. An dieser Tradition wurde festgehalten, und auch heute noch können die Besucher authentisch erleben, wie gut der Raum sowohl in ästhetischer wie auch in praktischer Hinsicht seine Funktion erfüllt.

Similar to La Mansana de Chinati, the Arena's courtyard was laid with pathways in brick, embedded in gravel. Judd designed a large table with benches to be placed in the southwest corner, near the entrance to the kitchen. To the west of the Arena, outside the courtyard, a second table with benches was placed close to a plastered adobe barbecue pit.

Judd allowed access to the interior of the Arena from the east, west, and north facades through center-hinged, quartered wood and glass doors. He closed some of the former openings on the ground level in order to focus the natural light source and have it enter solely through the three revolving doors plus, most importantly, through the long rows of clerestory windows above. The walls were painted white. This large space is furnished with tables and chairs designed by Judd. He paid particular attention to the floor, preserving the long concrete strips that were originally the foundation for the wooden beams supporting the gymnasium's floor, and then filling the spaces between the strips with gravel. On either end, Judd had new concrete floors poured, dovetailing them with the existing strips. The larger of these new floors is reserved for dining, while the smaller strip to the northern end is the entrance area. A sculpture by David Rabinowitch is placed here. On the southern side of the building we find several smaller rooms, one containing the kitchen and pantry, the other a bathroom and an office. A wooden staircase leads up to a loft with a bed and another sculpture by David Rabinowitch. From here, two doors permit access to an outdoor wooden deck overlooking the bath and courtyard below. Judd chose the Arena to host his annual Open House celebrations. The tradition continues, and today visitors can still experience firsthand how well the space works in both an aesthetic and a practical sense.

Arena.
Tables, chairs, bed and doors by Donald Judd, view to south.

Tisch, Stühle, Bett und Türen von Donald Judd, nach Süden.

THE CHINATI FOUNDATION

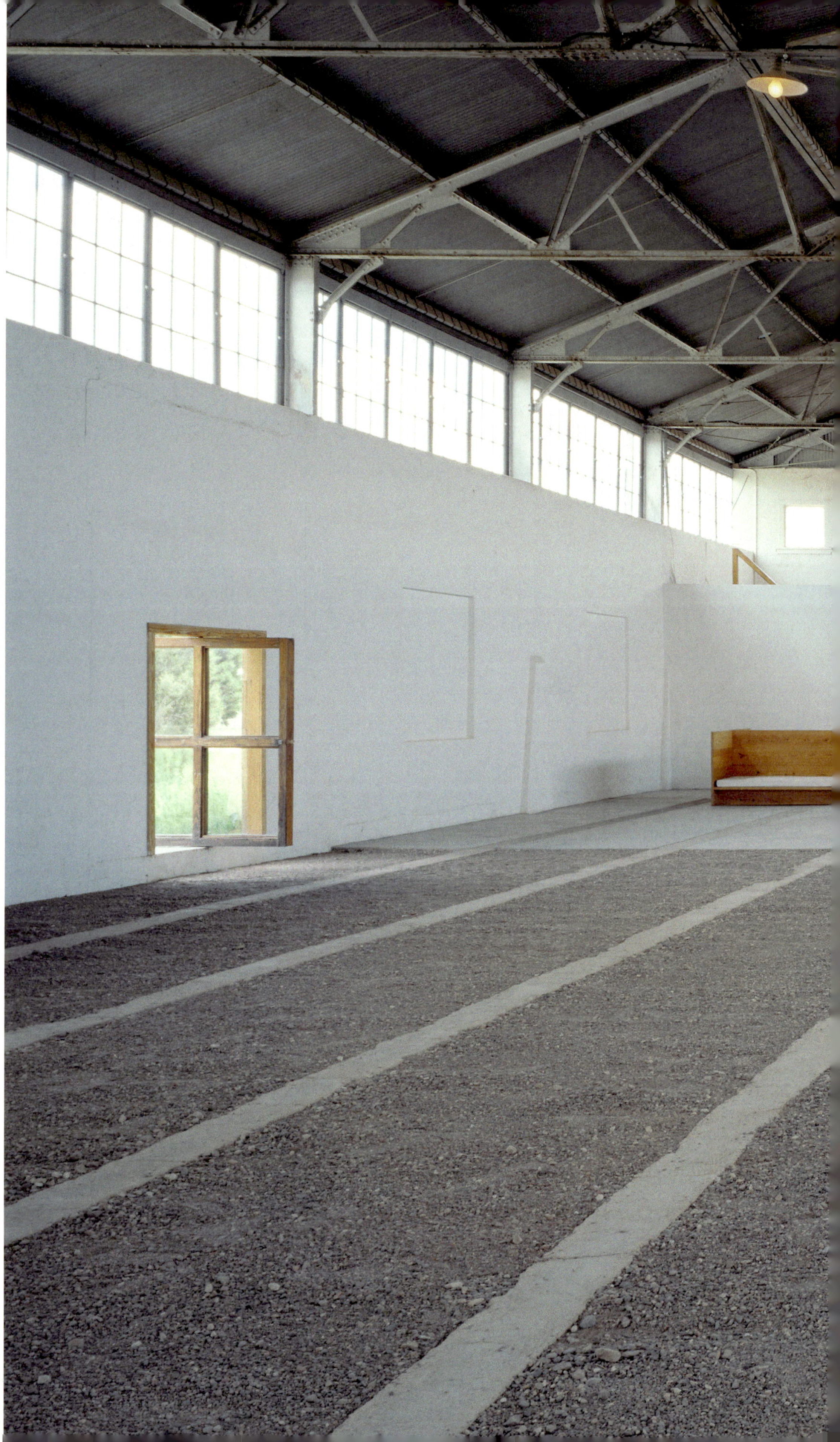

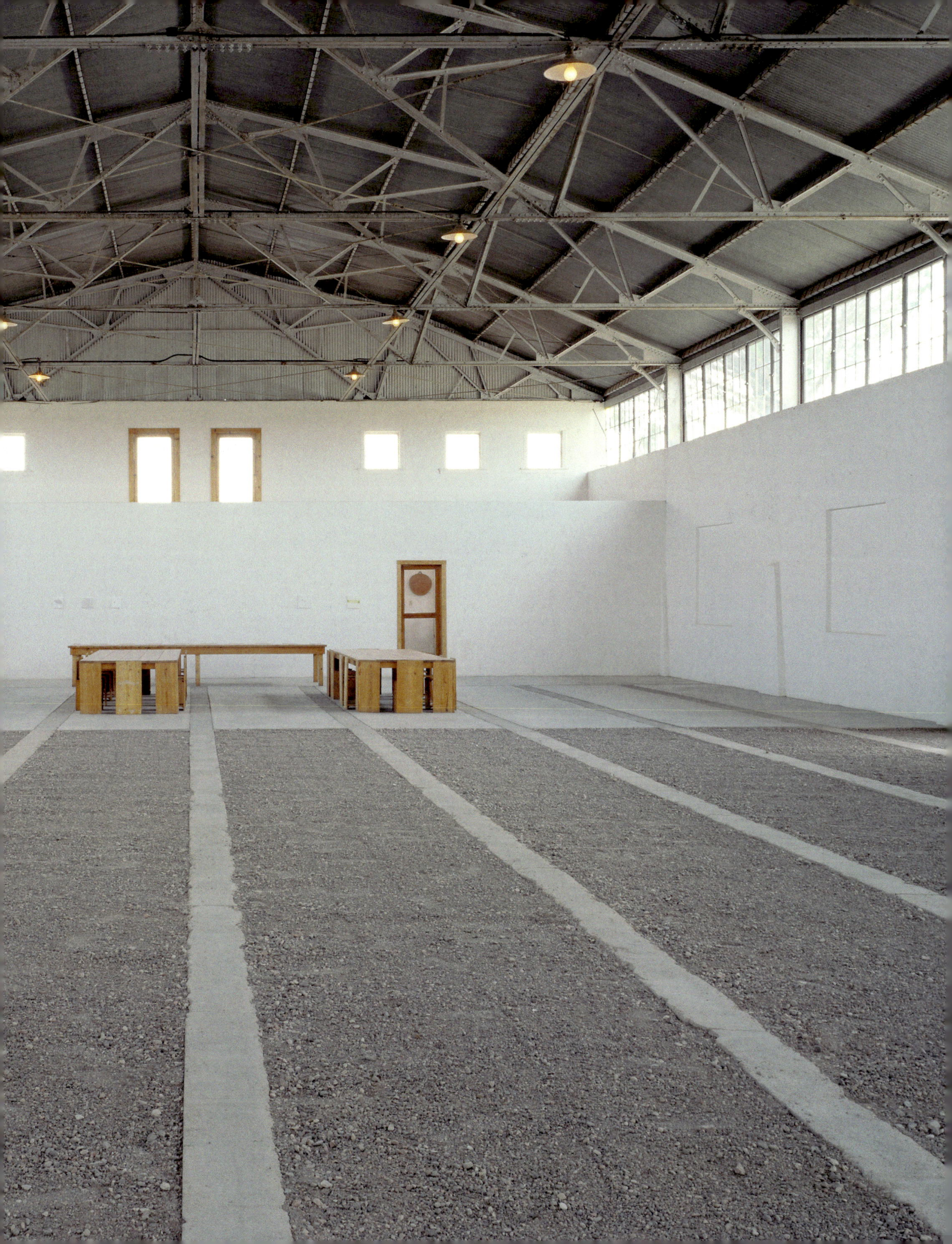

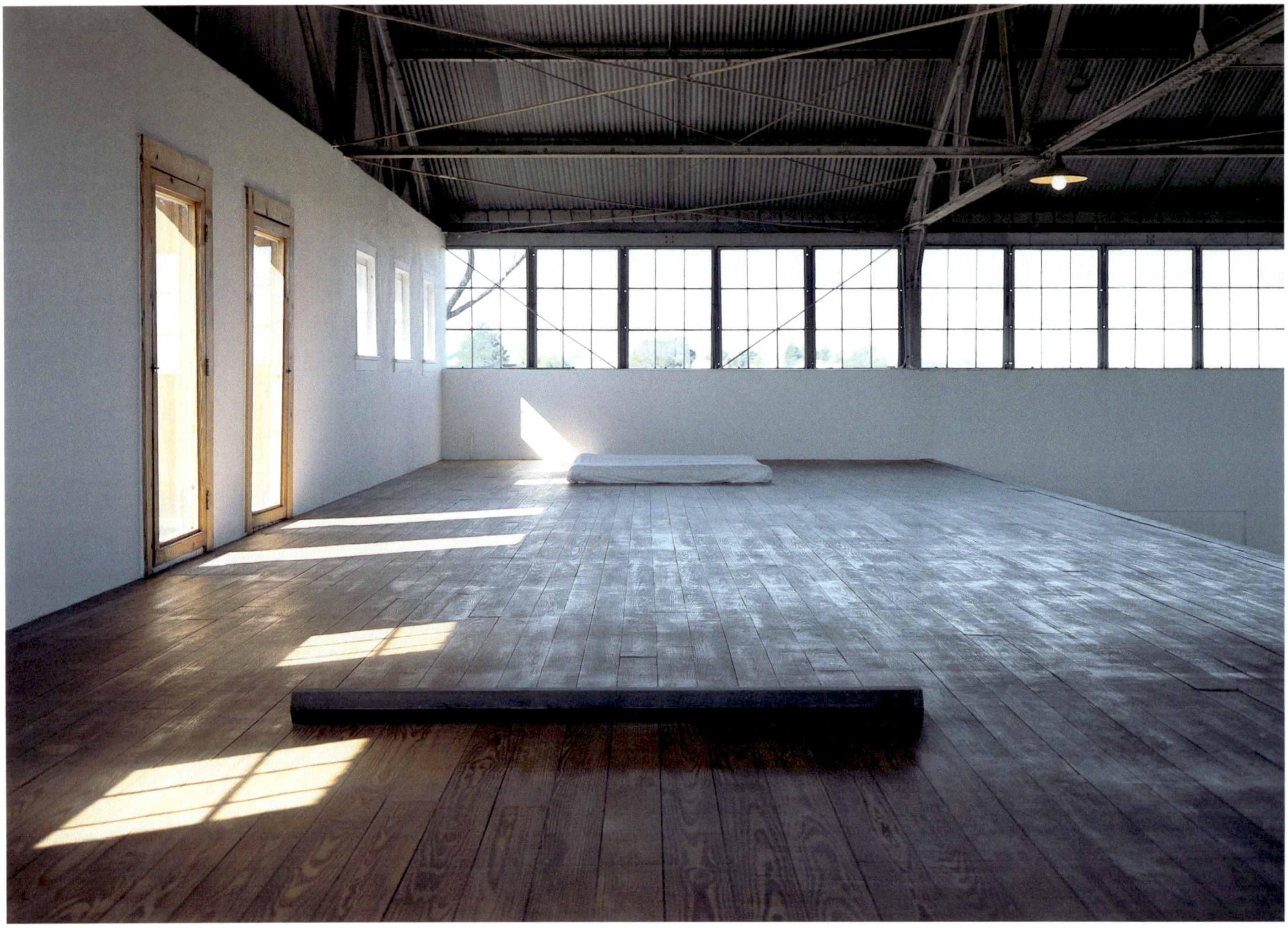

Arena.
Loft, second floor, with sculpture by David Rabinowitch, view to west.

Loft, Obergeschoss mit Skulptur von David Rabinowitsch, nach Westen.

Arena.
Before renovation, riding practice circa 1950. View to northeast.

Vor der Renovierung Reithalle, ca. 1950, nach Nordosten.

THE CHINATI FOUNDATION

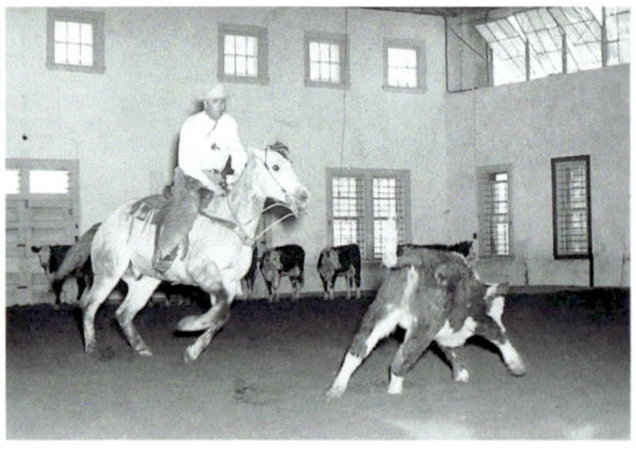

Arena.
Tables, chairs, and doors by Donald Judd, view to north.

Tisch, Stühle und Türen von Donald Judd, nach Norden.

THE CHINATI FOUNDATION

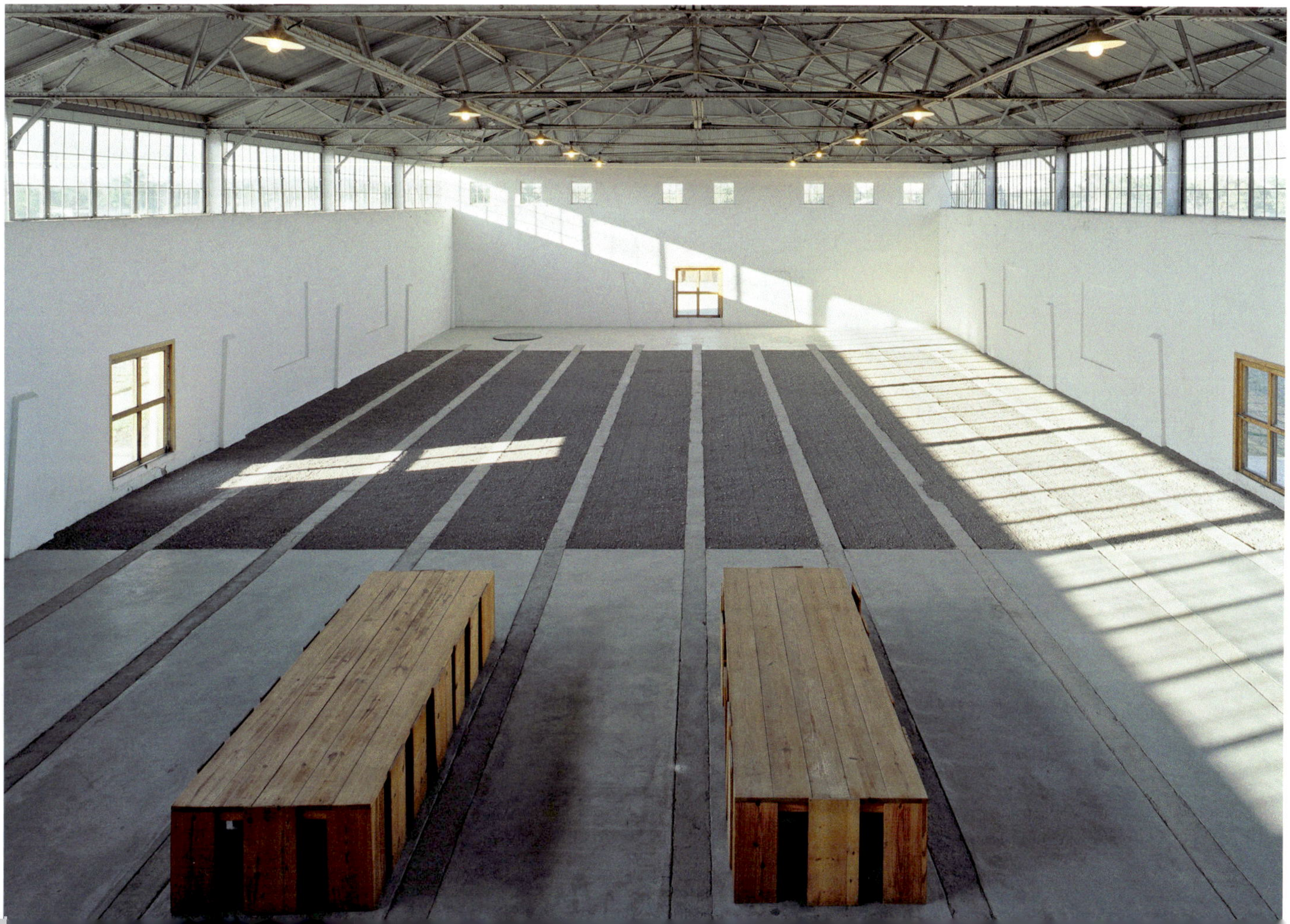

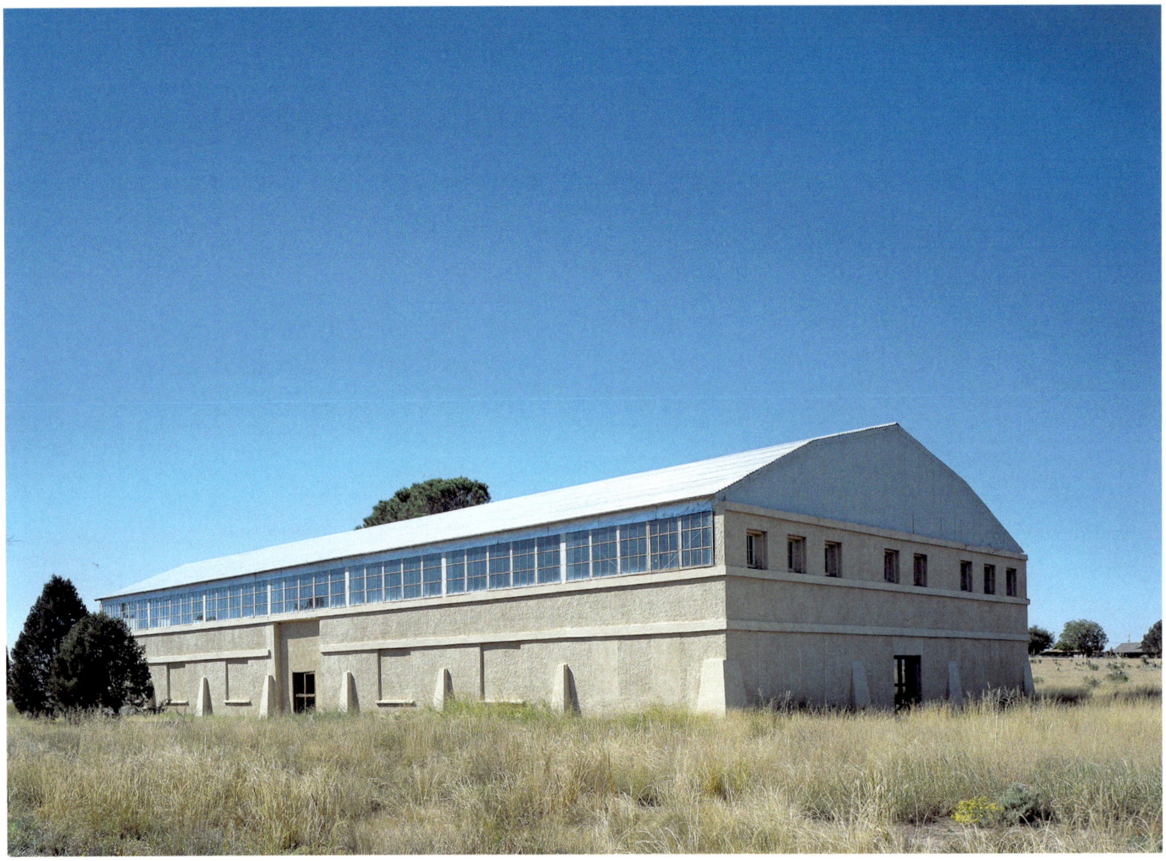

Arena.
View to southwest.
Nach Südwesten.

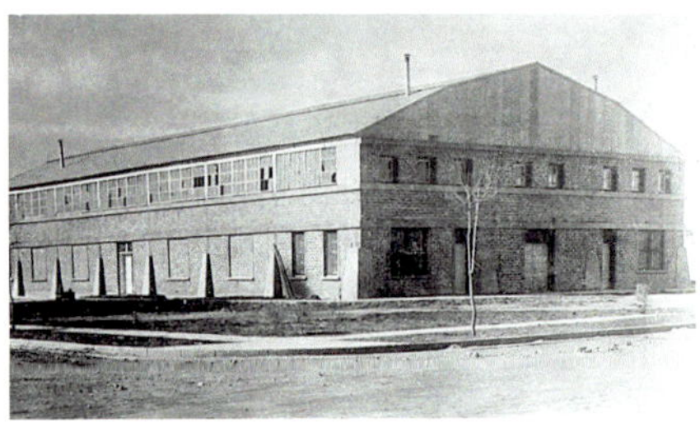

Arena.
Circa 1930, view to southwest.
Ca. 1930, nach Südwesten.

THE CHINATI FOUNDATION

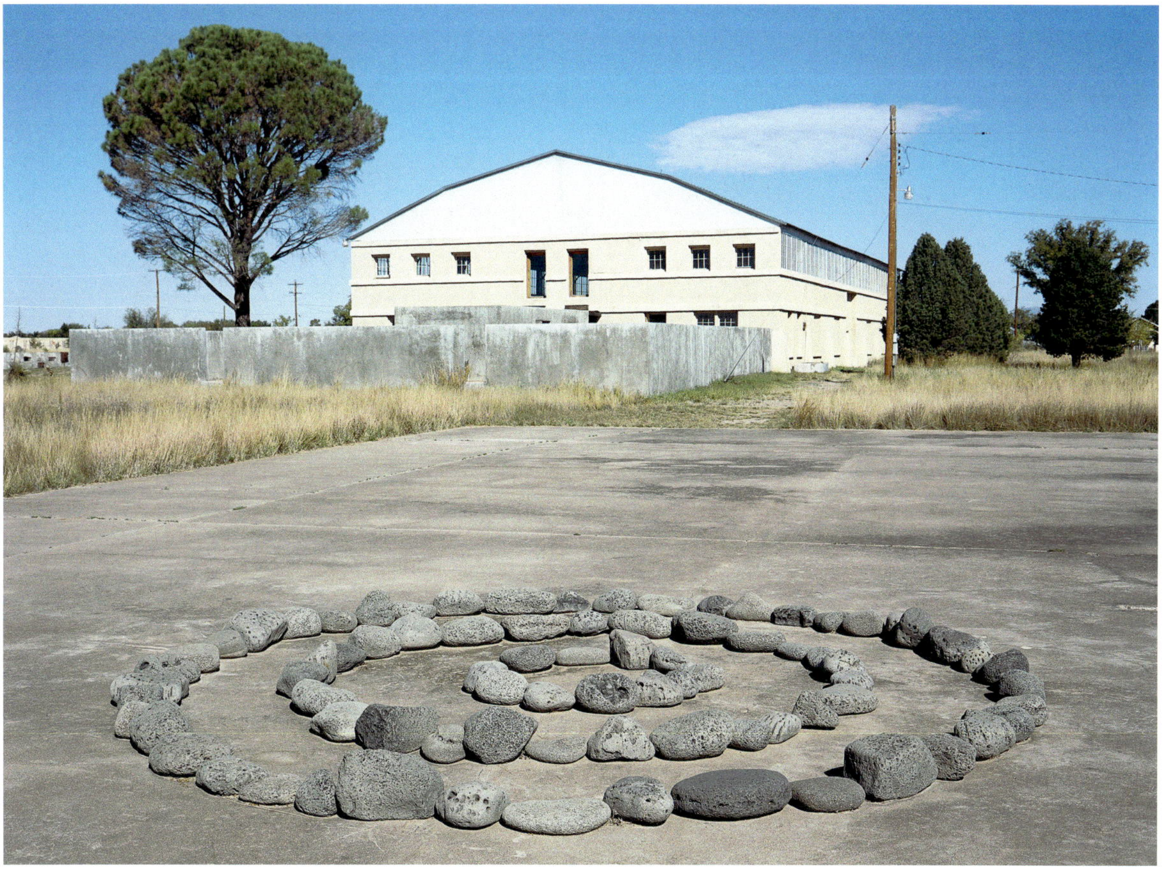

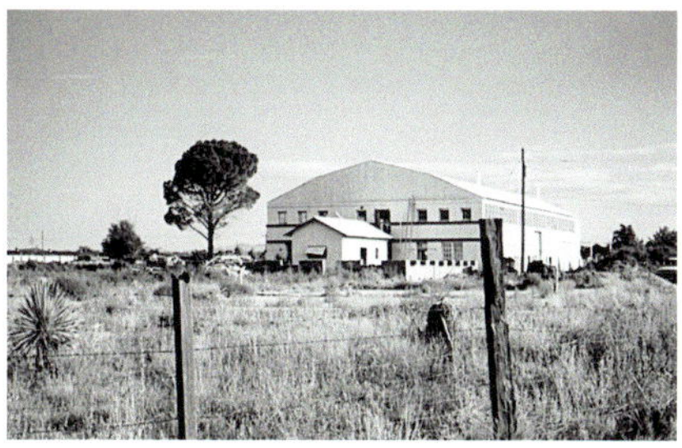

Arena.
Foreground with Sea Lava Circles, by Richard Long, background Arena, view to northwest.

Vordergrund mit Sea Lava Circles von Richard Long. Im Hintergrund die Arena, nach Nordwesten.

Arena.
Before renovation, circa 1980, view to northwest.

Vor der Renovierung, ca. 1980, nach Nordwesten.

THE CHINATI FOUNDATION

Arena.
Table, benches and barbecue pit by Donald Judd, view to west.

Tisch, Bank und Grill von Donald Judd, nach Westen.

Arena.
Before renovation courtyard, castellated adobe walls circa 1981. View to southwest.

Vor der Renovierung. Innenhof, Lehmziegel-mauern mit Zinnen, ca. 1981, nach Südwesten.

THE CHINATI FOUNDATION

Arena.
Brick pathway between Arena and courtyard, view to west.

Ziegelsteinweg zwischen Arena und Innenhof, nach Westen.

THE CHINATI FOUNDATION

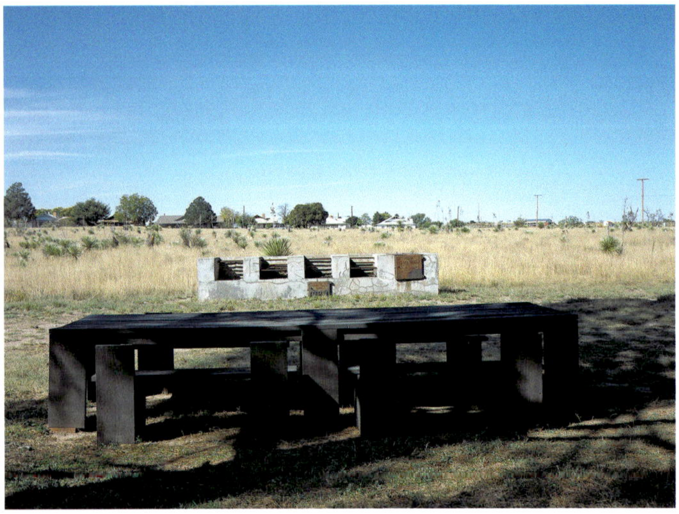

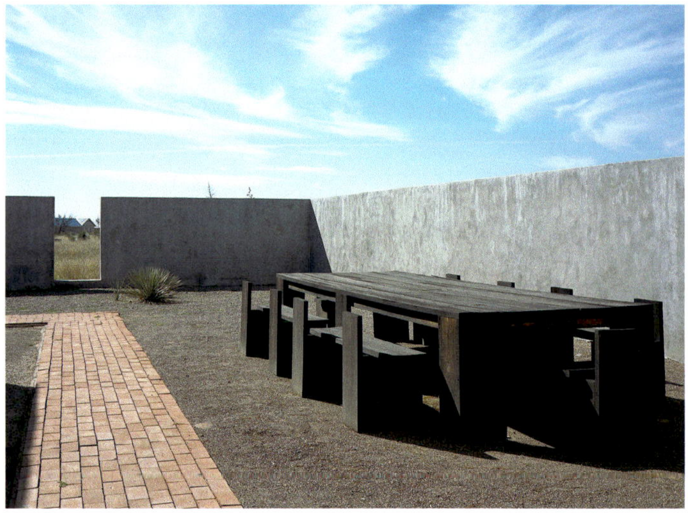

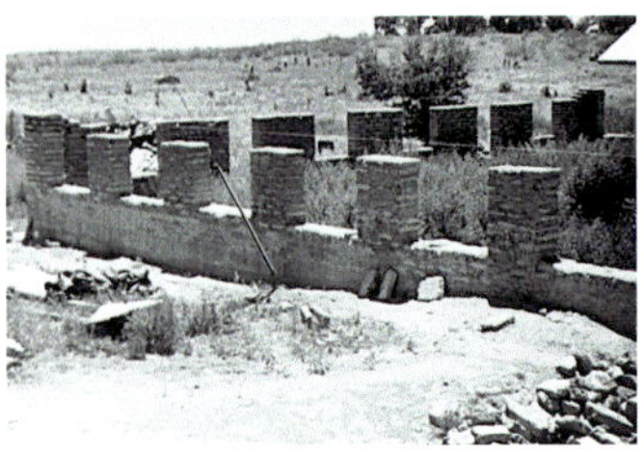

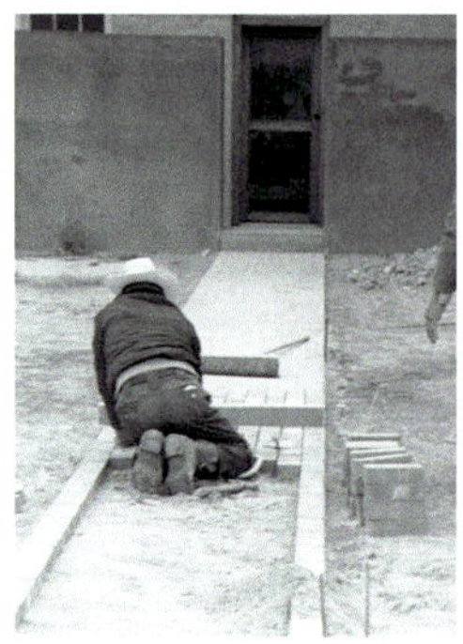

Arena.
Courtyard with table and benches by Donald Judd, view to southwest.

Innenhof mit Tisch und Bänken von Donald Judd, nach Südwesten.

Arena.
Courtyard, construction of brickpathway, circa 1981. View to north.

Innenhof, Bau des Ziegelsteinwegs, ca. 1981, nach Norden.

THE CHINATI FOUNDATION

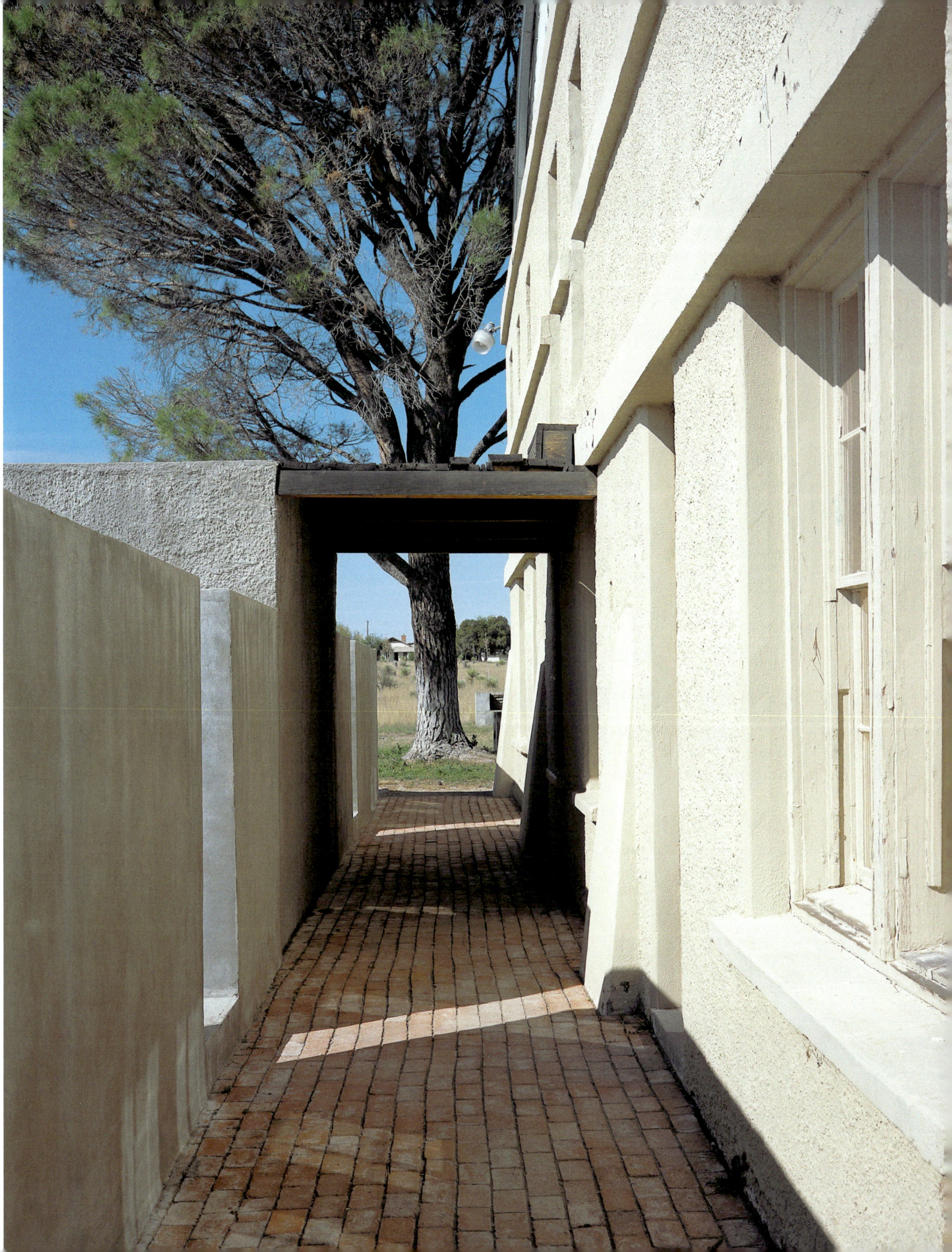

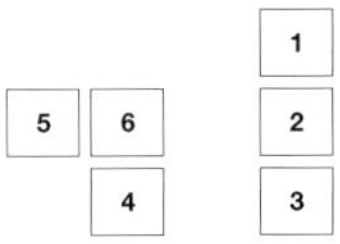

1 **Arena, second floor, plan**
Grundriss Obergeschoss

2 **First floor, plan**
Grundriss Erdgeschoss

3 **Section A-A**
Schnitt A-A

4 **Section B-B**
Schnitt B-B

5 **South elevation**
Südansicht

6 **West elevation**
Westansicht

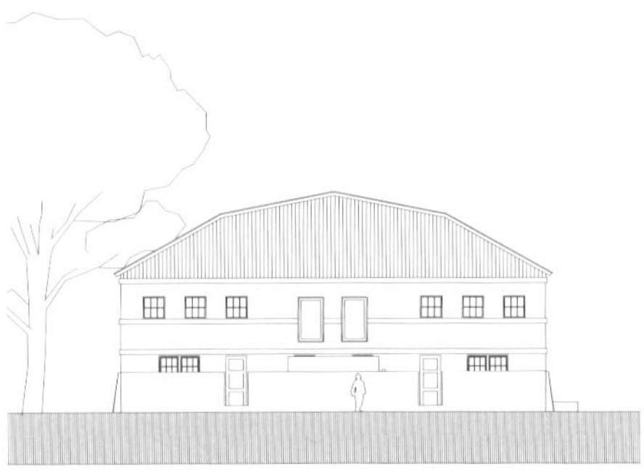

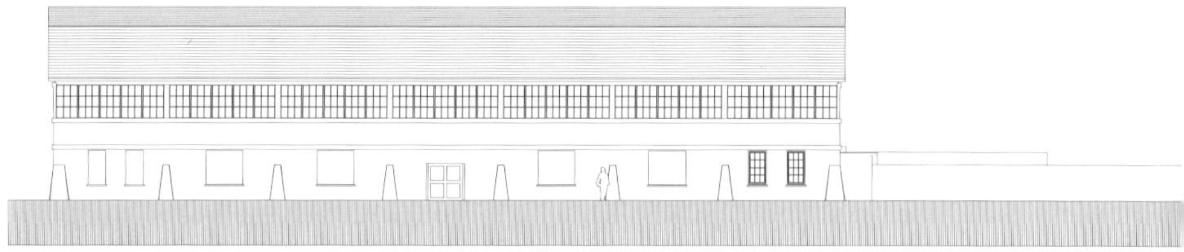

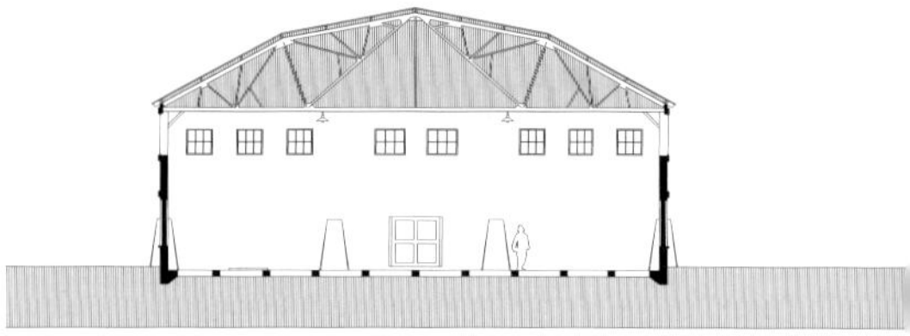

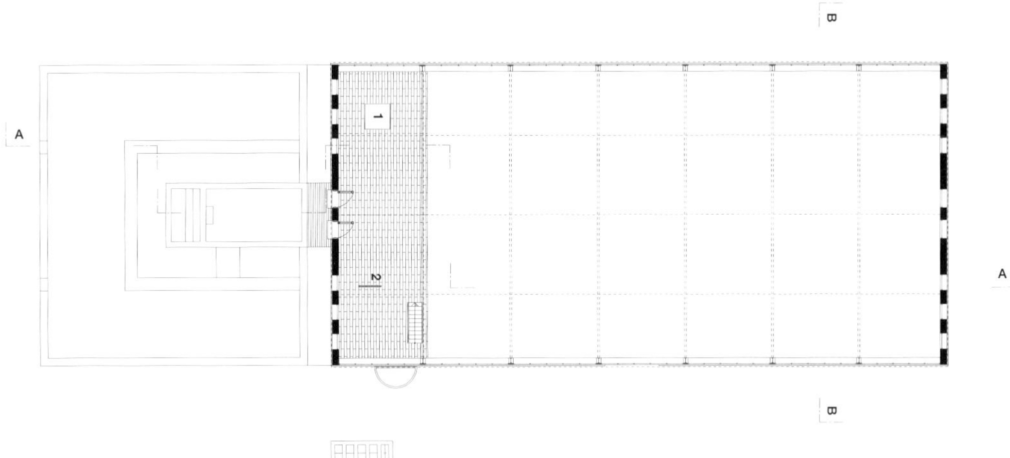
B
A
1
2
A
B

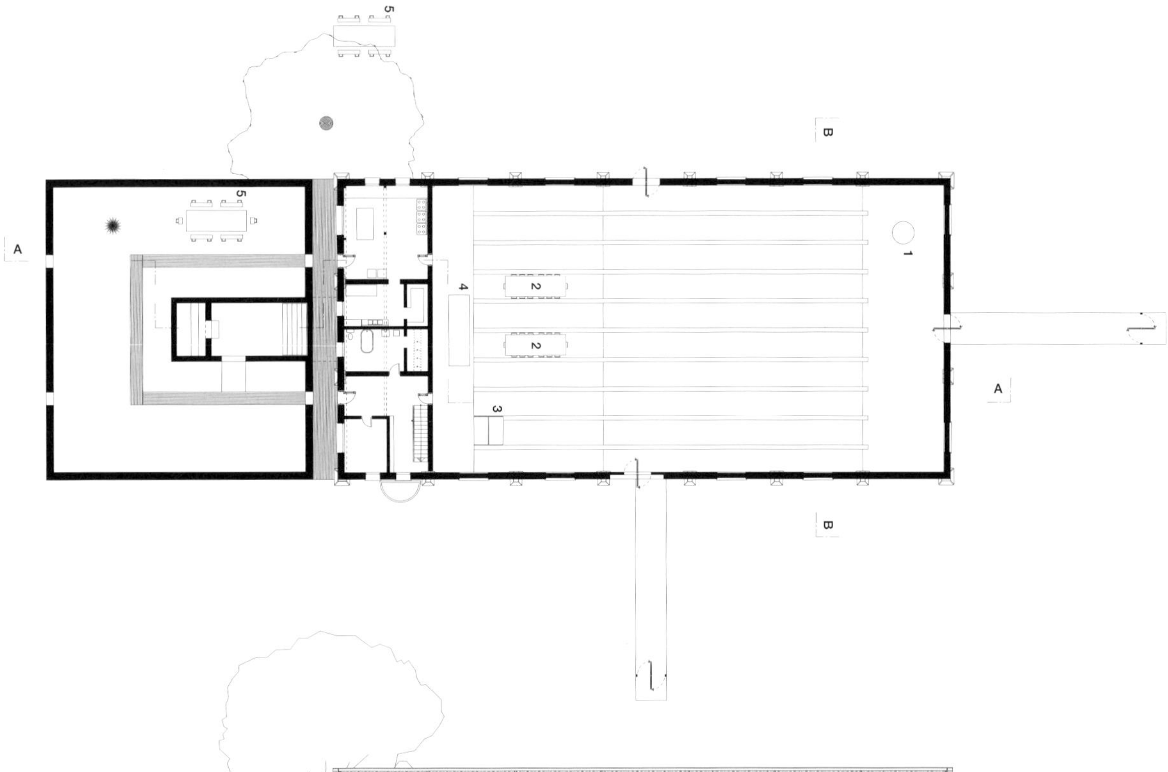
5
B
5
A
4
2
2
1
3
A
B

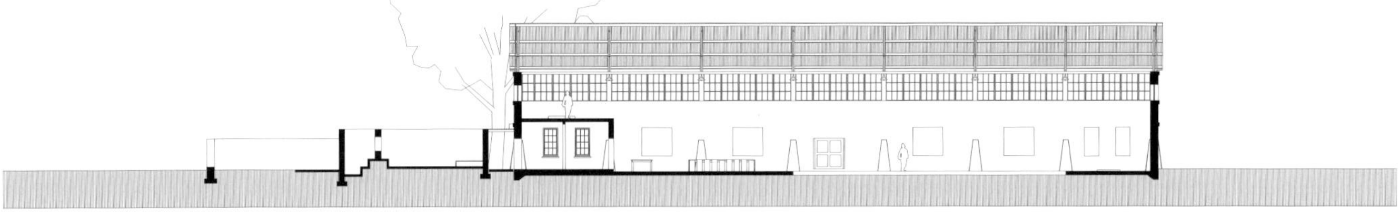

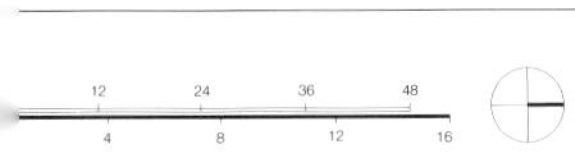
12 24 36 48
4 8 12 16

DAS CHAMBERLAIN-GEBÄUDE

THE CHAMBERLAIN BUILDING

Das Chamberlain-Gebäude liegt im Zentrum von Marfa, dort, wo sich die Highland Avenue und die Eisenbahngleise kreuzen. Es besteht aus drei zusammenhängenden Gebäuden unterschiedlicher Länge und Breite mit einer Gesamtlänge von ca. 97 m (320 ft). Ursprünglich waren die Bauten Sitz der Marfa Wool & Mohair Company und enthielten Büro- und Lagerräume. Heute sind sie Teil der Chinati Foundation und bieten Raum für 24 Skulpturen von John Chamberlain.

Dem Besucher, der sich dem Bau von Süden her nähert, fallen die Sotol-Pflanzen, eine einheimische Agavenart, ins Auge. Vier Reihen dieser Agaven pflanzte Judd entlang der Südgrenze der Parzelle, parallel zu den Eisenbahnschienen, fünf weitere Reihen entlang der Ostgrenze, um damit einen optischen Schutzschild zwischen dem Gebäude und dem Verkehr zu schaffen. Nach Nordwesten entwarf Judd einen Innenhof mit einer Umfriedungsmauer aus Lehmziegeln, der zwei bestehende Bäume einbezieht und den Perimeter des breiteren Teils der Gebäude fortsetzt. Der Kiesbelag des Bodens schafft ein einheitliches Erscheinungsbild und ist ein wirksames Entwässerungsmittel.

Die Gebäude sind auf einem durchlaufenden Betonboden ca. 1,20 m (4 ft) über dem Straßenniveau errichtet. Man betritt sie von der Ostseite her durch eine von Judds Drehtüren aus Holz und Glas. An drei Haupträume schließen sich zwei kleinere Bereiche

The Chamberlain Building is located in the center of Marfa, at the junction of Highland Avenue and the railroad tracks. It consists of three contiguous buildings differing in length and width, measuring 320 feet in total length. The buildings were originally the seat of the Marfa Wool & Mohair Company, accommodating offices and a warehouse; they are now part of The Chinati Foundation and house twenty-four sculptures by John Chamberlain.

Approaching the building from the south, the visitor notices the sotols Judd had planted in four rows along the railroad tracks on the southern boundary and in five rows along the eastern boundary, creating a visual shield between the traffic and the building. To the northwest Judd designed a courtyard with a wall built in adobe that would integrate two existing trees and continue the perimeter of the wider part of the building. Gravel covers the ground, homogenizing the appearance and serving as an effective means of drainage.

The buildings are raised on a continuous concrete floor four feet above street level and are accessed on the east side through one of Judd's center-hinged wood and glass doors. There are three primary spaces along with two smaller areas and a small guest room. Large windows bring natural light into the first space on the north, south, east, and by the entrance. Four works by John Chamberlain are exhibited in this first room, along with

und ein kleines Gästezimmer an. Der erste Raum erhält Tageslichtbeleuchtung durch den Eingang sowie von Norden, Süden und Osten durch große Fenster. In diesem ersten Raum sind drei Arbeiten von John Chamberlain ausgestellt, zusammen mit seiner *Barge Marfa*, die von einer Video-Installation flankiert wird. Die Wände und die verputzte Decke sind weiß gestrichen. Die kleinere Raumgröße bereitet die Besucher auf die üppigen Raumvolumina vor, die sie als Nächstes erleben. Bevor man diese Räume erreicht, geht man durch einen schmalen Korridor mit drei von Judds Drehtüren. Die nördliche Tür führt in einen kleineren Ausstellungsraum, der durch ein Oberlicht beleuchtet wird, und in ein Schlafzimmer mit Bad. Die südliche Tür führt in einen ähnlichen, doch etwas größeren Ausstellungsraum mit drei Wandskulpturen. Den größten Raum betritt man durch die Drehtür im Westen. Dort sind acht große Skulpturen von John Chamberlain aufgestellt. Ein unverkleidetes stählernes Deckengerüst mit grauem Anstrich verklammert Bauwerk und Dach. Acht Oberlichter und vier große Fenster – zwei an der Nordwand, zwei nach Süden – und eine Tür in der Nordwestecke erlauben Tageslichteinfall. Die Wände sind lehmziegelfarben gestrichen.

Der weiter westlich gelegene Ausstellungsraum ist schmaler, das Dach und seine Stützen sind aus Holz. Hier werden, durch vier Oberlichter erhellt, sechs von Chamberlains Boden- und Wandarbeiten präsentiert. Die vier Fenster sind nach Norden und Süden gerichtet. Eine Tür, die nach Westen in den hinter dem Bau gelegenen Innenhof führt, ist auf der Korridor-Eingangs-Achse platziert.

Es ist Judd gelungen, ein Bauwerk, das als schwieriger Raum gelten könnte – aus Gründen der unterschiedlichen Länge, Höhe und Breite der Teilgebäude sowie der unmittelbaren Nähe der Eisenbahn –, in einen erfolgreichen Ausstellungsbereich zu verwandeln, in dem die drei Räume einerseits geschlossener wirken und andererseits doch die Präsentation kleinerer Werkgruppen pro Raum erlauben. Die Geräuschkulisse der vorüberfahrenden Züge intensiviert das Erlebnis nur, und für Augenblicke kann der Betrachter nichts anderes tun, als zu beobachten, wie der Zug die Szene beherrscht. Einen Moment lang ist der Zug im Rahmen der Fenster *das* Ereignis – eine Erinnerung an die Entstehung der Stadt.

his *Barge Marfa*, which is flanked by a video installation. The walls and plasterboard ceiling are painted white. With its smaller volume, this room prepares visitors for the grand spaces they will experience next. Before reaching the spaces, one walks through a narrow corridor with three of Judd's revolving doors. The door to the north provides access to a smaller exhibition space, lit by a skylight, and a bedroom with bath. The door to the south provides access to a similar but slightly larger exhibition space, where three wall sculptures are exhibited. Access to the largest space is through the center-hinged door to the west. Here, eight large sculptures by Chamberlain are displayed. An exposed metal ceiling system painted gray supports the structure and roof. Eight skylights and four large windows—two on the north wall, two on the south—and a door in the northwest corner allow natural light into the space. The walls are painted adobe color.

The exhibition space further west is narrower; the roof and its supports are made of wood. Six of Chamberlain's floor and wall works are exhibited here, lit by four skylights. Four windows are on the north and south, plus a door on the west. The door provides access to the courtyard to the rear and is on axis to the corridor and the point of entry.

What could be considered a difficult space—because of the differences in width, height and length of each individual structure, plus the proximity of the railroad—Judd was able to transform into a successful exhibition area, where the three spaces become more coherent yet allow for the display of smaller groups per space. The sound generated by passing trains creates a spectacle that only adds to the experience, and momentarily the viewer can do nothing but watch the train take center stage. For a moment the train becomes the event, framed by the windows—a reminder of how the town came into existence.

Chamberlain Building. View to southwest.

Chamberlain-Gebäude, nach Südwesten.

Chamberlain Building. View to southeast.

Chamberlain-Gebäude, nach Südosten.

THE CHINATI FOUNDATION

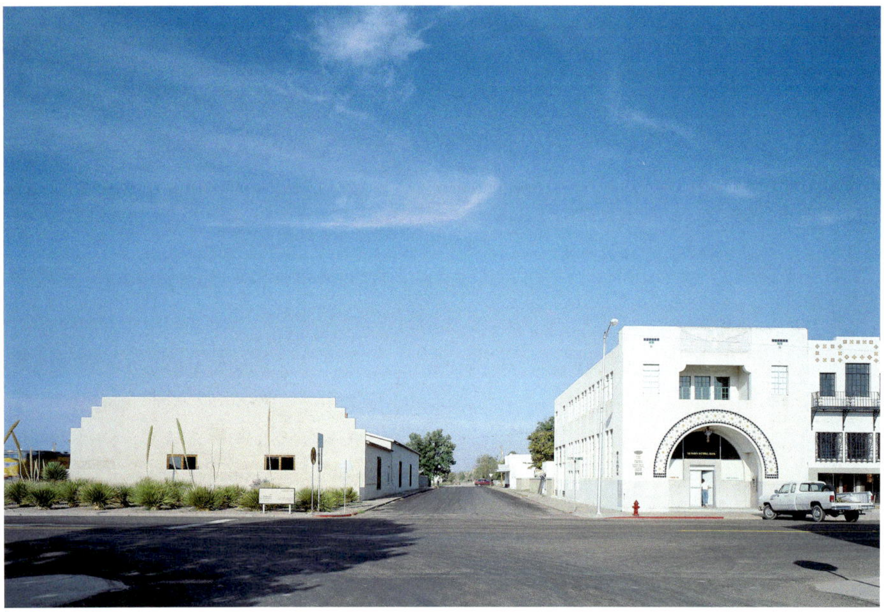

View of Chamberlain Building and Architecture Studio. View to west.

Chamberlain-Gebäude und Architekturstudio, nach Westen.

THE CHINATI FOUNDATION

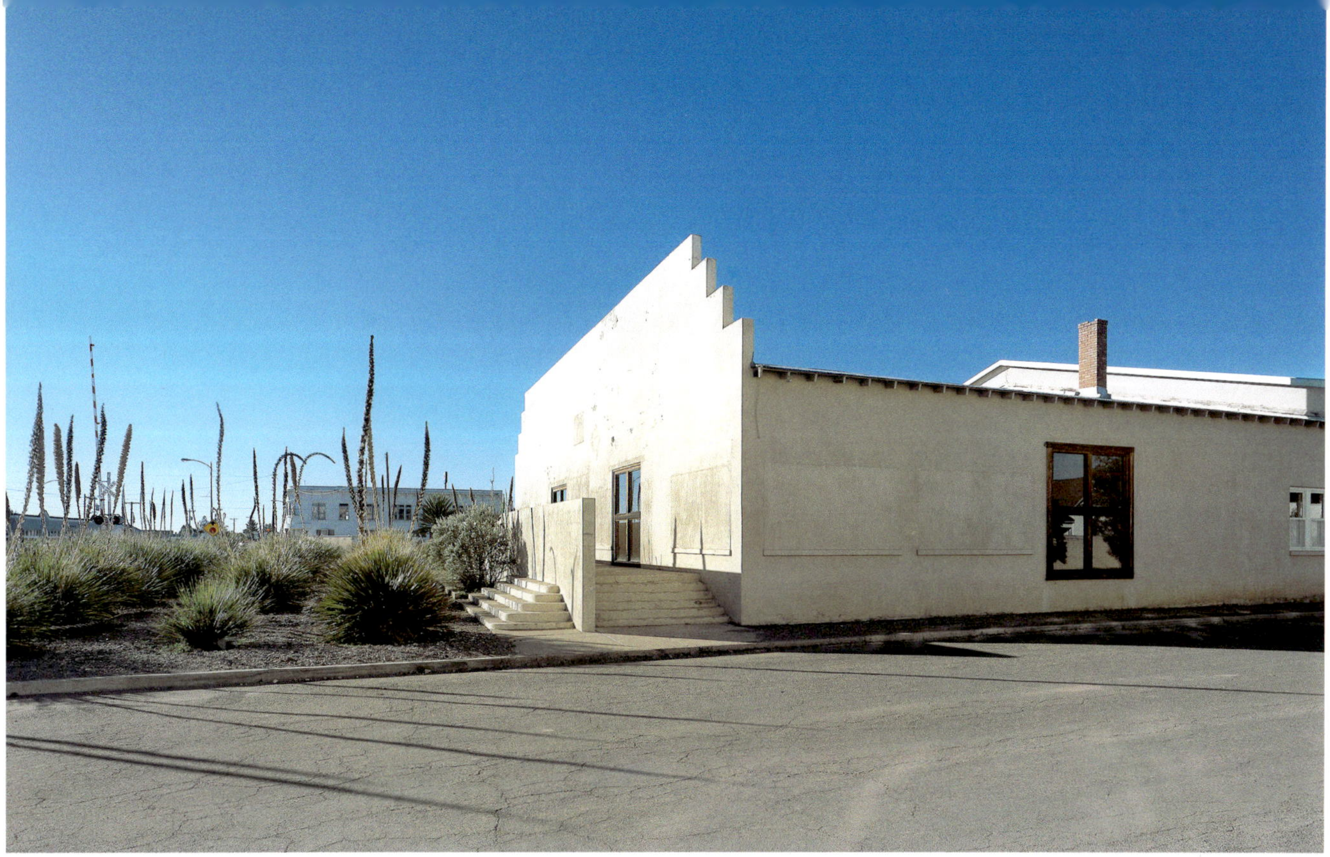

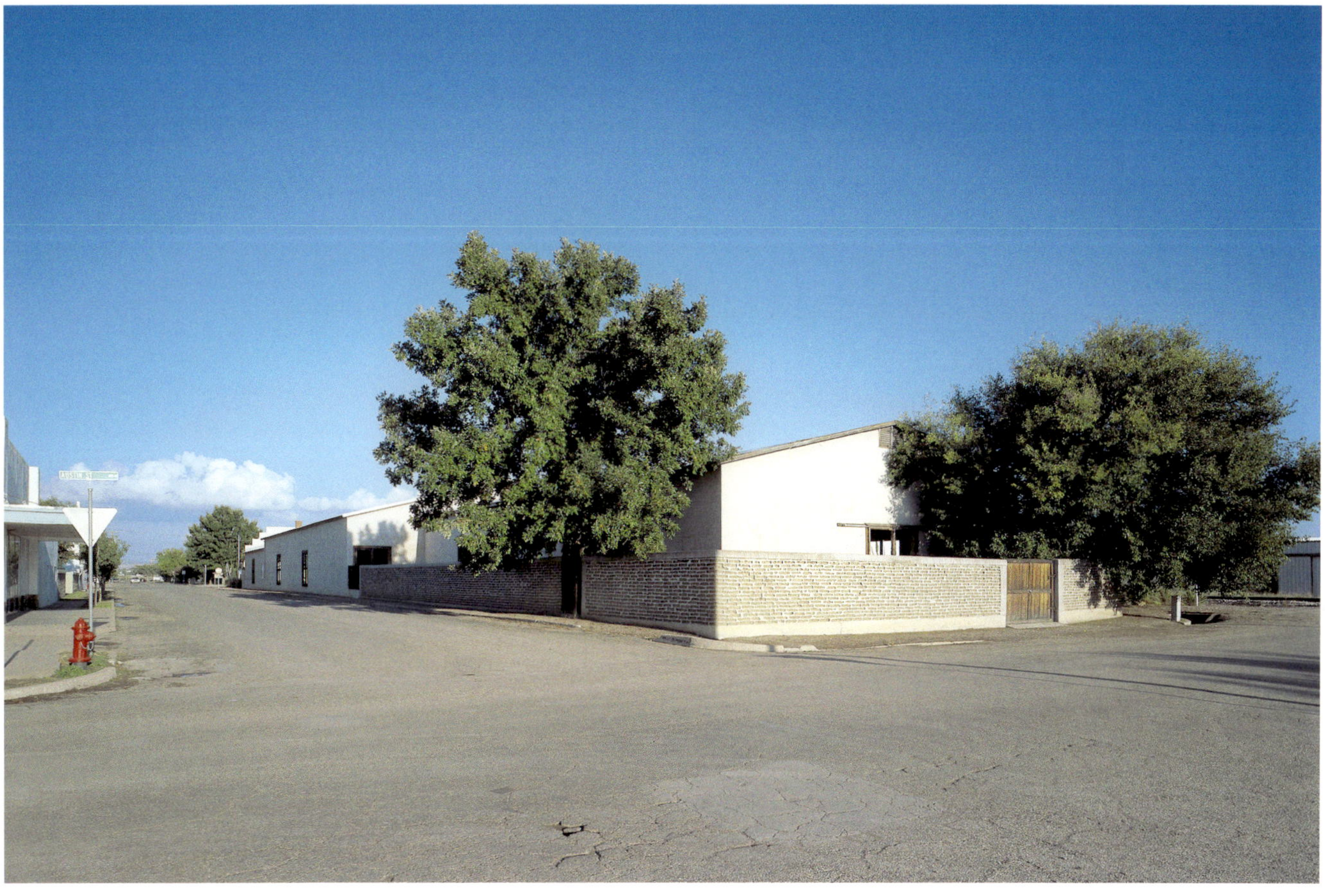

Chamberlain Building. First space with works by John Chamberlain, view to northeast.

Chamberlain-Gebäude. Erster Raum, mit Skulpturen von John Chamberlain, nach Nordosten.

THE CHINATI FOUNDATION

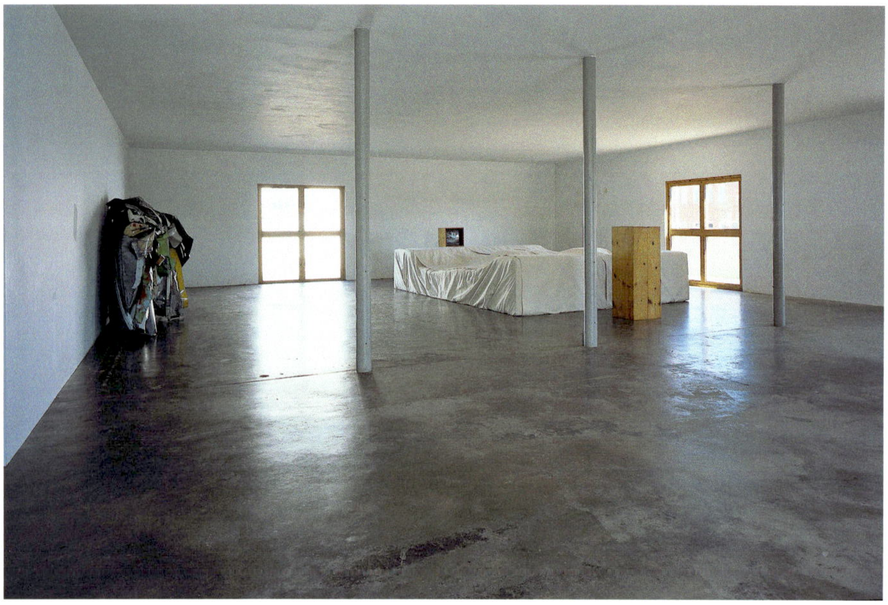

Chamberlain Building, with revolving doors by Donald Judd between first and second space, view to west.

Chamberlain-Gebäude, mit Drehtüren von Donald Judd zwischen dem ersten und zweiten Raum, nach Westen.

THE CHINATI FOUNDATION

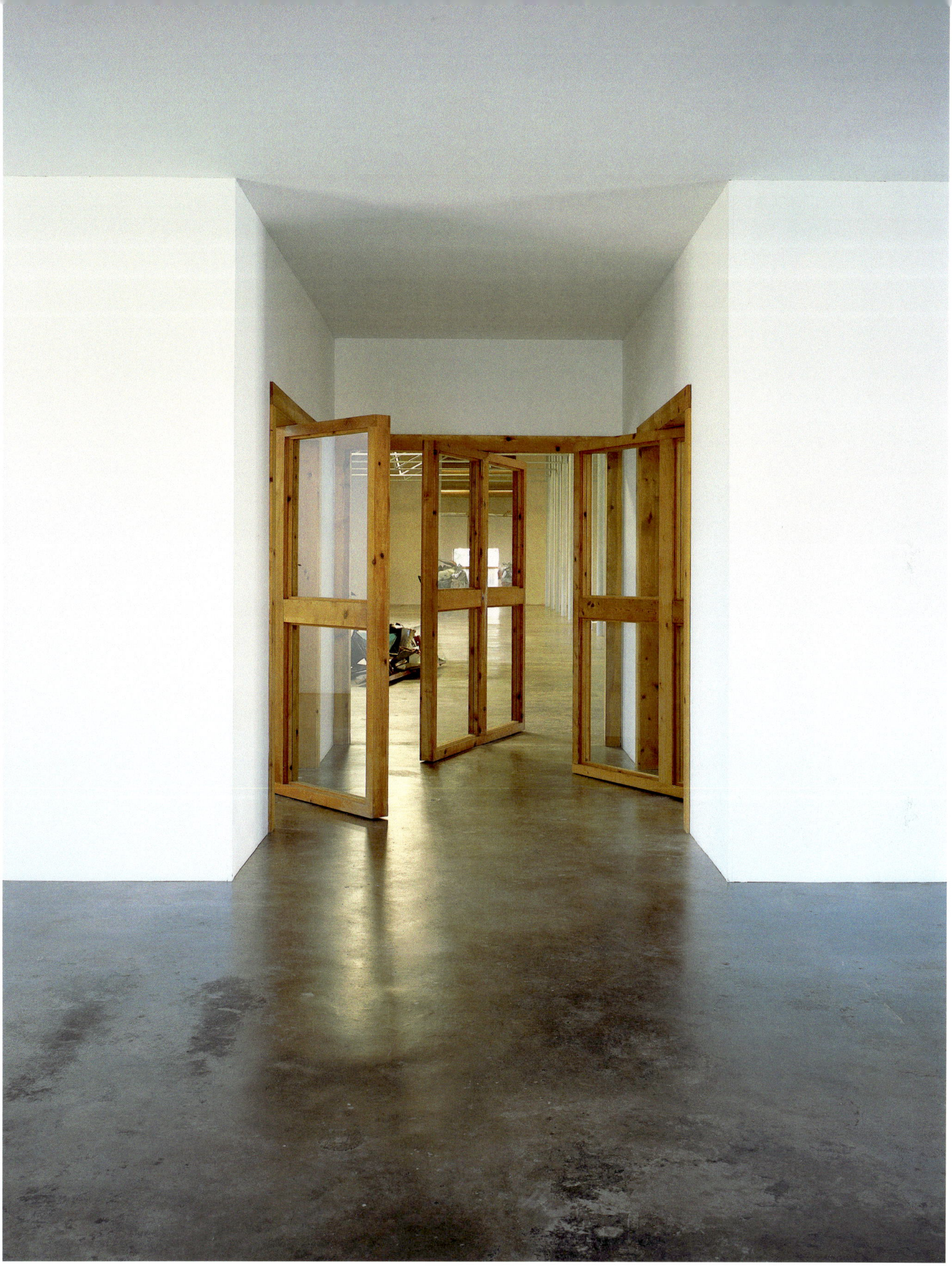

Chamberlain Building. Second space with sculptures by John Chamberlain, view to west.

Chamberlain-Gebäude. Zweiter Raum, mit Skulpturen von John Chamberlain, nach Westen.

Chamberlain Building. Second space with sculptures by John Chamberlain, view to east.

Chamberlain-Gebäude. Zweiter Raum, mit Skulpturen von John Chamberlain, nach Osten.

THE CHINATI FOUNDATION

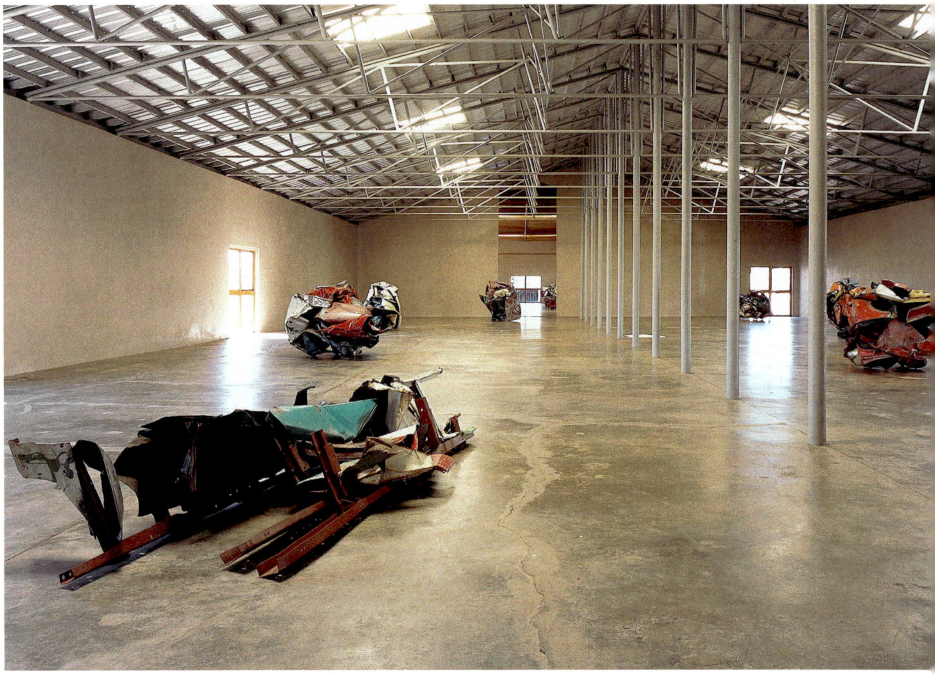

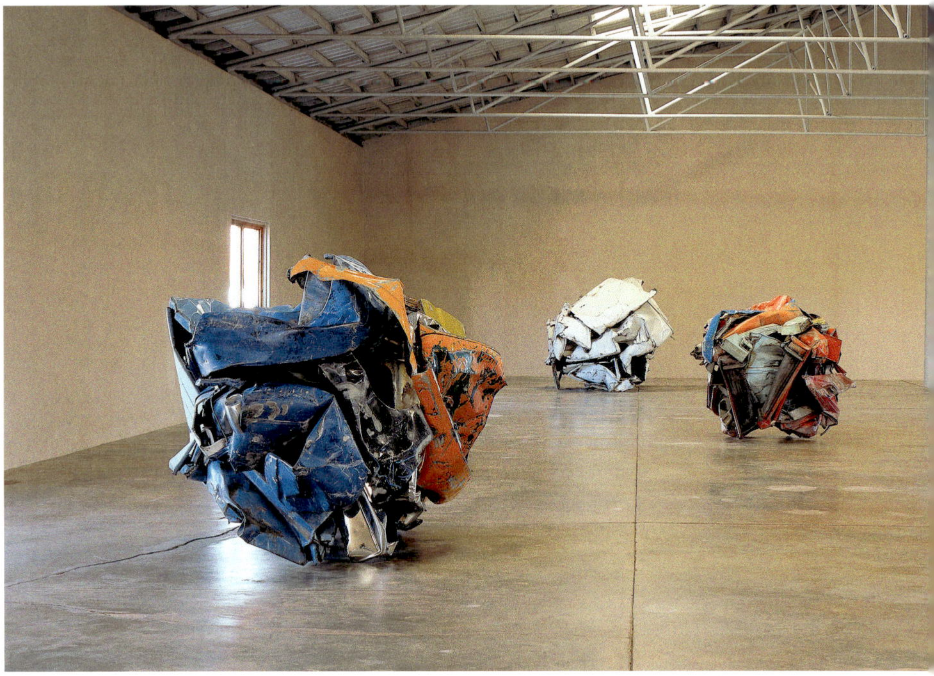

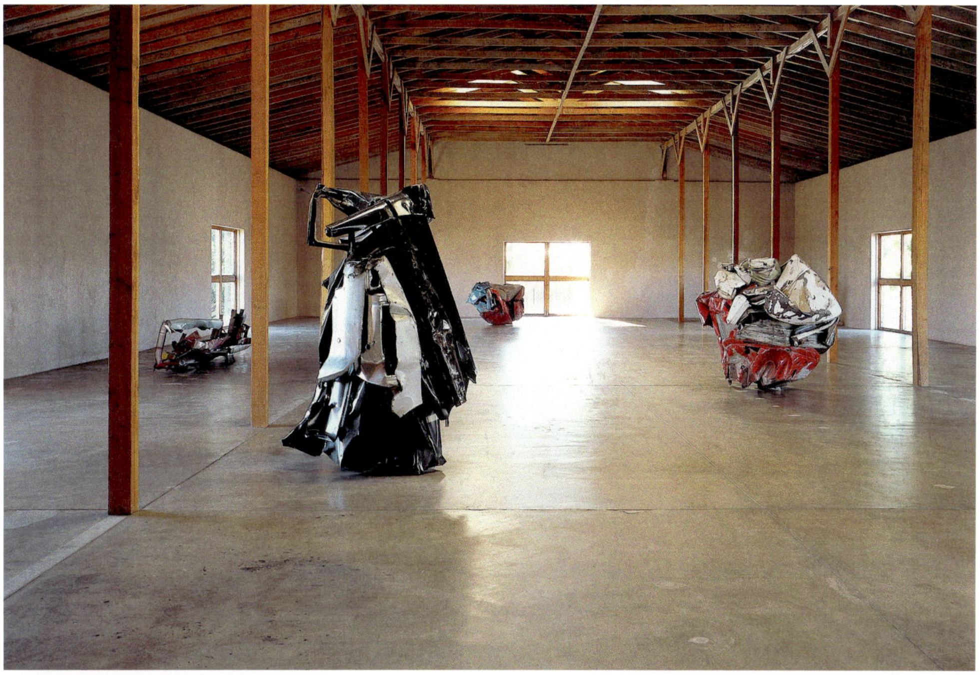

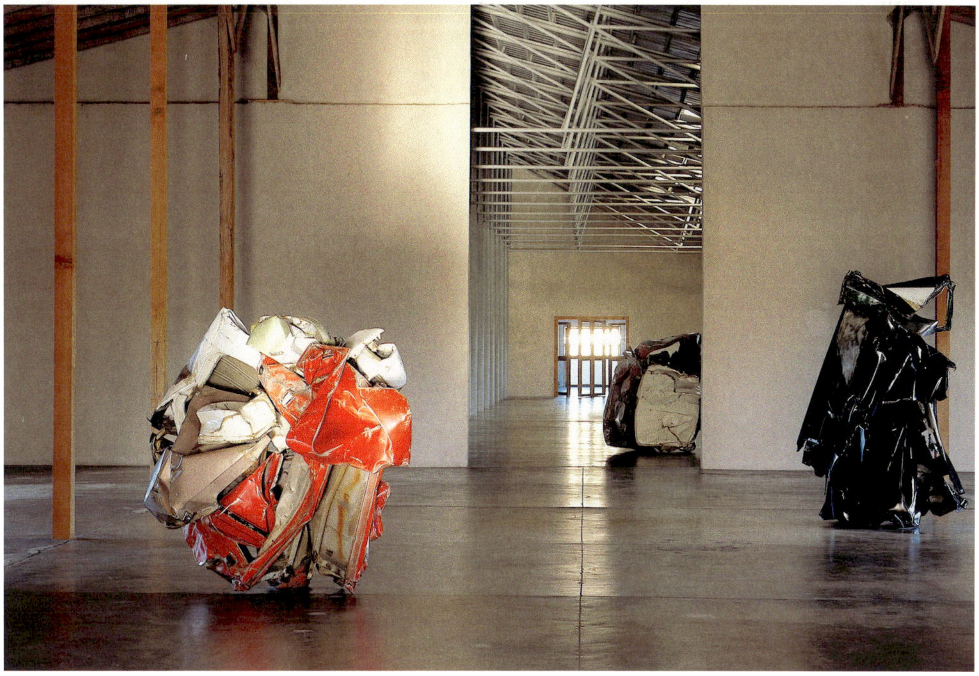

Chamberlain Building. Third space with sculptures by John Chamberlain, view to west.

Chamberlain-Gebäude. Dritter Raum, mit Skulpturen von John Chamberlain, nach Westen.

Chamberlain Building. Third space with sculptures by John Chamberlain, view to east.

Chamberlain-Gebäude. Dritter Raum, mit Skulpturen von John Chamberlain, nach Osten.

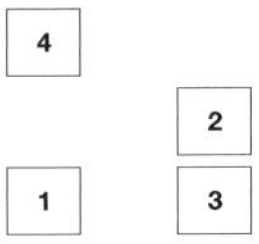

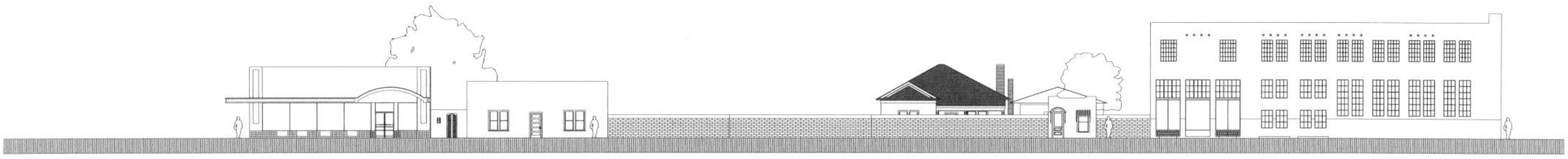

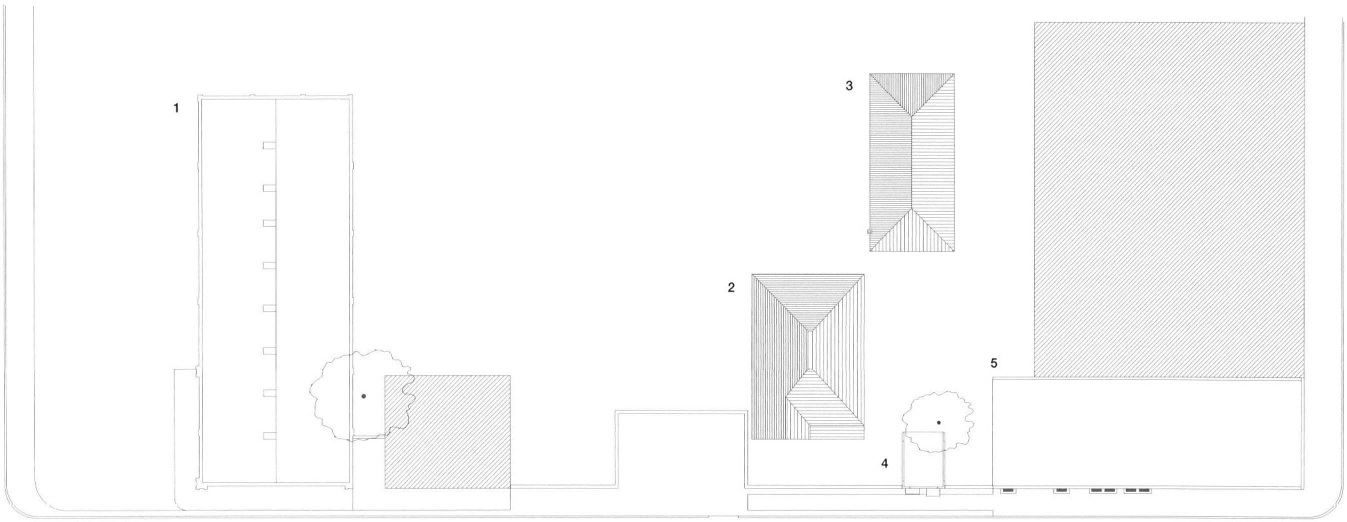

OAK STREET

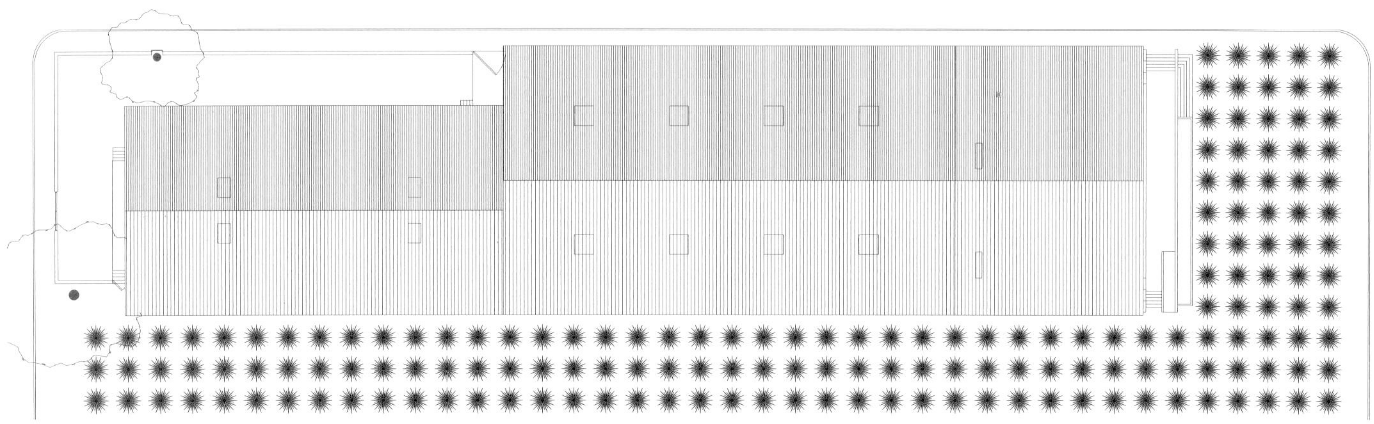

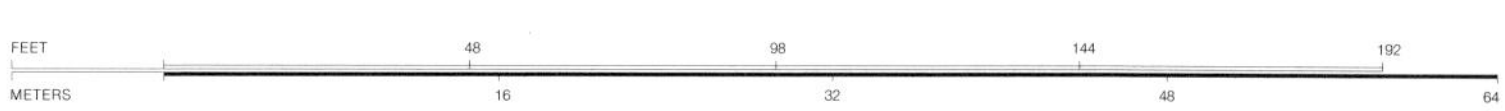

1 **Site plan Oak Street**
Situationsplan Oak Street

2 **Chamberlain Building Floor plan**
Chamberlain-Gebäude. Grundriss

3 **Chamberlain Building Section A-A**
Chamberlain-Gebäude. Schnitt A-A

4 **Buildings on Oak Street. South elevation**
Gebäude an der Oak Street. Südansicht

1.1 **The Art Studio**
Kunstatelier

1.2 **The Cobb House**
Haus Cobb

1.3 **The Whyte Building**
Whyte-Gebäude

1.4 **The Gate House**
Pförtnerhaus

1.5 **Architecture Studio**
Architekturstudio

2.1 **Dumb Name (One for Maurice), 1980–81**

2.2 **Barge Marfa, 1983**

2.3 **Aba Funn, 1979**

2.4 **Zia Lightning Field Forever, 1979**

2.5 **Small Monument to a Swiss Monument, 1979–82**

2.6 **Patino Nuevo, 1975**

2.7 **Kunstecher, 1977**

2.8 **I, Mencius, 1975**

2.9 **Four Polished Nails, 1979**

2.10 **Gondola Ezra Pound, 1982**

2.11 **Falfurrias, 1972**

2.12 **Bushland-Marsh, 1972–73**

2.13 **Papalote Goliad, 1972–75**

2.14 **Chili Terlingua, 1972–74**

2.15 **Iraan Crocket, 1972–75**

2.16 **Tapawingo, 1972**

2.17 **Glasscock-Notrees, 1972–74**

2.18 **Tongue Pictures, 1979**

2.19 **Gondola William Carlos Williams, 1982**

2.20 **Panna Normanna, 1972**

2.21 **Broken Toe, 1980–81**

2.22 **International 500, 1972–73**

2.23 **Roxanne Loup, 1979**

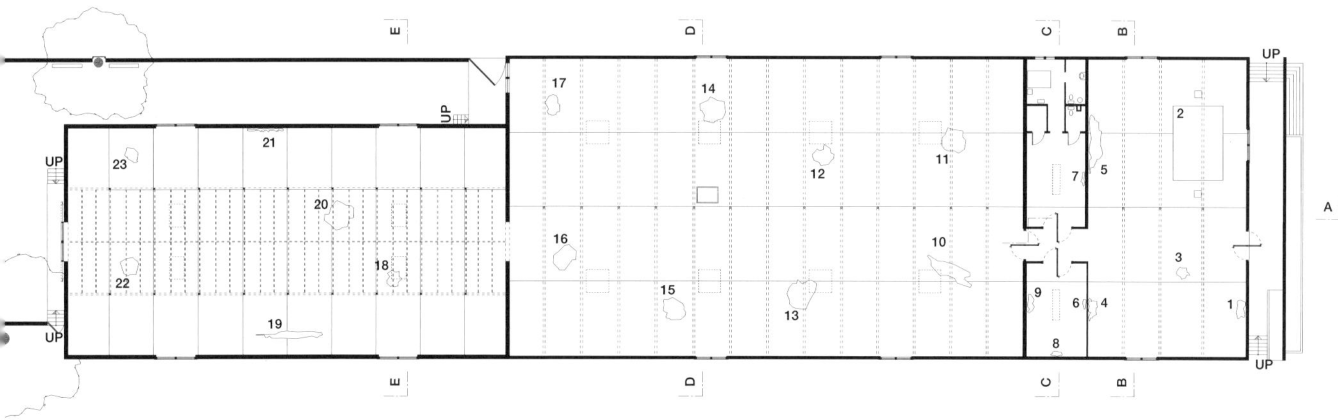

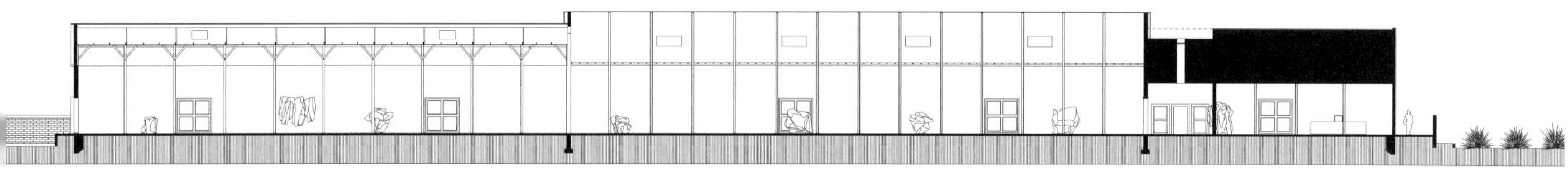

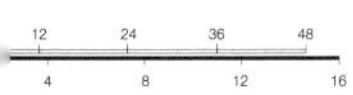

1 2 5 6

3 4 7

8

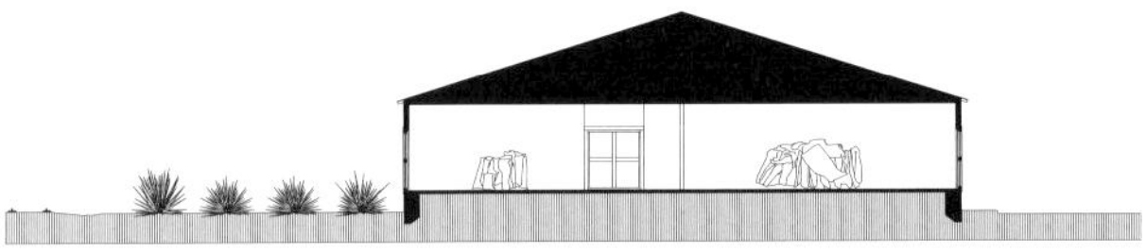

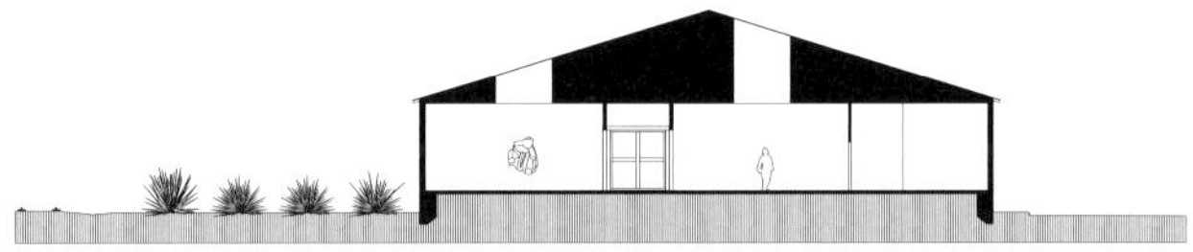

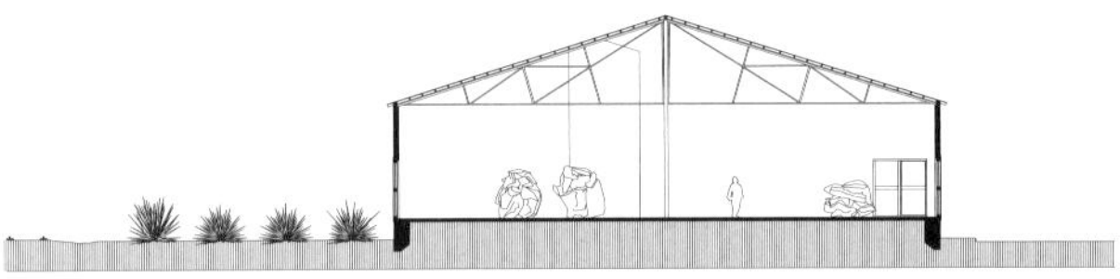

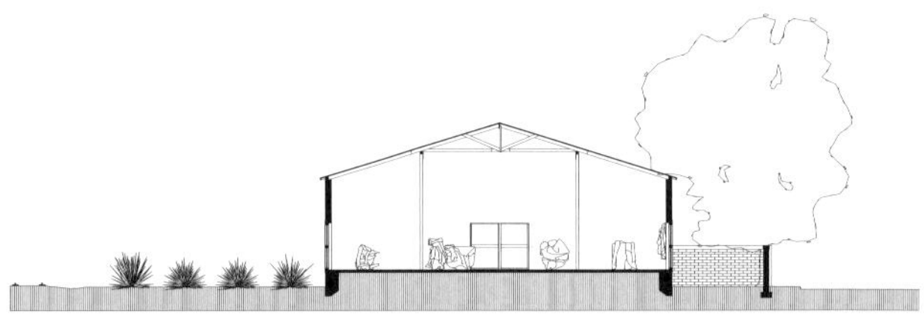

1 **Chamberlain Building Section B-B**
Chamberlain-Gebäude. Schnitt B-B

2 **Section C-C**
Schnitt C-C

3 **Section D-D**
Schnitt D-D

4 **Section E-E**
Schnitt E-E

5 **West elevation**
Westansicht

6 **East elevation**
Ostansicht

7 **North elevation**
Nordansicht

8 **South elevation**
Südansicht

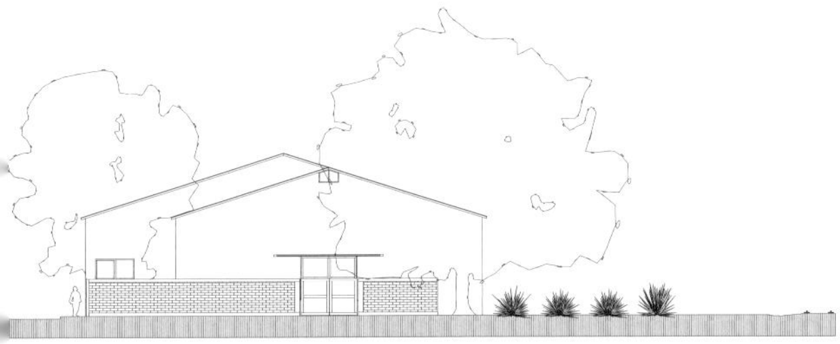

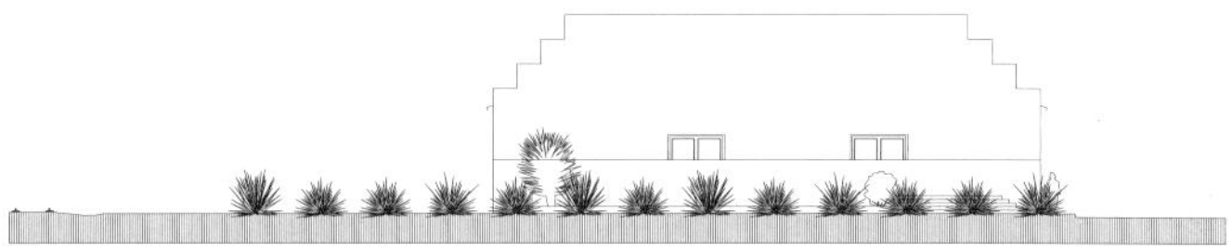

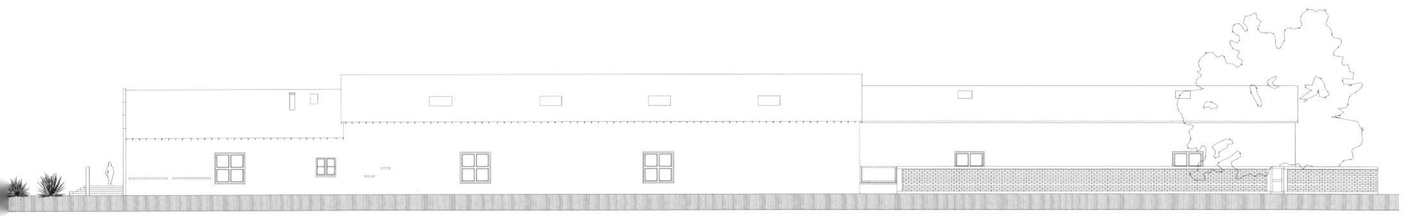

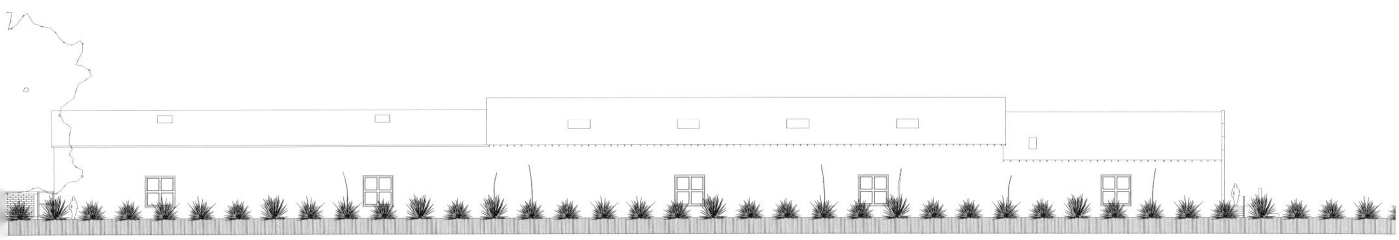

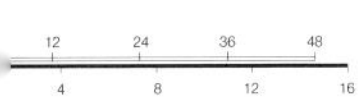

DAS ARCHITEKTURSTUDIO

Das Gebäude der Marfa National Bank wurde 1931 nach einem Entwurf des Architekten Leighton Green Knipe[1] errichtet. Judd erwarb es 1989 und gab ihm nach der Renovierung den Namen Architekturstudio. Es liegt unmittelbar nördlich des Chamberlain-Gebäudes an der Nordwestecke der Kreuzung von Oak Street und Highland Avenue. Die Bank ist ein zweigeschossiges Gebäude mit Zwischenetage und Kellergeschoss. Die Mauern sind aus Stahlbeton. Die Außenschicht des Gebäudes ist weißer Putz mit Verzierungen und Gestaltungselementen aus Keramikfliesen.

Im Gebäudeinneren wurden in der früheren Schalterhalle der Bank die ursprünglichen Verkleidungen entfernt, darunter die abgehängte Decke, welche die Klimaanlage enthielt, und es präsentierte sich ein etwa 5 m (17 ft) hoher Raum mit Pfeilern und einem Wandgemälde des Architekten. Die Renovierung und Einrichtung des restlichen Gebäudes hat Judd weitgehend zu Ende geführt; nicht so die dieses zentralen Raumes. Verschiedene Möbelstücke sind etwas willkürlich in der Halle verteilt – Tische und Stühle von Judd neben historischen Stücken und Prototypen von Gerrit-Rietveld-Bänken, einem Tisch mit Schemel von Alvar Aalto sowie einem Freischwinger von Mies van der Rohe. An den Wänden hängen ein paar Bilder und Reliefs von Judd aus den Jahren 1961/62. Eine schmale Treppe führt ins Mezzanin, vormals das Büro des Bankdirektors, das mit einem alten russischen Tisch samt Stühlen und mit Bildern von Josef Albers, Theo van

THE ARCHITECTURE STUDIO

The Marfa National Bank building, designed by the architect Leighton Green Knipe[1] and built in 1931, was acquired by Judd in 1989 and subsequently renovated and named by him Architecture Studio. It is located on the northwest corner of Oak Street and Highland Avenue, just north of the Chamberlain Building. The Bank is a two-story structure with a mezzanine and basement. Walls are made of reinforced concrete. The exterior finish of the building is white plaster, with ornamentation and detail work in ceramic tiles.

Inside, the former bank lobby is now stripped of previous coverings, including the dropped ceiling which housed the A/C system, revealing a 17-foot-tall space with columns and a wall painting by the architect. While the renovation and installation of the rest of the building was largely completed by Judd, this principal space was not. Several pieces of furniture are somewhat randomly displayed—tables and chairs by Judd alongside historic pieces and prototypical Gerrit Rietveld benches, an Alvar Aalto table and stool, and a Mies van der Rohe cantilever chair. There are a number of paintings and reliefs by Judd dating from 1961/62. A narrow staircase leads to the mezzanine level, formerly the bank director's office, which is furnished with a historic Russian desk and chairs, and paintings by Josef Albers, Theo van Doesburg, Larry Bell, and Antonio Calderara. Behind the main hall, on the ground level, is another tall room where Judd

Doesburg, Larry Bell und Antonio Calderara eingerichtet ist. Im Erdgeschoss schließt sich an die Haupthalle ein weiterer großer Raum an, in dem zwei Bilder und ein Relief von Judd sowie zwei Radierungen von Rembrandt zusammen mit zwei Möbelstücken ihren Platz gefunden haben.

Während im Erdgeschoss und Zwischenstockwerk der Bank eindrückliche Kunstwerke ausgestellt sind, zeigt sich im Obergeschoss, warum das Gebäude seinen Namen erhielt.

Eine steile Treppe führt vom Westzimmer ins Obergeschoss, wo sich von Osten nach Westen eine Flucht von sieben Büros über die gesamte Länge des Gebäudes (ca. 29 m / 96 ft) erstreckt. In diesen Zimmern ist Judds Sammlung von Möbeln der Moderne untergebracht, darunter Tische und Stühle von Alvar Aalto und Gerrit Riedvelts Rot-Blau-Stuhl, je zwei Exemplare seines Stuhls Zig-Zag und seines Beugelstuhls (*Beugelstoel*) sowie der Berliner Stuhl und der Kratstuhl. Daneben finden sich zahlreiche Exemplare von Judds eigenen Möbelentwürfen. Judd benutzte die Reihe der Büros zur Systematisierung seiner Bauprojekte. An den Bürowänden hängen seine Entwurfszeichnungen und Skizzen sowie Plakate für Ausstellungen seiner architektonischen Projekte, aber auch Arbeiten anderer Künstler und Architekten. Eines der Büros enthält Originalmöbel Mies van der Rohes, darunter drei Freischwinger und einen Tisch, ergänzt durch drei Bleistiftzeichnungen des Architekten. Im Raum auf der Ostseite stehen ein Bett, entworfen von Judd, sowie Möbel von Aalto und Rietveld; daneben sind Drucke von Josef Albers und Henri Matisse zu sehen. Von einer Loggia auf der Seite der Highland Avenue überblickt man die Hauptstraße von Marfa.

Zurück im Erdgeschoss, öffnet sich am Fuß der Treppe eine Tür zu einem Innenhof, der zu drei weiteren von Judd renovierten Gebäuden führt: zum Pförtnerhaus im Süden, Haus Cobb im Westen und zum Whyte-Gebäude im Norden. Dort hat Judd durch den Bau einer Lehmziegelmauer entlang der Oak Street einen urbanen „Raum im Raum" gebildet. Damit war der Innenhof geschaffen und zwischen den drei zuvor unverbundenen Gebäuden eine optische und physische Beziehung hergestellt.

1 Lee Glascock Bennett, *History of the Marfa National Bank, the First Hundred Years*, Austin, Texas, 2007, S. 61.

placed two paintings, one relief and two etchings by Rembrandt together with two pieces of furniture.

While the ground floor and mezzanine level of the Bank exhibit impressive works, the second floor reveals why the building was named the Architecture Studio.

A steep staircase leads from the west room to the second floor, where an enfilade of seven offices stretches the full length of the building (96 feet) east to west. These rooms house Judd's collection of Modernist furniture, including tables and chairs by Alvar Aalto, and Gerrit Rietveld's Red and Blue chair, two versions each of his Zig-Zag chair and his Beugelstoel, as well as his Berlin and Crate chairs. One also finds numerous examples of Judd's own furniture design. Judd used the row of offices to organize his architectural projects. The office walls are hung with drawings, sketches, and exhibition posters for his architectural works. One also finds works by other artists and architects. One office houses period pieces by Mies van der Rohe, including three cantilever chairs and a table, complemented by two of the architect's pencil drawings. The room on the east side holds a bed designed by Judd as well as furniture by Aalto and Rietveld, plus prints by Josef Albers and Henri Matisse. A porch facing Highland Avenue provides a view to the principal street of Marfa.

Back on the ground floor, a door at the bottom of the staircase opens onto a courtyard which leads to three additional buildings that were renovated by Judd: the Gatehouse to the south, the Cobb House to the west, and the Whyte Building to the north. Here Judd defined an urban "space within a space" by building an adobe wall along Oak Street, thus creating the courtyard and establishing a visual and physical relationship between these previously unrelated buildings.

1 Bennett, Lee Glascock. *History of the Marfa National Bank, the First Hundred Years*, Nortex Press (Austin, Texas, 2007), p. 61.

The Marfa National Bank.
Circa 1950.
View to northwest.

Ca. 1950.
Nach Nordwesten.

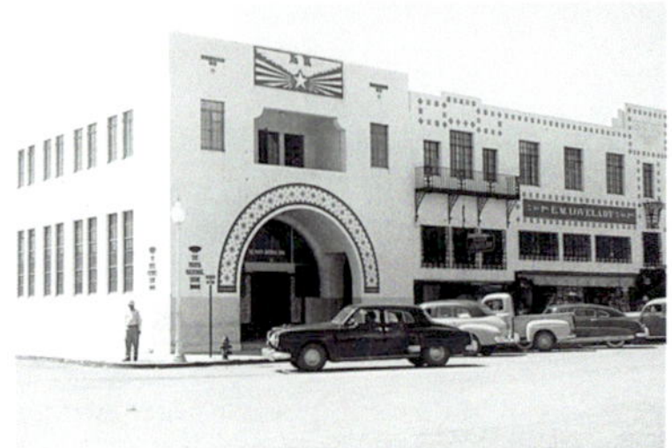

Architecture Studio.
First floor, main hall with painting by Donald Judd, untitled, 1961, table and chairs by Donald Judd, view to east.

Architekturstudio.
Erdgeschoss, Haupthalle, mit Bild von Donald Judd, ohne Titel, 1961, Tisch und Stühlen von Donald Judd, nach Osten.

JUDD FOUNDATION

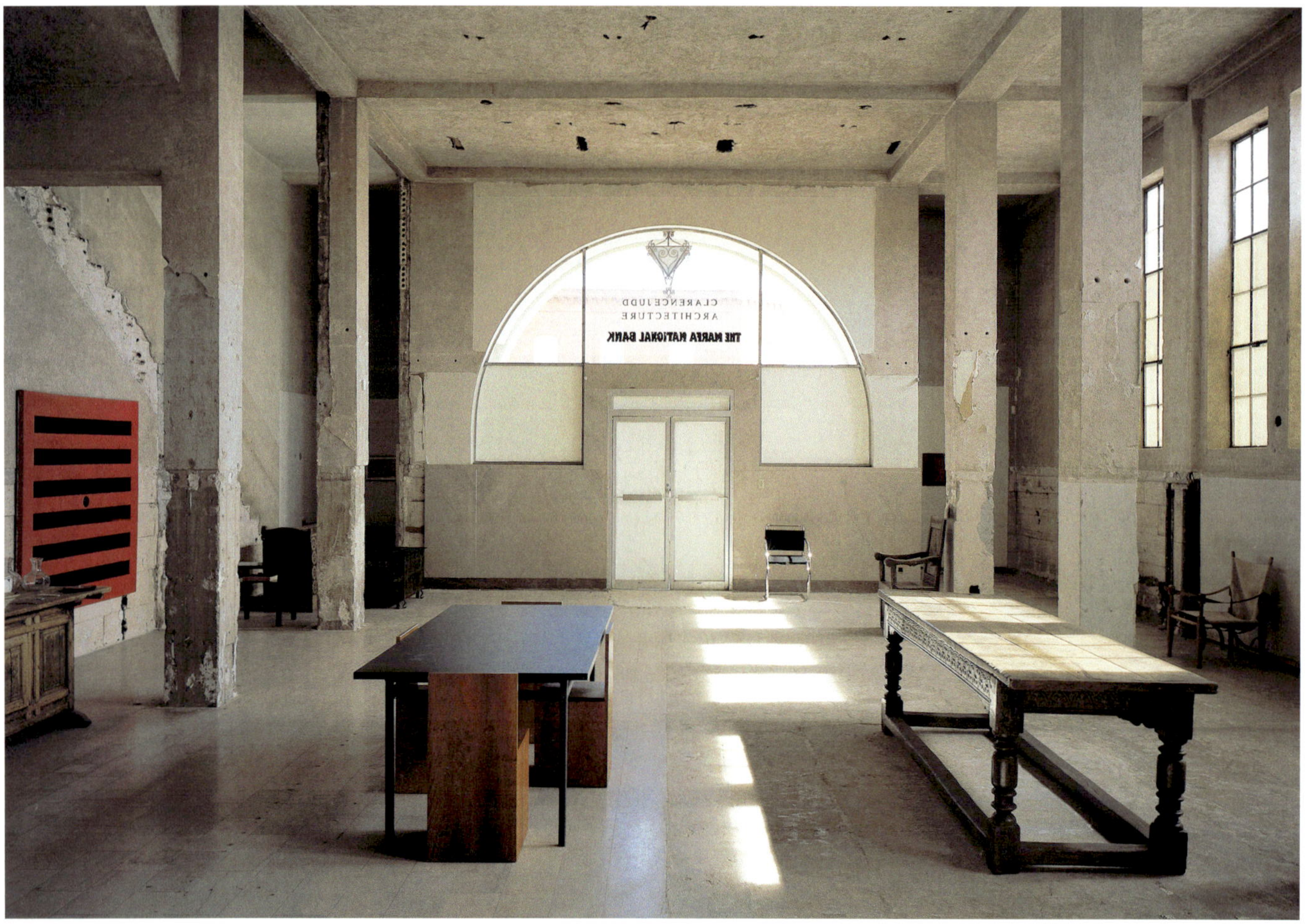

Architecture Studio. First floor, main hall with painting by Donald Judd, untitled, 1961, table and chairs by Donald Judd, view to northwest.

Architekturstudio. Erdgeschoss, Haupthalle, mit Bild von Donald Judd, ohne Titel, 1961, Tisch und Stühlen von Donald Judd, nach Nordwesten.

JUDD FOUNDATION

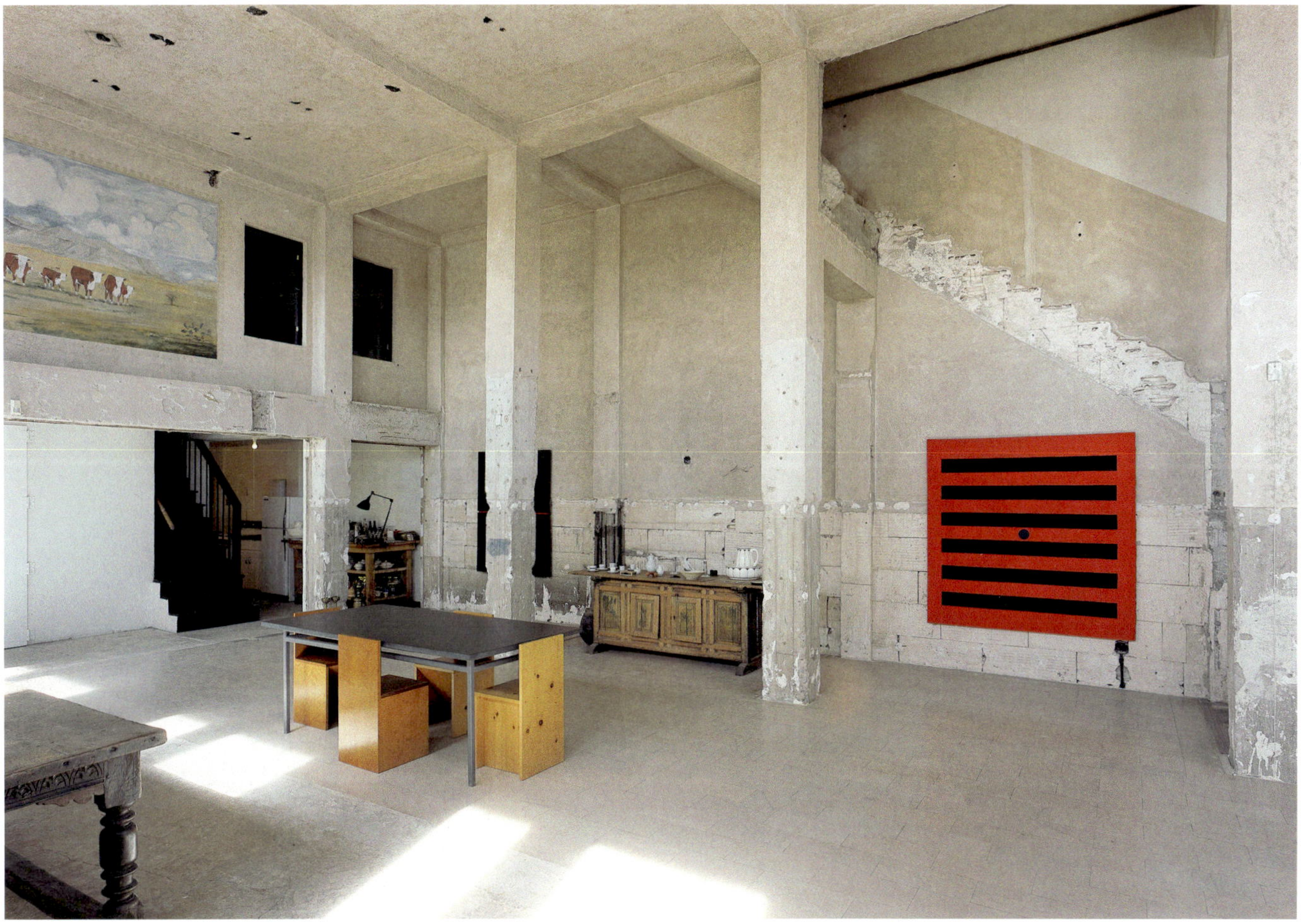

Architecture Studio. Second floor, with table by Donald Judd, view to east.

Architekturstudio. Obergeschoss, mit Tisch von Donald Judd, nach Osten.

Architecture Studio. Second floor, with shelf by Donald Judd, view to west.

Architekturstudio. Obergeschoss, mit Regal von Donald Judd, nach Westen.

Architecture Studio. Second floor, with table and chair by Donald Judd, view to east.

Architekturstudio. Obergeschoss, mit Tisch und Stuhl von Donald Judd, nach Osten.

JUDD FOUNDATION

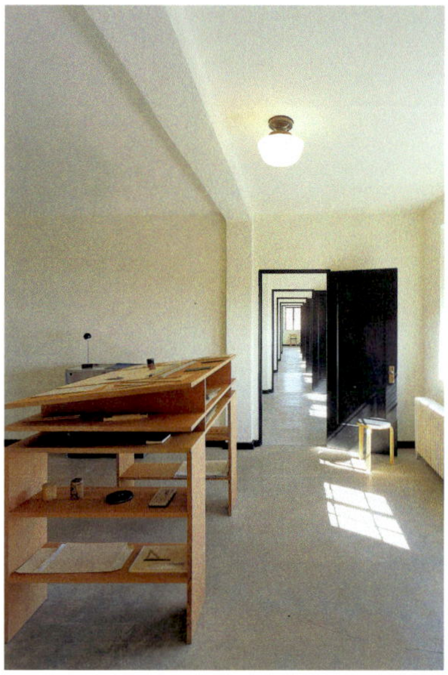

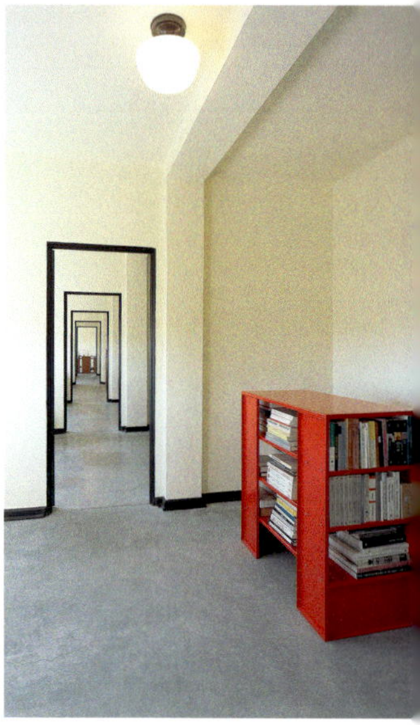

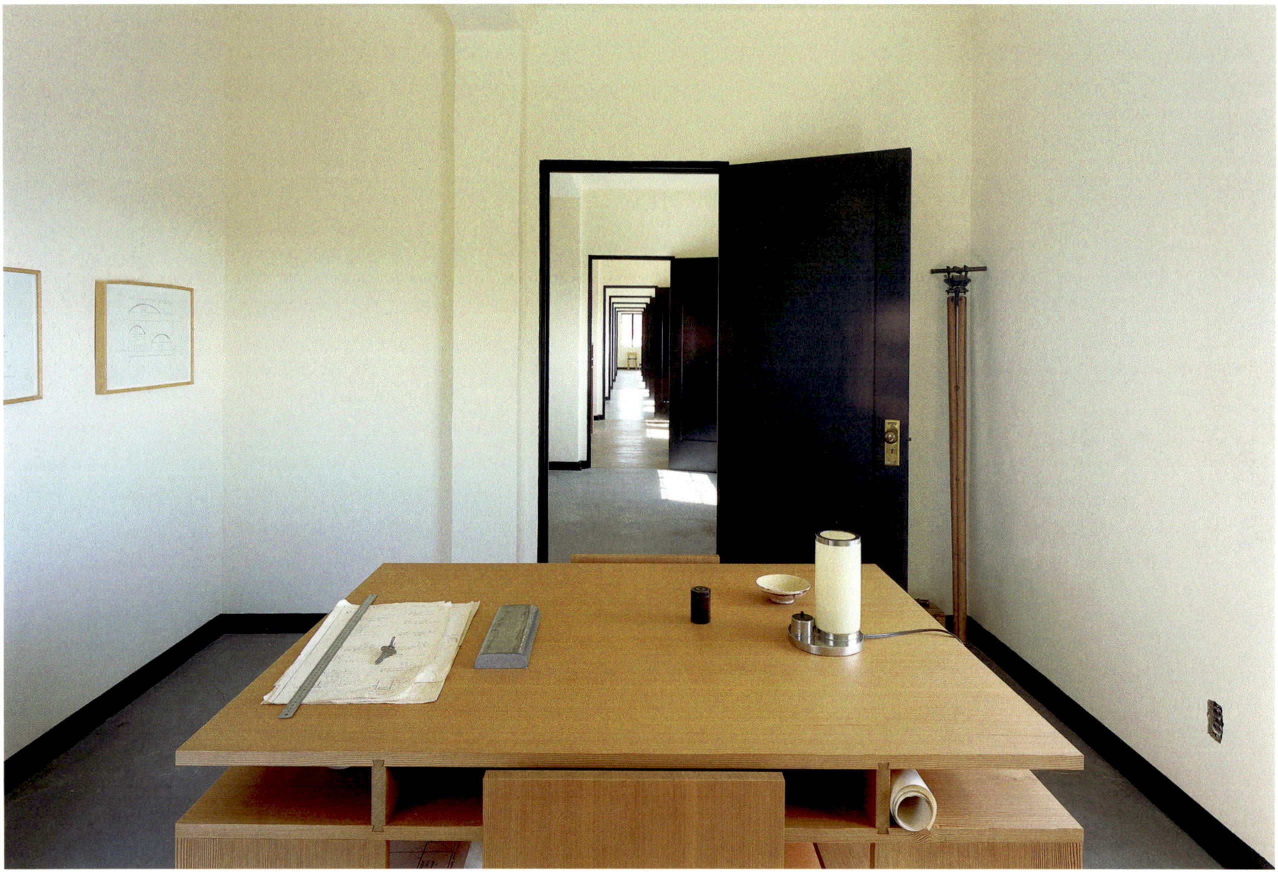

Architecture Studio. Second floor, with table by Donald Judd, view to south.

Architekturstudio. Obergeschoss, mit Tisch von Donald Judd, nach Süden.

JUDD FOUNDATION

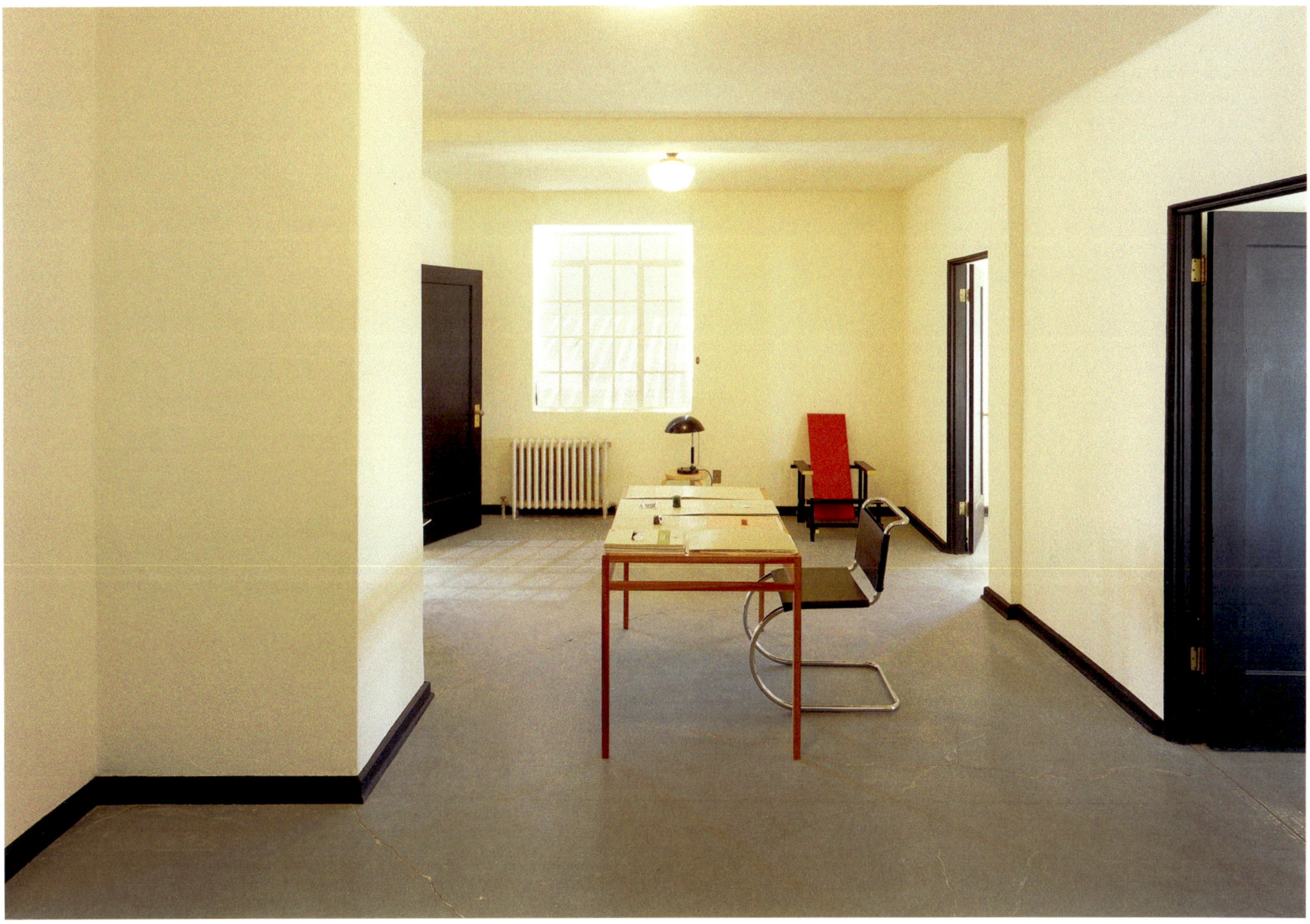

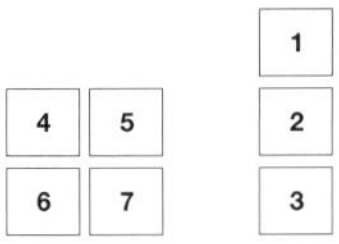

1 **Architecture Studio Second floor, plan**
Architekturstudio Grundriss Obergeschoss

2 **Mezzanine, plan**
Grundriss Zwischengeschoss

3 **First floor, plan**
Grundriss Erdgeschoss

4 **East elevation**
Ostansicht

5 **South elevation**
Südansicht

6 **Section B-B**
Schnitt B-B

7 **Section A-A**
Schnitt A-A

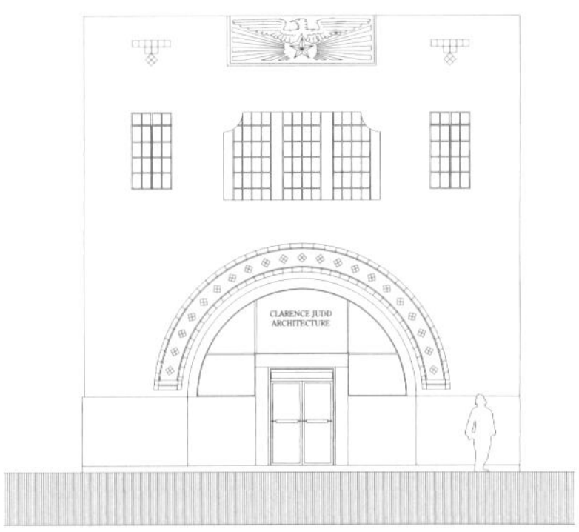

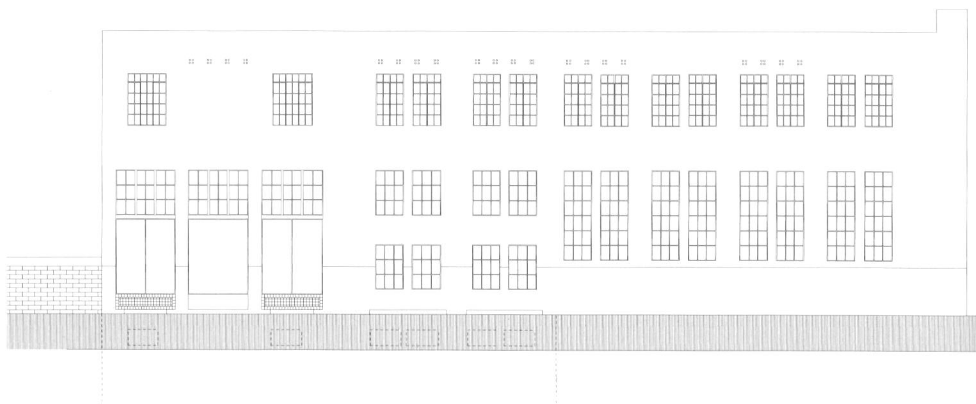

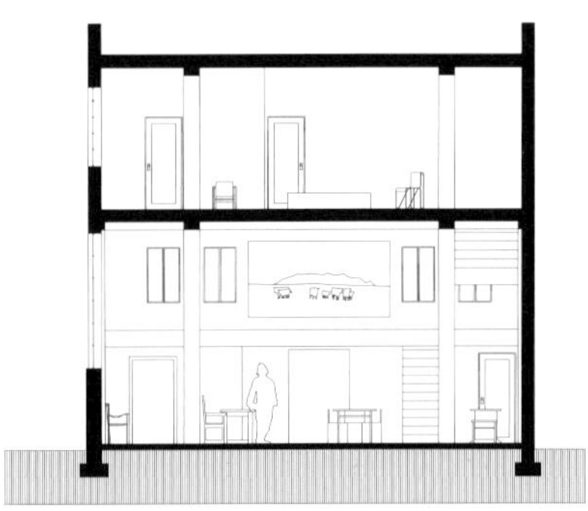

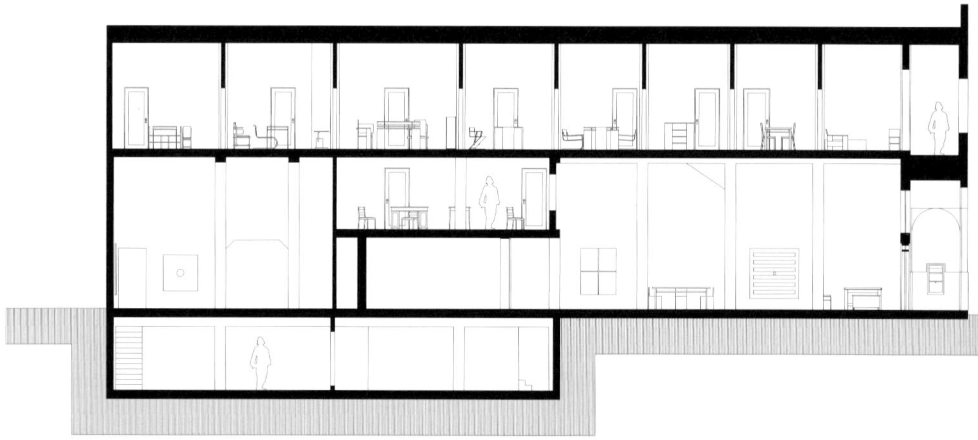

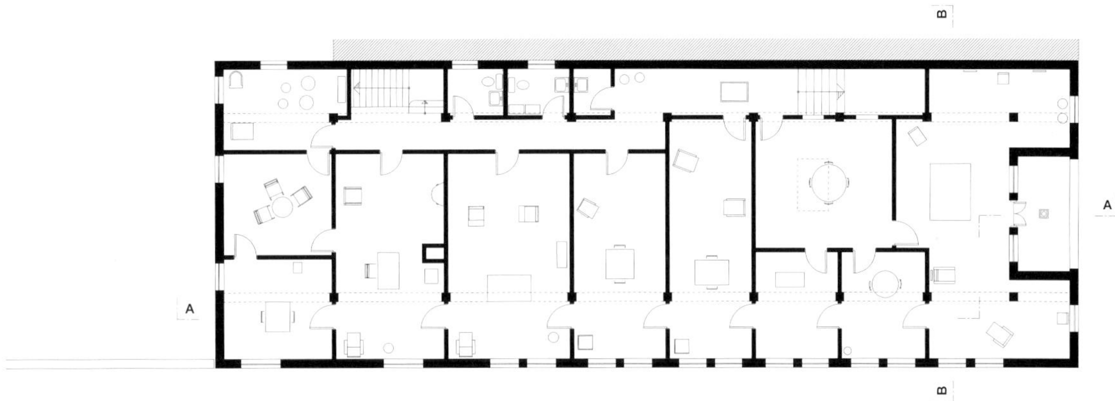
B
A
A
B

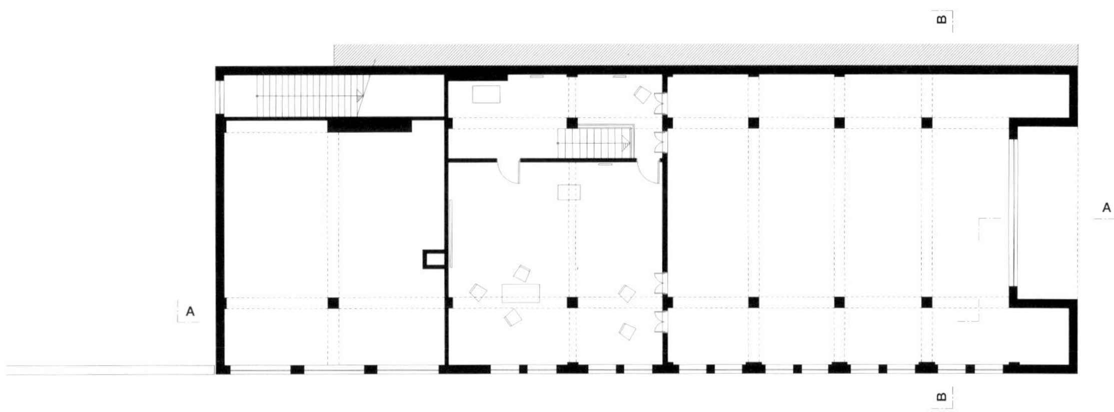
B
A
A
B

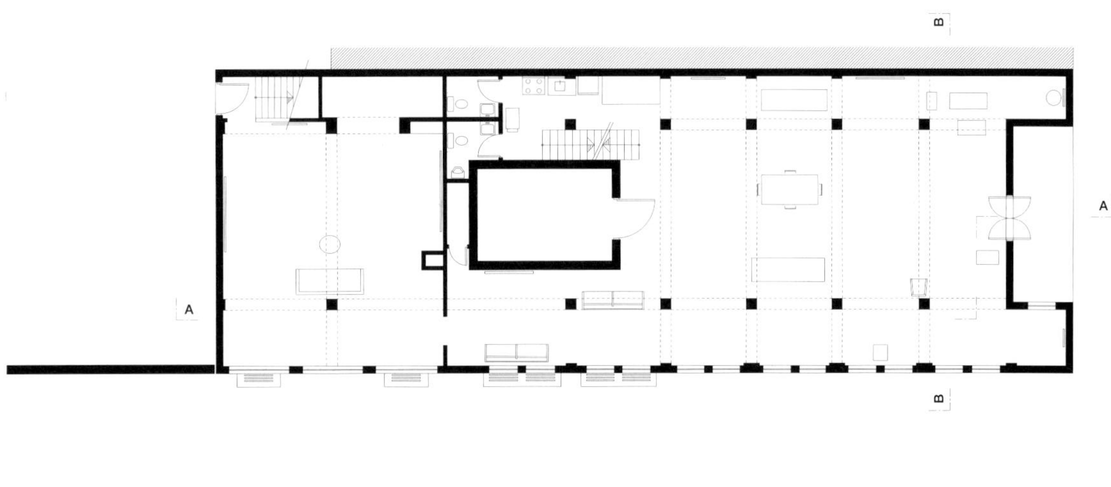
B
A
A
B

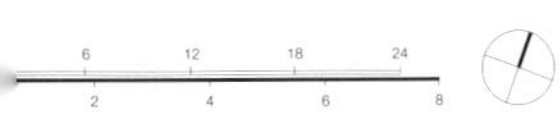
6 12 18 24
2 4 6 8

DAS WHYTE-GEBÄUDE

Das nach einem früheren Eigentümer benannte Whyte-Gebäude liegt im Nordwesten des Architekturstudios und gegenüber dem Chamberlain-Gebäude jenseits der Oak Street. Es ist Teil eines Ensembles verschiedener von Judd adaptierter Bauten, zu denen auch das Architekturstudio, das Pförtnerhaus und Haus Cobb gehören. Das Whyte-Gebäude, ursprünglich ein Zweckbau, besteht aus einem einzigen Raum mit Adobe-Mauerwerk und einem Dach aus verzinktem Wellblech. Eine im Zentrum der Südfassade positionierte Drehtür gewährt Zugang und ermöglicht zugleich Tageslichteinfall. Der Innenraum, Wände und Decke, ist sandfarben verputzt. Hier sind drei Gemälde und ein Relief von Judd aus den Jahren 1960, 1961 und 1962 ausgestellt, zusammen mit Möbeln, die Rudolph Schindler in den frühen 1920er-Jahren für sein Haus an der Kings Road in West Hollywood entworfen hat, darunter zwei Slingstühle, zwei Hocker, zwei Ottomanen und ein Ruhebett sowie eine Stehlampe, ein Entwurf Schindlers für Haus Wolfe aus den Jahren 1928/29.

Das Whyte-Gebäude ist von bescheidener Größe, und auch sein architektonischer Wert müsste als bescheiden gelten, wären nicht Judds Eingriff, seine Kunst und Schindlers Möbel. Judd wusste zweifellos, dass Schindler einer der ersten modernen Architekten Amerikas war, die eine radikal neue Vorstellung vom Raum lanciert hatten. Sein Strandhaus Lovell von 1926 (Philip Lovell Beach House) zum Beispiel war ein meisterhaftes Experiment mit expressiven Volumen. Schindler hatte für dieses Gebäude ein offen liegendes Betontragwerk entworfen, in das er eine Reihe verzahnter Volumen einschob – ein bis dahin beispielloses Modell räumlicher Beziehungen. Seine Raumkonzepte können als unmittelbare Vorgänger mancher Architektur-Ikone des 20. Jahrhunderts betrachtet werden, darunter Ludwig Mies van der Rohes Barcelona-Pavillon und Le Corbusiers Villa Savoye. In Schindler hatte Judd mit seinem Sinn für Volumen im Unterschied zu Masse und seiner Sensibilität für Raumbeziehungen zweifellos einen Geistesverwandten gefunden.

THE WHYTE BUILDING

The Whyte Building, named after a previous owner, is located northwest of the Architecture Studio and across the street from the Chamberlain Building. It is one of a complex of several buildings Judd adapted, including the Architecture Studio, the Gatehouse, and the Cobb House. The Whyte Building originally served as a utilitarian structure; it is one room, built of adobe, covered by a corrugated galvanized sheet-metal roof. A revolving door, placed in the center of the south facade, provides access and allows daylight to flow into the space. The interior walls and ceiling are plastered in a sand color. Three paintings and one relief by Judd dating from 1960, 1961 and 1962 are exhibited here, together with furniture by Rudolf Schindler designed in the early 1920s for his house on Kings Road, including two sling chairs, two stools, two ottomans, and a daybed, as well as a floor lamp which Schindler designed for Wolfe House in 1928–29.

The Whyte Building is modest in scale and would be modest in architectural value if not for Judd's intervention, his art, and Schindler's furniture. Judd must have known that Schindler was one of America's first modern architects who radically changed concepts of space. His 1926 Lovell Beach House, for example, was a virtuoso essay in expressive volumes. Here Schindler created an exposed armature of reinforced concrete into which he slid a series of interlocking volumes, creating an unprecedented example of spatial relationships. His ideas about space preceded many iconic masterpieces of the twentieth century, including Ludwig Mies van der Rohe's Barcelona Pavilion and Le Corbusier's Villa Savoie. Judd—with his own sense of volume, as opposed to mass, and his sensitivity to spatial relationships—no doubt found a kindred spirit in Schindler.

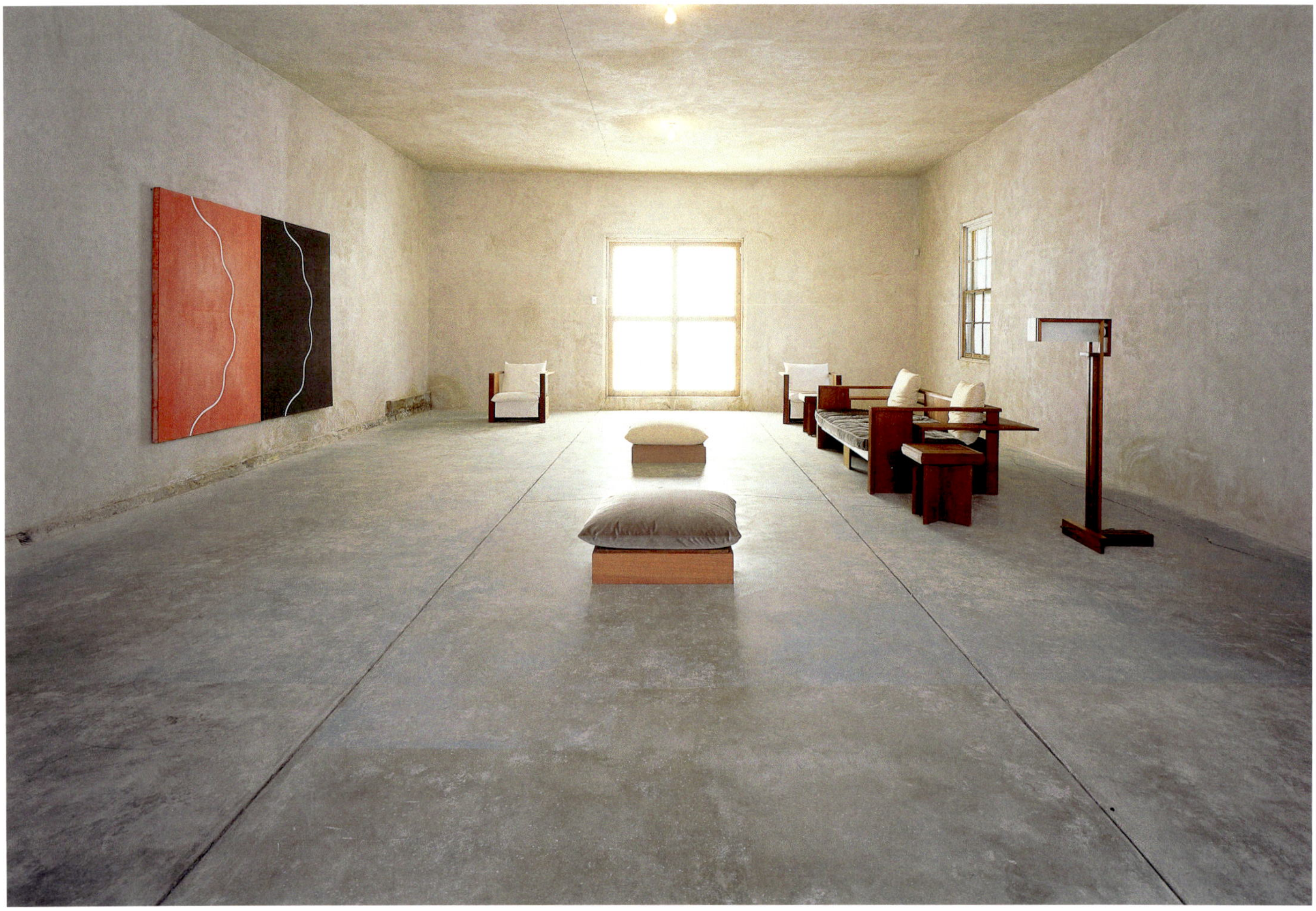

Whyte Building, with works by Donald Judd, untitled, 1961 and furniture by Rudolph M. Schindler, view to south.

Whyte-Gebäude, mit Arbeiten von Donald Judd, ohne Titel, 1961 und Möbeln von Rudolph M. Schindler, nach Süden.

JUDD FOUNDATION

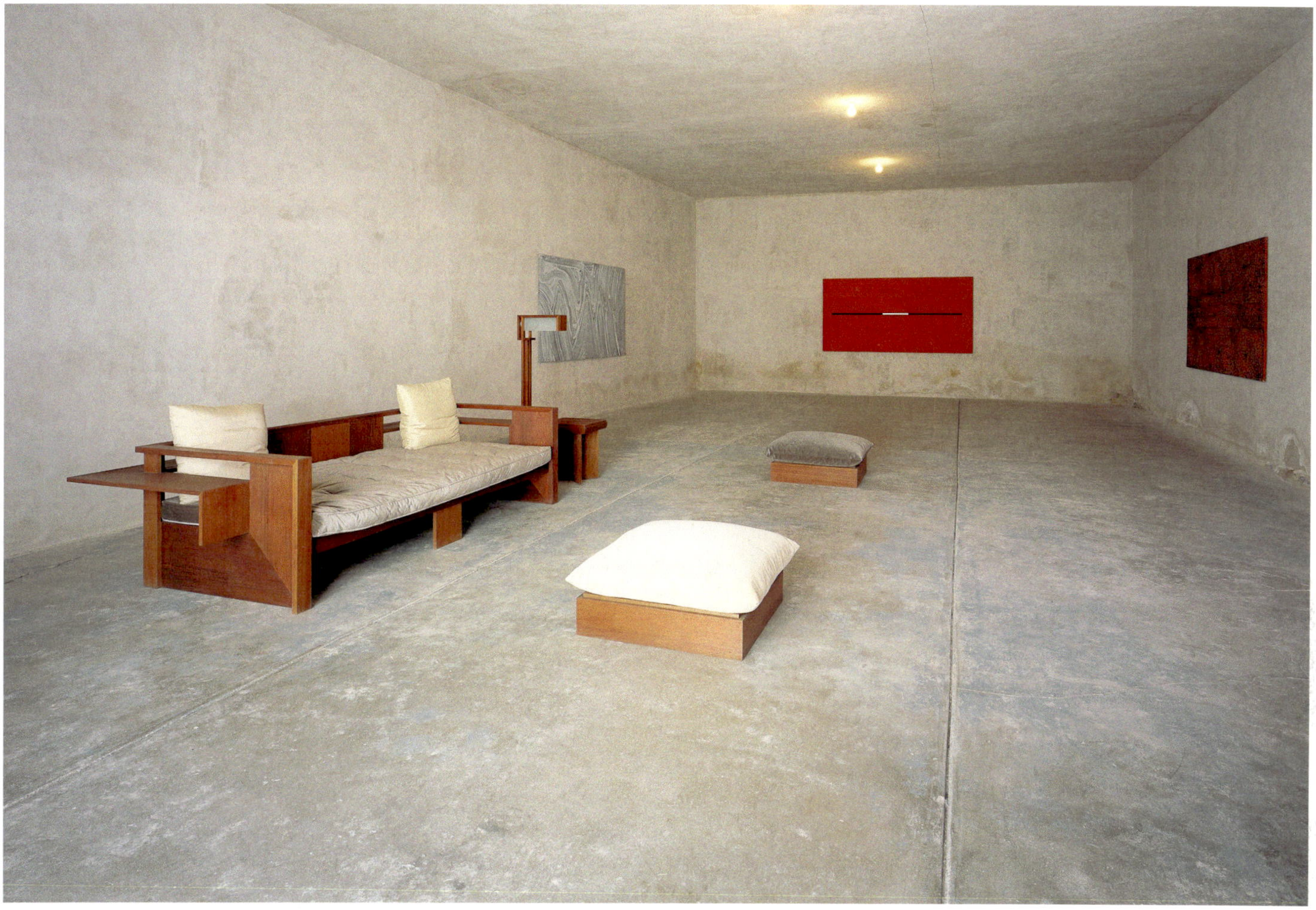

Whyte Building, with works by Donald Judd, untitled, 1960; untitled, 1962; untitled, 1961; and furniture by Rudolph M. Schindler, view to northwest.

Whyte-Gebäude, mit Arbeiten von Donald Judd, ohne Titel, 1960, 1962, 1961, und Möbeln von Rudolph M. Schindler, nach Nordwesten.

JUDD FOUNDATION

1 **The Whyte Building**
Whyte Gebäude

2 **The Cobb House**
Haus Cobb

The Gate House
Pförtnerhaus

3 **The Architecture Studio**
Architekturstudio

4 **The Whyte Building. Plan**
Whyte-Gebäude. Grundriss

5 **The Whyte Building. Section with east elevation of Gate and Cobb House**
Whyte-Gebäude. Schnitt mit Ostansicht des Pförtnerhauses und Haus Cobb

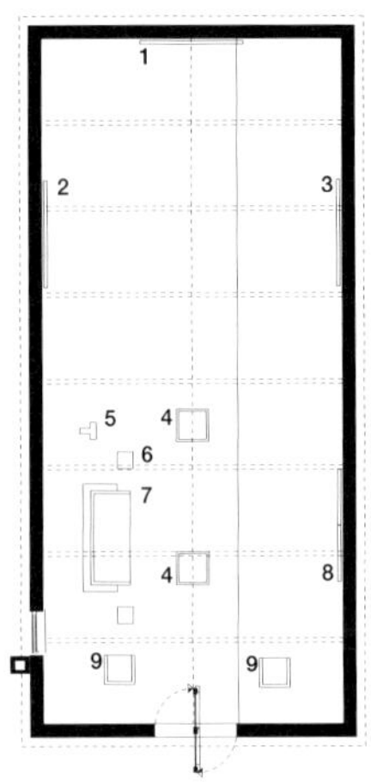

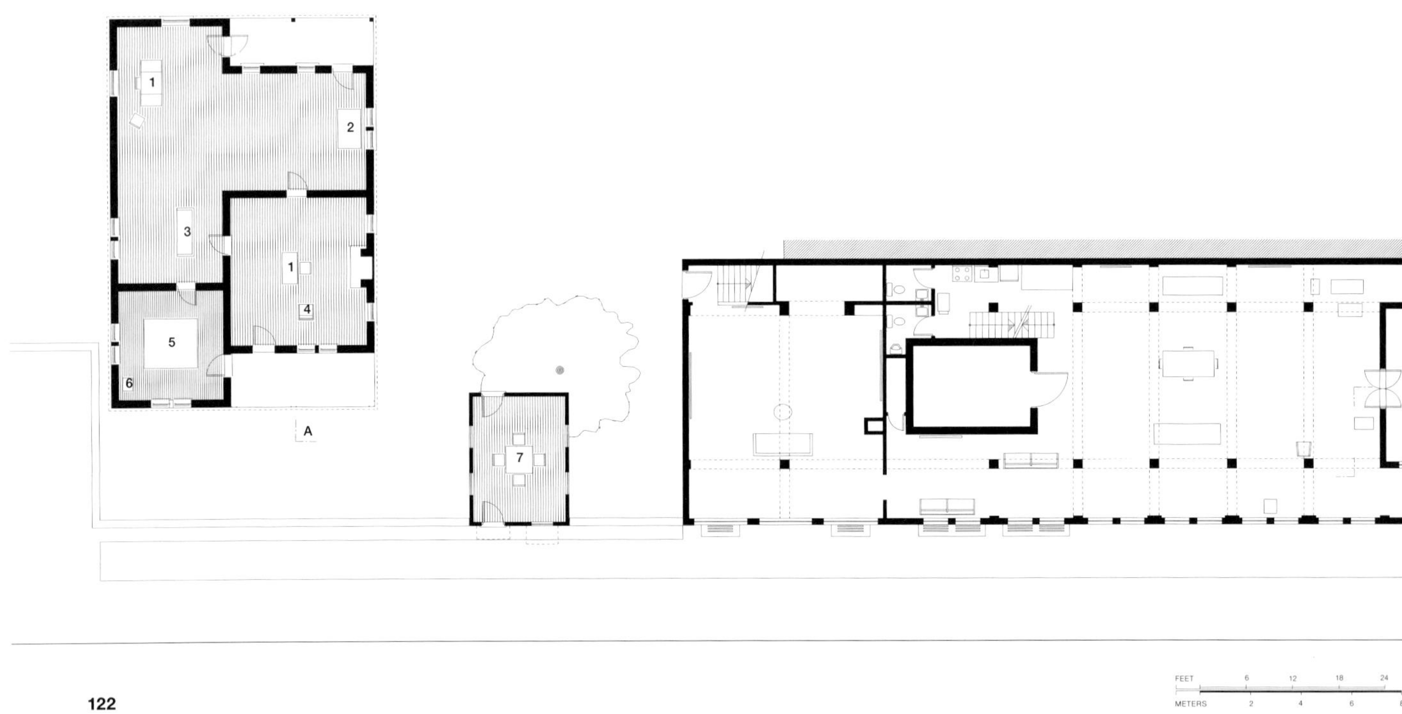

1.1 **Donald Judd, untitled, 1962**
Ohne Titel, 1962

1.2 **Donald Judd, untitled, 1960**
Ohne Titel, 1960

1.3 **Donald Judd, untitled, 1961**
Ohne Titel, 1961

1.4 **Rudolph M. Schindler Ottoman, 1921–22**
Polsterhocker, 1921–1922

1.5 **Rudolph M. Schindler Standing Lamp, 1928–29**
Stehlampe, 1928–1929

1.6 **Rudolph M. Schindler Stool, 1921–22**
Hocker, 1921–1922

1.7 **Rudolph M. Schindler Sofa, 1921–22**
Sofa, 1921–1922

1.8 **Donald Judd, untitled, 1961**
Ohne Titel, 1961

1.9 **Rudolph M. Schindler Sling Chair, 1921–22**
Sling Chair, 1921–1922

2.1 **Antique Table and Chairs**
Antiker Tisch und Stühle

2.2 **Antique Chest**
Antike Truhe

2.3 **Antique Sofa**
Antikes Sofa

2.4 **Antique upholstered Armchair**
Antiker Polstersessel

2.5 **Donald Judd Bed**
Bett

2.6 **Antique Side Table**
Antiker Beistelltisch

2.7 **Donald Judd Table and Chairs**
Tisch und Stühle

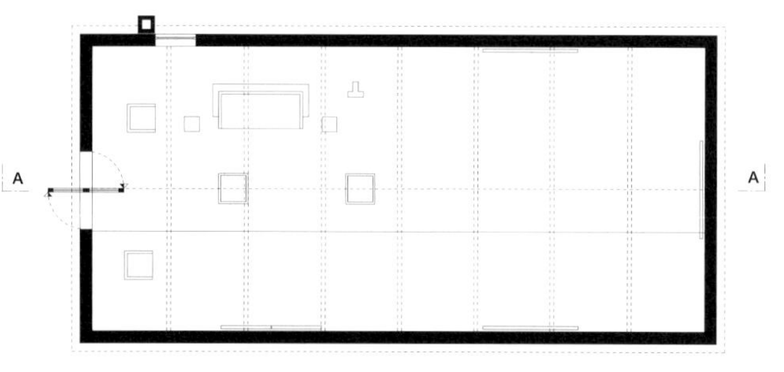

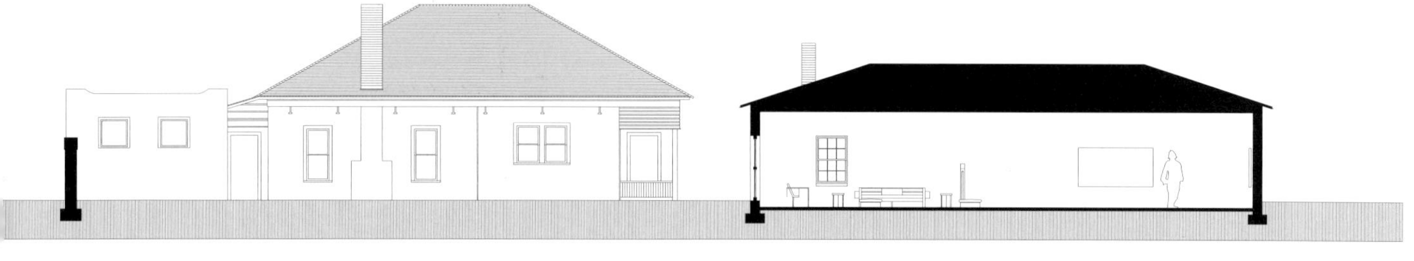

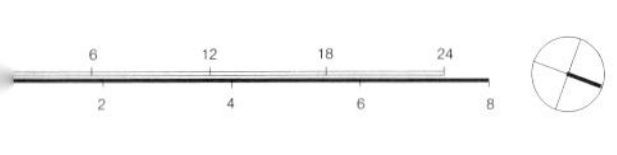

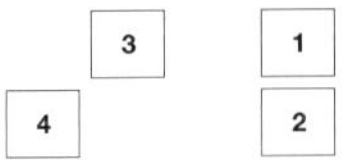

1 **Gate House, Cobb House and Whyte Building. East elevations**
Pförtnerhaus, Haus Cobb und Whyte-Gebäude. Ostansichten

2 **Whyte Building, Gate House and Architecture Studio. West elevations**
Whyte-Gebäude, Pförtnerhaus und Architekturstudio. Westansichten

3 **Whyte Building, Cobb House. North elevations**
Whyte-Gebäude, Haus Cobb. Nordansichten

4 **Whyte Building, South elevation**
Whyte-Gebäude. Südansicht

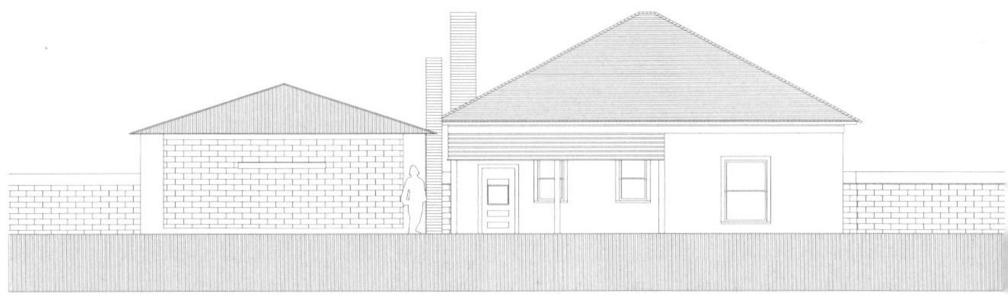

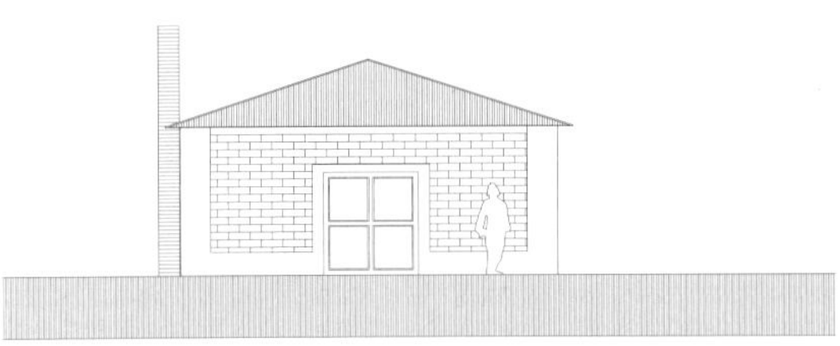

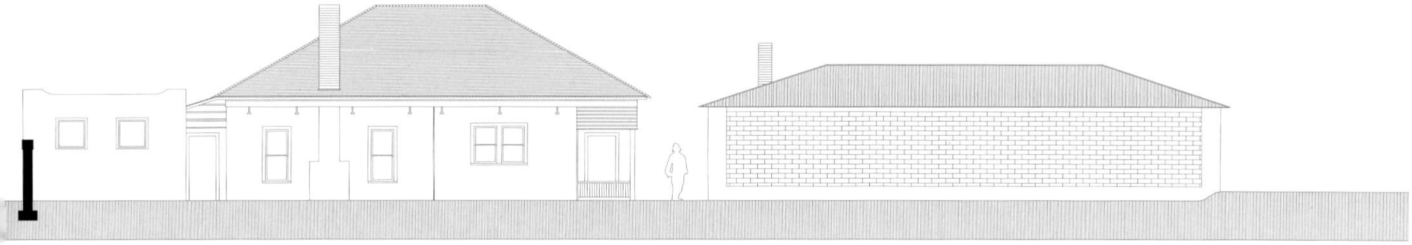

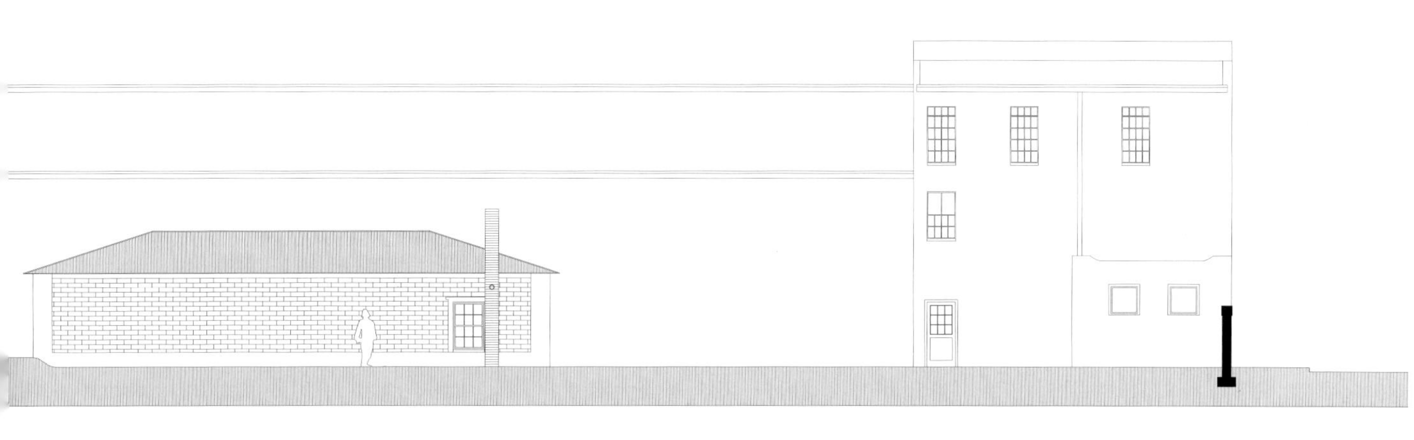

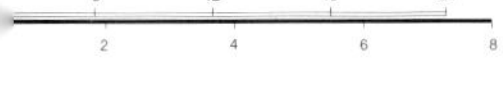
6
12
18
24
2
4
6
8

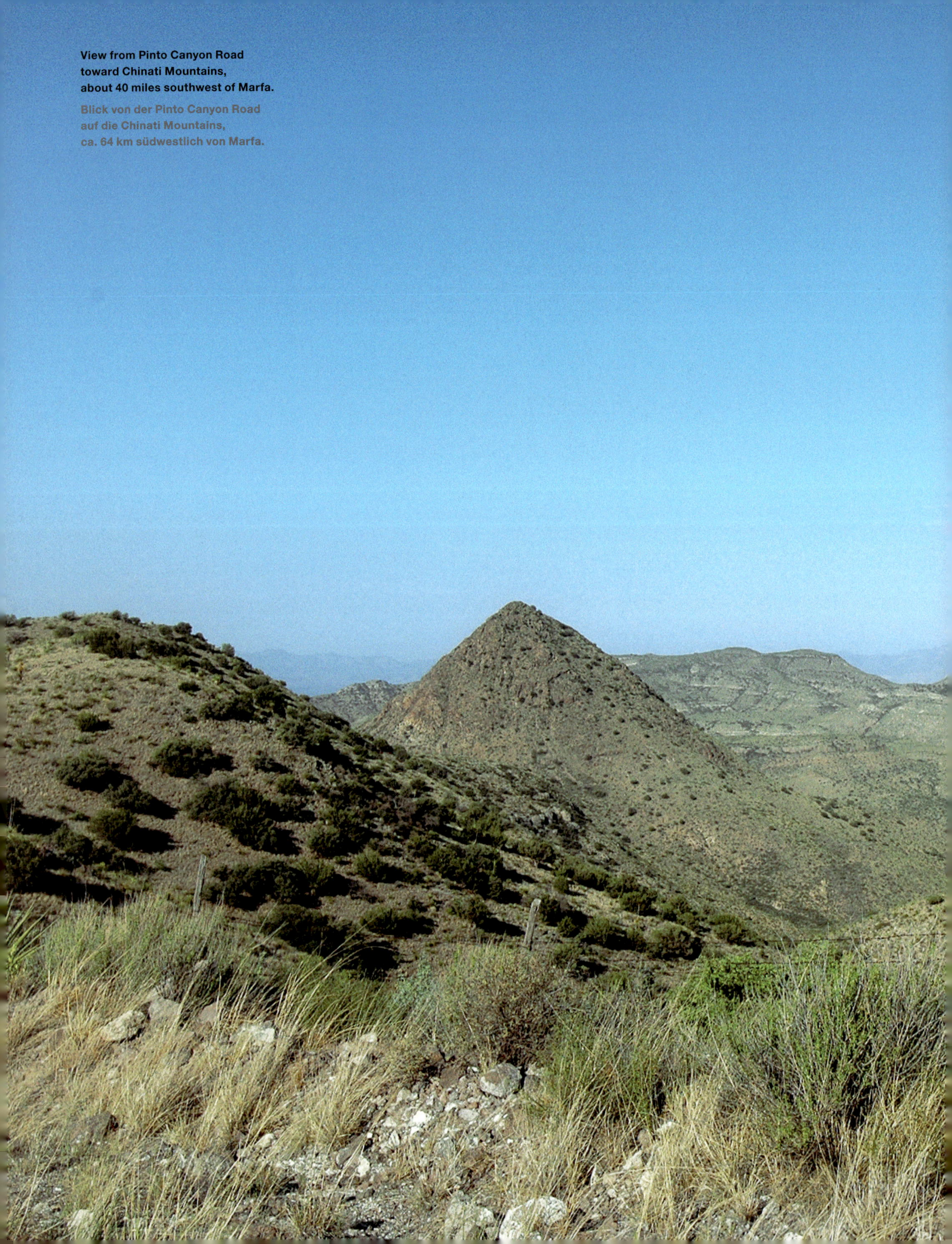

View from Pinto Canyon Road
toward Chinati Mountains,
about 40 miles southwest of Marfa.

Blick von der Pinto Canyon Road
auf die Chinati Mountains,
ca. 64 km südwestlich von Marfa.

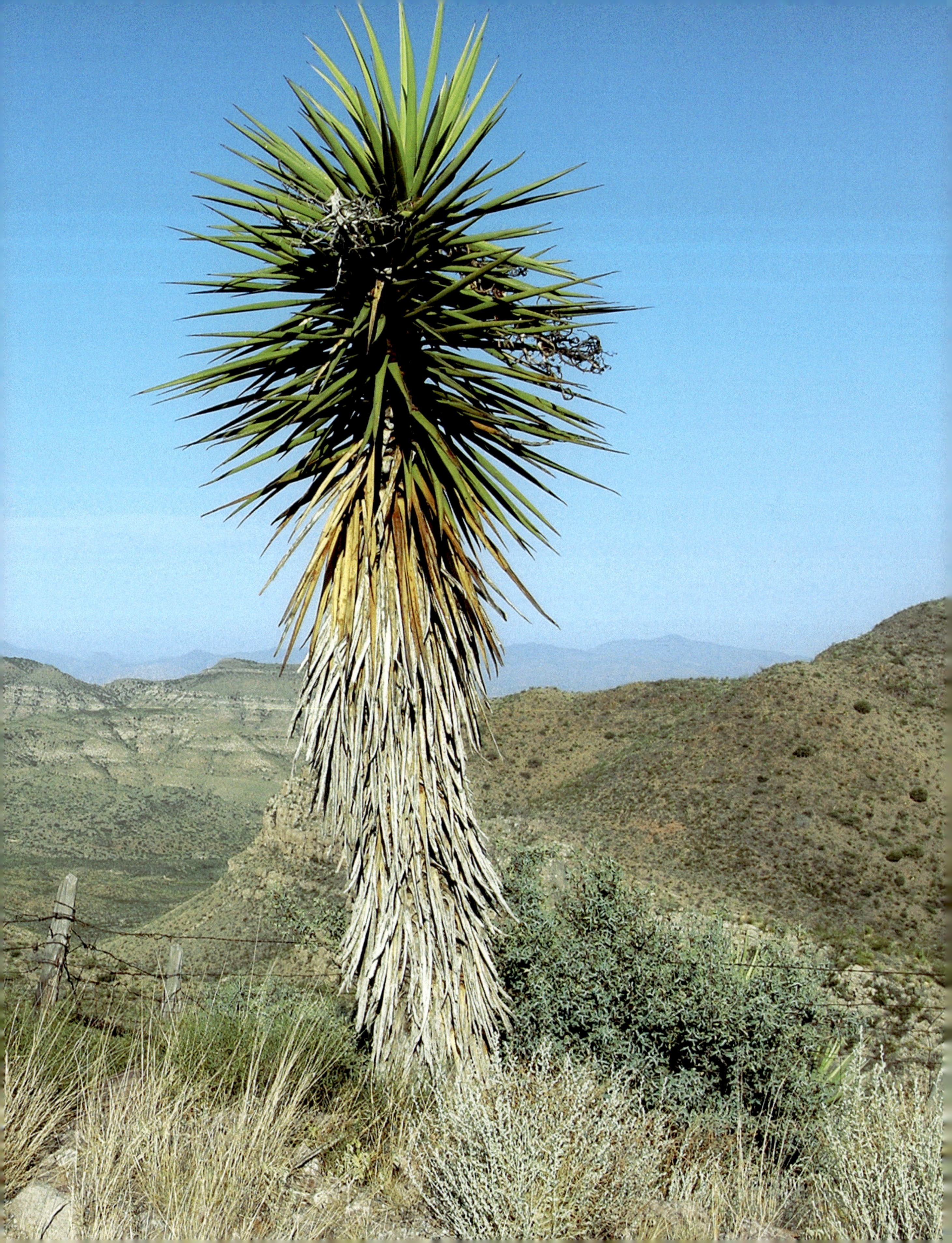

CASA MORALES, AYALA DE CHINATI

Drei Jahre nachdem er sein erstes Gebäude in Marfa erworben hatte, kaufte Donald Judd 1976 mit der Casa Morales das erste seiner Ranchhäuser. Obwohl ihm der Block in Marfa als Hauptwohnsitz in Texas diente, fühlte er sich von dem Landstrich südlich des Candelaria Rim angezogen, diesem abgelegenen, rauen Gebirgszug in der Wüste, der sich durch den Pinto Canyon bis über die Chinati Mountains erstreckt. Judds Liebe zu diesem Land und der Kultur im Grenzbereich zwischen den USA und Mexiko sowie zur Abgeschiedenheit dieser Gegend inspirierte ihn zu bemerkenswerten architektonischen Eingriffen, die er an den bescheiden wirkenden Gehöften der ehemaligen Schaf- und Ziegenfarmen vornahm. Die Casa Morales befindet sich auf einer

Casa Morales is the first ranch house Donald Judd acquired in 1976, three years after purchasing his first building in Marfa. While Judd's primary residence in Texas was the Block in Marfa, he was attracted to the land south of Candelaria Rim, the rugged remote desert mountains that stretch through Pinto Canyon and Chinati mountains. His affection for the land and border culture between the US and Mexico and the remoteness of the land led Judd to create remarkable architectural interventions on seemingly modest homesteads of former goat and sheep ranches. Casa Morales is situated on a slightly sloped natural terrace on the western slope of the Sierra Parda, about 5¼ miles linear distance west from Chinati Peak and 6¾ east from the US-Mexican border.

etwas abschüssigen natürlichen Terrasse an der Westflanke der Sierra Parda, etwa 8,5 Kilometer Luftlinie westlich des Chinati Peak und knapp 11 Kilometer östlich der Grenze zu Mexiko.

Reist man über die Pinto Canyon Road an, so erreicht man die Casa Morales von Nordwesten kommend über einen Weg, der nur äußerst wohlwollend als Schotterpiste bezeichnet werden kann. Streckenweise verschwindet dieser Weg im Nichts, dann nimmt man nur Dornenbüsche wahr, die ihre Kratzer an den Türen des Geländewagens hinterlassen. Das spärliche Gras, das sich äußerst mühsam einen Platz zum Wachsen erkämpft, lässt erahnen, wie schwer es einst für die Bauern gewesen sein muss, auf diesem Land ihren Lebensunterhalt zu erwirtschaften. Nach einem steilen Anstieg gelangt man dank Allradantrieb auf eine leicht geneigte natürliche Hochebene. Die Casa Morales umfasst das Ranchhaus, ein kleines Lagergebäude, *Tiendita* genannt, und eine ziemlich große Tränke mit Windrad.

Ursprünglich wurde die Casa Morales in den 1940er-Jahren als Einraumhaus mit einer Grundfläche von 9,2 × 4,3 Metern (30 × 14 ft) aus lokalem Gestein erbaut. Einige Zeit später, jedoch noch bevor Judd das Anwesen kaufte, wurden zwei weitere Räume und ein kleines Badezimmer an der Nordseite angefügt. Über die gesamte Länge der Südfassade erstreckt sich eine 2,5 Meter (8 ft) breite Veranda. Judd fertigte Zeichnungen für weitere Räume und ein Studio an, eingerahmt von Terrassen, Pergolen und Wasserbecken. Eine niedrige Trockenmauer fasst das gesamte Anwesen mit seinen Gärten ein.

Schon bald nach dem Kauf skizzierte Judd, wie die Casa Morales renoviert und für seine Zwecke verändert werden sollte. Es existieren einundachtzig[1] Zeichnungen mit verschiedenen Entwürfen, deren älteste aus dem Oktober 1976 stammt. Eine Handvoll dieser Zeichnungen, die im Archiv der Judd Foundation lagern, werden Lauretta Vinciarelli zugeschrieben, einer aus Italien stammenden Künstlerin und Architektin, die in den Siebziger- und Achtzigerjahren des vorigen Jahrhunderts für rund zehn Jahre privat und beruflich Judds Partnerin war. Die fundierte Recherche der Kunsthistorikerin Rebecca Siefert zu Vinciarelli lässt deren Einfluss auf Judds Wirken, nicht nur auf seine Architektur, sondern auch auf seine Möbelentwürfe und Kunstwerke, insbesondere die Drucke[2], in ganz neuem Licht erscheinen.

After leaving Pinto Canyon Road, Casa Morales is approached from the northwest on what can generously be described as a dirt road at best, but sometimes becomes no road at all, only thorny shrubs that scratch the sides of the pick-up truck. The sparse grass, barely negotiating space to grow, allows one to imagine what it must have been like for the ranchers trying to make a living of this land. After a steep climb in a four-wheel drive one arrives at a slight sloping natural terrace. Casa Morales is comprised of the ranch house and a small storage building called a *tiendita,* and a sizable stock tank with a windmill.

Casa Morales was originally built as a one-room house in the 1940s' made of local rock encompassing an area of 30 × 14 feet. Later, but before Judd acquired it, two rooms and a small bathroom were added to the north side of the ranch house. To the south an 8-foot-wide porch stretches over the full length of the south façade of the house. Judd made drawings for additional rooms and a studio enclosed by porches, pergolas, and pools. The compound and its gardens are bounded by a low dry-laid rock wall.

Soon after acquiring the property Judd made drawings to renovate and adapt Casa Morales for his use. Eighty-one[1] drawings are known to exist of various design schemes, the earliest dating to October 1976. A handful of those drawings, archived at the Judd Foundation, are credited to Lauretta Vinciarelli, the Italian-born artist and architect who was Judd's partner in work and life for a decade during the seventies and eighties. Art historian Rebecca Siefert's important research on Vinciarelli sheds new light on how she influenced Judd's work, not only his architecture but also his furniture design and artwork, especially, his prints[2]. The collaboration between Judd and Vinciarelli clearly goes beyond that previously known of besides the two unrealized projects, for Providence (1984) and Cleveland (1986), for which Judd credited Vinciarelli as a collaborator[3].

As with the other ranch houses, Casa Perez and Las Casas, many of Judd's architectural ideas remain unfinished. Judd altered the south-facing 8-foot-wide porch. He removed the ten red-painted columns built of two combined 2 × 4s and replaced them with five 4 × 4 columns. The porch roof rests on 4 × 4 beams cantilevering 4 feet on each side. The most striking alteration to

Die Zusammenarbeit von Judd und Vinciarelli ging eindeutig über das bisher Erforschte und die beiden nicht verwirklichten Projekte für Providence (1984) und Cleveland (1986) hinaus, für die Judd Vinciarelli als Mitwirkende[3] ausgewiesen hatte.

Wie bei den anderen beiden Ranchhäusern, Casa Perez und Las Casas, blieben viele von Judds architektonischen Ideen unvollendet. Er veränderte die 2,50 Meter (8 ft) breite Veranda auf der Südseite, indem er die zehn rotlackierten Stützen aus je zwei 38 × 89 Millimeter (2 × 4 in) großen Bohlen durch fünf 89 × 89 Millimeter (4 × 4 in) starke Stützen ersetzte. Die Balken, auf denen das Verandadach ruht, haben einen Querschnitt von 89 × 89 Millimetern (4 × 4 in) und kragen an den Seiten um jeweils um 1,20 Meter (4 ft) aus. Die markanteste Veränderung im Inneren ist die Kiefernholzverkleidung der Decke, die der Unterseite der Dachbinder folgt und den Raum überraschend stattlich wirken lässt. Auf der Ostseite befindet sich die von Judd entworfene Küchentheke mit Spüle und offenen Regalen darunter. Es gibt zwei Öfen in diesem Raum, einen zum Kochen und einen zum Heizen, sowie einen zylindrischen *White Frost*-Eisschrank aus dem frühen zwanzigsten Jahrhundert, in dem vor der Erfindung des Kühlschranks Lebensmittel und Getränke gekühlt wurden. An der Südwand steht eine Bank von Gustav Stickley. Ein Tisch, Stühle, eine Anrichte und ein Bücherregal vervollständigen den Raum. In den einstigen Fenstern gen Norden hängen Stoffbänder aus rot-schwarzem Schottenkaro und bieten den dahinter angrenzenden Schlafzimmern etwas Sichtschutz. Im östlichen Schlafzimmer befindet sich ein von Judd entworfenes niedriges Bett, das durch eine Wand mit Tür vom Schlafzimmer seiner Kinder Flavin und Rainer abgetrennt ist. Das Kinderzimmer ist mit einem ebenfalls von Judd entworfenen Stockbett mit Leiter, einem Bücherregal und einem Stehpult mit Staufach möbliert. Beide Räume verfügen über einen Holzofen, und die Zimmerdecken sind mit Kiefernbrettern verkleidet. Der Fußboden im Kinderzimmer ist ebenfalls mit Kiefernholz ausgelegt, in Judds Schlafzimmer ist er jedoch aus unbehandeltem Beton. Das Ranchhaus schließt mit einem Badezimmer in der nordwestlichen Ecke ab, das nur vom Kinderzimmer aus zugänglich ist.

In der *tiendita* südöstlich des Hauptgebäudes lagern Werkzeuge und andere Gerätschaften für den Ranchbetrieb. Judd

the interior is the pine-clad ceiling which follows the underside of the roof framing, giving the space a surprising splendor. To the east is a Judd-designed kitchen counter with sink and open shelves beneath. The room contains two stoves, one for cooking, the other for heating and a cylindrical *White Frost* ice box from the early 1900 which served to keep food and drinks cool before the invention of the modern refrigerator. Along the south wall is a Gustav Stickley bench. A table, chairs, a credenza, and a bookshelf complete the space. In the two former windows to the north, ripped red and black tartan strips hang from the window heads, offering some visual privacy to the adjacent bedrooms. The east bedroom contains a low Judd-designed bed on the west side, which is separated by a wall and door from the bedroom for his children Flavin and Rainer. This room is furnished by a Judd-designed bunk bed with ladder, a bookshelf, and a standing desk with storage compartment. Both rooms are equipped with a wooden stove and a horizontal pine cladded ceiling. The children's bedroom has a pine floor while Judd's bedroom floor is of untreated concrete. The ranch house ends with a bathroom on the northwest corner accessible only from the children's bedroom.

At the *tiendita,* located to the southeast of the main house, ranch tools and other equipment are stored. Judd extended the roof of the *tiendita* to the east and added a counter with open storage shelves beneath, running along the south, east, and north walls. He placed a sink in the shaded east portion of the counter. Looking north, the mountain panorama unfolds, a magnificent vista before which to perform the morning grooming and start the day.

Casa Morales is the only Judd ranch house that presently does not feature any artwork of his or by others. During Judd's lifetime, an etching by Francisco Goya was displayed near the entrance of the children's bedroom. Judd's bedroom contains a geological map of a portion of west Texas. The hanging of the red and black tartan strips in the north windows of the main room were part of a family ritual that marked each new year visiting Casa Morales the arrival and departure at ranch. The strips were knotted onto the ranch gate below Casa Morales and later hung from simple nails at the windows.

verlängerte das Dach der *tiendita* gen Osten und fügte entlang der Süd-, Ost- und Nordwand eine lange Werkbank mit offenen Regalen hinzu. In diese setzte er an der schattigen Ostseite ein Waschbecken ein, wo man bei der morgendlichen Körperpflege mit einem spektakulären Blick auf das Bergpanorama in den Tag starten kann.

Die Casa Morales ist das einzige von Judds Ranchhäusern, in dem momentan keine Werke von ihm selbst oder anderen Künstlern ausgestellt sind. Zu Judds Lebzeiten schmückte eine Radierung von Francisco de Goya den Hauptraum. In seinem Schlafzimmer hängt eine geologische Karte von Westtexas. Das Anbringen der Schottenkarobänder an den einstigen Fensteröffnungen des Hauptraums war ein Familienritual, das jedes Jahr beim Besuch der Casa Morales die Ankunft und Abreise markierte. Die Bänder wurden zunächst ans Tor unterhalb der Casa Morales geknotet und später mit einfachen Nägeln an den Fenstern angebracht.

1 Momentan befasst sich die Judd Foundation damit, Judds architektonische Zeichnungen zu katalogisieren. Diese Arbeiten waren zum Zeitpunkt der Veröffentlichung dieses Buches noch nicht abgeschlossen, weshalb die exakte Anzahl der Zeichnungen für die Casa Morales abweichen kann.

2 Rebecca Siefert. *„Lauretta Vinciarelli, Into the Light: Her Collaborations with Donald Judd.“* Woman's Art Journal. Bd. 38, Nr. 1 (Frühjahr–Sommer 2017), S. 20–27.

3 *Donald Judd. Architektur,* Marianne Stockebrand, Herausgeberin. Dritte Ausgabe, (Ostfildern bei Stuttgart, Cantz, 1992) und Donald Judd. *Donald Judd Writings*. Hrsg. von Flavin Judd und Caitlin Murray. Hrsg. Judd Foundation und Zwirner Books, New York, 2016.

1 Currently the Judd Foundation is in the process of cataloging Judd's architectural drawings. This process is not completed at the time of the publishing of this book, so the exact total number of drawings attributed to Casa Morales may vary.

2 Siefert, Rebecca. *"Lauretta Vinciarelli, Into the Light: Her Collaborations with Donald Judd.", in:* Woman's Art Journal. Vol. 38, no. 1 (Spring-Summer 2017): p. 20–27

3 *Donald Judd. Architektur,* Marianne Stockebrand, editor. 3rd ed. (Ostfildern near Stuttgart, Cantz, 1992) and reprinted in Judd, Donald. *Donald Judd Writings*. Judd, Flavin. and Murray, Caitlin. Ed. Judd Foundation and Zwirner Books, New York, 2016.

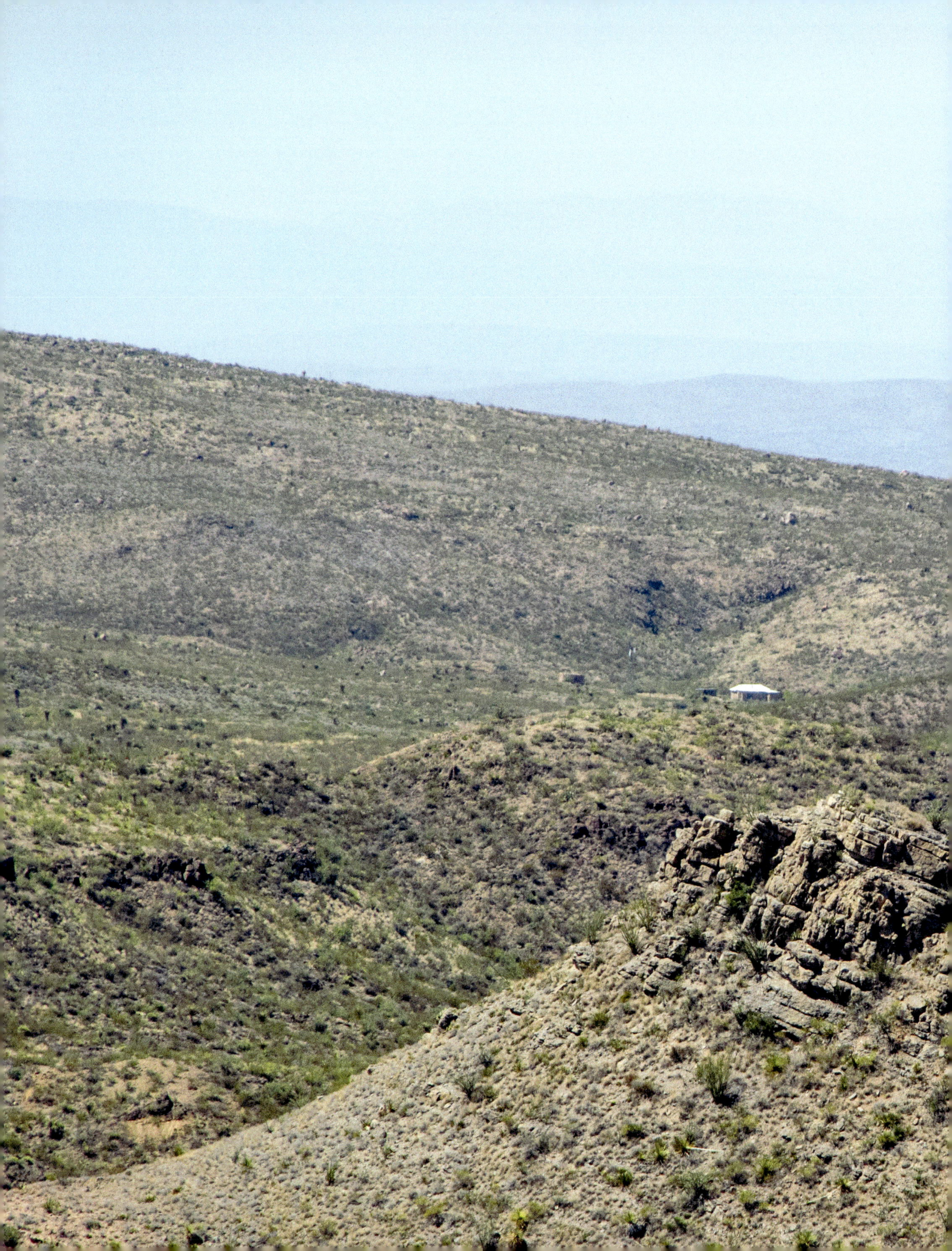

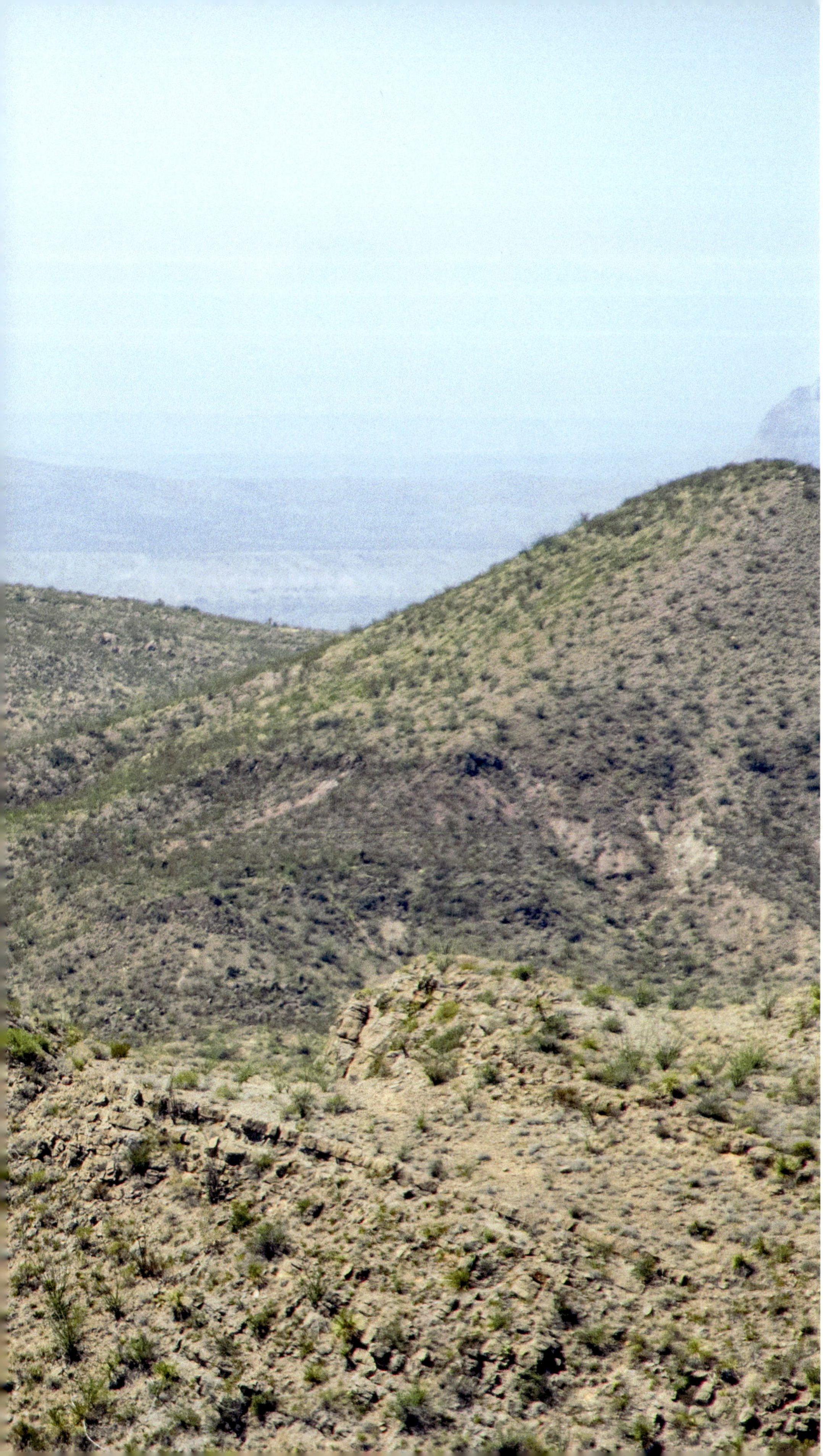

Casa Morales of Ayala de Chinati with Sierra Grande mountain range in the background, view to southwest.

Casa Morales of Ayala de Chinati mit dem Sierra Grande Gebirgszug im Hintergrund, Blick nach Südwesten.

JUDD FOUNDATION

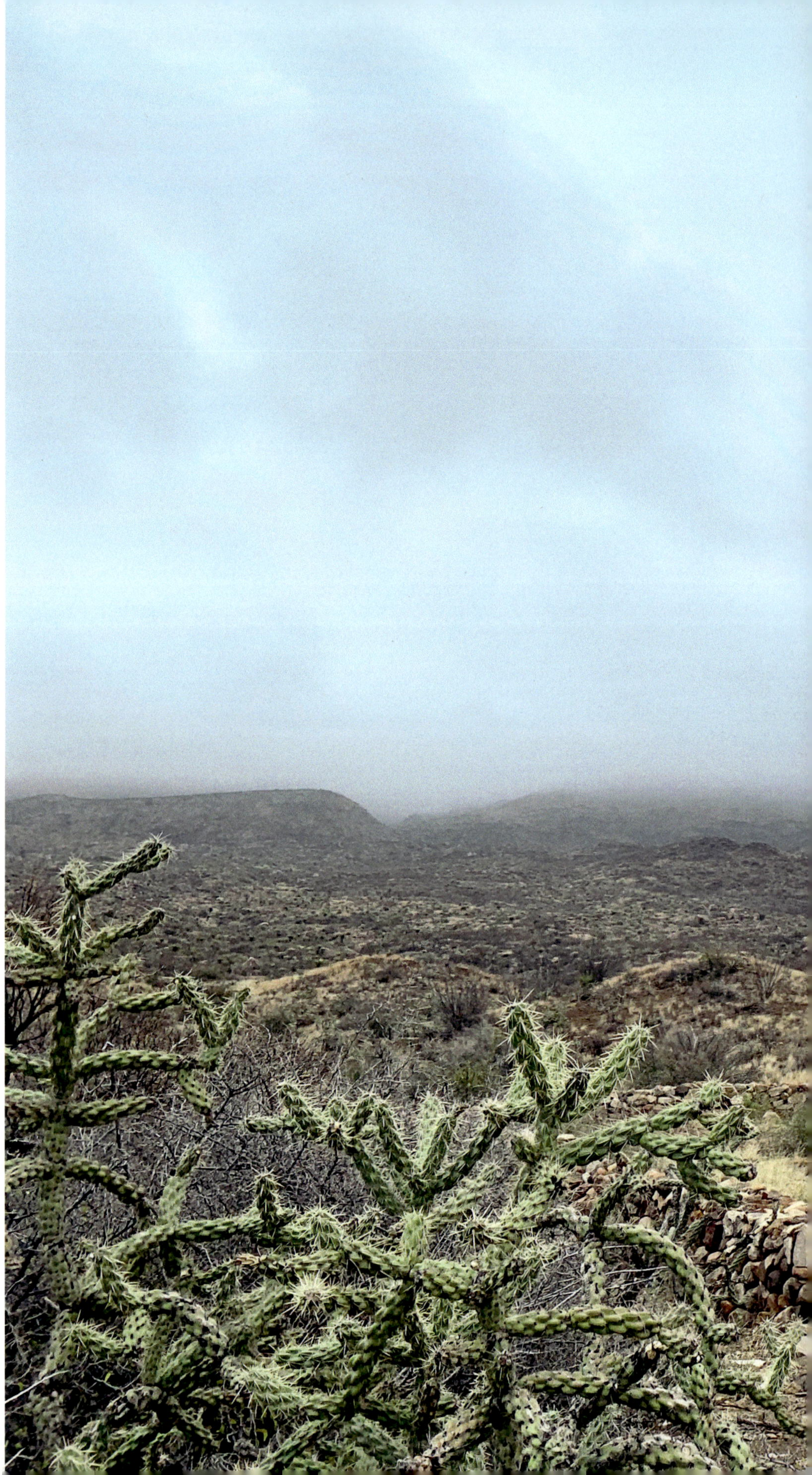

Casa Morales of Ayala de Chinati with stock tank and windmill and the Sierra Parda mountains in the clouds, view to southeast.

Casa Morales of Ayala de Chinati mit Tränke und Windrad und den Sierra Parda Bergen hinter den Wolken, Blick nach Südosten.

JUDD FOUNDATION

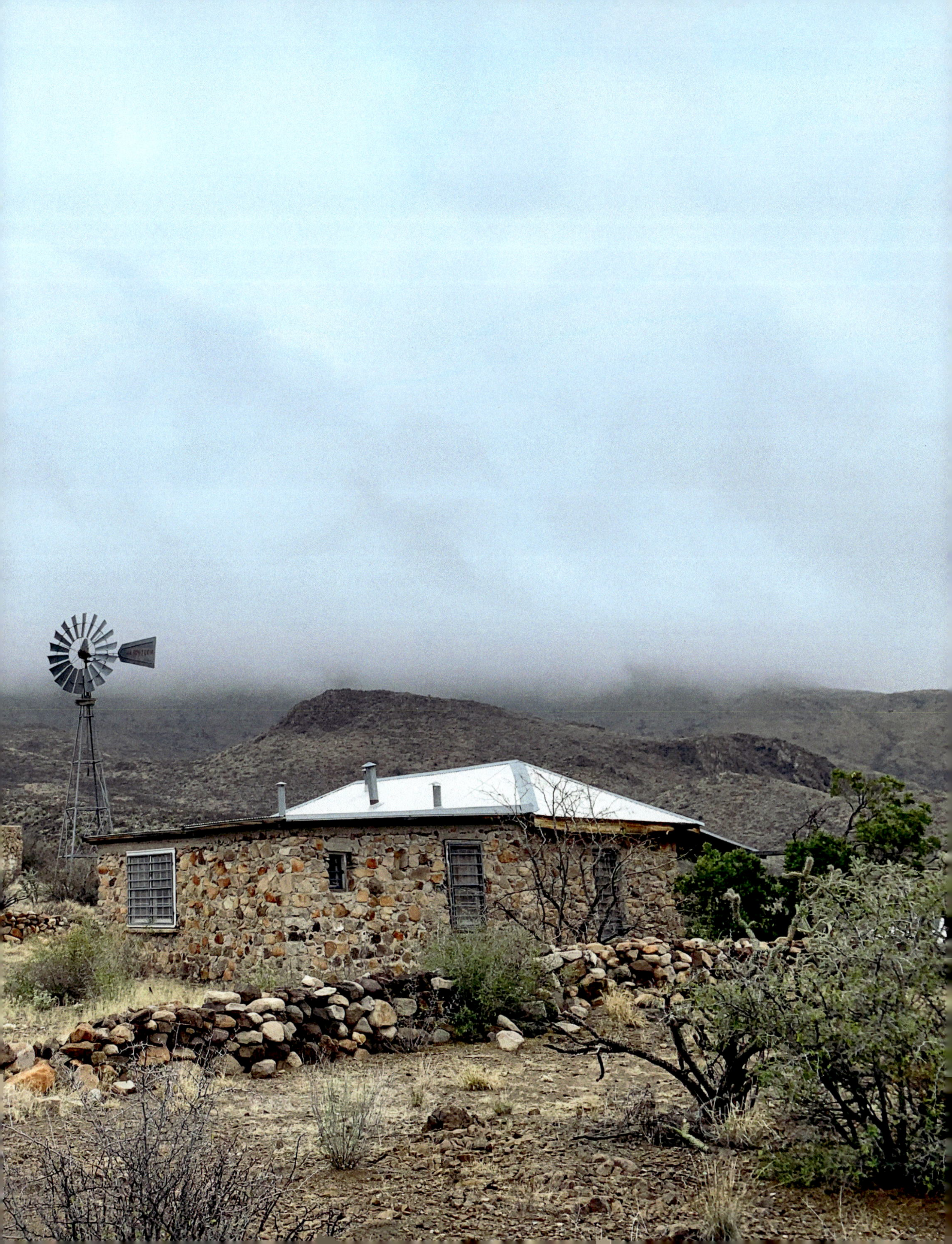

Casa Morales with dry-laid rock wall, view to north.

Casa Morales mit Trockenmauer, Blick nach Norden.

JUDD FOUNDATION

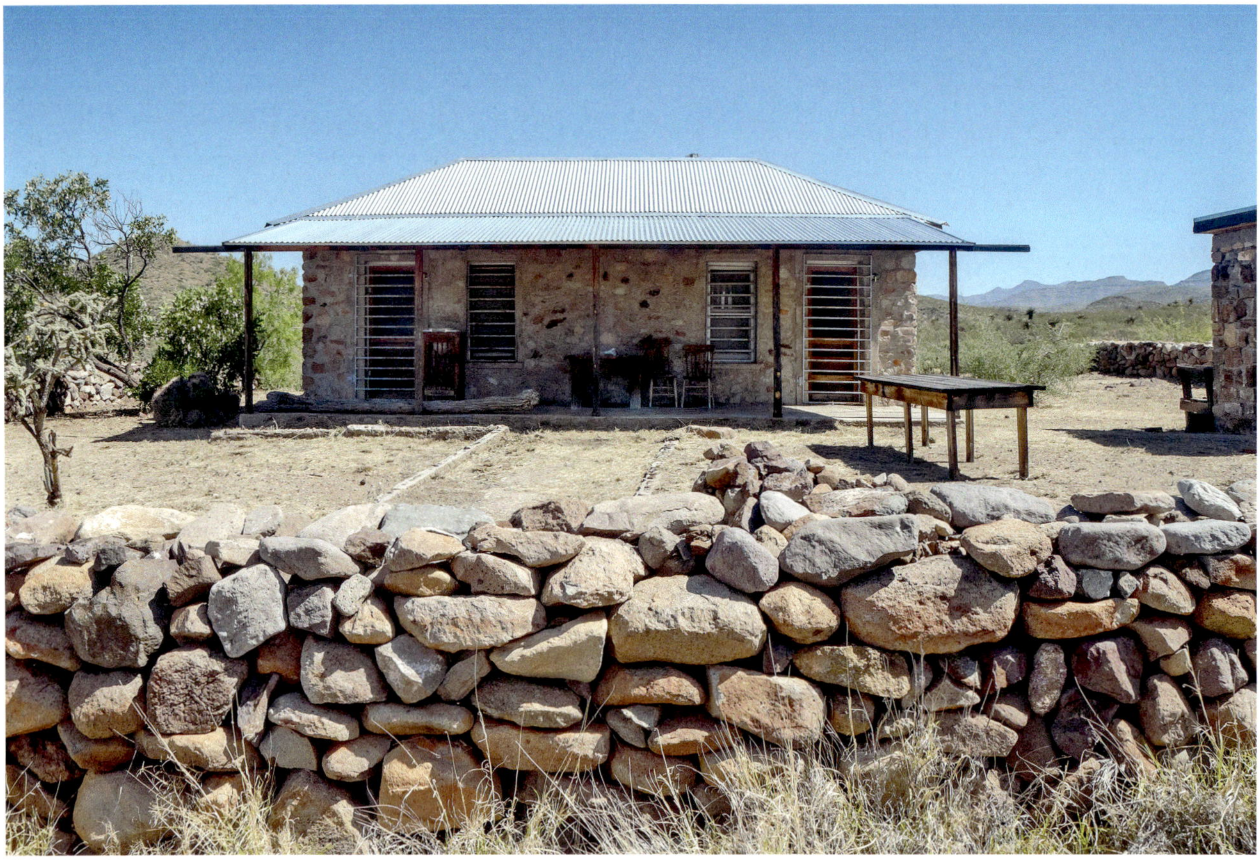

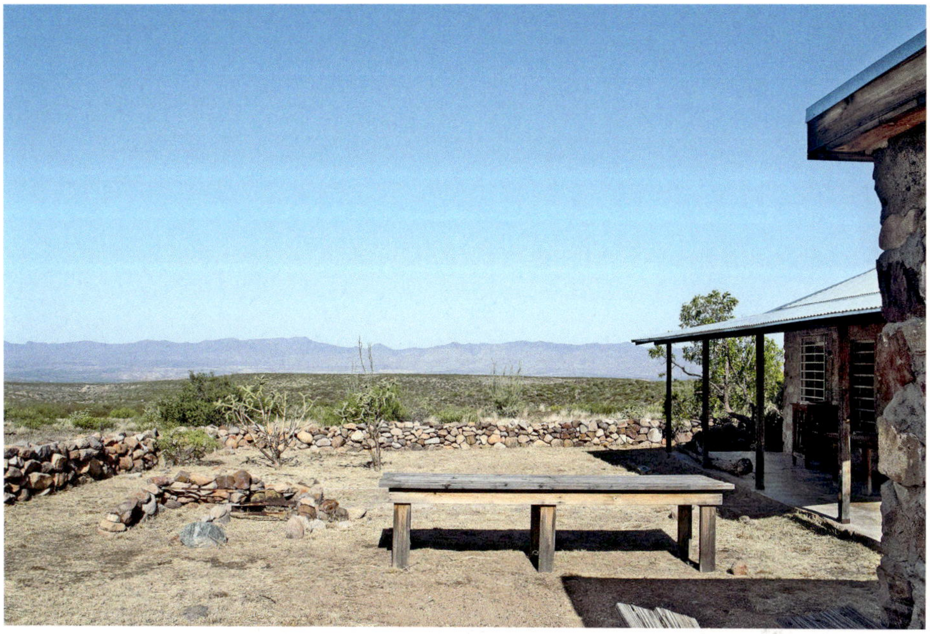

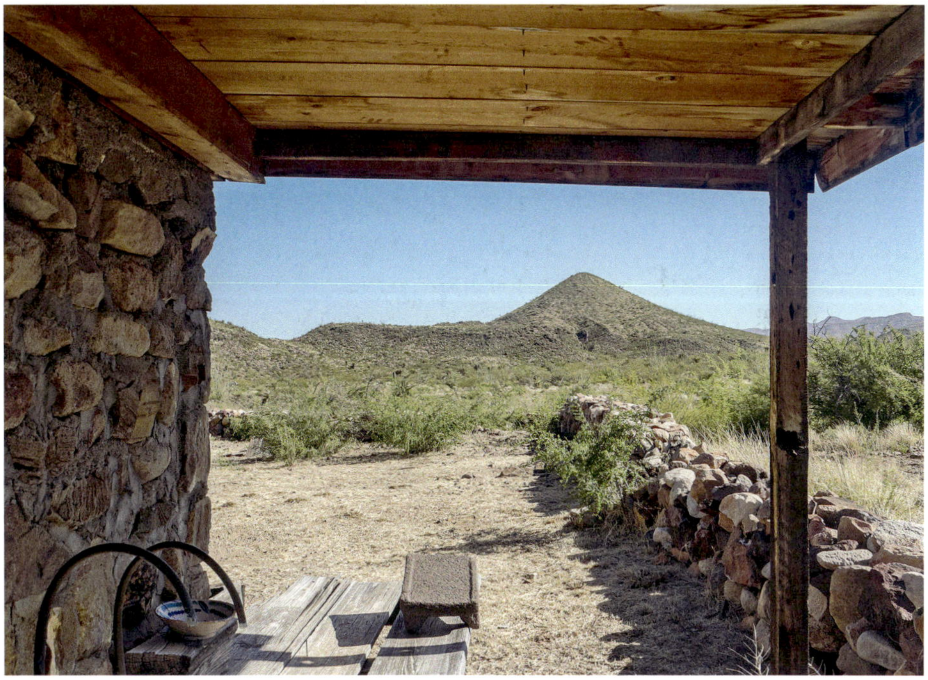

Casa Morales with porch, table, and barbecue pit by Donald Judd, view to west.

Casa Morales mit Veranda, Tisch und Grillstelle von Donald Judd, Blick nach Westen.

Casa Morales, tiendita with sink and counter by Donald Judd, view to north.

Casa Morales, Tiendita mit Waschbecken, Werkbank von Donald Judd, Blick nach Norden.

JUDD FOUNDATION

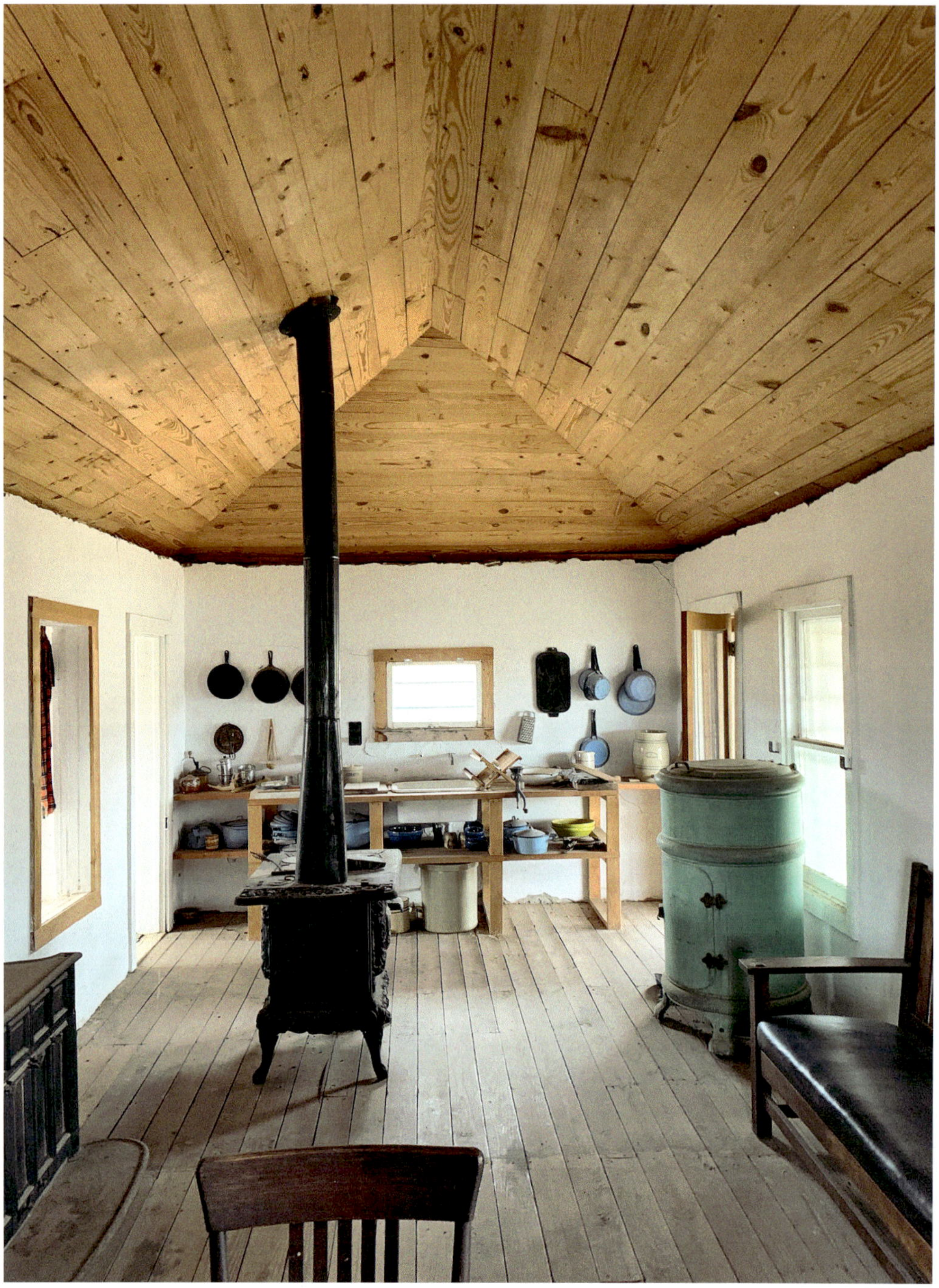

Casa Morales, main room, view to east. Notice the tartan strip in the window to the left.

Casa Morales, Hauptraum, Blick nach Osten. Man beachte die Schottenkarobänder im Fenster links.

JUDD FOUNDATION

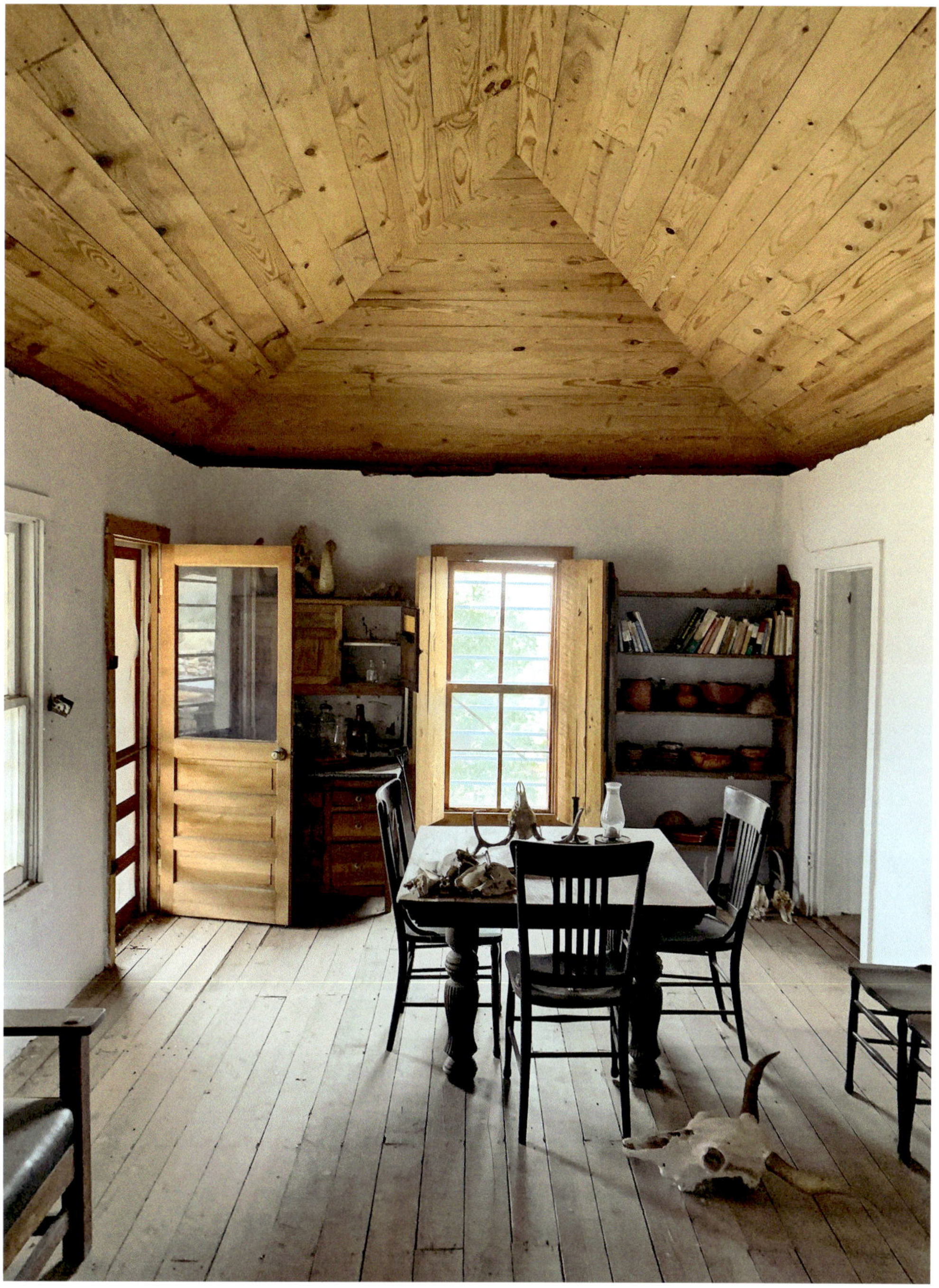

**Casa Morales,
main room, view to west.**

Casa Morales,
Hauptraum,
Blick nach Westen.

JUDD FOUNDATION

1 | 2

1 **Contour Lines, landscape around Casa Morales**
Höhenlinien, Landschaft um Casa Morales

2 **Site plan, Casa Morales**
Situationsplan, Casa Morales

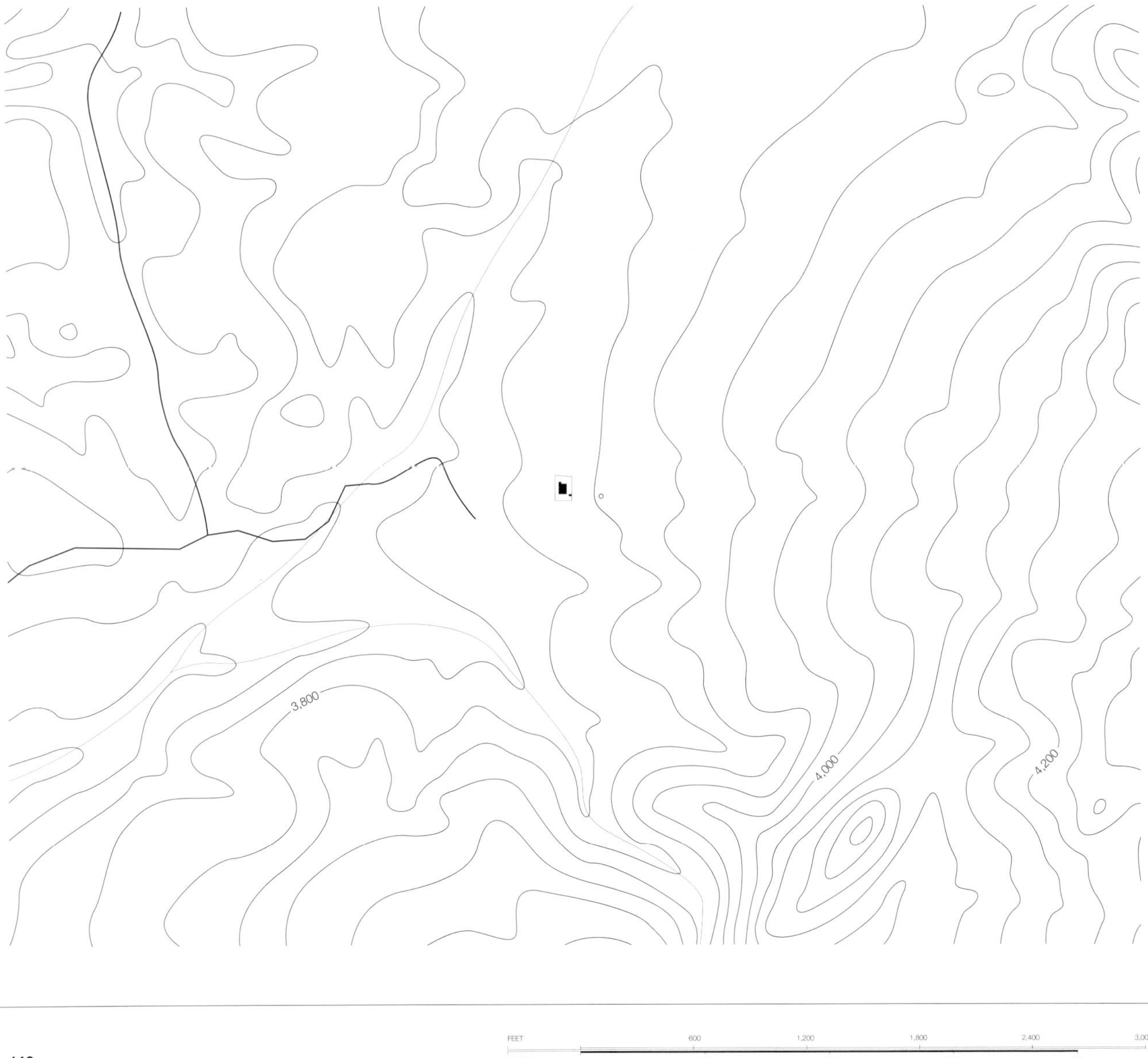

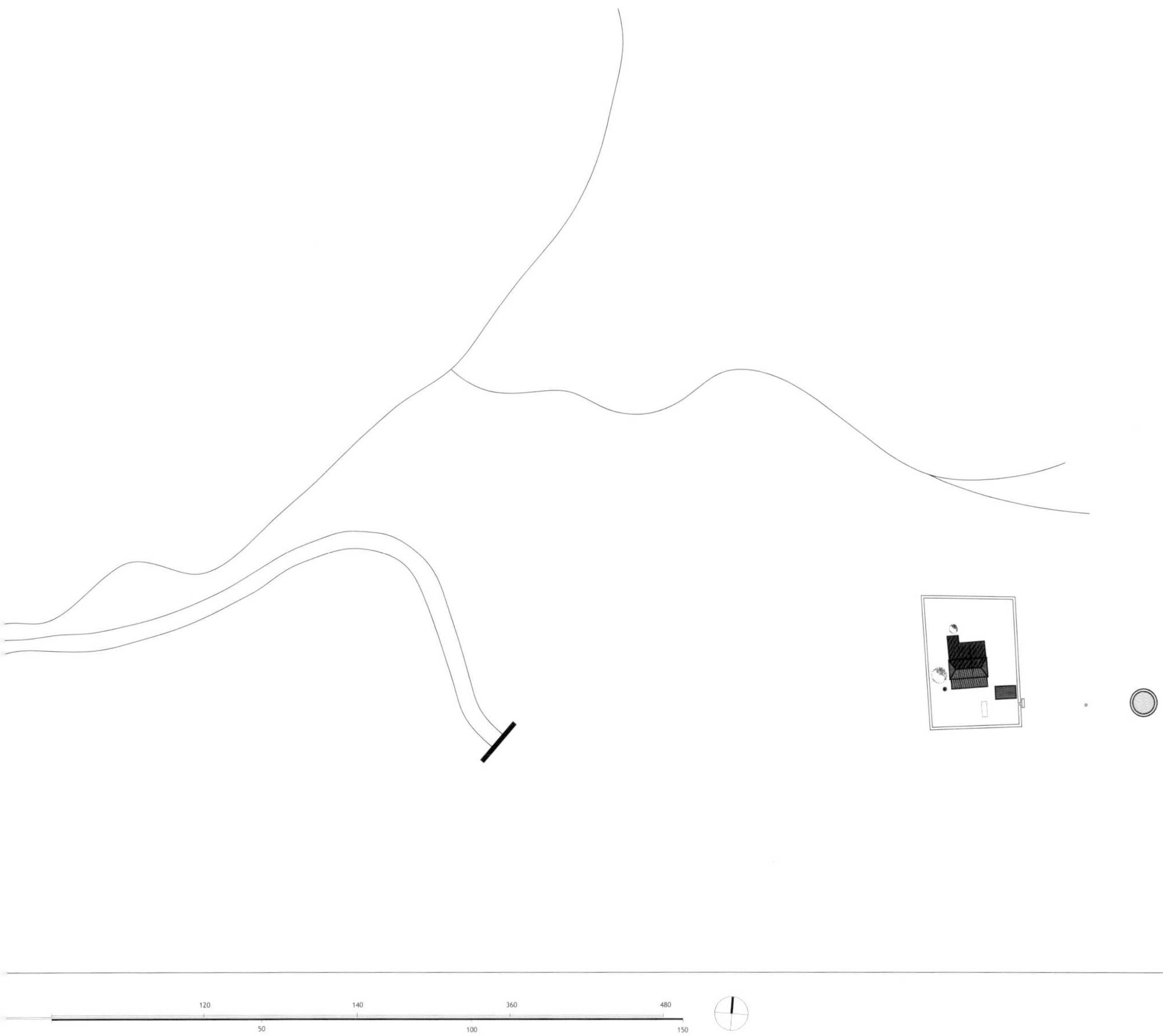
120
140
360
480
50
100
150

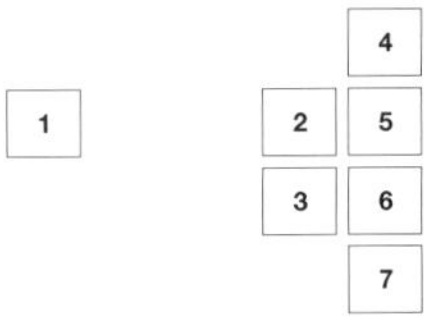

1 **Casa Morales, plan**
Casa Morales, Grundriss

2 **Casa Morales, section A-A**
Casa Morales, Schnitt A-A

3 **Casa Morales, section B-B**
Casa Morales, Schnitt B-B

4 **Casa Morales, south elevation**
Casa Morales, Südansicht

5 **Casa Morales, east elevation**
Casa Morales, Ostansicht

6 **Casa Morales, north elevation**
Casa Morales, Nordansicht

7 **Casa Morales, west elevation**
Casa Morales, Westansicht

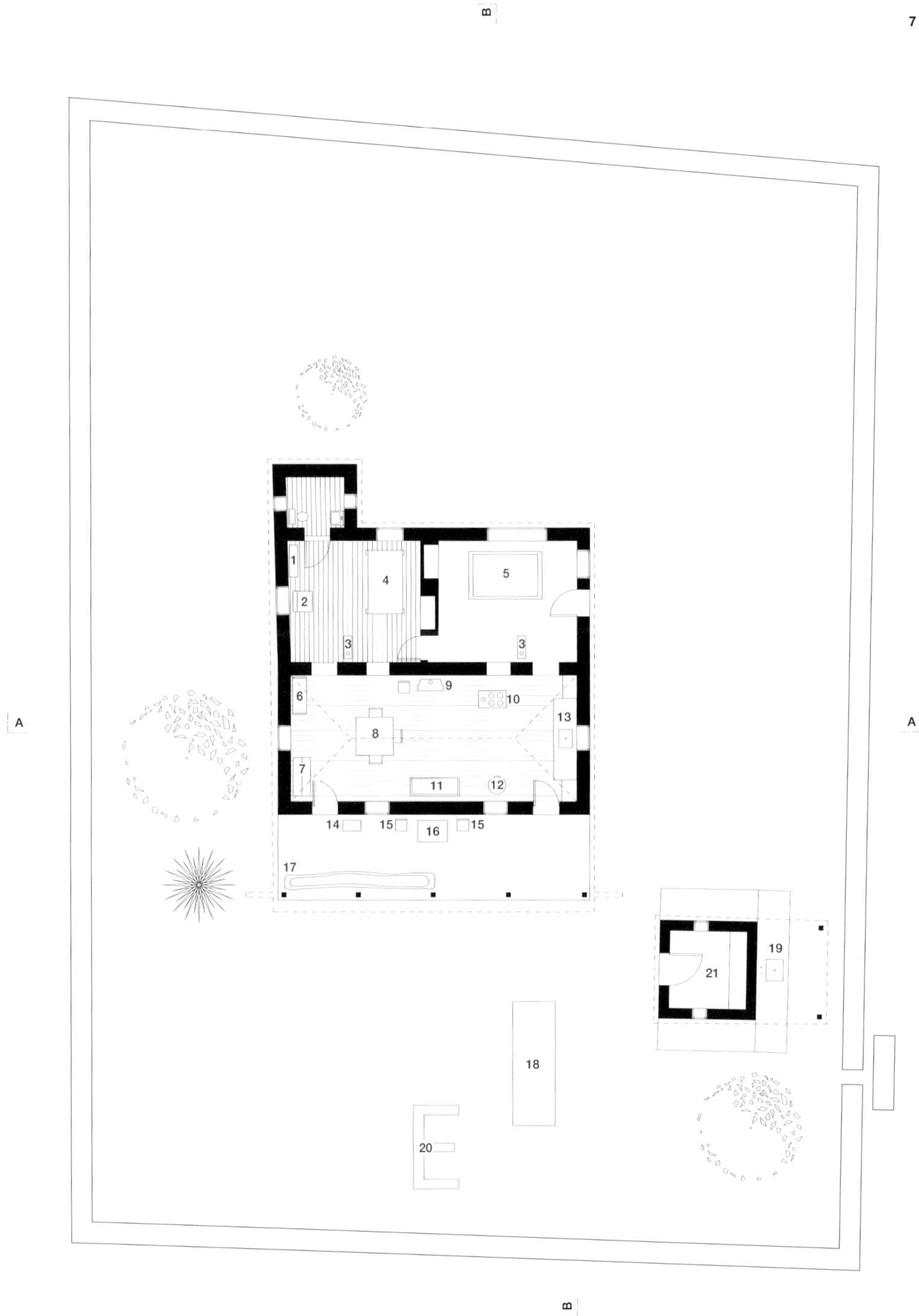

FEET 8 16 24 32 40
METERS 3 6 9 12

1.1 **Bookshelf**
Bücherregal

1.2 **Standing Desk**
Stehpult

1.3 **Wood Stove**
Holzofen

1.4 **Donald Judd, Bunk Bed**
Donald Judd, Stockbett

1.5 **Donald Judd, Bed**
Donald Judd, Bett

1.6 **Bookshelf**
Bücherregal

1.7 **Credenza**
Küchenbuffet

1.8 **Table and Chairs**
Tisch und Stühle

1.9 **Wood Stove**
Holzofen

1.10 **Kitchen Stove**
Küchenofen

1.11 **Gustav Stickley, Bench**
Gustav Stickley, Bank

1.12 **Antique Ice Box**
Historische Eistruhe

1.13 **Donald Judd, Kitchen Sink and Counter**
Donald Judd, Küchentheke und Spüle

1.14 **High Table**
Hoher Tisch

1.15 **Chair**
Stuhl

1.16 **Donald Judd, Table**
Donald Judd, Tisch

1.17 **Animal Food Trough**
Futtertrog

1.18 **Donald Judd, Table**
Donald Judd, Tisch

1.19 **Donald Judd, Outdoor Counter with Sink**
Donald Judd, Werkbank mit Waschbecken

1.20 **Fire Pit**
Feuerstelle

1.21 **Tiendita**
Tiendita

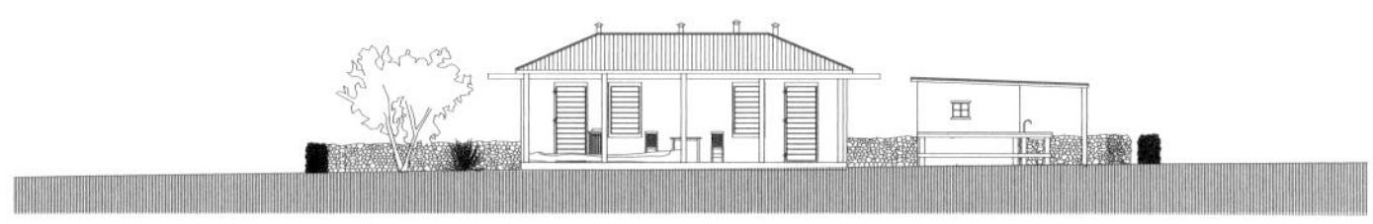

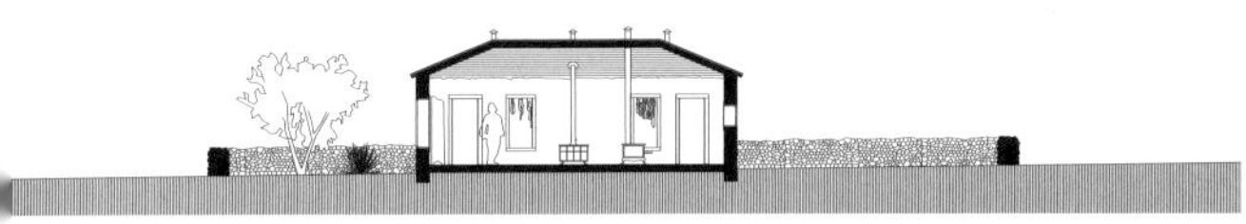

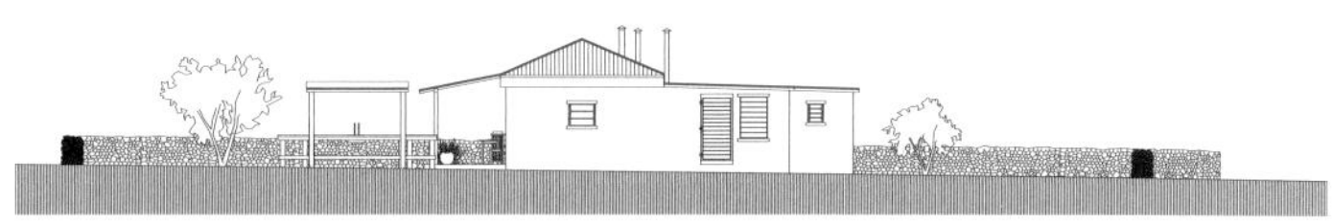

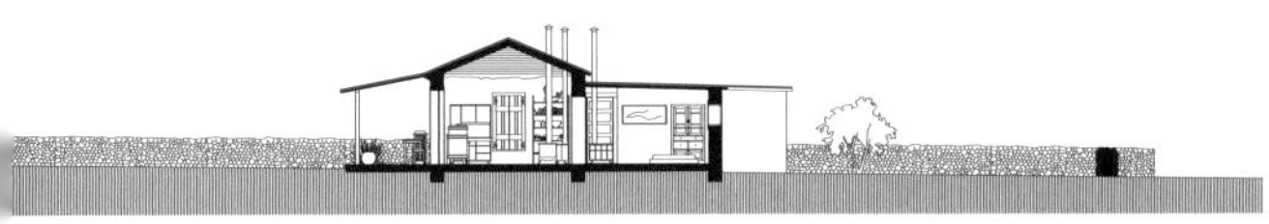

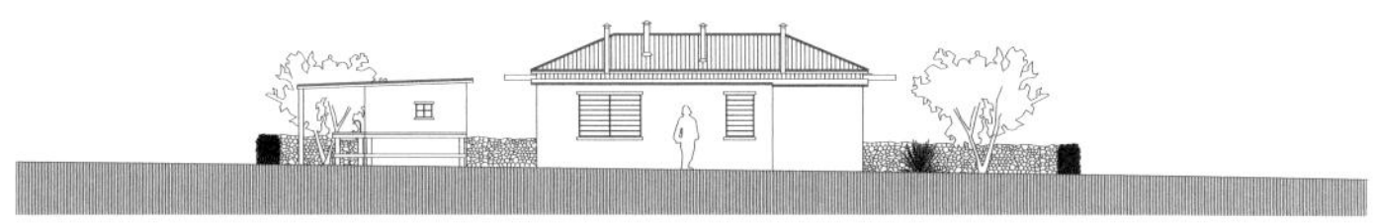

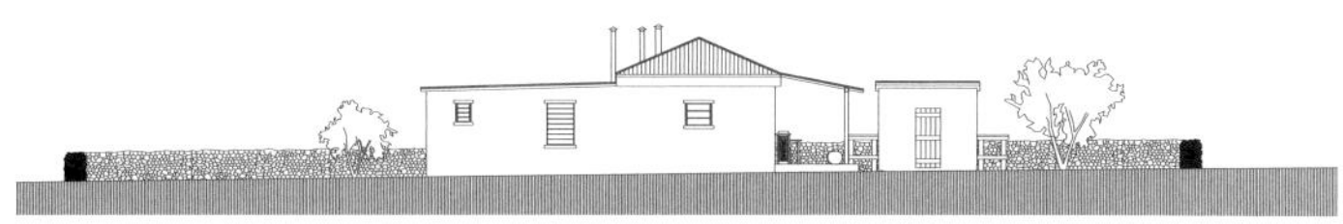

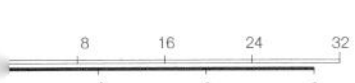

CASA PEREZ, AYALA DE CHINATI

Südlich des Pinto Creek und der Pinto Canyon Road auf einer erhöhten Ebene inmitten des Pinto Canyon befindet sich die Casa Perez. Sie ist das einzige der drei Ranchhäuser, das über elektrischen Strom verfügt, den es der Überlandleitung verdankt, die entlang der Pinto Canyon Road bis nach Ruidosa am Rio Grande verläuft und die Ferienanlage an den benachbarten Chinati-Thermalquellen versorgt. Die Sohle des Canyons ist dort, wo das Ranchhaus erbaut wurde, erstaunlich eben, spärlich mit Gras bewachsen und liegt etwa 6 Meter (20 ft) höher als die Pinto Canyon Road. Gegenwärtig besteht die Casa Perez aus dem in den 1940er-Jahren erbauten Haupthaus mit vier rechteckigen, etwa gleich großen Räumen und einer nach Westen ausgerichteten Veranda. Bedenkt man die eher ungewöhnliche Form des Daches und die Öffnung in der Westwand der Küche, die einst vermutlich als Fenster diente, ist zu vermuten, dass der Gebäudegrundriss anfangs eine L-Form aufwies.

Nordöstlich des Ranchhauses befinden sich ein voll funktionstüchtiger runder Wassertank und ein Windrad, an dem Judd drei hölzerne Plattformen in unterschiedlichen Höhen anbringen ließ, die Zugang zum Tank gewähren. Die nordwestliche Grundstücksgrenze markierte Judd mit einer selbst entworfenen Holzbank, die in seinem Möbelverzeichnis mit der Nummer 26 vermerkt ist. Dieses Möbelstück ist ein Ensemble aus Tisch und Bank, das zum Sitzen, Schreiben und Nachdenken einlädt. Östlich dieser Bank steht eine eckige Betontränke aus den Tagen der Viehwirtschaft, und die niedrige Trockenmauer gen Süden orientiert sich in Abmessung und Ausrichtung an den Pergolen, die den Garten schützen. Die mit Eisenstangen eingezäunten Koppeln im Nordosten sind Überbleibsel der kurzzeitigen viehwirtschaftlichen Nutzung des Pinto Canyon. Im Gegensatz zur Casa Morales konnten die Farmer in diesem Teil des Canyons durchaus ihren Lebensunterhalt mit der Aufzucht von Rindern und Pferden bestreiten.

Casa Perez is situated south of Pinto Creek and Pinto Canyon Road on an elevated natural terrace in the center of Pinto Canyon. Of the three ranch houses, Perez is the only one with electricity, which is fed by the powerline that follows Pinto Canyon road and serves the nearby Chinati Hot Springs, ending in Ruidosa on the Rio Grande. The canyon floor on which the ranch house is situated rises about 20 feet from Pinto Canyon Road and is surprisingly level and sparsely covered with grass. Today Casa Perez is comprised of the main ranch house made of adobe from the 1940s with four rectangular rooms of similar dimensions and a west-facing porch. Based on the rather unusual shape of the roof and the opening in the west wall of the kitchen which perhaps served as a window originally, the ranch house at first might have started out with an L-shaped floor plan.

To the northeast of the ranch house is a fully operational circular stock tank and a windmill where Judd added three wooden platforms of various heights, allowing access to the stock tank. To the northwest, Judd marked the edge of the property with a Judd-designed wooden bench, labeled in the Judd furniture index as number 26. This furniture piece is a combination of bench and table where one could sit, write, and think. To the east of the bench rests a box-shaped concrete stock tank from the ranching days and to the south of the bench is a low dry rock wall following the same outer proportions and orientation as the nearby pergolas protecting a garden. To the northeast a series of iron pipe fenced corrals are the remnants of the short-lived ranch life in Pinto Canyon. Unlike at Casa Morales, in this part of the canyon ranchers were able to make a living by raising larger animals such as livestock and horses.

Judd's interventions at the main house are subtle but remarkable. He emptied the four rooms and designed a west-facing kitchen counter incorporating an electric stove, range and sink with open shelves beneath. The dining area contains wood-

Judds Eingriffe am Haupthaus sind trotz ihrer Subtilität erstaunlich. Er räumte alle vier Zimmer komplett leer und entwarf eine nach Westen ausgerichtete Küchentheke mit integriertem Elektroherd, Backofen und Spüle sowie mit offenen Regalen darunter. Die Holzmöbel im Essbereich stammen vermutlich aus Schweden, und eines seiner Kunstwerke aus Aluminium und roten Acrylplatten aus dem Jahr 1985 schmückt die Wand. Im Schlafzimmer, das in Richtung Nordosten von der Küche abgeht, befindet sich ein von Judd entworfenes Bett mit einer an den Bettrahmen montierten Leselampe, und in der Ecke steht ein Stuhl. Über dem nach Osten weisenden Fenster hängt ein mehrfarbiges Werk von Judd aus dem Jahr 1987 und an der Westwand eine Radierung von Francisco de Goya mit dem Titel *Mala Noche* aus dem Zyklus *Los Caprichos*. Die Ausstattung des nordwestlichen Schlafzimmers umfasst ein von Judd entworfenes Doppelbett, einen mexikanischen Kleiderschrank, einen Ofen und ein kleines Holzregal mit Büchern über Kunst, Architektur und Natur, das ebenfalls aus einem seiner Entwürfe entstanden war. In allen Räumen außer der Küche wurden die ursprünglichen Holzdecken und Betonböden beibehalten. In der Küche sind die Decke sowie alle Innenwände mit Gipsplatten verkleidet und in mattem Weiß gestrichen. Die anderen Decken und sämtliche Böden erhielten einen Anstrich in Battleship Grey. Alle vier Innenräume strahlen eine besondere Eleganz aus. Durch ihre Deckenhöhe von 3 Metern (9 ft 7 in), dank der es in den heißen Sommern nahe der mexikanischen Grenze im Gebäudeinneren angenehm kühl bleibt, wirken sie größer, als sie tatsächlich sind. Diese lichte Höhe ist für ein so abgelegenes Haus eine Besonderheit; die Räume in den anderen Farmhäusern, Morales und Las Casas, sind mit nur rund 2,10 Metern deutlich niedriger.

Ähnlich wie beim Block in Marfa plante Judd östlich der Casa Perez einen separaten Bau mit Verschattung, in dem Bad und Lager untergebracht sind. Jedoch wählte er hier als Baumaterial Holz statt Lehmziegeln. Die Konstruktion selbst ist eine Abwandlung des Ensembles aus Pergola, Tisch und Bank, das er neben dem Schwimmbecken am Block errichtet hatte. Die Bodenplatte des Badezimmers der Casa Perez besteht aus gegossenem Ortbeton, aus dem Judd eine einfache rechteckige Mulde ausgespart hat – seine Interpretation einer Badewanne. In

en furniture, possibly from Sweden, and an aluminum with red acrylic sheet Judd wall piece from 1985. The bedroom to the northeast of the kitchen contains a Judd-designed bed, a task lamp mounted on the frame of the bed, and a domestic chair in the corner. A multicolor Judd piece from 1987 is placed above the window facing east and a Francisco Goya etching titled *Mala Noche* from *Los Caprichos* is placed on the west wall. The northwest bedroom is furnished with a Judd-designed double bed, a Mexican armoire, a stove, and a small wooden Judd-designed bookshelf containing art, architecture, and nature related book titles. Except for the kitchen, all rooms have their original wooden ceilings and concrete floors. The kitchen ceiling is made of gypsum board painted in flat white, as are all the interior adobe walls. The other ceilings and all floors are painted in battleship grey. All four interior spaces radiate a certain grandeur. The rooms appear larger than they are because the ceiling height is 9 feet 7 inches, which helped keep the rooms cooler during the hot summers on the Mexico border. This is noteworthy for a house in such a remote location; at the other ranch houses, Morales and Las Casas, the original ceiling heights are much lower at around 7 feet.

Similarly, as at the Block in Marfa, Judd designed a detached bathroom and storage structure with shade east of Casa Perez. This time the material of the bathroom and storage room is not adobe but rather wood. The structure is a variation of the pergola, table and bench combination Judd built at the Block next to the swimming pool. At Casa Perez, the bathroom floor is a poured-in-place concrete slab from which Judd carved out a simple void in the shape of a rectangular box—his interpretation of a bathtub. A commode is in one corner, and a concrete sink is resting on a wooden Judd-designed shelf in another corner of the space. Several small wooden containers, typically found in farmsteads of the Swiss Alps and utilized as milk containers for various purposes, are used here as water containers for showering and grooming.

Two additional pinewood seating and shading structures, slightly different from each other, stretch along the western side of the terrace, offering opportunities for gatherings. To the north is a small garden surrounded by a low dry-laid rock wall about

der einen Ecke steht eine Kommode, und in einer anderen Ecke ruht ein Betonwaschbecken auf einem von Judd selbst entworfenen Holzregal. Diverse kleine Holzbehälter, wie sie häufig auf den Almen in den Schweizer Bergen zu finden sind, wo sie als Milchkannen dienen, werden hier als Wasserbehälter zum Duschen und für die Körperpflege genutzt.

Zwei weitere Sitzgelegenheiten mit Schatten spendenden Konstruktionen, die sich nur leicht voneinander unterscheiden, sind an der Westseite der Veranda angegliedert und laden zum Beisammensein ein. Gen Norden befindet sich ein kleiner Garten mit einer 0,80 Meter hohen Trockenmauer als Einfassung, die der an der Casa Morales ähnelt. Da der Garten unterhalb der Viehtränke liegt, kommt ihm das von dort überlaufende Wasser zugute.

Wie schon bei den anderen Gebäuden, die Judd in Marfa besaß, wurden viele seiner skizzierten architektonischen Ideen nie umgesetzt. Für die Casa Perez hatte er ein 6 Meter langes und 5 Meter (19,69 × 16,4 ft) breites Studio mit von Süden nach Norden geneigtem Pultdach entworfen. Die Südwand sollte 4 Meter (13,12 ft) und die Nordwand 3 Meter (9,84 ft) hoch sein. Dieses Studio wäre über fünf jeweils nur 25 Zentimeter schmale Fenster, die sich an der Nordwand vom Boden bis zur Decke erstrecken sollten, mit natürlichem Licht erhellt worden. Der Eingang war über zwei je 1 Meter (3,28 ft) breite Türen von Süden geplant.[1]

Da sich die Casa Perez etwa auf Höhe der Talsohle befindet, wirkt das Land hier anders auf den Besucher als bei der Casa Morales oder Las Casas – der Blick auf die umgebenden Berge im Nordwesten und Südosten vermittelt ein Gefühl der Intimität. Jedes Jahr, meistens im Herbst, veranstaltet die Judd Foundation ein öffentliches Event in der Casa Perez, einen Ranchtag. Obwohl diese Ranch in jeder Hinsicht als abgelegen bezeichnet werden kann, ist sie doch für Besucher am einfachsten zu erreichen und bietet den Gästen einen kleinen Einblick in Judds Leben im Pinto Canyon. Darüber hinaus kann man sich hier ein Bild davon machen, wie das Leben der ehemaligen Rancherfamilien Prieto und Perez ausgesehen haben muss.

1 *Donald Judd. Architektur,* Marianne Stockebrand, Herausgeberin, Dritte Ausgabe, (Ostfildern bei Stuttgart, Cantz, 1992), S. 59.

two and a half feet high, similar to the dry-laid rock wall at Casa Morales. A garden is downslope from the stock tank that benefits from the water run-off.

As with the other ranch houses and the buildings Judd owned in Marfa, many of Judd's sketched architectural ideas never became built form. At Casa Perez, Judd made drawings for a 6 meter by 5 meter rectangular studio (19.69 feet by 16.4 feet) with a 'shed' roof sloping south to north. The south wall ceiling height was to be 4 meters (13.12 feet) and the north wall ceiling height was shown to be 3 meters (9.84 feet). The studio would have been naturally illuminated from the north with five narrow windows 0.25 meters wide (9.84 inches) stretching from floor to ceiling. The studio would have been accessed from the south by two doors, each 1 meter (3.28 feet) wide.[1]

Because Casa Perez is located near the bottom of the valley, it makes the experience of the land different than at Casa Morales or at Las Casas—more intimate because of the vistas to the mountains surrounding the valley to the northwest and southeast. Judd Foundation holds an annual public event at Casa Perez, typically in the fall; a ranch day. Although remote by any standards, Casa Perez is the ranch most easily accessible to the public and offers the visitor a glimpse of what Judd's life in Pinto Canyon was like. In addition, guests can also imagine of what the homesteaders' the Prieto and Perez families' lives, must have been during the ranching years.

1 *Donald Judd. Architektur,* Stockebrand, Marianne, Editor. 3rd ed. (Ostfildern near Stuttgart, Cantz, 1992), p. 59.

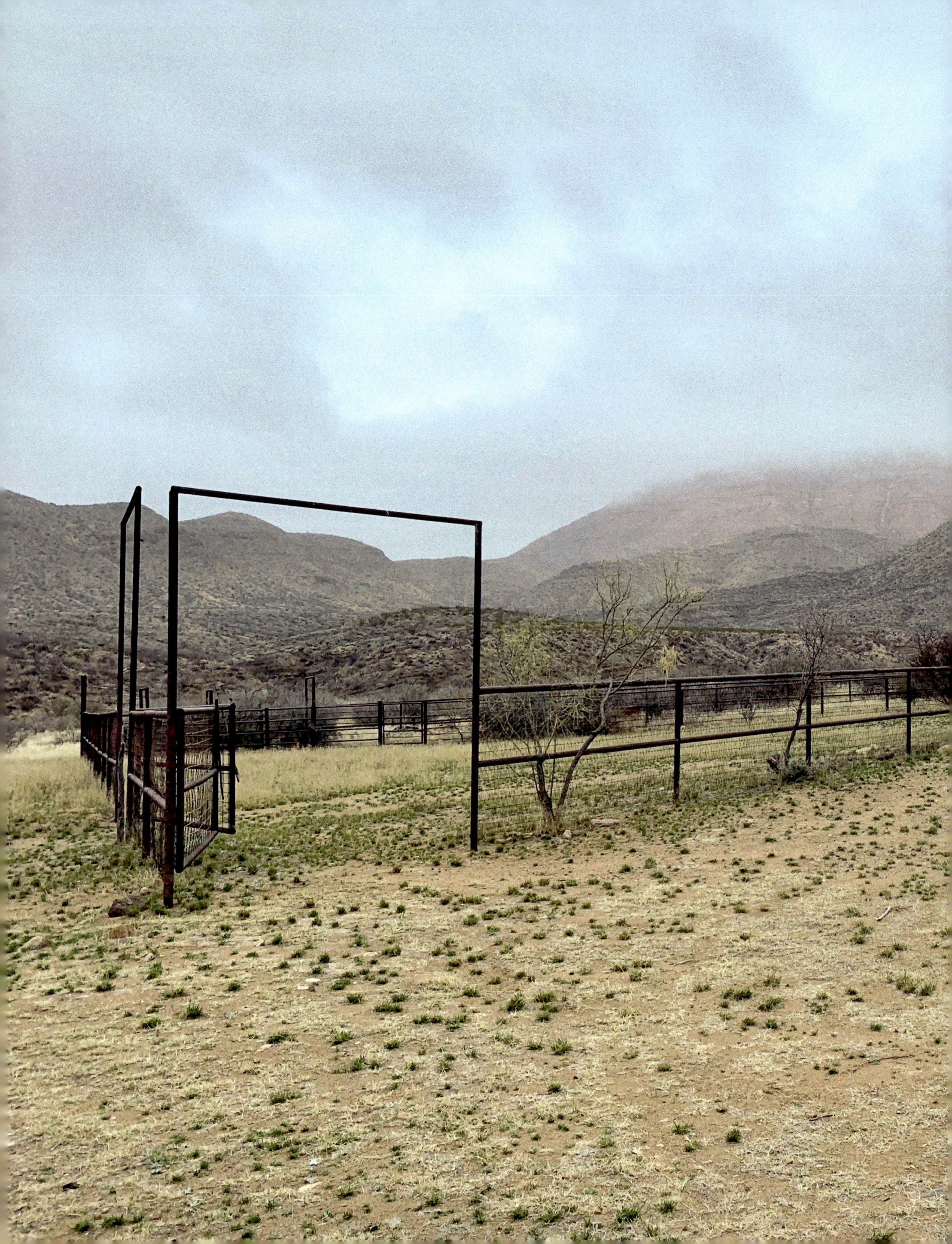

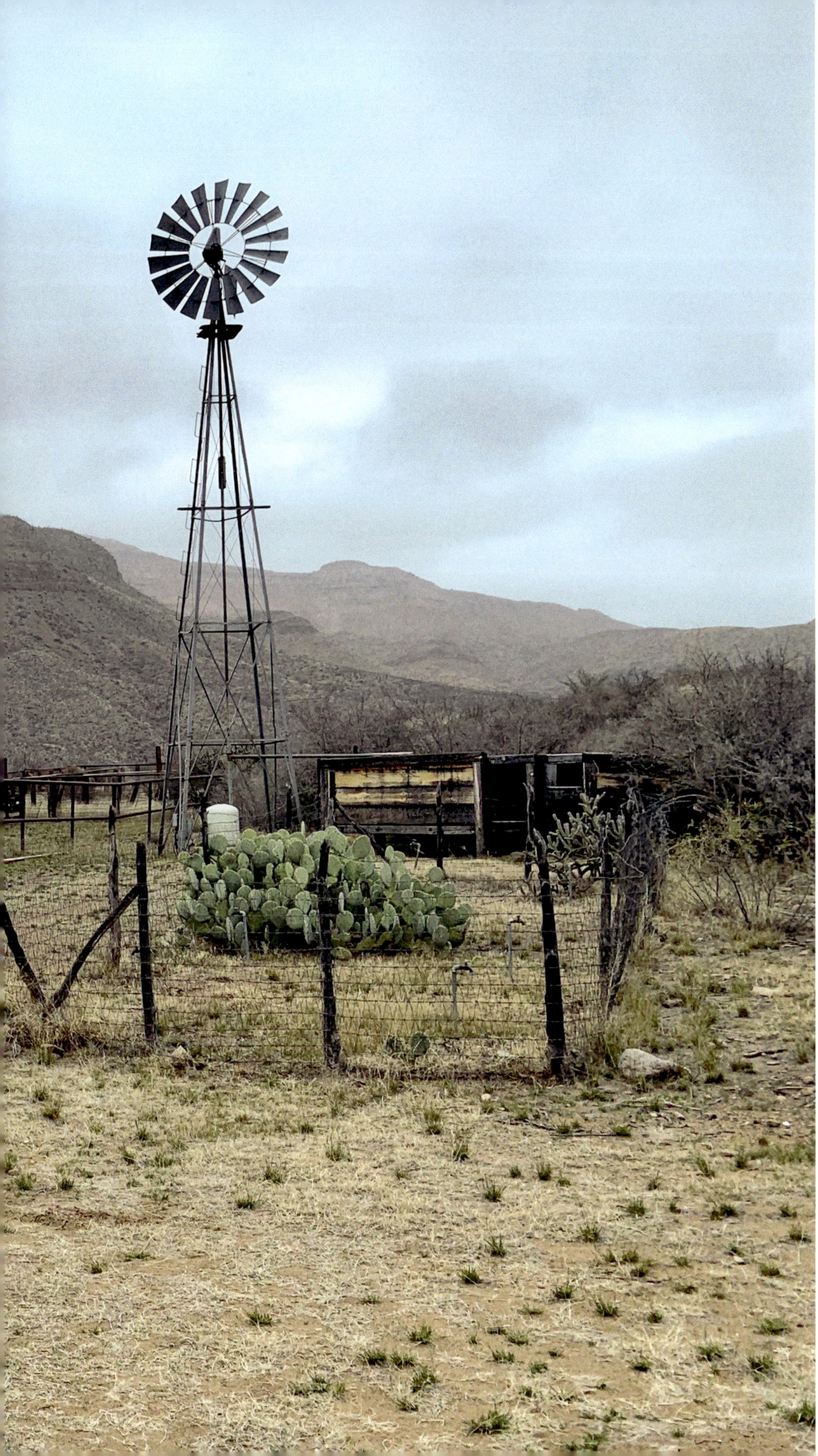

Casa Perez, Ayala de Chinati, corrales, windmill, and stock tank with wooden platforms by Donald Judd, view to northeast.

Casa Perez, Ayala de Chinati, Koppel, Windrad und Wassertanks mit Holzpodesten von Donald Judd, Blick nach Nordosten.

JUDD FOUNDATION

Casa Perez, Ayala de Chinati, view to northeast.

Casa Perez, Ayala de Chinati, Blick nach Nordosten.

JUDD FOUNDATION

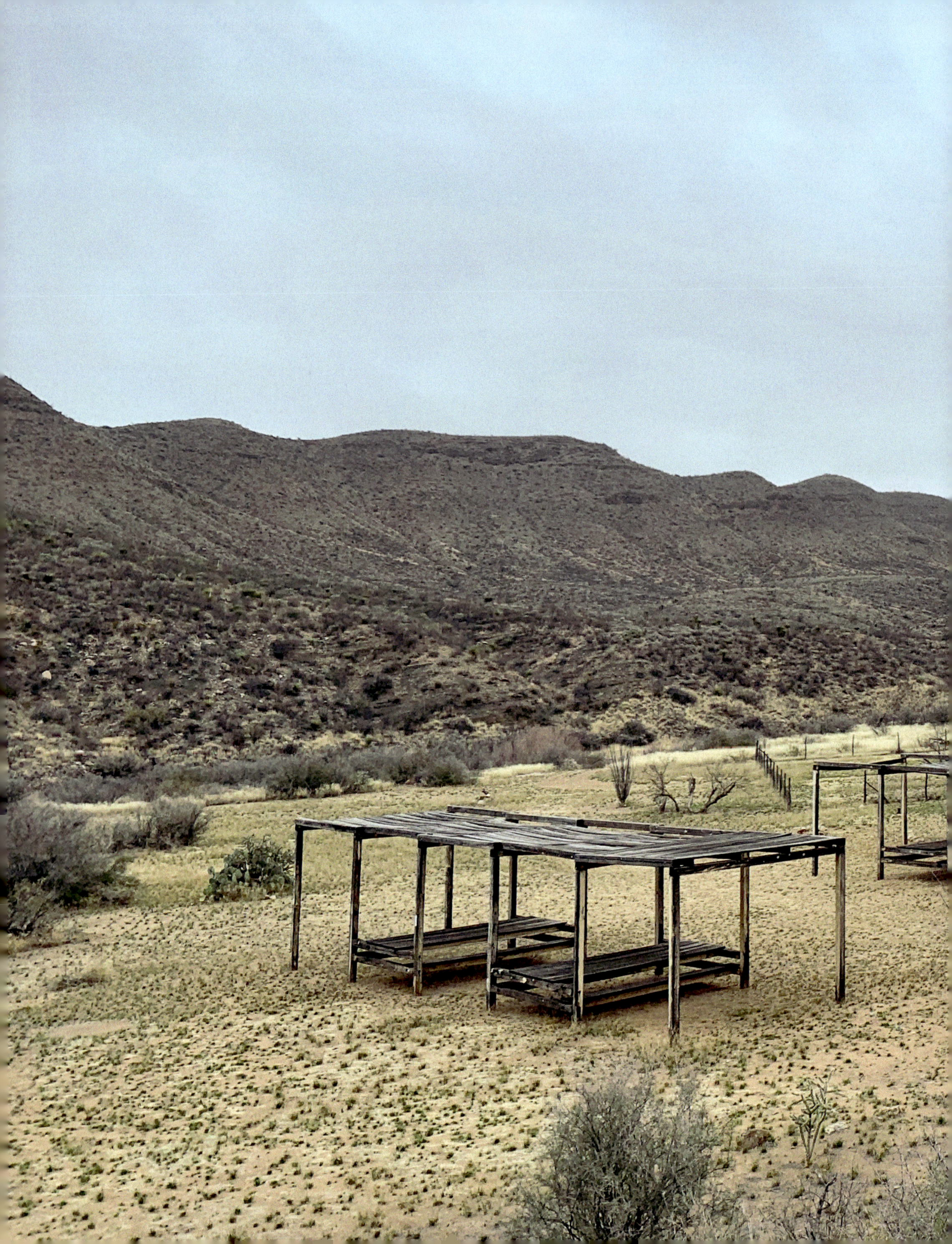

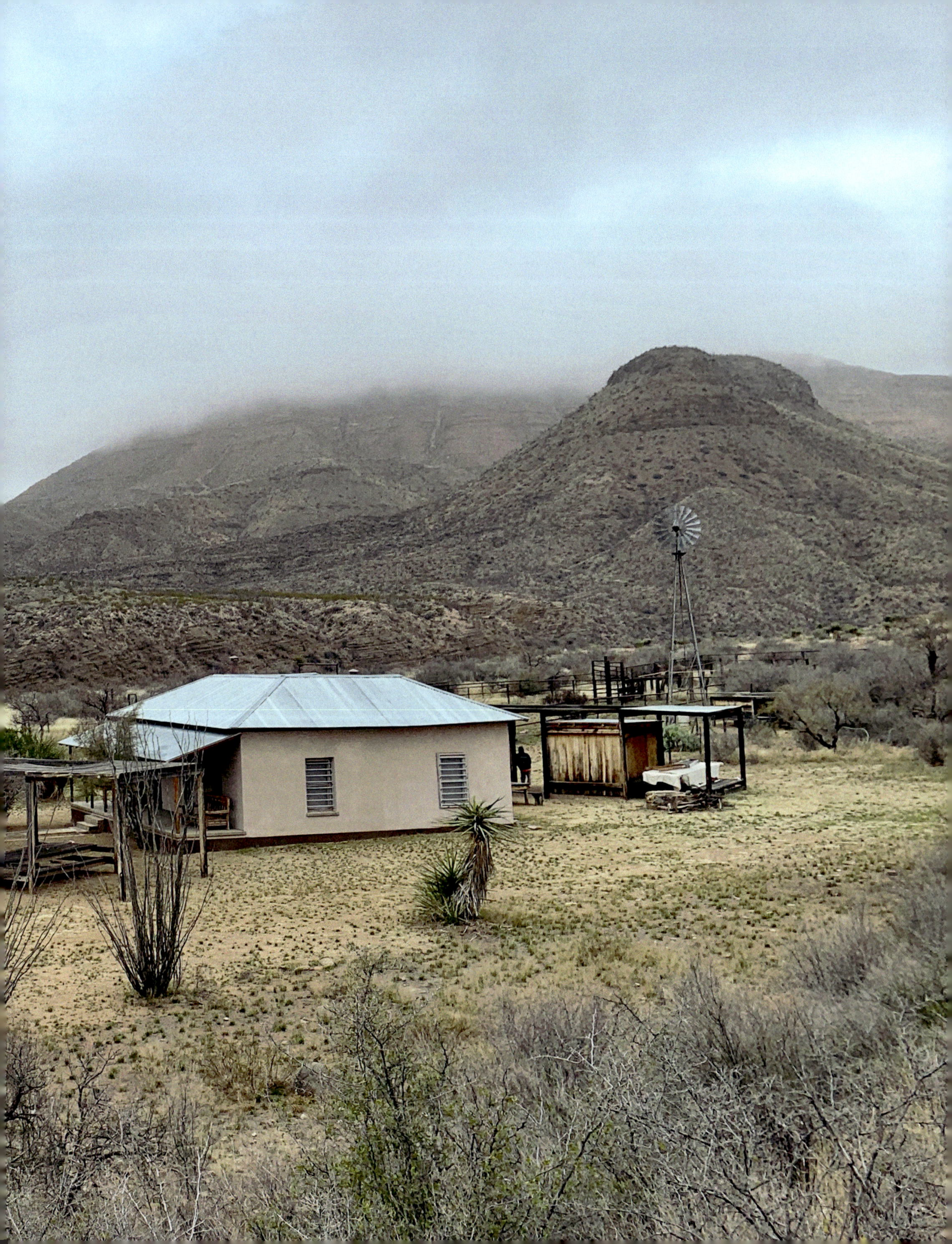

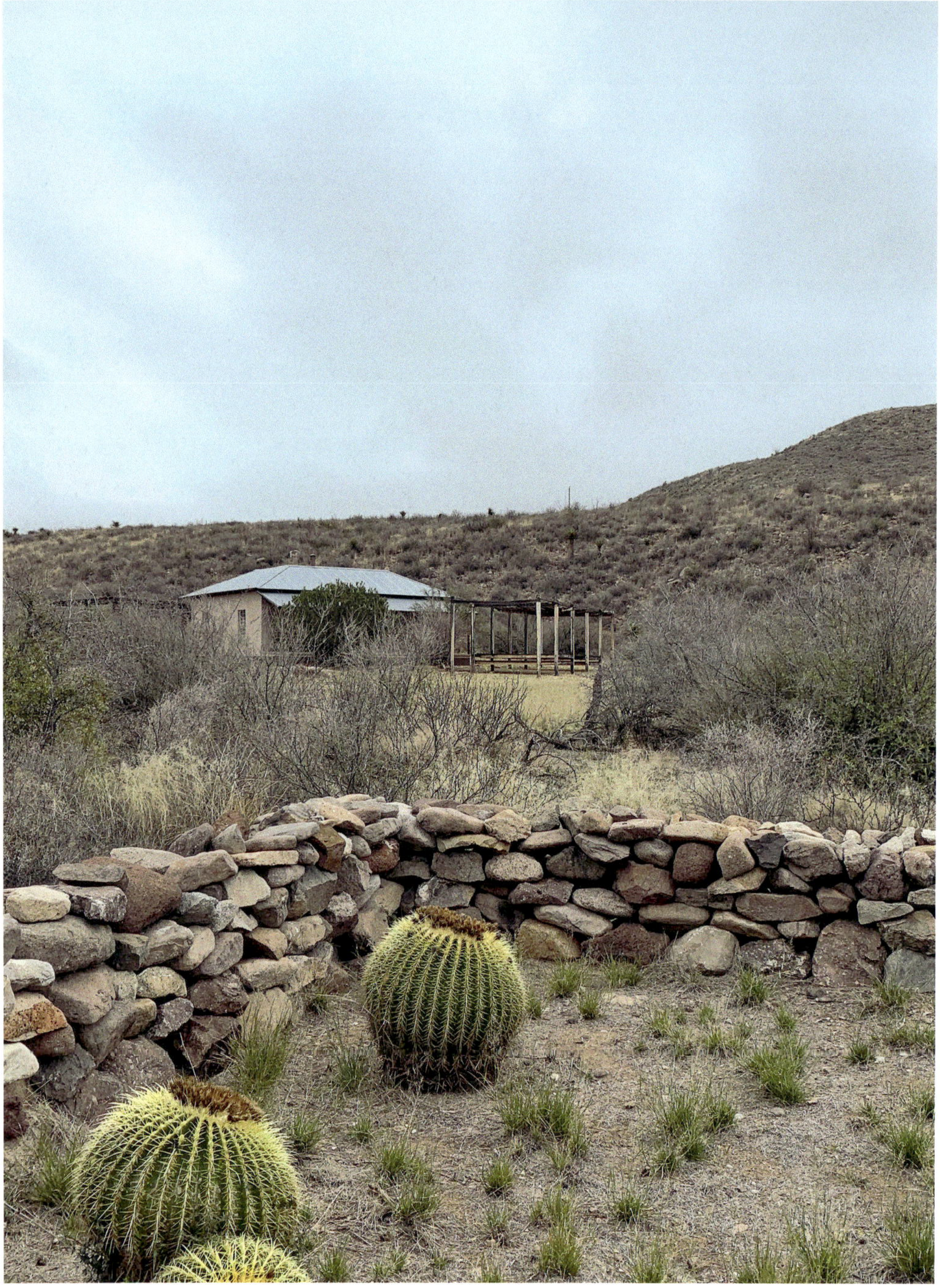

Casa Perez, with garden, view to southeast.

Casa Perez, mit Garten, Blick nach Südosten.

JUDD FOUNDATION

Casa Perez, with bench by Donald Judd, view to northwest.

Casa Perez, mit Bank von Donald Judd, Blick nach Nordwesten.

JUDD FOUNDATION

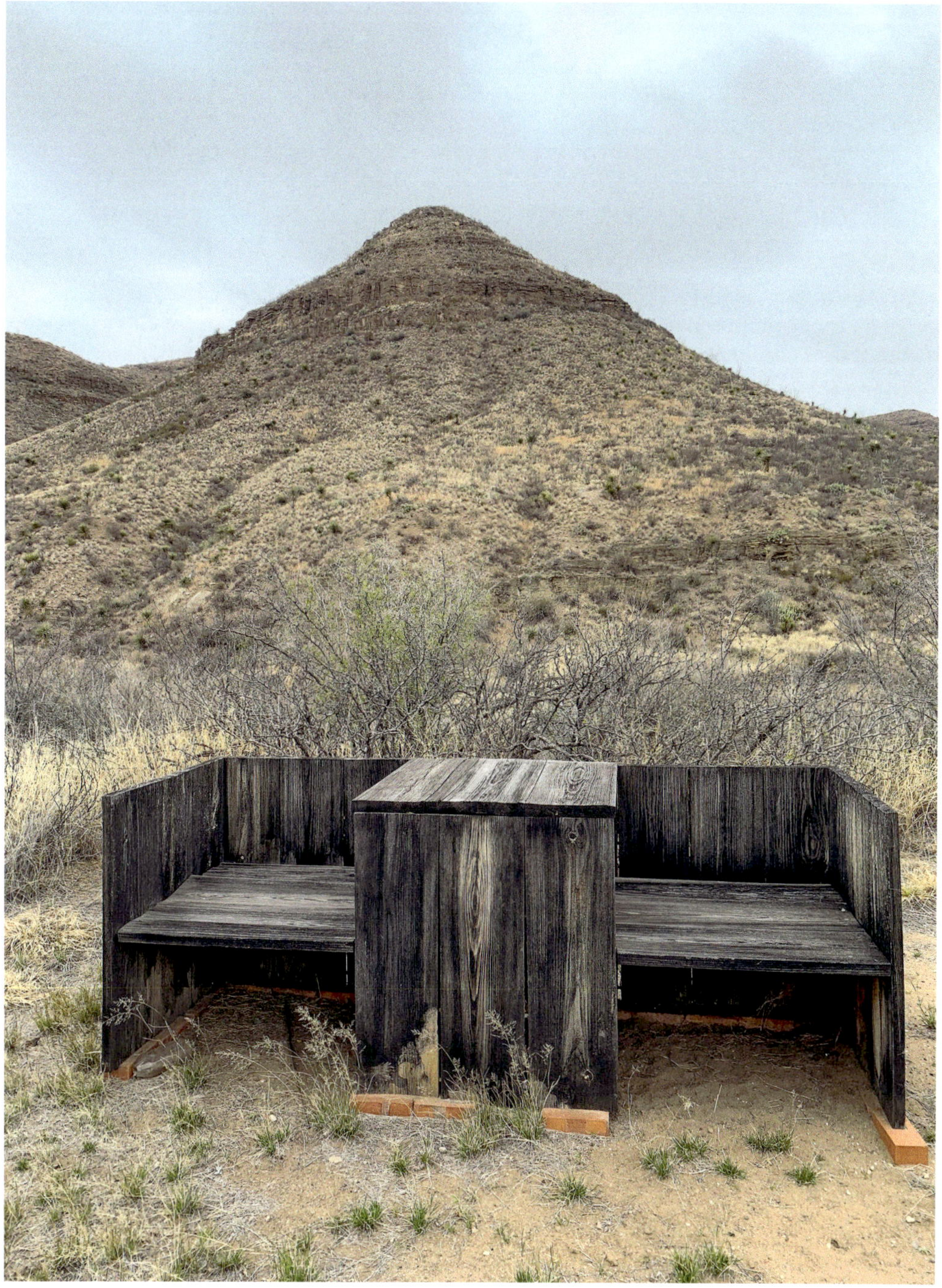

Casa Perez, with corrales and stock tank, view to northeast.

Casa Perez, mit Koppel und Wassertank, Blick nach Nordosten.

JUDD FOUNDATION

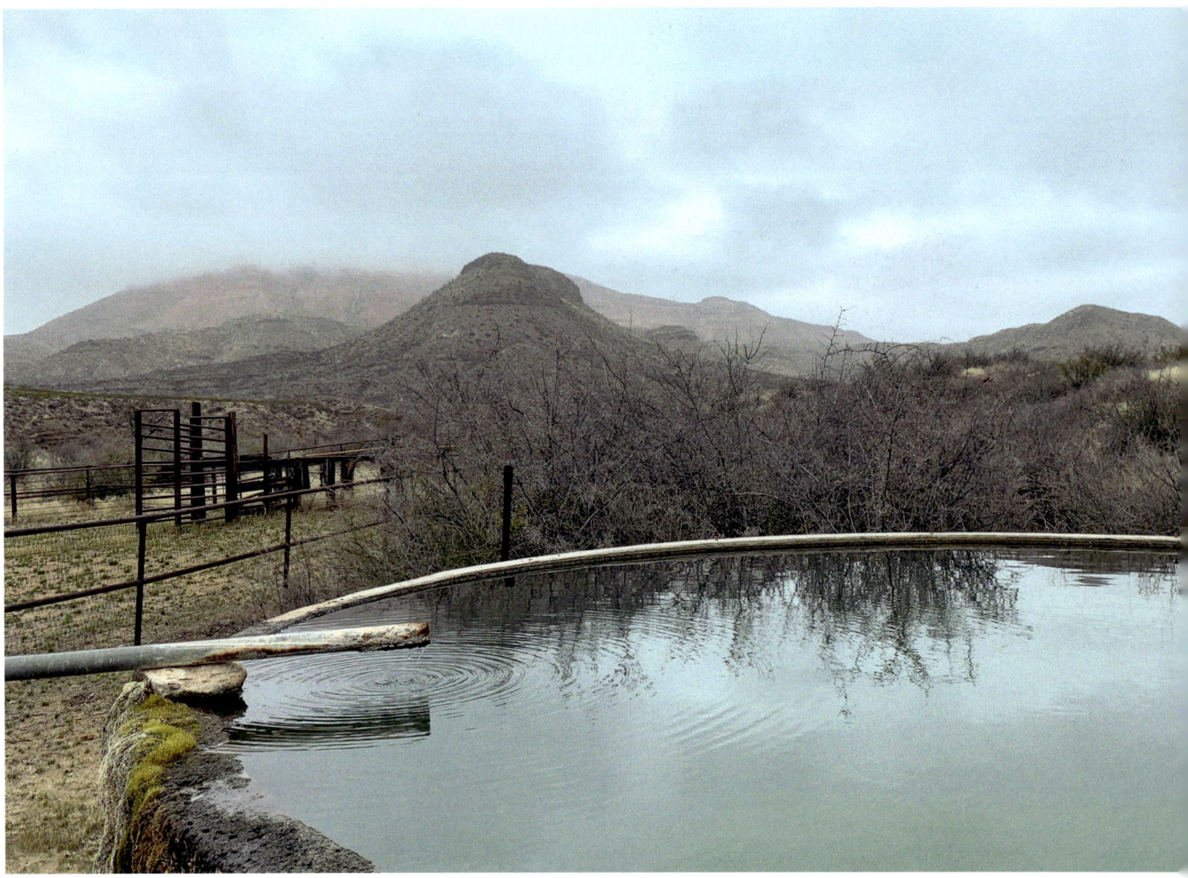

Casa Perez, with windmill, view to northwest.

Casa Perez, mit Windrad, Blick nach Nordwesten.

JUDD FOUNDATION

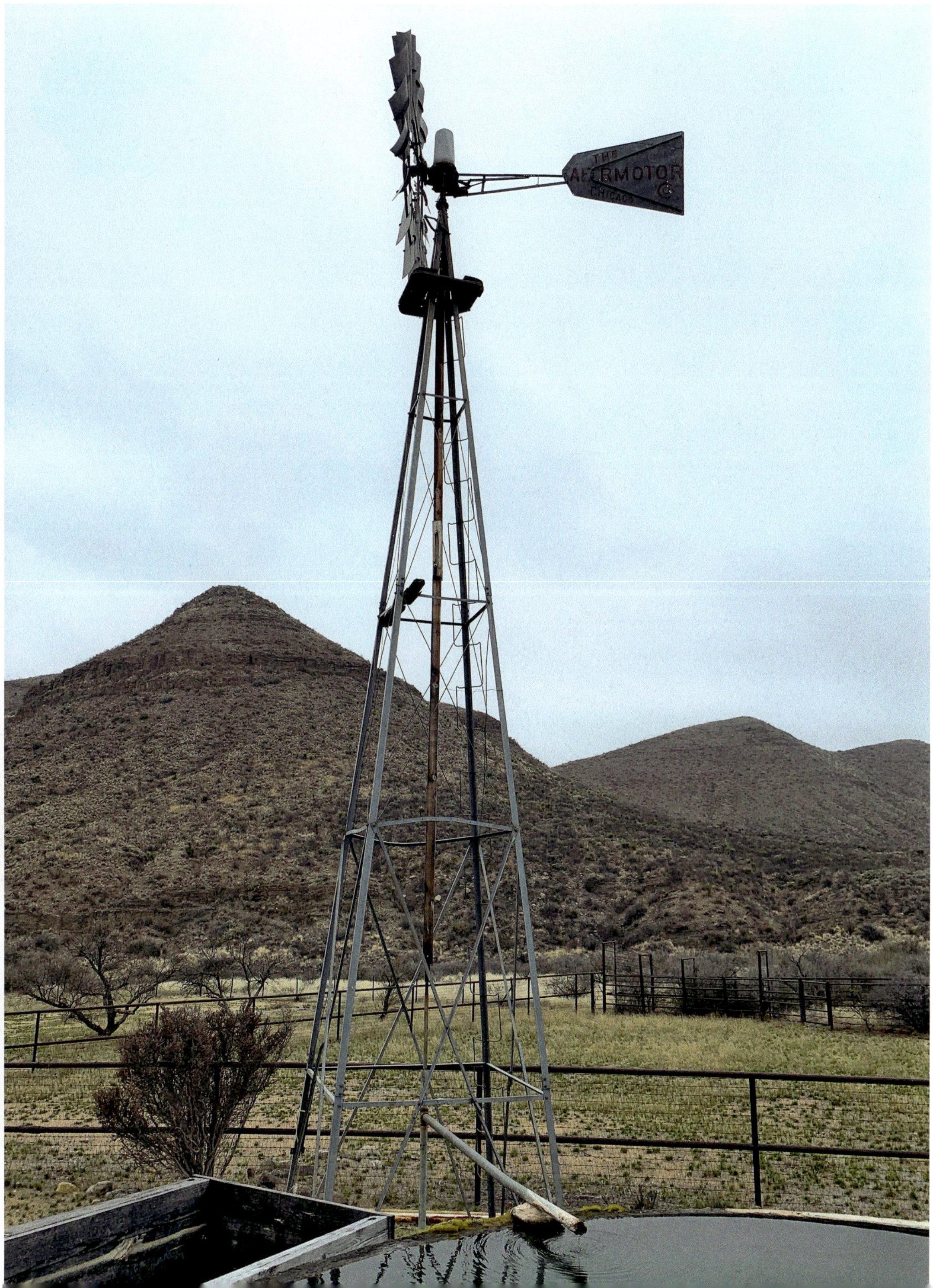

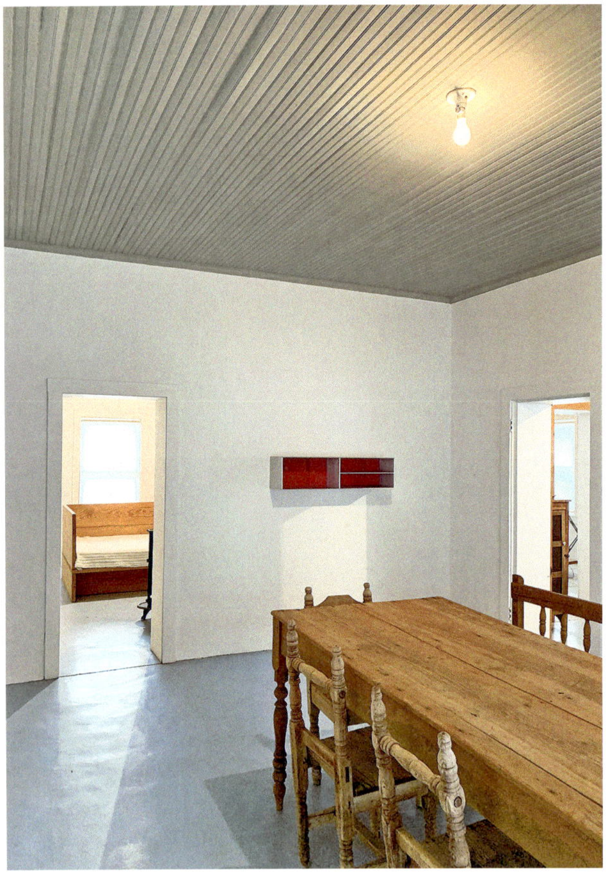

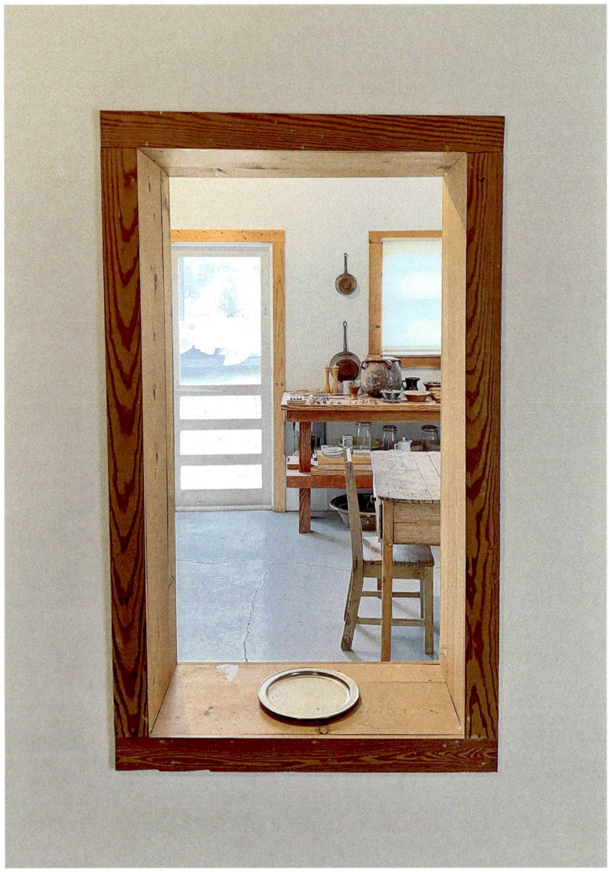

**Casa Perez,
with Donald Judd,
untitled, 1985,
view to northeast.**

Casa Perez,
mit Donald Judd,
ohne Titel, 1985,
Blick nach Nordosten.

**Casa Perez,
window towards kitchen,
view to east.**

Casa Perez,
Fenster zur Küche,
Blick nach Osten.

JUDD FOUNDATION

Casa Perez, kitchen counter by Donald Judd, table and chairs possibly from Sweden, view to south.

Casa Perez, Küchentheke von Donald Judd Tisch und Stühle wahrscheinlich aus Schweden, Blick nach Süden.

JUDD FOUNDATION

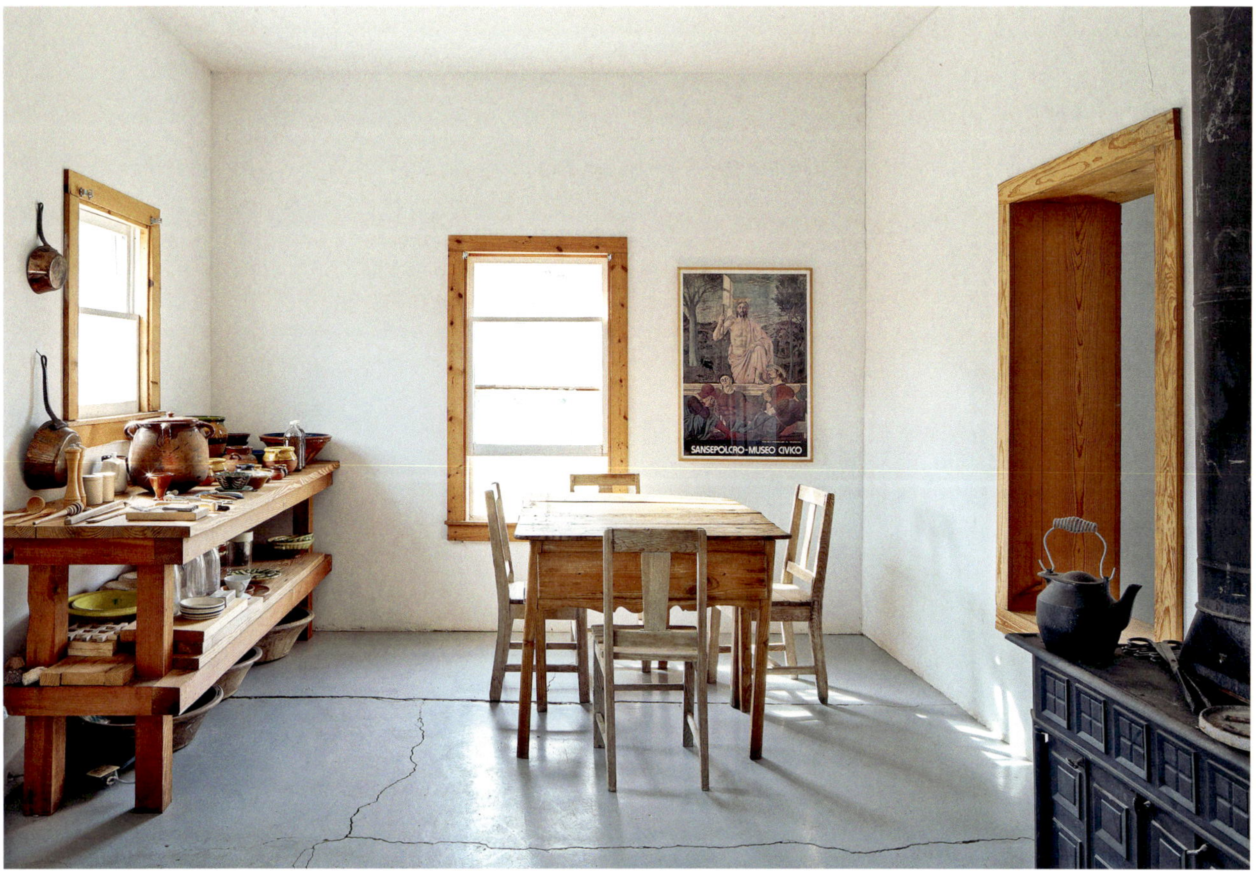

1 **Contour Lines, Landscape around Casa Morales**
Höhenlinien, Landschaft um Casa Morales

2 **Site plan, Casa Morales**
Situationsplan, Casa Morales

1

2

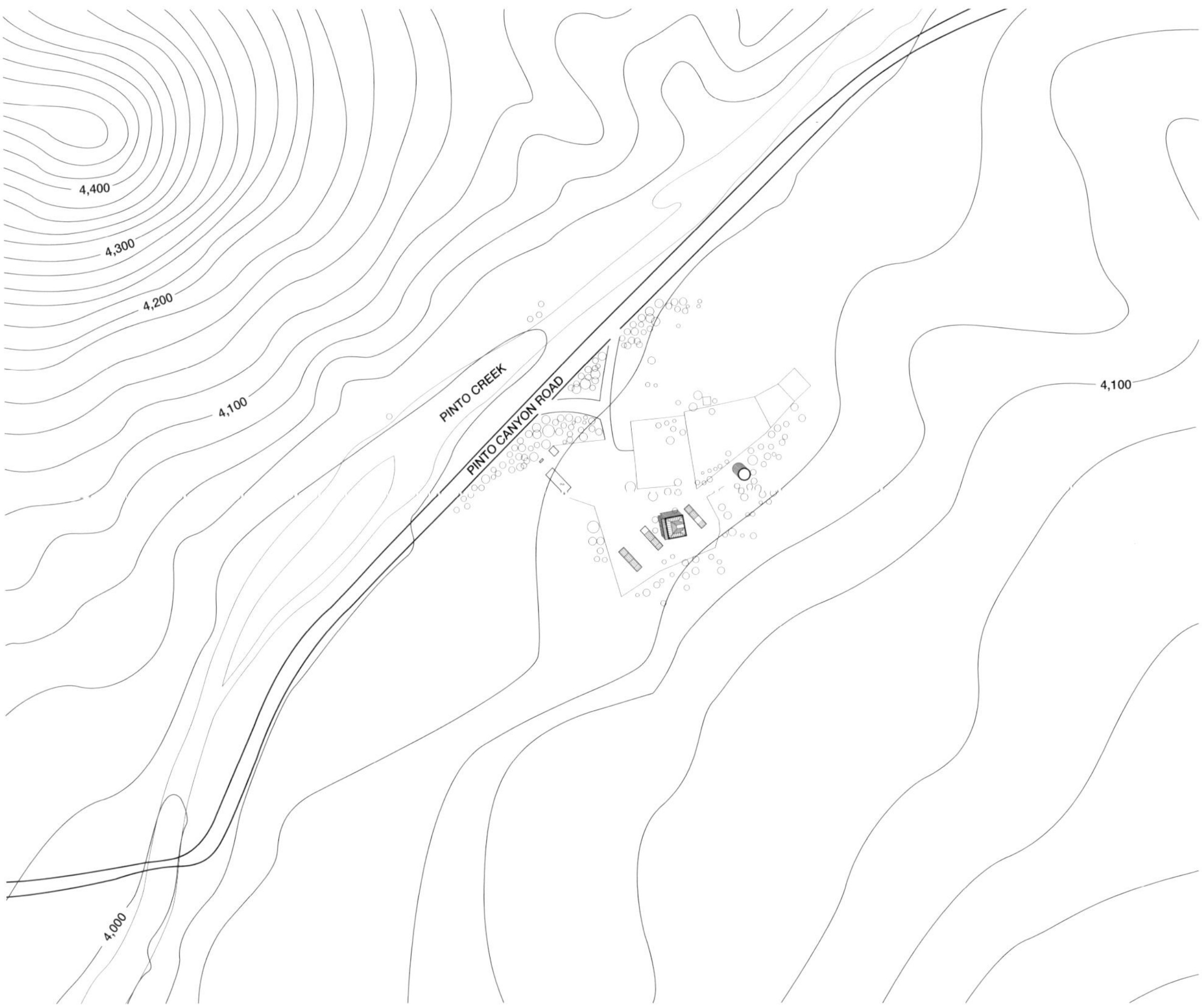

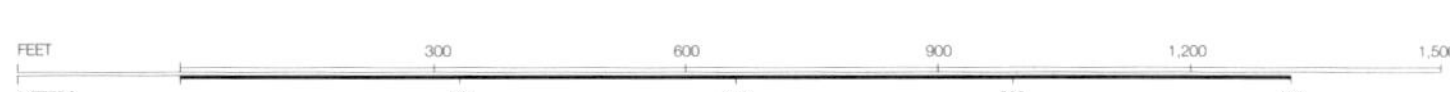

2.1 Main House
Haupthaus

2.2 Shading Structure
Pergola

2.3 Bathroom
Badezimmer

2.4 Storage
Lagerraum

2.5 Picnic Table
Picknicktisch

2.6 Windmill
Windrad

2.7 Stock Tank
Wassertank

2.8 Gate
Tor

2.9 Corrals
Tiergehege

2.10 Fire Pit
Feuerstelle

2.11 Garden
Garten

2.12 Donald Judd, Bench
Donald Judd, Bank

2.13 Stock Tank
Wassertank

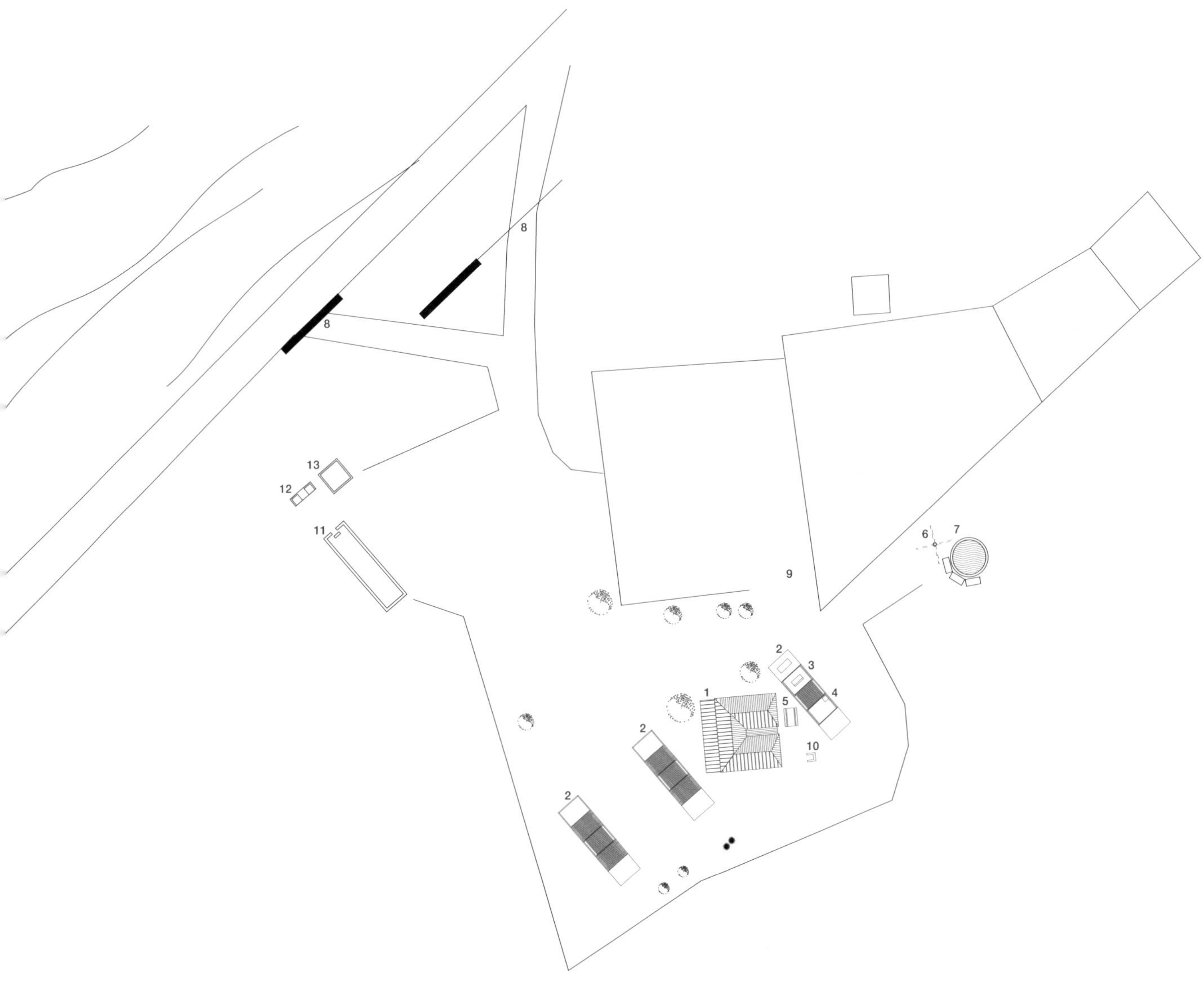

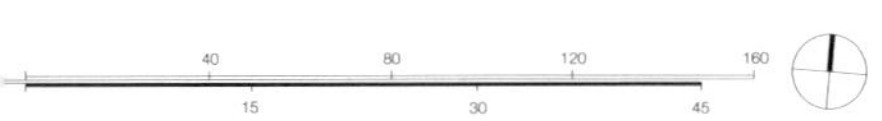

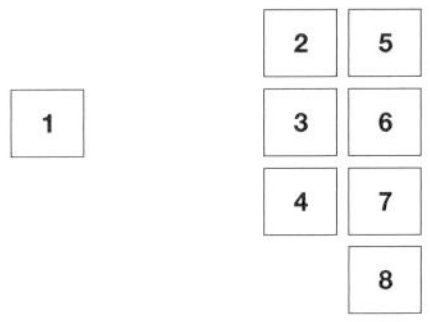

1 **Site plan, Casa Perez**
Situationsplan, Casa Perez

2 **Casa Perez, section A-A**
Casa Perez, Schnitt A-A

3 **Casa Perez, section B-B**
Casa Perez, Schnitt B-B

4 **Casa Perez, section C-C**
Casa Perez, Schnitt C-C

5 **Casa Perez, south elevation**
Casa Perez, Südansicht

6 **Casa Perez, west elevation**
Casa Perez, Westansicht

7 **Casa Perez, north elevation**
Casa Perez, Nordansicht

8 **Casa Perez, east elevation**
Casa Perez, Ostansicht

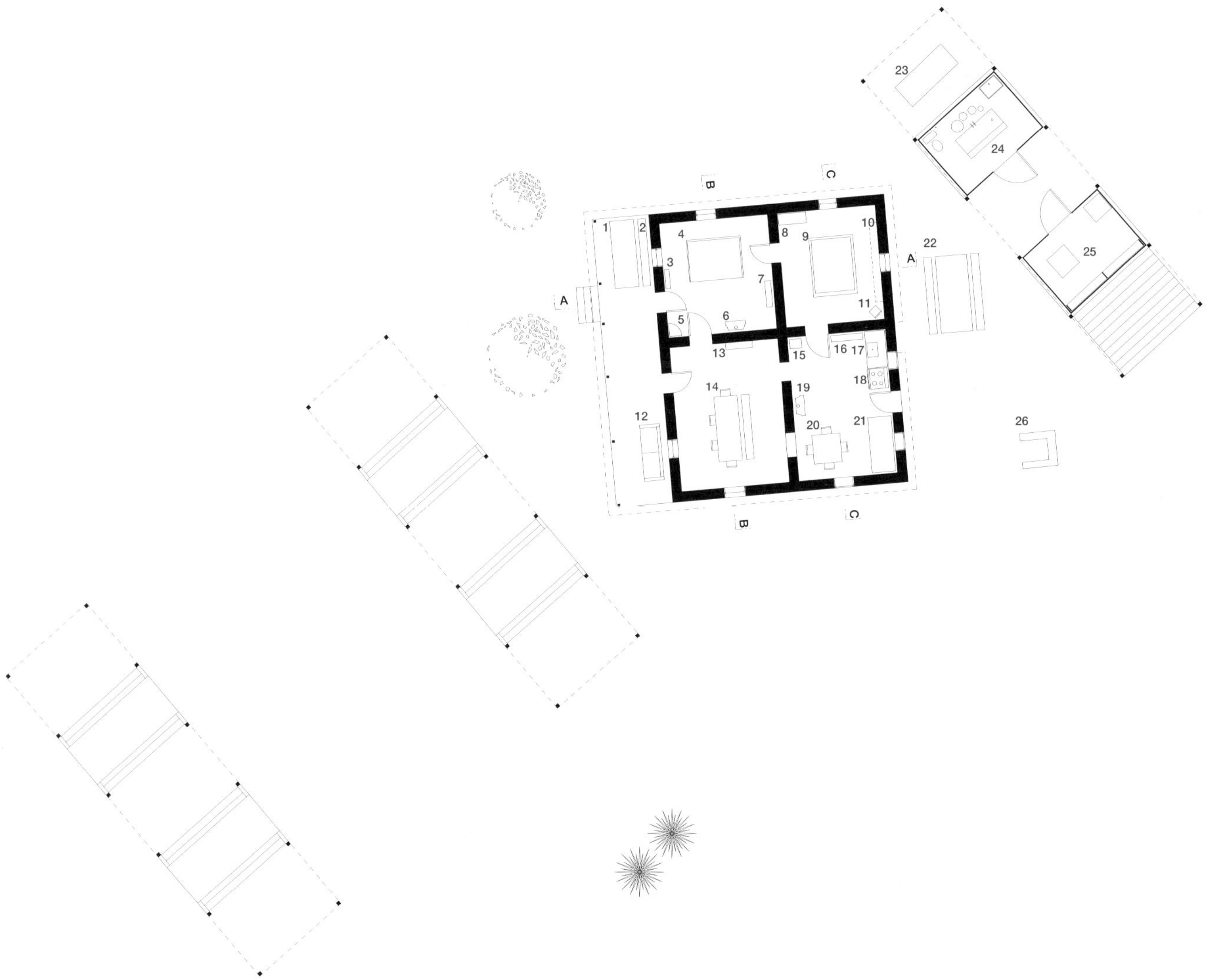

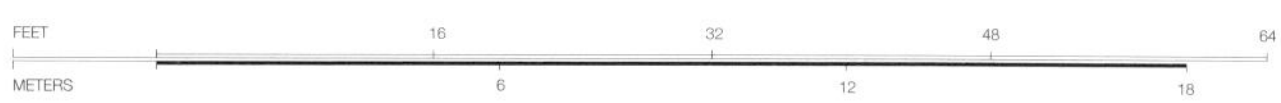

1.1 **Donald Judd, Table**
Donald Judd, Tisch

1.2 **Donald Judd, Bench**
Donald Judd, Bank

1.3 **Donald Judd, Bookshelf**
Donald Judd, Bücherregal

1.4 **Donald Judd, Bed**
Donald Judd, Bett

1.5 **Corner Table**
Ecktisch

1.6 **Wood Stove**
Holzofen

1.7 **Mexican Armoire**
Mexikanischer Kleiderschrank

1.8 **Chest**
Truhe

1.9 **Donald Judd, Bed**
Donald Judd, Bett

1.10 **Donald Judd, untitled, 1987**
Donald Judd, ohne Titel, 1987

1.11 **Chair**
Stuhl

1.12 **Sofa**
Sofa

1.13 **Donald Judd, untitled, 1985**
Donald Judd, ohne Titel, 1985

1.14 **Table, Chairs, and Bench**
Tisch, Stühle und Bank

1.15 **Pie Safe**
Fliegenschrank

1.16 **Donald Judd, Shelf**
Donald Judd, Regal

1.17 **Donald Judd, Kitchen Sink and Counter**
Donald Judd, Spüle und Theke

1.18 **Kitchen Stove**
Herd

1.19 **Wood Stove**
Holzofen

1.20 **Table and Chairs**
Tisch und Stühle

1.21 **Donald Judd, Counter and Shelf**
Donald Judd, Theke und Regal

1.22 **Donald Judd, Table**
Donald Judd, Tisch

1.23 **Donald Judd, Table**
Donald Judd, Tisch

1.24 **Bathroom**
Badezimmer

1.25 **Tiendita**
Tiendita

1.26 **Fire Pit**
Feuerstelle

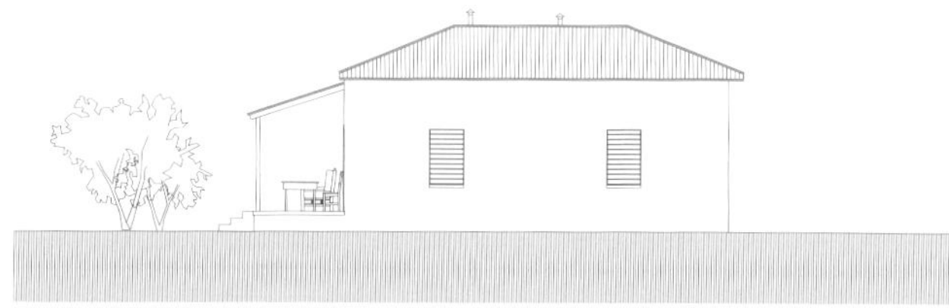

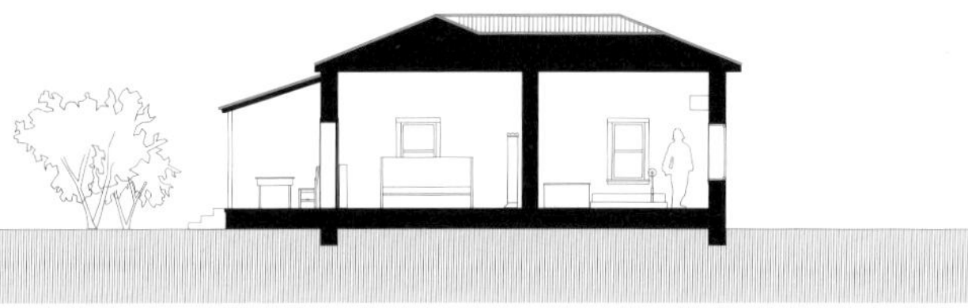

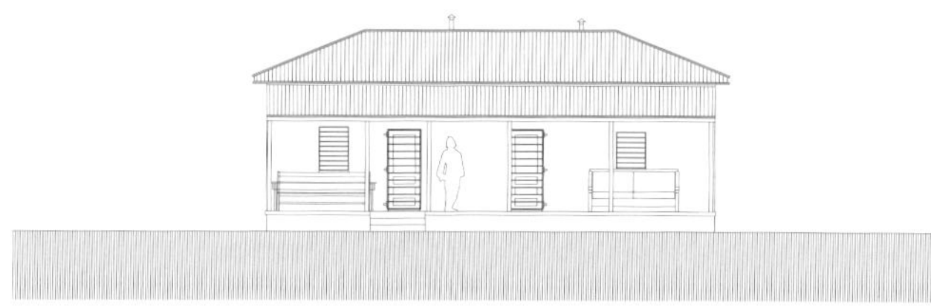

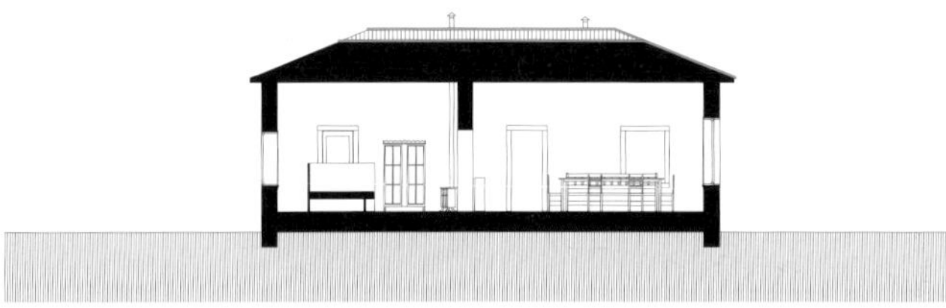

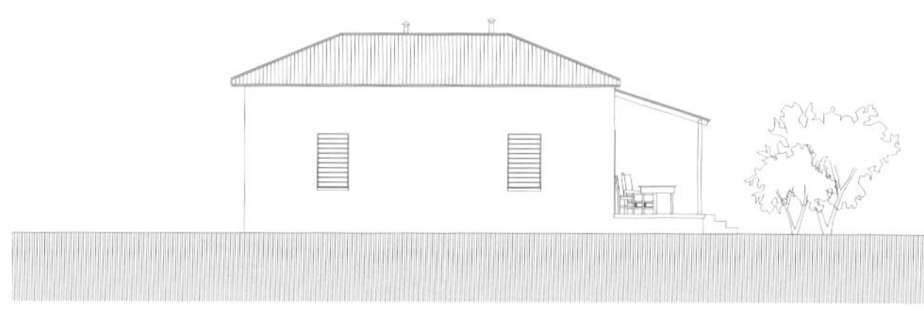

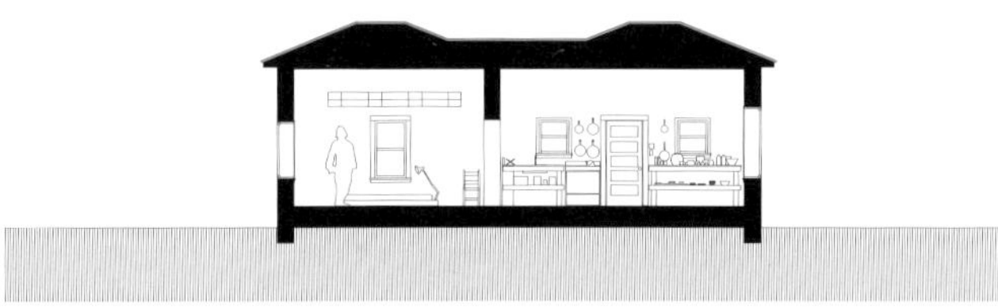

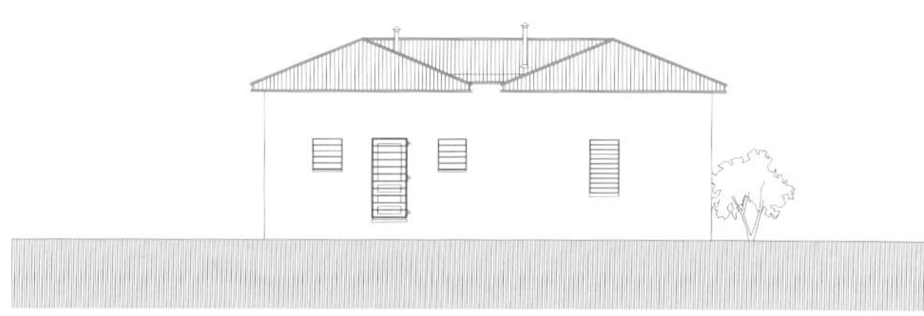

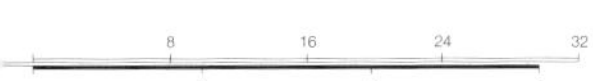

LAS CASAS, AYALA DE CHINATI

Las Casas liegt in der Nähe der Chinati Mountains, etwa 96 km südwestlich von Marfa unweit der Grenze zu Mexiko. Las Casas ist das abgelegenste von Judds drei Ranchhäusern, denen er den gemeinsamen Namen Ayala de Chinati gab. Nach Las Casas führt eine dreistündige Fahrt – zweckmäßigerweise in einem Fahrzeug mit Vierradantrieb – über meist ungepflasterte Straßen und Feldwege. Las Casas ist auf einer natürlichen Terrasse angelegt, hinter der sich im Nordwesten ein Gebirgszug erstreckt. Vier Gebäude gehören zu diesem Ensemble: das Hauptgebäude mit Wohnräumen, das Gästehaus mit Küche, Esszimmer, Bad und Arbeitszimmer, das Studio sowie die Schlafbaracke, das einzige neue, von Judd entworfene Gebäude, dessen Erstellung aber nicht abgeschlossen wurde. Dazu kommen Zweck- oder Ranchanlagen, so ein früher noch erhaltener Wassertank, den Judd mit konzentrischen Ringmauern einfriedete, ein kreisförmiger Garten mit Bewässerungssystem, ein neuer, runder Wasserspeicher sowie eine Gruppe von drei nebeneinander liegenden Bauten, ebenfalls von Judd entworfen, die aber zu seinen Lebzeiten nicht

Las Casas lies near the Chinati Mountains some sixty miles southwest of Marfa, near the border to Mexico. Las Casas is the most remote of Judd's three ranch houses, which he collectively called Ayala de Chinati. Getting to Las Casas takes a three-hour drive, preferably in a four-wheel drive vehicle over mostly unpaved dirt roads. Las Casas is situated on a natural terrace with the mountain range rising toward the northwest. There are four buildings: the main house with living spaces; the guesthouse with kitchen, dining room, bathroom, and study; the studio; and the bunkhouse, the only new structure designed by Judd, which was begun but not finished. In addition to these buildings, there are utilitarian or ranch structures, including a previously extant stock tank that Judd surrounded with concentric walls; a circular garden with irrigation system; a new circular tank; plus a group of three adjacent structures that Judd designed but that remained unfinished during his lifetime. They were intended as a stable, a chicken coop and storage for ranch equipment. When viewed from the distance, the complex appears to be a small

mehr fertiggestellt wurden. Geplant waren sie als Stall, Hühnerstall und Lagerraum für Ranchgerät. Aus der Ferne betrachtet, wirkt der Komplex wie ein kleines Dorf. Von Judd gepflanzte Olivenbäume und verschiedene Kakteenarten ragen verstreut aus der rauen Wüstenlandschaft. Eine niedrige, l-förmige Stützmauer zieht sich an Hauptgebäude, Wassertank und Garten entlang.

Im Hauptgebäude wurde das Badezimmer entfernt und im Nordosten ein Schlafzimmer angebaut. Anders als die originalen Lehmziegelmauern sind die neuen Wände eine Holzrahmenkonstruktion. Das Haus ist mit Möbeln von Gustav Stickley ausgestattet und enthält Werke von Donald Judd. Außen ist das Gebäude verputzt und lehmziegelfarbig gestrichen; der Anstrich im Inneren ist ein mattes Weiß. Die Betonböden sind grau gestrichen. Eine weiße Decke aus Gipskarton verstärkt die kastenartige Wirkung der Zimmer. Sowohl auf der Nordost- als auch auf der Südwestseite des Hauptgebäudes hat Judd eine Veranda angebaut und der Landschaft damit einen Rahmen gegeben.

Im Gästehaus sind eine Küche, ein Essraum mit riesigem offenem Kamin sowie antikem Tisch und Bänken und ein Bad untergebracht. Ein weiterer Raum steht für Büroarbeiten zur Verfügung. Er enthält einen von Judd gestalteten Tisch, und an der Wand hängt eine Karte mit Sternbildern. An der Südwestseite des Gästehauses hat Judd eine Veranda angebaut, die wie die beiden Verandas am Haupthaus die volle Längsseite des Gebäudes einnimmt. Auf der Veranda ist ein Tisch mit Bank aufgestellt, beide von Judd entworfen. Im Haupthaus wie auch im Gästehaus hat Judd an der weißen Gipskartondecke zwar Beleuchtungskörper angebracht, doch wurde die Ranch nie ans Elektrizitätsnetz angeschlossen. Die einzig verfügbare Energiequelle war Propangas. Parallel zum Gästehaus steht im Nordosten ein zweites Gästehaus – sechs großzügig bemessene, etwa 3,6 m (12 ft) hohe Zimmer. Das zweite Gästehaus wurde nicht vollendet, doch weiß man, dass Judd geplant hatte, eine Variante seiner um die Mittelachse drehbaren Türen mit einem zusätzlichen Schirm einzusetzen. Ein Prototyp wurde zwar angefertigt, um die Realisierbarkeit zu testen, zur Herstellung der endgültigen Türen kam es aber nicht.

Südwestlich des Hauptgebäudes liegen die von früher noch vorhandenen *corrales*, die Tiergehege, mit ca. 1,8 m (6 ft) hohen

village. The harsh desert landscape is dotted with olive trees planted by Judd and various types of cacti. A low L-shaped retaining rock wall runs along the main house, the stock tank, and the garden.

In the main house the bathroom was removed and a bedroom added to the northeast. The original walls are made of adobe, whereas the new walls are made of wood-frame construction. The house is furnished with Gustav Stickley furniture, as well as artworks by Donald Judd. The exterior is plastered and painted in adobe color and the interior is painted flat white. The concrete floors are painted gray. A white plasterboard ceiling reinforces the boxy appearance of the rooms. Judd added a porch to both the northeast and southwest sides of the main house, framing the landscape.

The guesthouse contains a kitchen, a dining room with an enormous fireplace with an antique table and benches, and a bathroom, along with an office space furnished with a desk designed by Judd, where a map of the constellations is placed on the wall. On the southwest side of the guesthouse, Judd added a porch running the full length of the building, similar to the ones he added to the main house. Placed within the porch are a table and bench, both designed by Judd. In the main house and guesthouse, Judd installed light fixtures in the white plasterboard ceiling, but electricity was never brought to the ranch. The only available source of energy was propane gas. Parallel to the guesthouse to the northeast is the bunkhouse, consisting of six spacious rooms with 12-foot ceilings. The bunkhouse was not completed, but Judd had planned to install a variation of his center-hinged doors, which would have had an additional screen. A prototypical scale model of the door was made to test its feasibility, but the final doors were never produced.

To the southwest of the main house are the existing corrals with 6-foot-high walls built of black and white volcanic rocks from the area. The nearby walls of the three unfinished Judd designed structures are 12-foot-high, double the height of the corrals, and are built of a red/brown local rock. Rock-wall construction is a Hispanic masonry tradition, and Judd hired Mexican experts in rock work to build all the walls and additions. The studio, which was only minimally modified by Judd, had also

Mauern aus dem schwarzen und weißen Vulkangestein der Region. Die benachbarten Mauern der drei unvollendeten von Judd entworfenen Anlagen sind mit ihren etwa 3,6 m (12 ft) doppelt so hoch, und zu ihrem Bau wurde ein rotbraun gefärbtes lokales Gestein benutzt. Felsmauern sind eine hispanische Tradition, und Judd beschäftigte beim Bau aller Mauern und baulichen Erweiterungen mexikanische Spezialisten für die Bearbeitung von Natursteinen. Das Studio, das Judd nur minimal veränderte, war ebenfalls aus Felsgestein errichtet worden. Es liegt südwestlich der halbfertigen Natursteinmauern, von diesen an der schmalsten Stelle durch einen Abstand von nur ca. 70 cm (2 ft) getrennt. Im Studio sind mehrere Wandarbeiten von Judd ausgestellt; sechs gleichmäßig verteilte Oberlichter ermöglichen einen großzügigen Tageslichteinfall.

Judd betrachtete Las Casas als zweites Zuhause und hatte nach Auskunft seines Sohnes Flavin die Absicht, auch seine Bibliothek auf der Ranch unterzubringen. Unter den Büchern, die schon in Las Casas ihren Platz gefunden haben, sind Vitruvs *Zehn Bücher über die Architektur*, Albertis Werk *Über die Baukunst* und Palladios *Die vier Bücher zur Architektur*. Dieses bibliografische Destillat zeigt Judds Interesse für die Architektur und seine Wertschätzung der Klassiker der Baukunst mit dem Akzent auf Architekturgeschichte und Proportionslehre.

Viele der räumlichen und architektonischen Ideen, die Judd in Marfa entwickelte, kommen in der einen oder anderen Form auch in Las Casas zum Ausdruck, am deutlichsten in den sorgfältig komponierten Raumsequenzen zwischen alten und neuen Gebäuden und ihrer Beziehung zum Standort. Las Casas ist so in die Landschaft gesetzt, dass die kilometerweite Sicht zum Horizont orchestrale Vielfalt gewinnt. Judd hat die vorhandenen Bauten durch neue Gebäude erweitert und dabei den Standort und die landschaftliche Umgebung durch den nur minimalen Charakter seiner Interventionen intakt gehalten. Steht man auf der Veranda seines Hauses, fällt der Blick nach Südwesten auf ein Gelände unberührter Natur, das sich ohne Unterbrechungen oder Eingriffe von Menschenhand bis hinunter zum Rio Grande und weiter über die Grenze hinaus bis zu den fernen Bergketten Mexikos zieht. Hier ist Donald Judds letzte Ruhestätte, in der unendlichen Weite der Landschaft um Las Casas.

been constructed of rock. It is situated to the southwest of the unfinished rock walls, with a distance of only two feet between them at the narrowest point. Several wall works by Judd are displayed inside; six evenly spaced skylights provide plenty of natural light.

Judd considered Las Casas another home and according to his son Flavin, intended to bring his library to the site. Among the books already at Las Casas are Vitruvius' *Ten Books on Architecture*, Alberti's *On the Art of Building*, and Palladio's *The Four Books of Architecture*. This distilled selection shows Judd's interest in architecture and his appreciation of the classics, with an emphasis on architectural history and proportion theory.

Many of the spatial and architectural ideas that Judd developed in Marfa are again expressed in some form at Las Casas, most noticeably in the careful sequencing of spaces between old and new structures and their relationship to the site. Las Casas is situated in the landscape in a way that orchestrates views for miles into the horizon. He expanded the existing buildings with new structures, preserving the site and the landscape through minimal interventions. Standing on the porch of Judd's house, one sees to the southwest a landscape flowing without interruption or human interventions down to the Rio Grande and beyond the border to the distant Mexican mountain ranges. Donald Judd's final resting place is here, in the vast unending landscape that unfolds around Las Casas.

Las Casas.
View of ranch
to west.

Las Casas.
Blick auf die Ranch,
nach Westen.

JUDD FOUNDATION

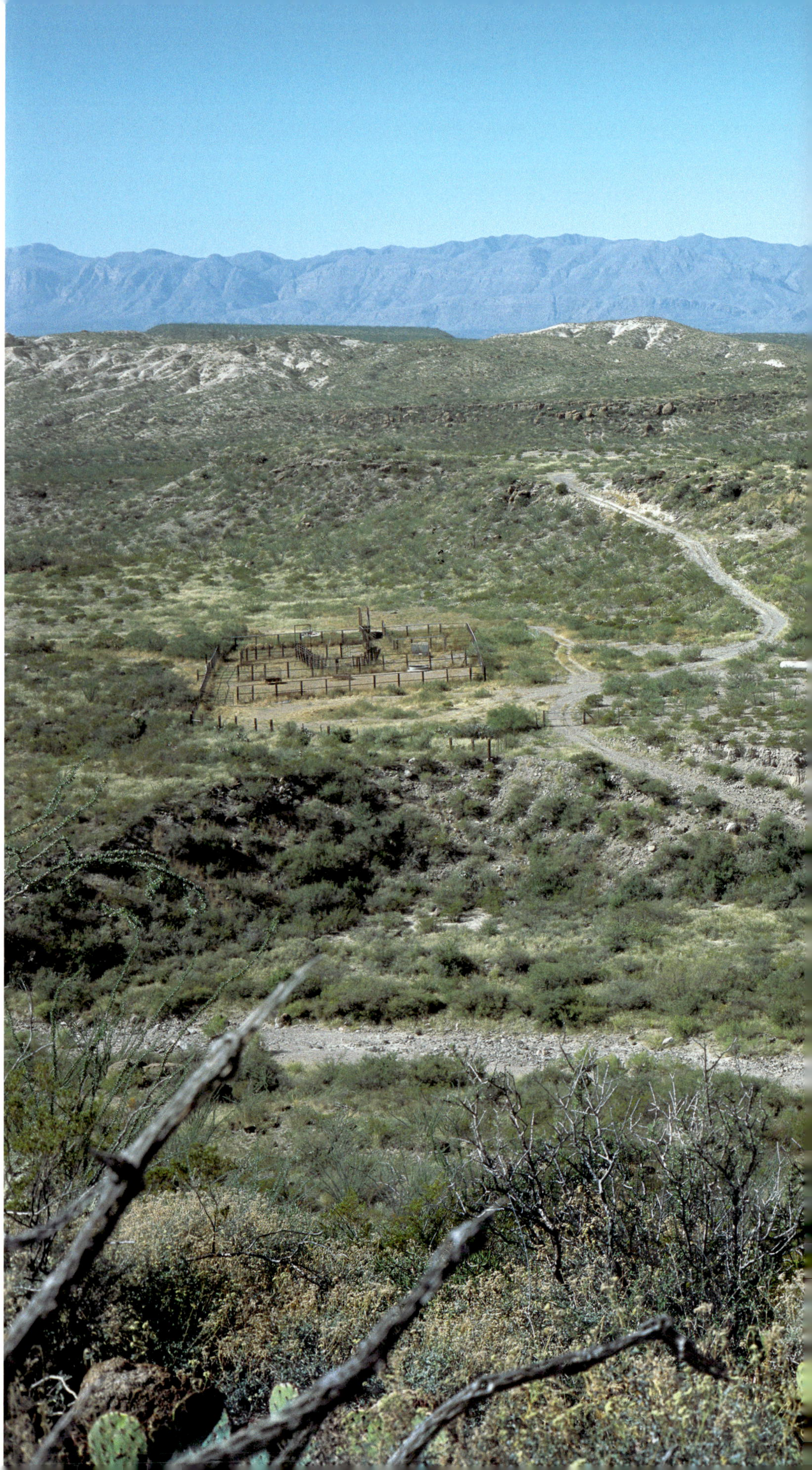

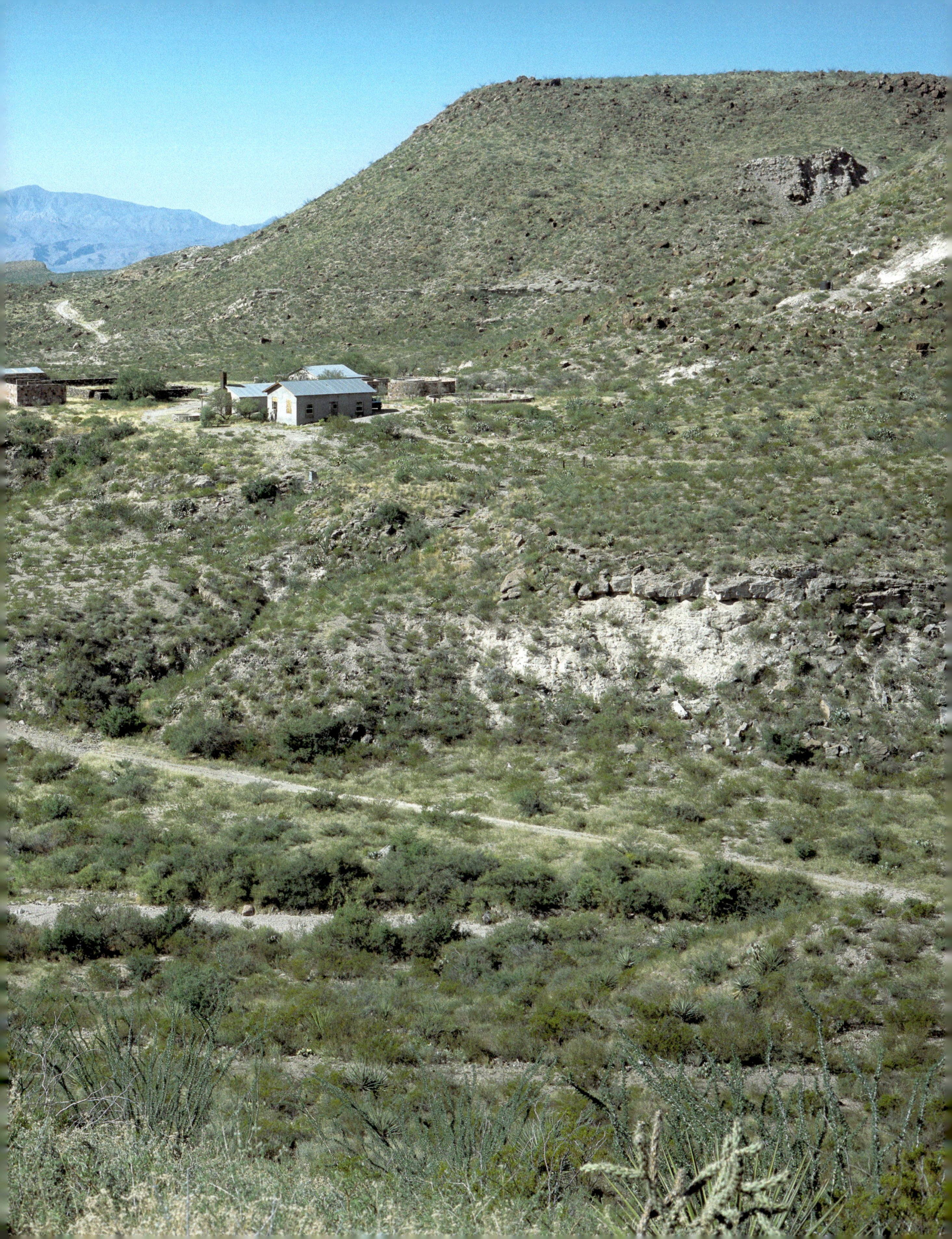

Las Casas. View of ranch to southeast.

Blick auf die Ranch, nach Südosten.

JUDD FOUNDATION

Las Casas. Stock tank with concentric walls, view to southeast.

Wasserspeicher mit konzentrischen Mauern, Blick nach Südosten.

View of walls, studio and corrales to southwest.

Blick auf Mauern, Studio und Tiergehege, nach Südwesten.

View of walls and studio, to north.

Blick auf Mauern und Studio, nach Norden.

JUDD FOUNDATION

Stock tank with concentric walls, view to northeast.

Wasserspeicher mit konzentrischen Mauern, nach Nordosten.

Walls, view to southwest.

Mauern nach Südwesten.

View of corrales, walls and studio, to southeast.

Blick auf Tiergehege, Mauern und Studio, nach Südosten.

JUDD FOUNDATION

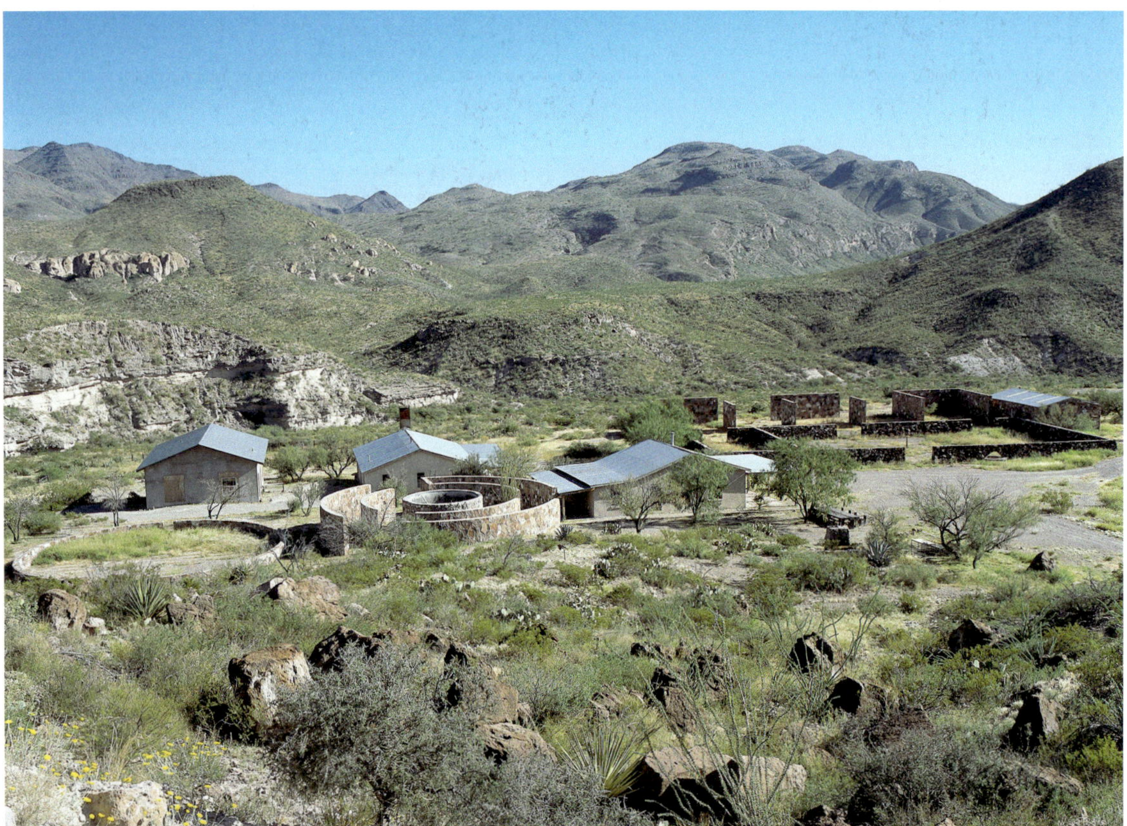

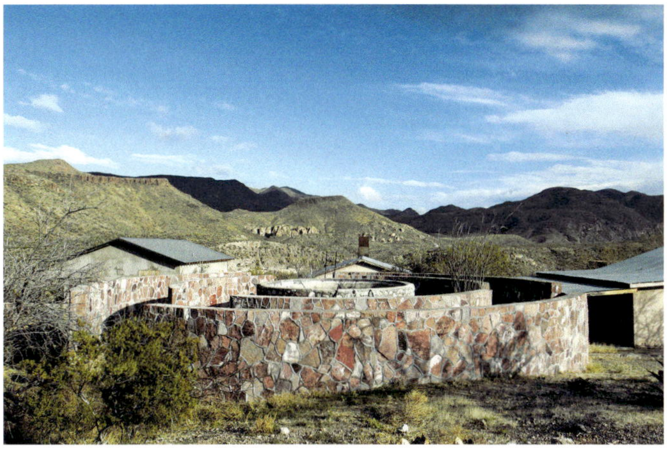
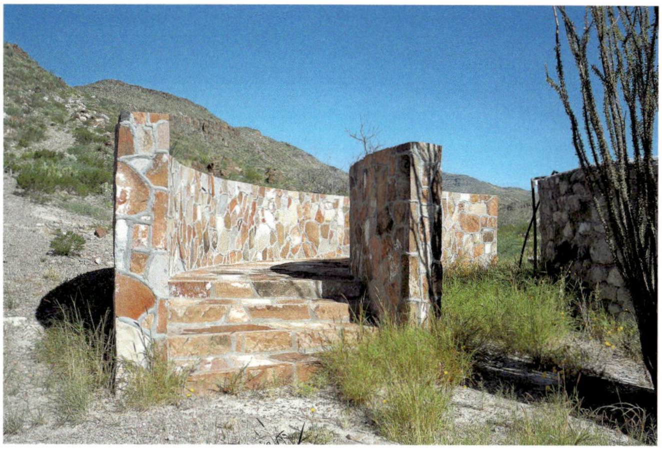
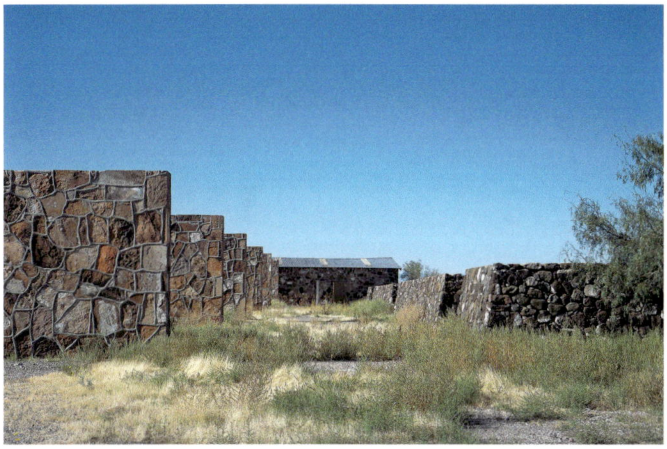
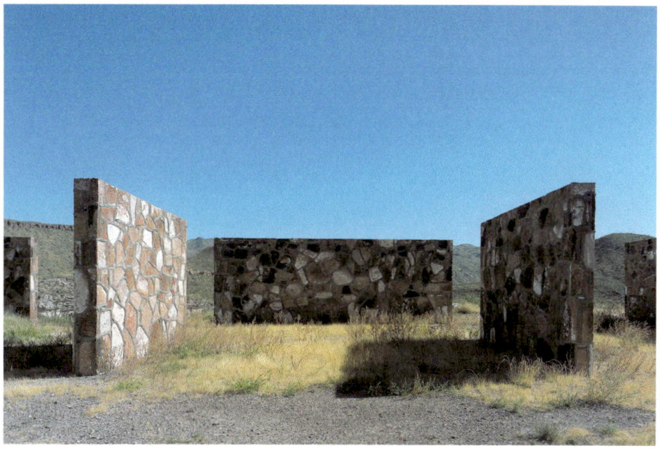
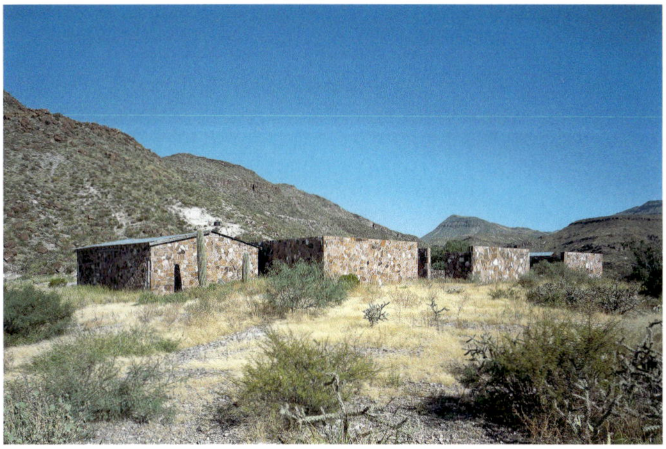
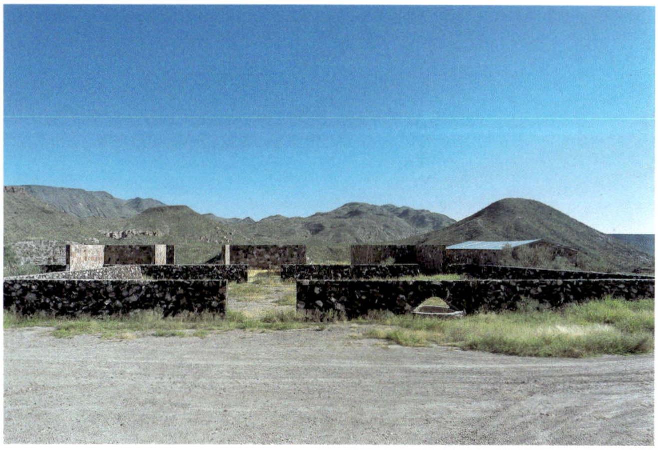

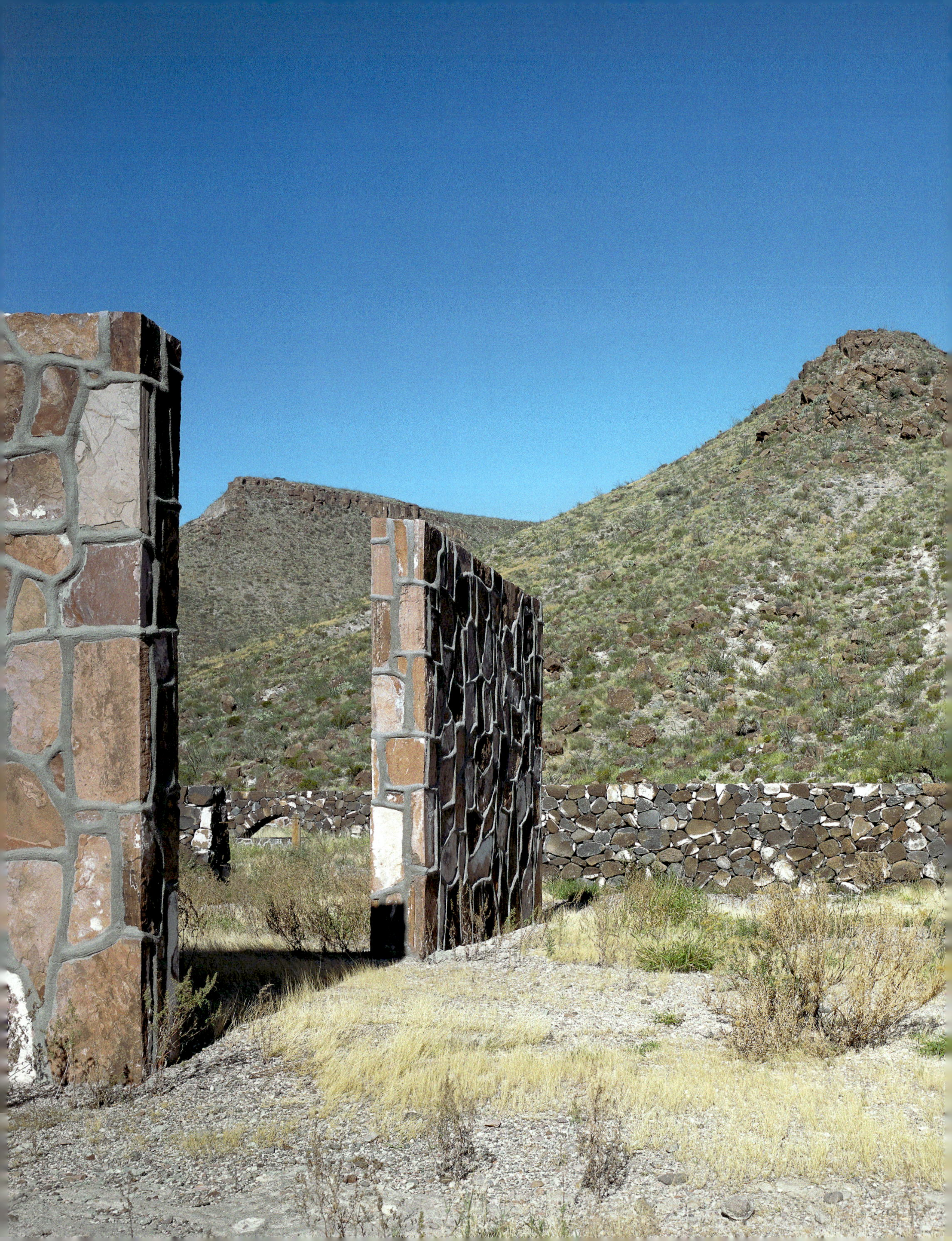

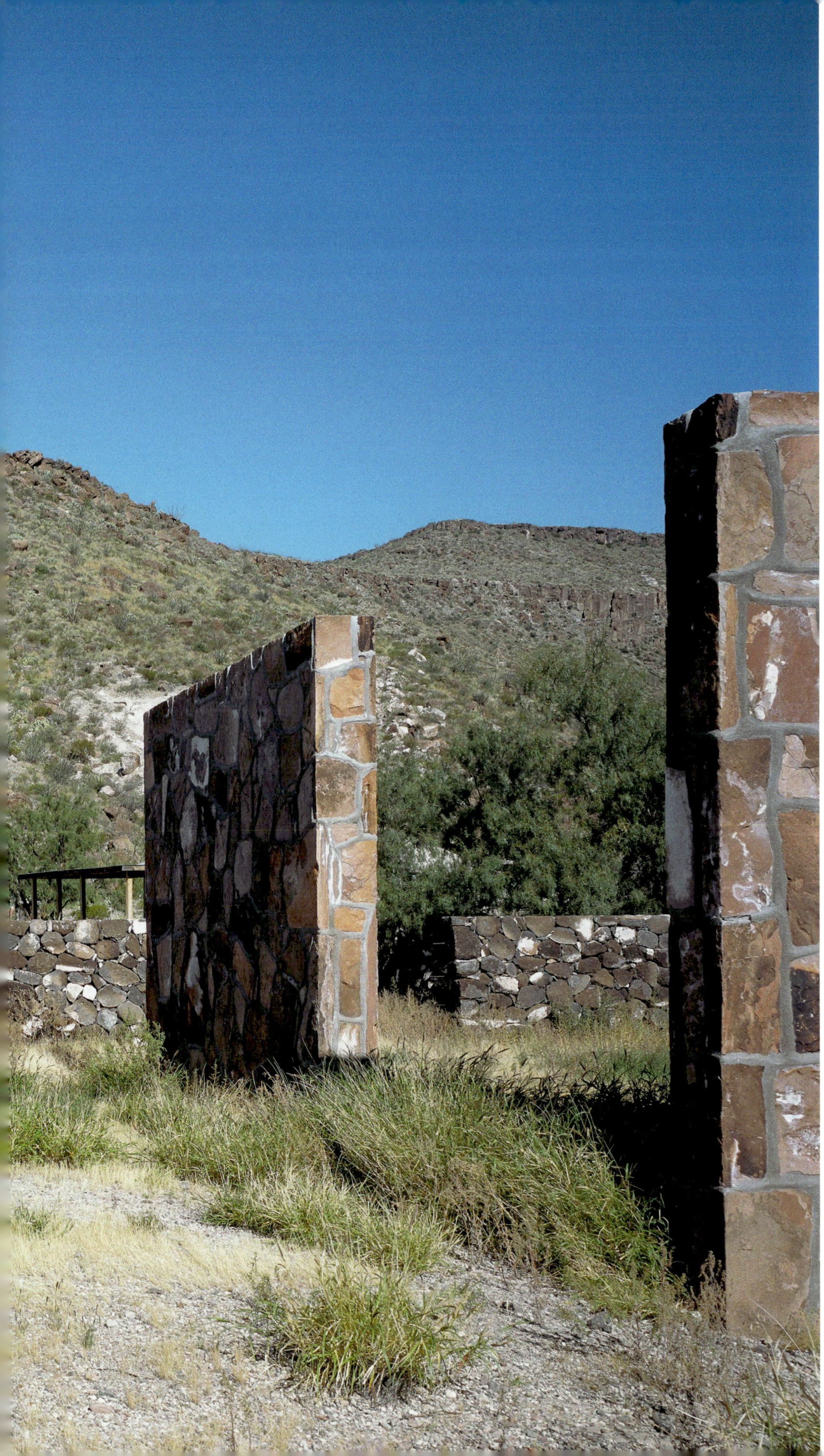

Las Casas. View of walls and corrales, to northwest.

Las Casas. Blick auf Mauern und Tiergehege, nach Nordwesten.

JUDD FOUNDATION

Las Casas. View of walls and corrales, to west.

Las Casas. Blick auf Mauern und Tiergehege, nach Westen.

JUDD FOUNDATION

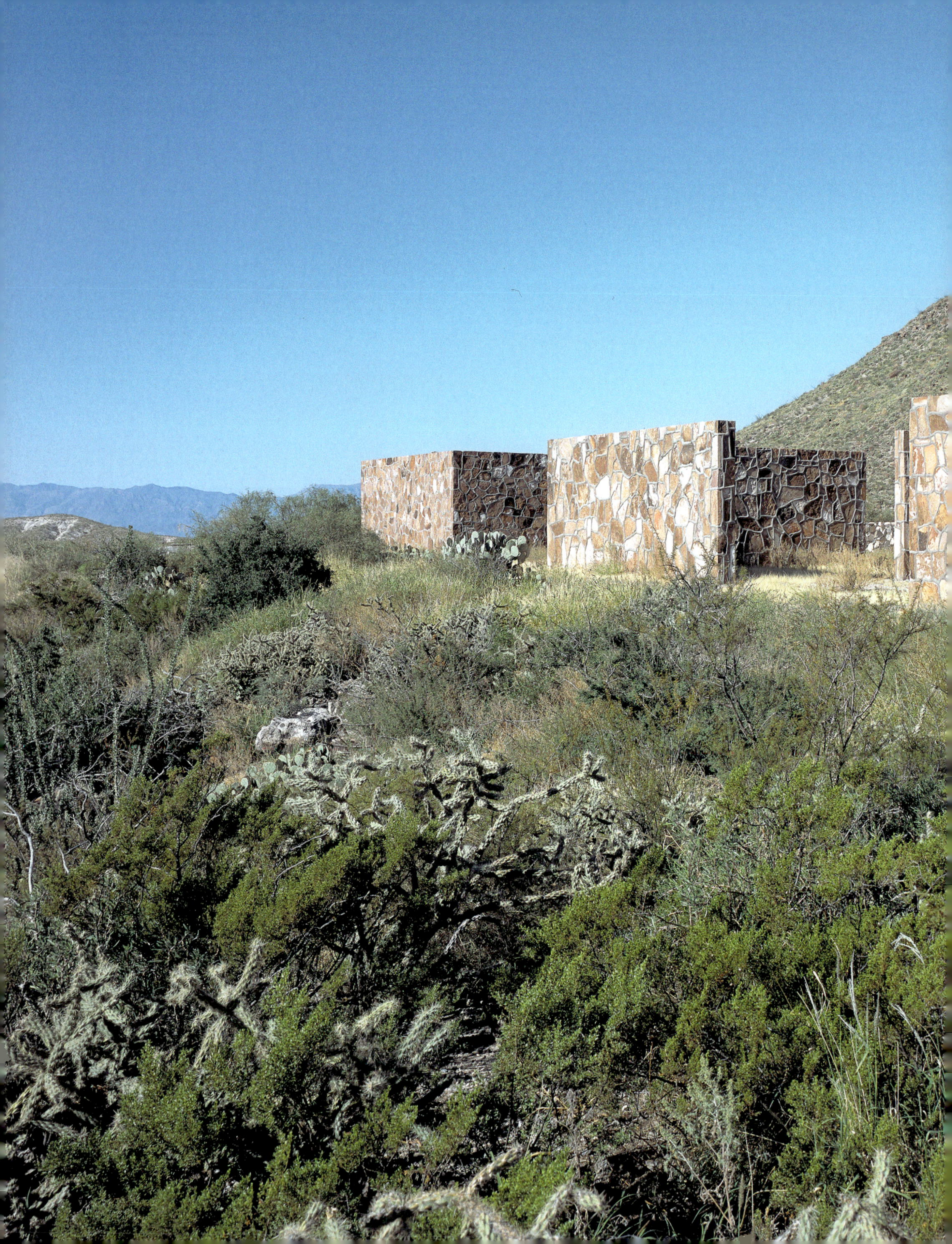

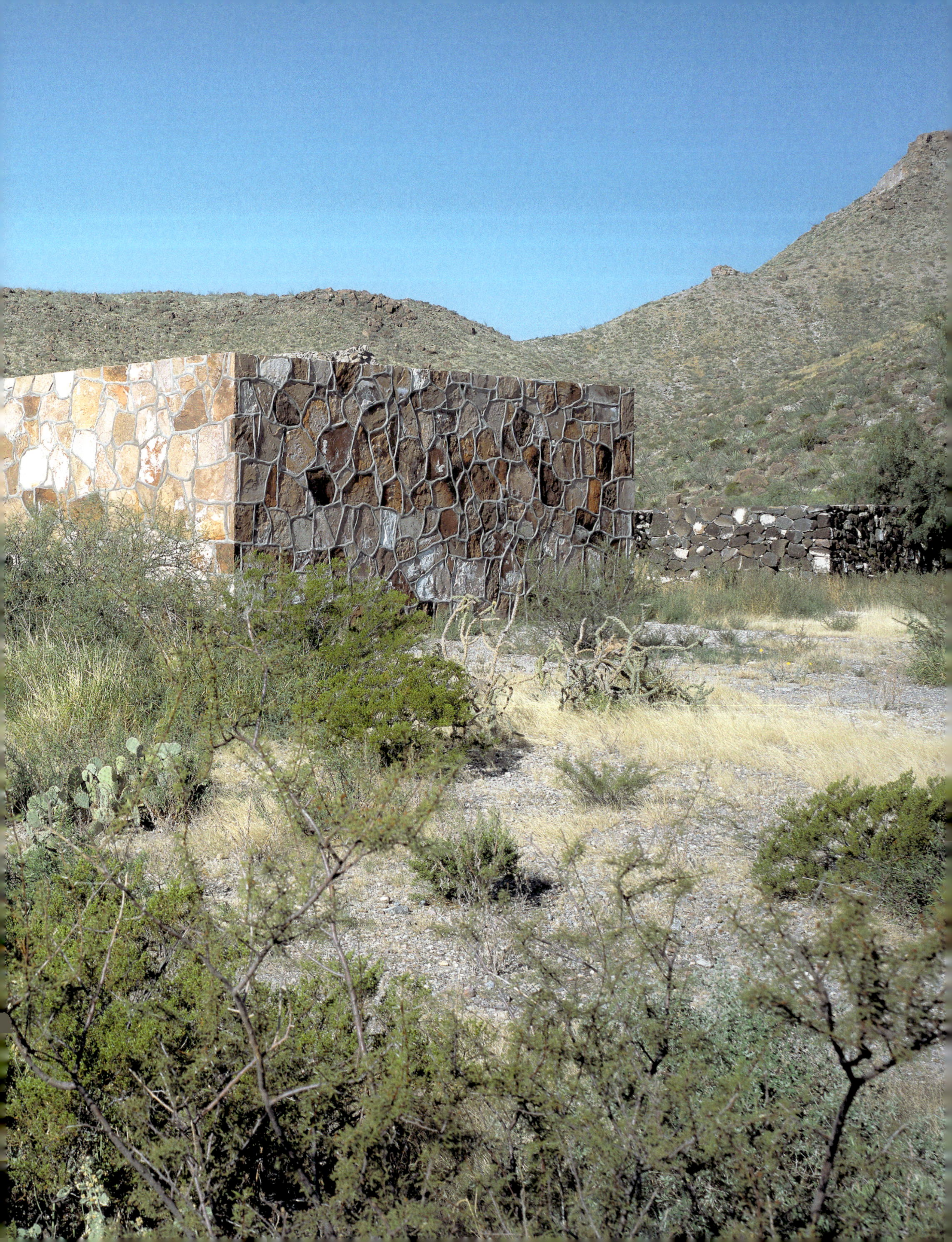

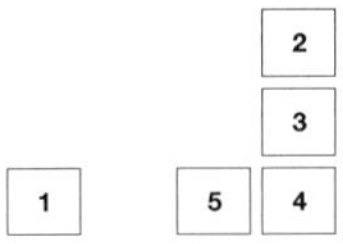

1 **Site plan, Las Casas**
Situationsplan, Las Casas

2 **Main House, plan**
Haupthaus, Grundriss

3 **Main House, section A-A**
Haupthaus, Schnitt A-A

4 **Main House, southeast elevation**
Haupthaus, Südostansicht

5 **Main House, southwest elevation**
Haupthaus, Südwestansicht

Olive tree
Olivenbaum

Mesquite tree
Mesquitbaum

Cactus
Kaktus

Desert agave
Wüstenagave

Ocotillo cactus
Ocatilla

Boulder
Steinblock

1.1 **Main House** Haupthaus

1.2 **Stock Tank** Wasserspeicher

1.3 **Concentric stone walls** Konzentrische Steinmauern

1.4 **Garden** Garten

1.5 **Guesthouse** Gästehaus

1.6 **Bunkhouse** Zweites Gästehaus

1.7 **Tank** Tank

1.8 **Studio** Studio

1.9 **Corrales** Tiergehege

1.10 **Walls (unfinished)** Mauern (nicht zu Ende geführt)

1.11 **Low retaining wall** Niedrige Stützmauer

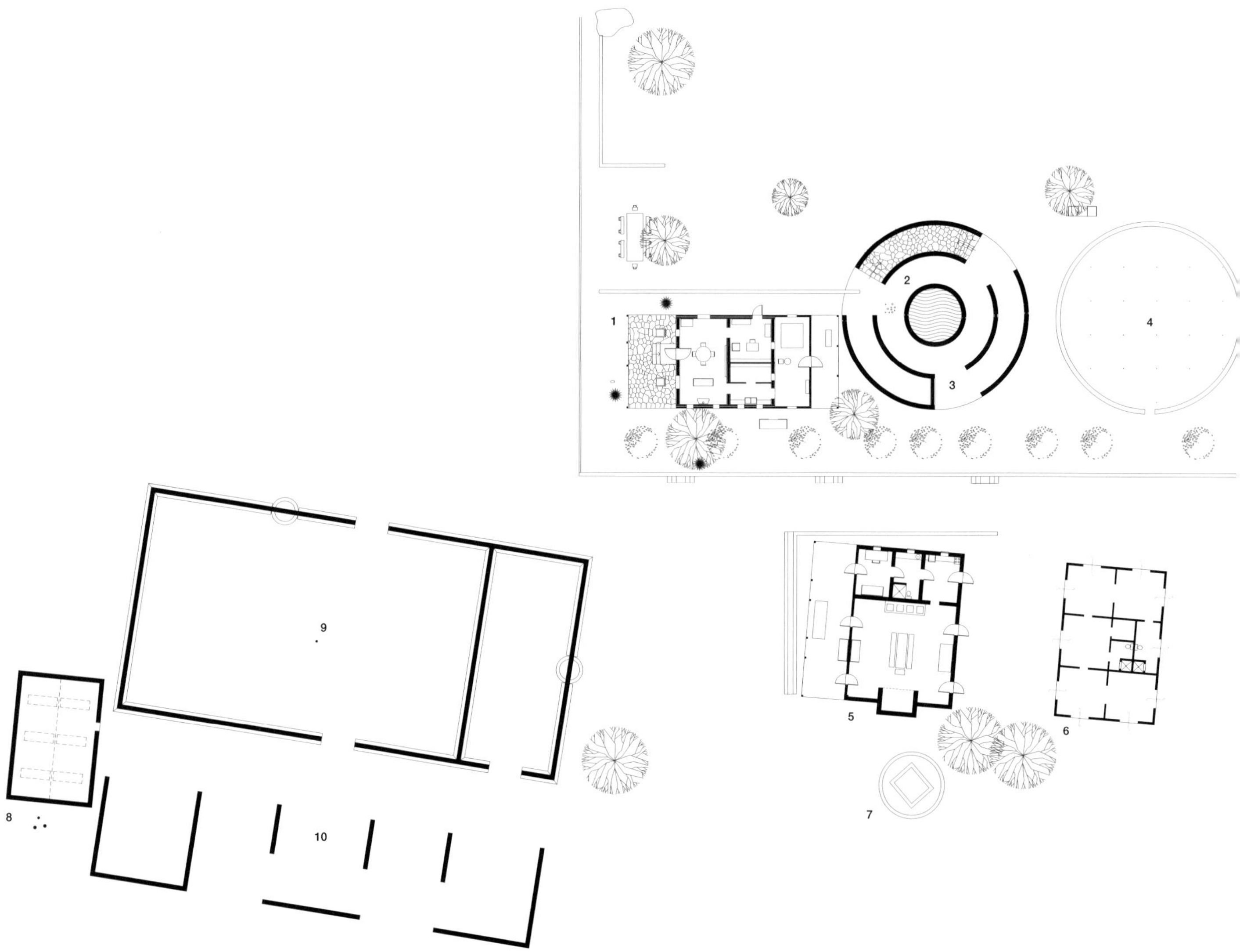

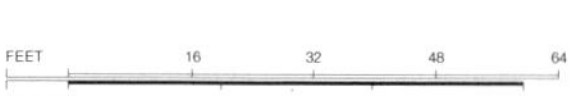

- 2.1 **Wooden Armchair** Holzsessel
- 2.2 **Insulated Icebox** Eisbox
- 2.3 **Gustav Stickley Table and Chairs** Gustav Stickley Tisch und Stühle
- 2.4 **Gustav Stickley Bench** Gustav Stickley Bank
- 2.5 **Stove** Ofen
- 2.6 **Donald Judd, untitled, 1987** Donald Judd, ohne Titel, 1987
- 2.7 **Gustav Stickley Bookcase** Gustav Stickley Bücherschrank
- 2.8 **Gustav Stickley Armchair** Gustav Stickley Sessel
- 2.9 **Gustav Stickley Table and Chair** Gustav Stickley Tisch und Stuhl
- 2.10 **Gustav Stickley Chest** Gustav Stickley Kommode
- 2.11 **Donald Judd Bookshelves** Donald Judd Bücherregale
- 2.12 **Donald Judd Bed** Donald Judd Bett
- 2.13 **Gustav Stickley Table and Chair** Gustav Stickley Tisch und Stuhl
- 2.14 **Donald Judd, untitled, 1987** Donald Judd, ohne Titel, 1987
- 2.15 **Donald Judd Table** Donald Judd Tisch
- 2.16 **Donald Judd Bench** Donald Judd Bank

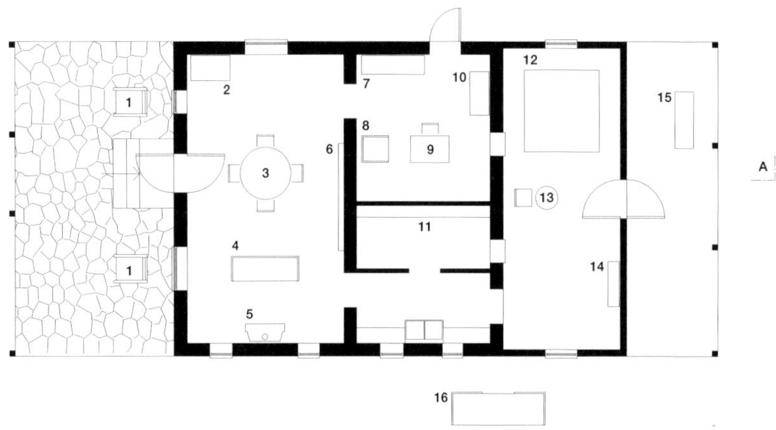

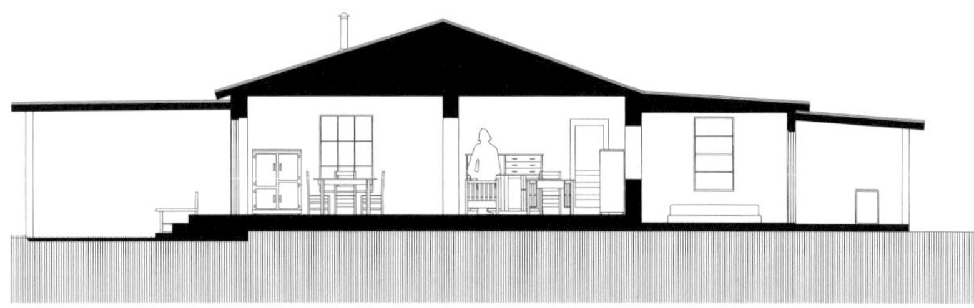

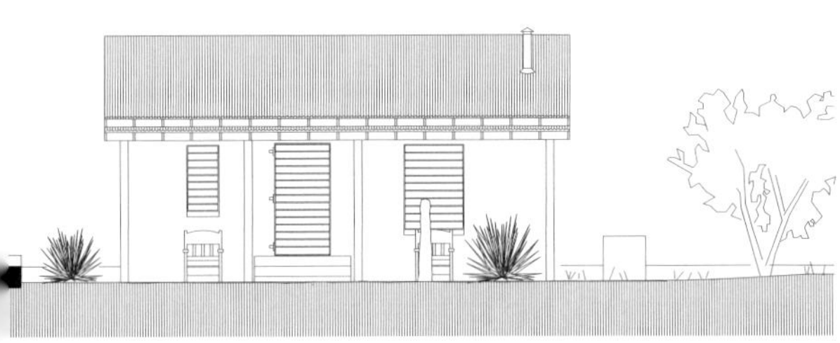

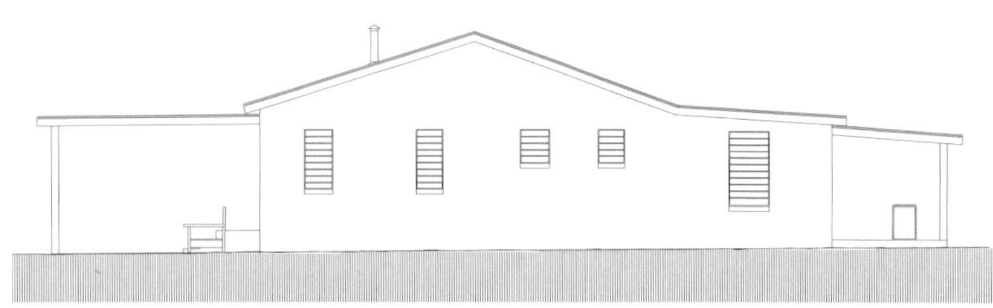

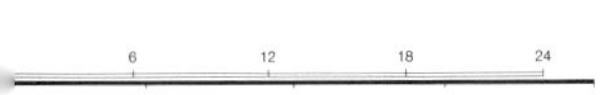

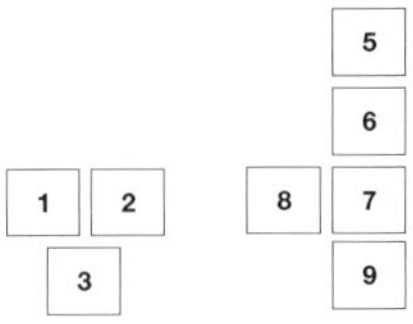

1 **Guesthouse, floor plan**
Grundriss Gästehaus

2 **Bunkhouse, floor plan**
Grundriss zweites Gästehaus

3 **Section A-A**
Schnitt A-A

4 **Studio, corrales and walls, floor plan**
Studio, Tiergehege und Mauern, Grundriss

5 **Studio and corrales, section A-A**
Studio und Tiergehege, Schnitt A-A

6 **Corrales, section B-B**
Tiergehege, Schnitt B-B

7 **Walls, studio and corrales, northeast elevations**
Mauern, Studio und Tiergehege, Nordostansicht

8 **Walls, studio and corrales, southeast elevations**
Mauern, Studio und Tiergehege, Südostansicht

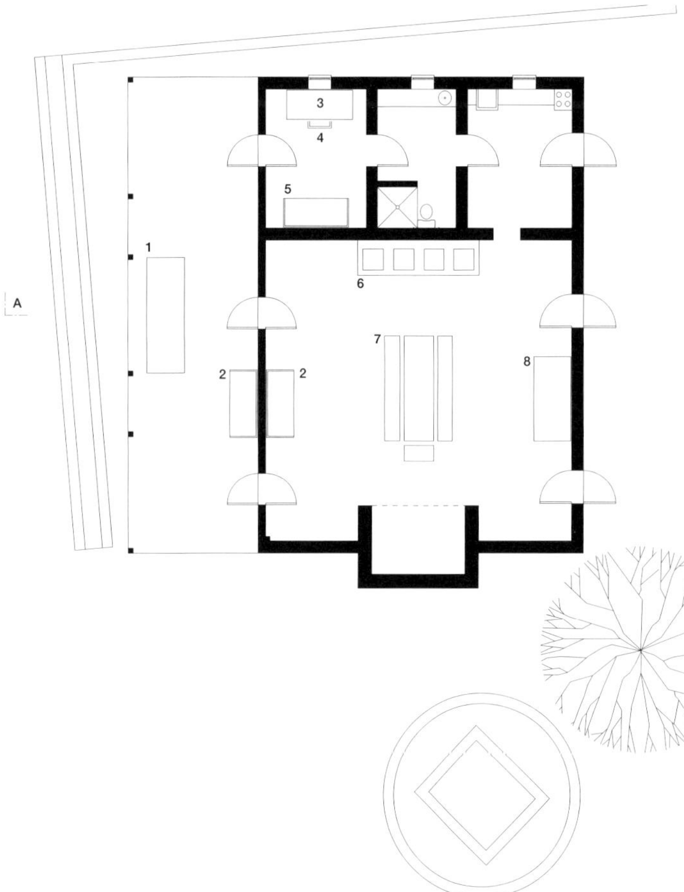

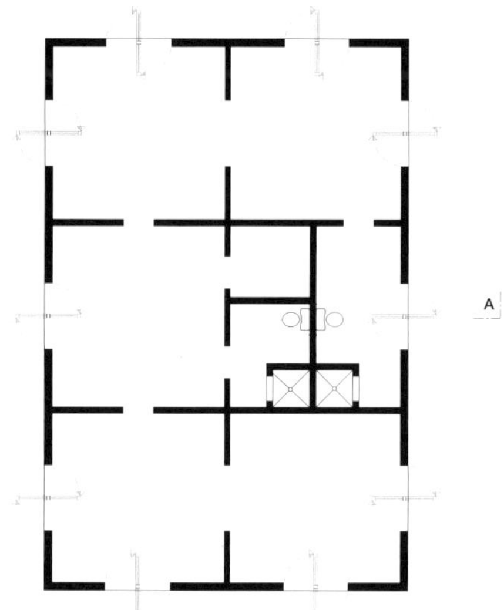

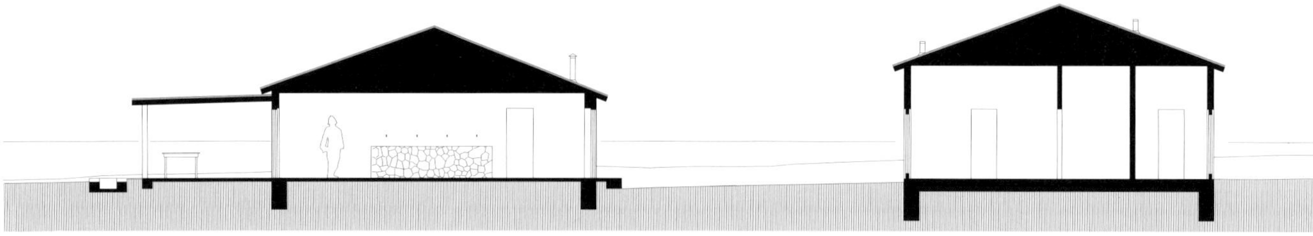

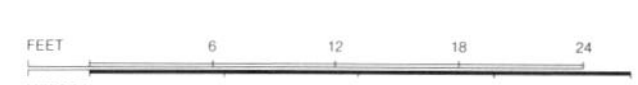

1.1 **Donald Judd**
Table Tisch

1.2 **Donald Judd**
Bed Bett

1.3 **Donald Judd**
Table Tisch

1.4 **Gustav Stickley**
Chair Stuhl

1.5 **Donald Judd**
Bed Bett

1.6 **Donald Judd**
Sink Spülbecken

1.7 **Antique Table and Benches**
Antiker Tisch und Bänke

1.8 **Donald Judd**
Table Tisch

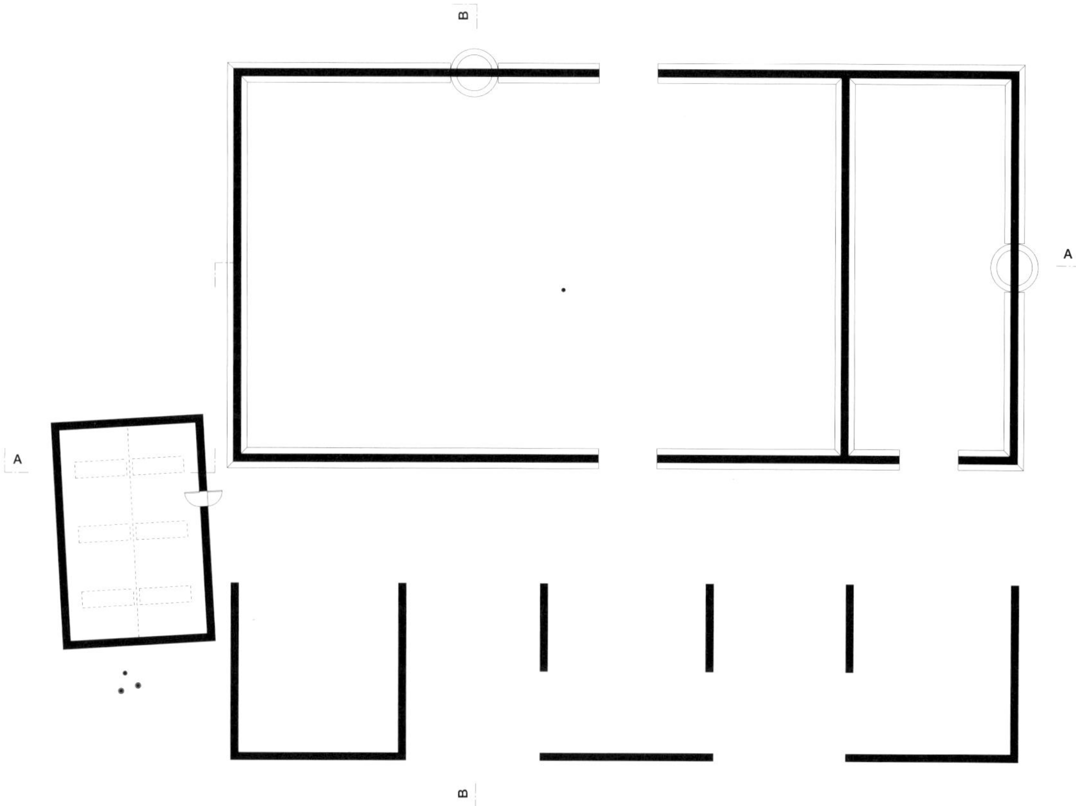

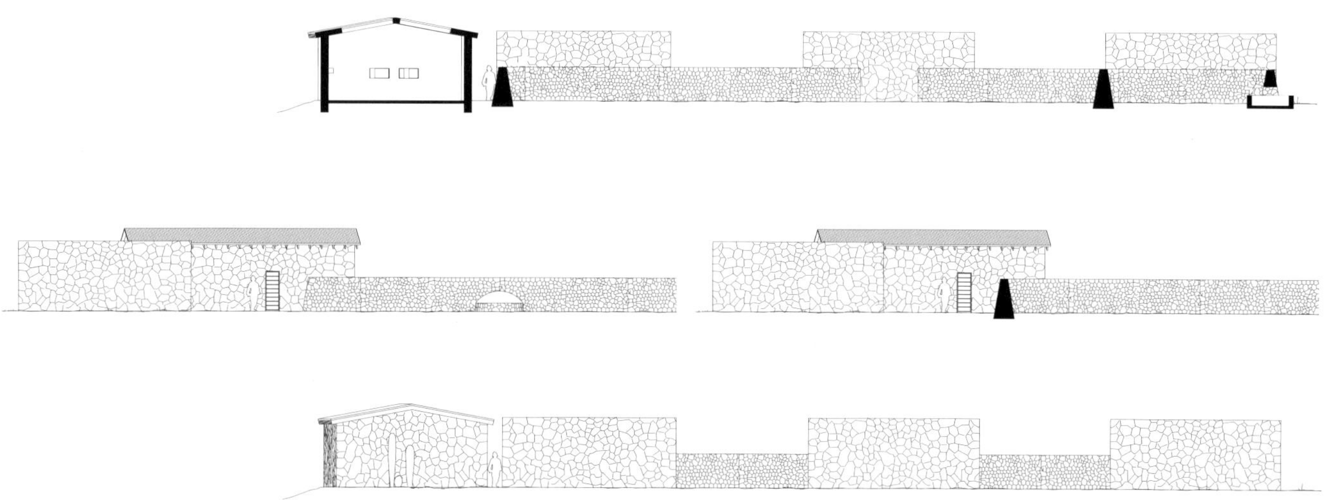

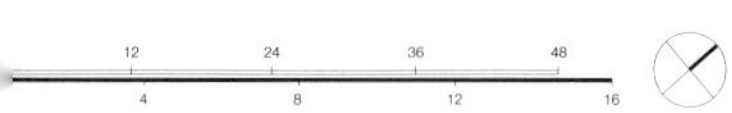

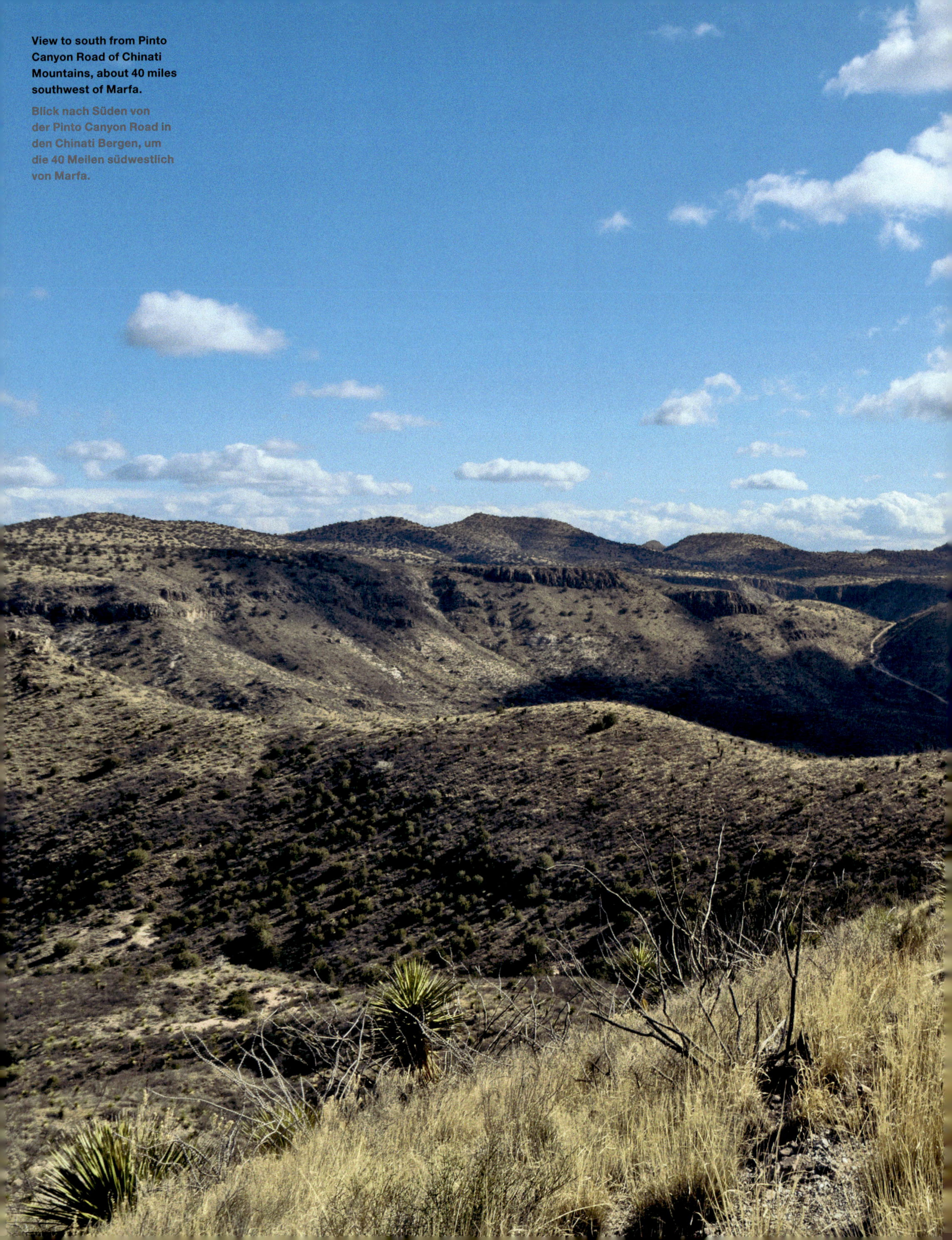

View to south from Pinto Canyon Road of Chinati Mountains, about 40 miles southwest of Marfa.

Blick nach Süden von der Pinto Canyon Road in den Chinati Bergen, um die 40 Meilen südwestlich von Marfa.

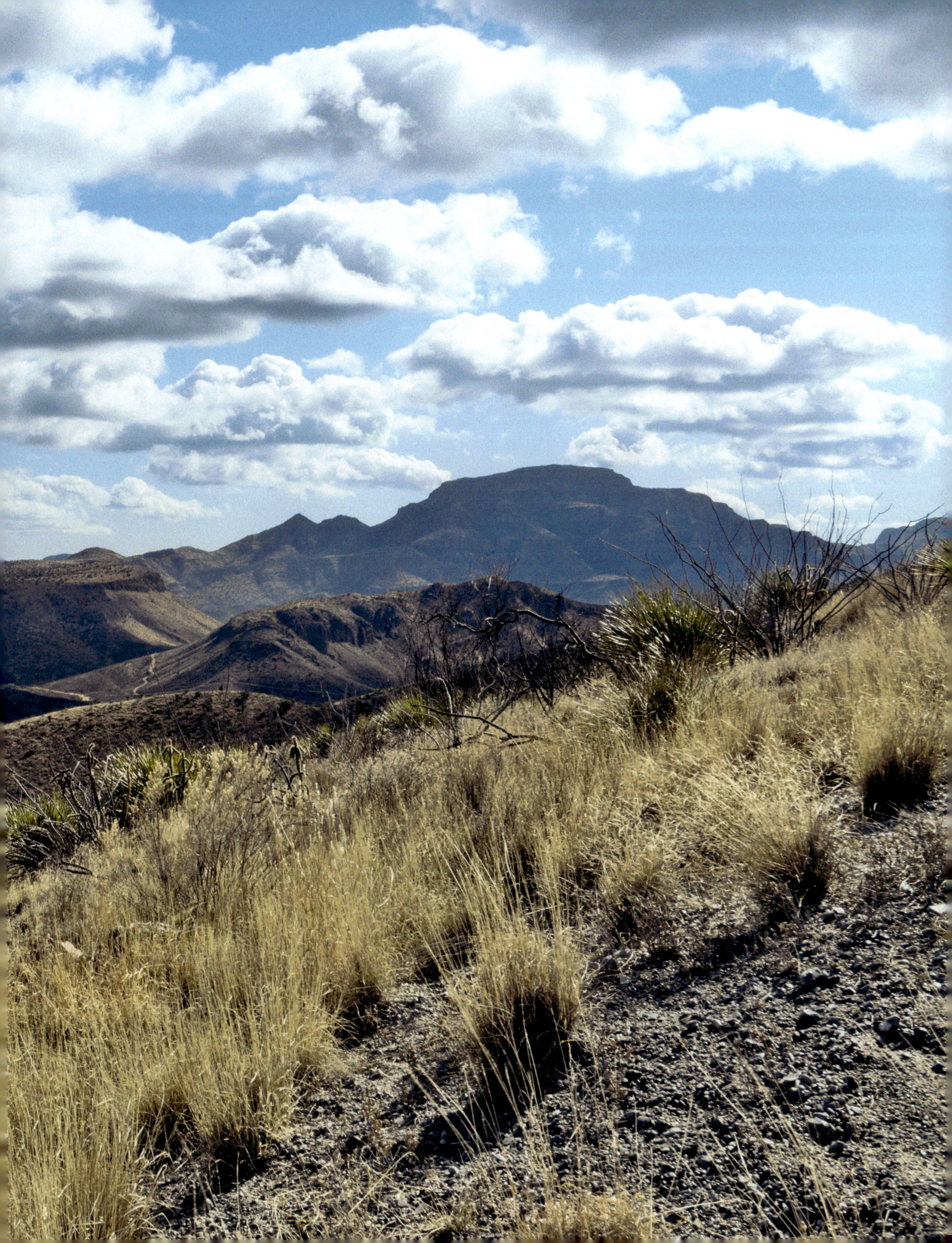

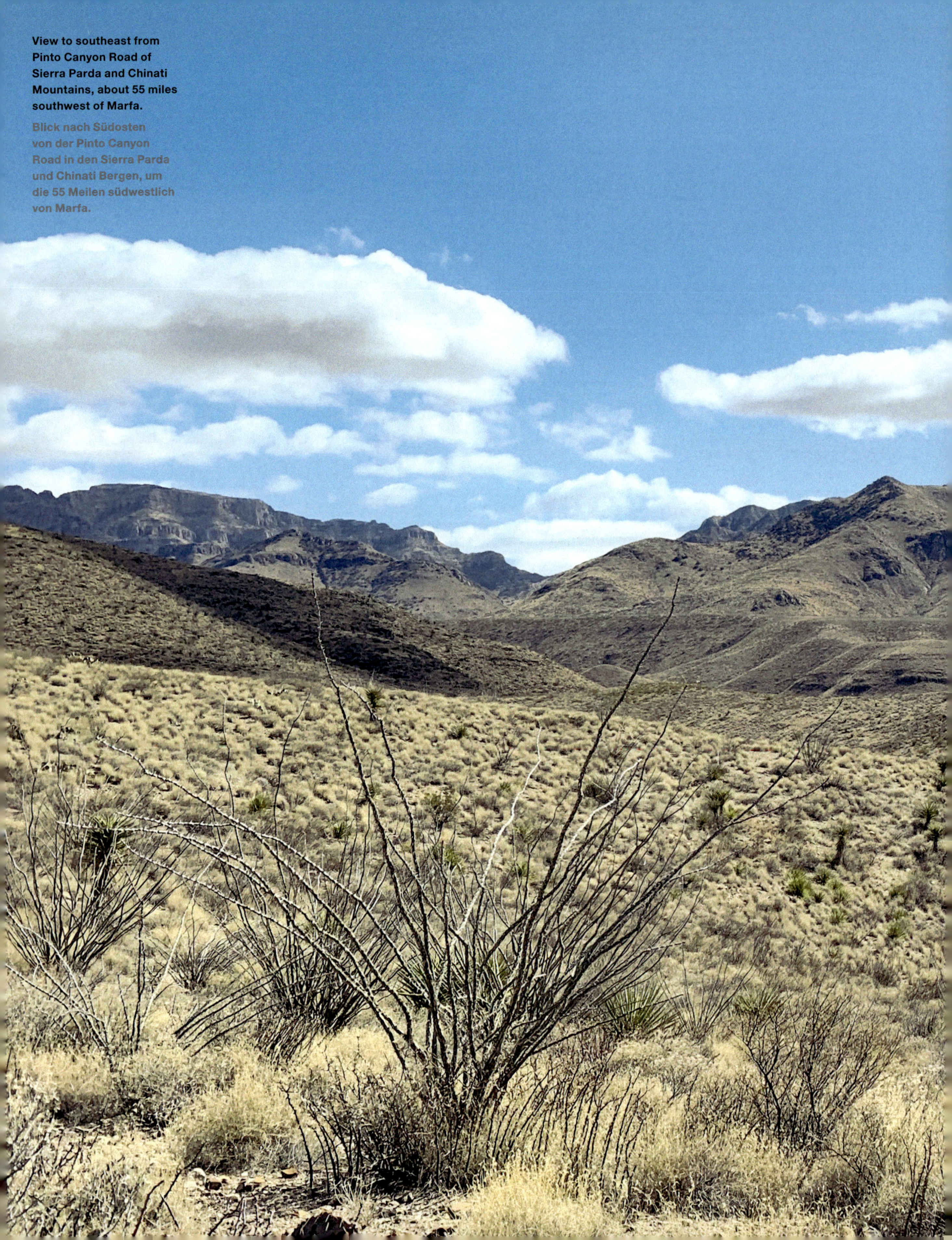

View to southeast from Pinto Canyon Road of Sierra Parda and Chinati Mountains, about 55 miles southwest of Marfa.

Blick nach Südosten von der Pinto Canyon Road in den Sierra Parda und Chinati Bergen, um die 55 Meilen südwestlich von Marfa.

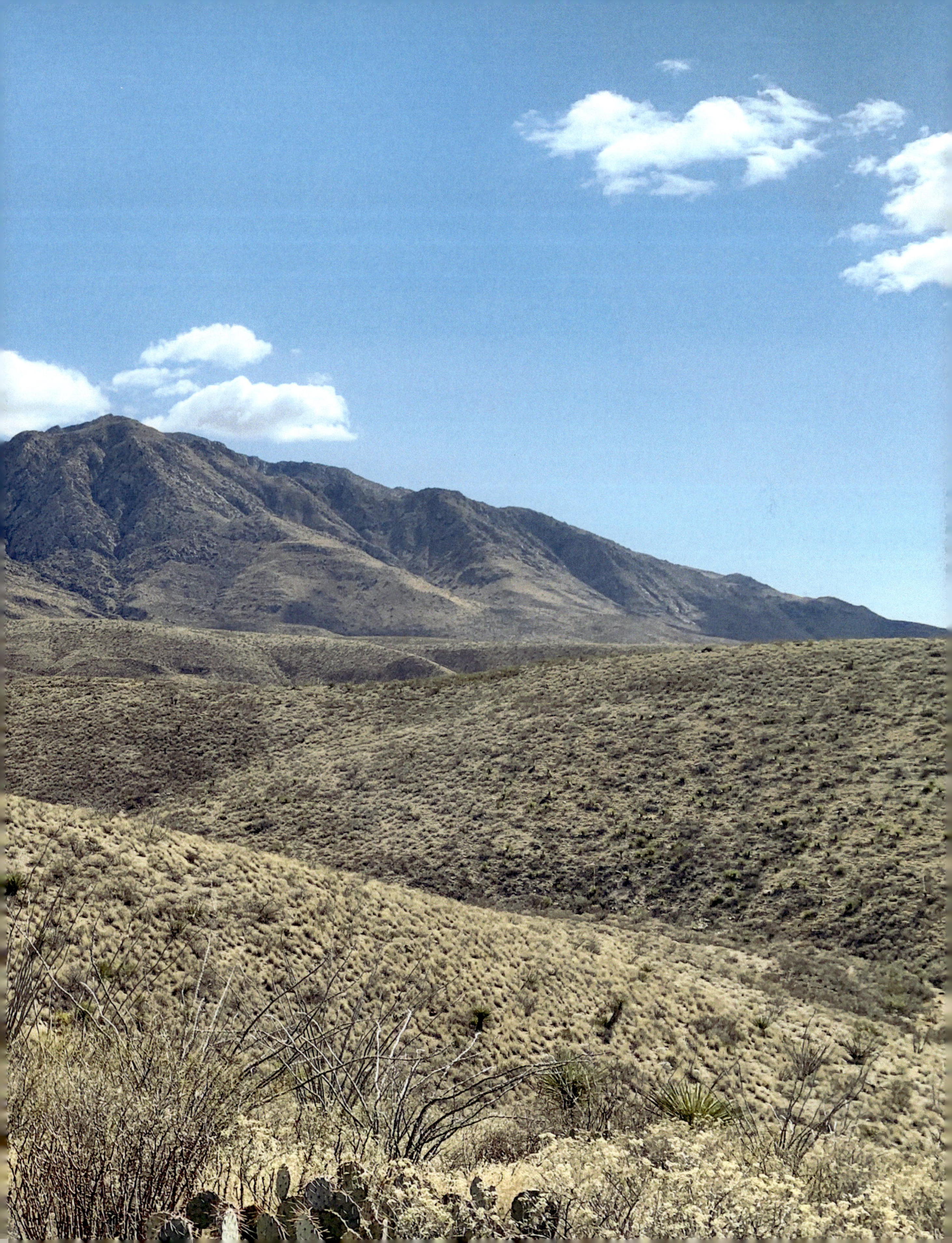

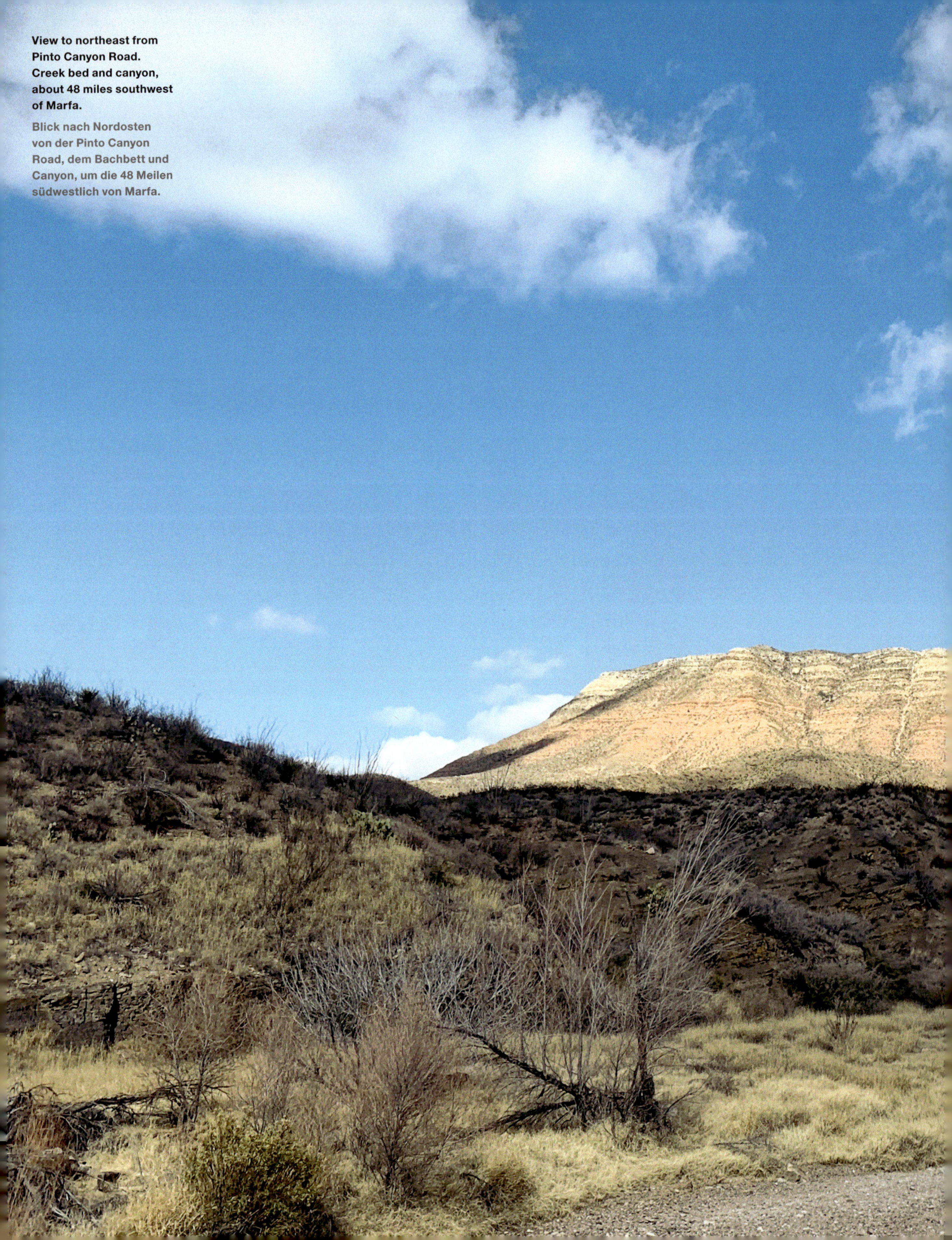

View to northeast from Pinto Canyon Road. Creek bed and canyon, about 48 miles southwest of Marfa.

Blick nach Nordosten von der Pinto Canyon Road, dem Bachbett und Canyon, um die 48 Meilen südwestlich von Marfa.

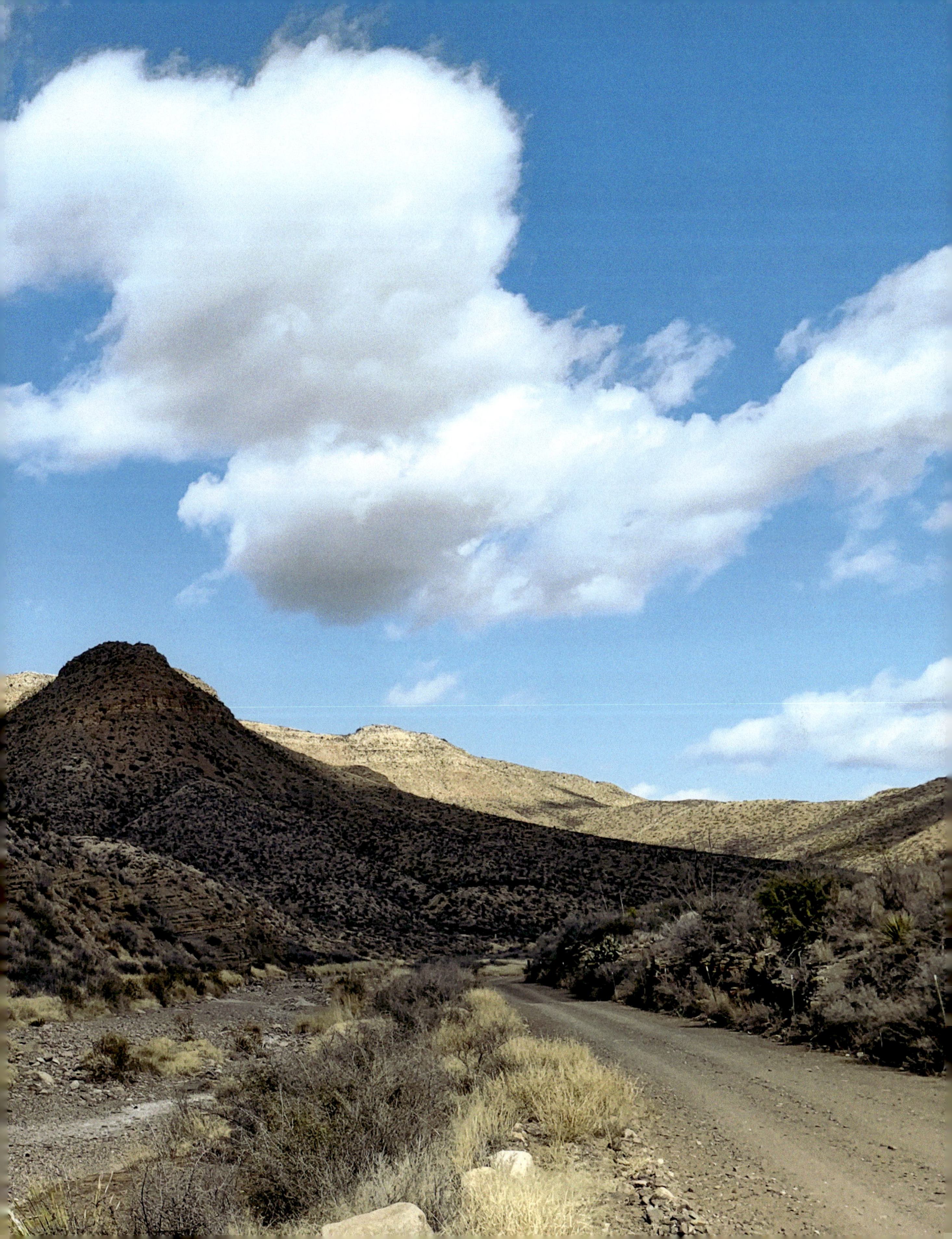

URS PETER FLÜCKIGER

NACHWORT AFTERWORD

Fast fünfzehn Jahre sind seit der Erstveröffentlichung von *Donald Judd Architecture in Marfa, Texas* bereits vergangen. Vor mehr als zwanzig Jahren haben wir mit tatkräftiger Unterstützung vieler Studierenden des College of Architecture der Texas Tech University damit begonnen, Vermessungen vor Ort durchzuführen und Zeichnungen der Gebäude anzufertigen, die Donald Judd in Marfa, Texas, umgebaut hat. Im Jahr 2016 wurden Casa Morales und Casa Perez vermessen und gezeichnet und 2017 folgte das Anwesen in der Spring Street 101 in New York. Wir verfolgten das Ziel, mithilfe der Zeichnungen – Grundrisse, Schnitte, Ansichten – die Positionen und Proportionen der Kunstwerke und Möbelstücke in Bezug zum Gebäude, zu dessen Kontext und dem umgebenden Land kenntlich zu machen.

Die in diesem Buch enthaltenen Zeichnungen basieren auf der jahrhundertealten Tradition der Parallelprojektion, die ihren Ursprung in der Renaissance hatte. Anschaulichkeit und Lesbarkeit der Darstellungen sind dabei von größter Bedeutung. Wir haben diese Zeichnungen angefertigt, weil keine Baubestandszeichnungen von Judds Gebäuden und deren Innenausstattung existierten. Ab etwa 1962 nannte Judd alle seine Kunstwerke „Ohne Titel", um jegliche Deutung und Assoziation, die über das reine Werk selbst hinausgehen, zu vermeiden. Wer Judds Kunst betrachtet, die immer auch den Raum ringsum einbezieht, sieht nur das, was er oder sie selbst sieht und was es für ihn persönlich bedeutet. In diesem Sinne werden wir den Zeichnungen außer den dargestellten Fakten auch keine Deutung zukommen lassen.

Seit unserer Vermessung der ersten Gebäude in Marfa ist der Besucherstrom in die Stadt stark angeschwollen. Die Chinati Foundation sowie die Judd Foundation unternehmen viel, um Judds Werk und Vermächtnis am Leben zu erhalten – seine Kunst ebenso wie die Kunst von anderen. Zahlreiche Gebäude, die Judd architektonisch umgestaltet hat, können von Interessierten besucht, bestaunt und erlebt werden. Um sie möglichst vielen Menschen zugänglich zu machen, haben beide Stiftungen ihr Personal aufgestockt, die Anzahl der geführten Besichtigungen erhöht und Forschern den Zugang zu ihren Archiven gewährt.

Die erste Ausgabe dieses Buchs aus dem Jahr 2007 endete mit Las Casas, dem dritten Ranchkomplex, den Judd kaufte.

More than a dozen years have passed since the publishing of the first edition of *Donald Judd Architecture in Marfa, Texas*. Over two decades ago with the help of many students from the College of Architecture at Texas Tech University we began taking on site measurements and making drawings of the buildings that Donald Judd altered in Marfa, Texas. In 2016 we measured and made drawings of Casa Morales and Perez and in 2017 of 101 Spring Street, New York. The aim was to reveal the positioning and proportions of the artwork and furniture in relation to the building, its context, and the land through drawings—plans, elevations, and sections.

The drawings in this book are rooted in the centuries old tradition of parallel projections originating in the European Renaissance. Clarity and readability of these drawings are of utmost importance. We produced these drawings because no *as built* drawings of the Judd buildings and its contents existed. Around 1962 Judd began naming his artwork "untitled" to avoid any meaning or association other than the work itself. Viewers of Judd's artwork, which always encompasses the space around the artwork itself, see what they see and whatever that means to them as individuals. Similarly, we do not impose or imply any meaning into the drawings other than what the drawings represent as the drawings themselves.

The stream of visitors to Marfa has increased substantially since the first buildings were measured. Both The Chinati Foundation and Judd Foundation made significant efforts to keep Judd's work and legacy alive—his art and the art of others. Many of Judd's architecturally altered buildings are open for the public to see and experience in person; and to facilitate more visitors, both foundations increased their staff, the frequency of scheduled tours, and opened their archives for scholars.

The first edition, published in 2007, concluded with the Las Casas, the third ranch house Judd acquired. This second and expanded edition of *Donald Judd Architecture in Marfa, Texas* gives me the opportunity to add chapters seven and eight; addressing Casa Morales and Casa Perez, the ranch houses Judd acquired in 1976 and 1982, respectively. This is significant since the Judd ranches are relatively unknown to the larger public. Judd purchased the first ranch, Casa Morales, three

Diese zweite und erweiterte Auflage von *Donald Judd Architecture in Marfa, Texas* bietet mir nun die Möglichkeit, die Kapitel sieben und acht hinzuzufügen, worin ich auf die beiden Ranchhäuser Casa Morales und Casa Perez eingehe, die Judd 1976 beziehungsweise 1982 erwarb. Diese Ergänzung erscheint mir wichtig, da Judds Ranchhäuser der breiteren Öffentlichkeit weitgehend unbekannt sind. Sein erstes Ranchhaus, die Casa Morales, kaufte er etwa drei Jahre, nachdem er sich im Block (La Mansana de Chinati) in Marfa niedergelassen hatte.

Judd gab seiner Ranch den Namen Ayala de Chinati nach dem Gebirgszug südwestlich von Marfa. Möchte man eines der Ranchhäuser besuchen, muss man sich auf eine Fahrt von anderthalb bis drei Stunden einstellen und am besten in einem Geländefahrzeug anreisen. Ayala de Chinati liegt in einem abgelegenen Landstrich südwestlich des Rimrocks und keine zehn Meilen nördlich des Rio Grande, dem Grenzfluss zwischen den USA und Mexiko. Die Gegend ist atemberaubend, gebirgig, rau und manchmal furchteinflößend, aber vor allem unerbittlich. Fährt man ab Marfa auf der Ranch Road 2810 gen Südwesten, erreicht man nach etwa 32 Meilen die Südspitze des Rimrocks, wo die holprige zweispurige Asphaltstraße in eine Schotterpiste übergeht, die steil in den Pinto Canyon führt und stellenweise gerade breit genug für ein Fahrzeug ist. Diese Straße ist die Verbindung zwischen Marfa und der Ortschaft Ruidosa, Texas, die am Nordufer des Rio Grande liegt. Die Fahrt dorthin lohnt sich und entschädigt den Besucher mit einer prächtigen Aussicht auf Berge, Canyons und über den Rio Grande hinweg bis nach Mexiko.

Über Jahrhunderte war die Gegend um den Pinto Canyon sporadisch von indigenen Stämmen besiedelt. Archäologen fanden hier Artefakte, die sich bis ins elfte Jahrtausend vor Christus zurückdatieren lassen. Im mexikanisch-amerikanischen Krieg zogen Militärtruppen durch den Canyon. Und im späten 19. Jahrhundert versuchten angloamerikanische und hispanische Siedler hier ihr Glück mit Landwirtschaft und Bergbau, bis sie wegen Dürreperioden und immer geringer werdenden Erträgen infolge moderner Technologien in Ackerbau und Viehwirtschaft dieser Gegend endgültig den Rücken kehrten. Der Archäologe David Keller zeichnet in seinem Buch *In the Shadows*

years after settling at La Mansana de Chinati (The Block) in Marfa.

Judd named his ranch Ayala de Chinati after the nearby mountain range which is located southwest of Marfa. Depending on which ranch house you are planning to visit, the drive can take between one and a half to three hours, preferably in a 4 × 4 vehicle, to reach them. Ayala de Chinati is situated in the remote stretch of land southwest of the Rimrock and less than ten miles north of the Rio Grande, which is the border between the United States and Mexico. This land is gorgeous, mountainous, rugged, and sometimes scary—certainly unforgiving. Traveling 32 miles southwest of Marfa on Ranch Road number 2810, one reaches the most southern tip of the Rimrock where the rough paved two-lane road turns into a gravel road with a steep incline into Pinto Canyon leaving at times room for one vehicle only. The road connects Marfa to Ruidosa, Texas, located on the northern shore of the Rio Grande. The drive is well worth it and honors the visitor with a splendid view over mountains and canyons past the Rio Grande into Mexico.

The area of Pinto Canyon was sporadically inhabited by indigenous peoples for centuries. Archeologists have found artifacts that date as far back as 11,000 BC. During the Mexican-American War, military troops made their way through the canyon. Anglo and Hispanic settlers tried their luck as ranchers and miners in the late 19th century until droughts and thinner profit margins due to modern farming and ranching technologies made them abandon the area for more lucrative pursuits. Archeologist David Keller chronicles in his book *In the Shadows of the Chinatis*, the history of Pinto Canyon, with its habitants, geology, landscape, and the great biodiversity of the border region.[1]. Today, little ranching persists on the original farmsteads, many of these homes are not in use all year round. The Chinati Hot Springs, a small spa of warm mineral springs offers cabins for lodging and relaxation. The area today attracts predominantly adventurous tourists who are interested in nature and the outdoors and to a lesser extent, travelers who visit Marfa for the art. The three ranch houses are part of Judd Foundation and its personnel keeps up with their maintenance. Judd Foundation opens Casa Perez, the closest of the three ranch houses to Marfa, to

of the Chinatis die Geschichte des Pinto Canyons nach, berichtet von dessen Bewohnern, der Geologie und der Landschaft sowie von der enormen Biodiversität dieser Grenzregion.[1] Noch heute wird auf einigen der alten Ranches ein wenig Landwirtschaft betrieben, aber viele Gehöfte sind nicht ganzjährig bewohnt. Das kleine Thermalbad Chinati Hot Springs verfügt über warme Mineralquellen und bietet Ferienunterkünfte an. Hauptsächlich abenteuerhungrige Touristen, die an der Natur und an Unternehmungen unter freiem Himmel interessiert sind, werden von dieser Gegend angezogen; nur wenige Reisende, die Marfa der Kunst wegen besuchen, finden ihren Weg hierher. Die drei Ranchhäuser gehören der Judd Foundation, deren Personal sich auch um den Erhalt kümmert. Einmal pro Jahr lädt die Judd Foundation die Öffentlichkeit zu einem Ranch-Tag in die Casa Perez ein, da sie von den drei Ranchhäusern aus Marfa kommend am schnellsten zu erreichen ist. Bei diesem Event sind Vorträge über die Geschichte und Ökologie der Region zu hören und für Musik und das leibliche Wohl wird ebenfalls gesorgt. Wer zum ersten Mal dieses raue Grenzgebiet besucht, ist meist überrascht, dass sich Klima und Landschaft so stark von der Region um Marfa unterscheiden.

Im ersten Absatz des Kapitels *Wasserbecken-Sequenz* in dem 1989 erschienenen Buch *Donald Judd Architektur* schreibt Judd:

> In West-Texas gibt es viel freies Land, aber man kann nirgends hingehen. Für Menschen aus der Stadt ist das Land unzugänglich. Es gibt keine Parks mit öffentlichen Einrichtungen. Anderseits – so klein die Städte auch sein mögen – sind die meisten Leute durch und durch Stadtmenschen und nicht am Land interessiert.[2]

Judds Aussage gilt noch immer. Mehr als 95 Prozent der Landfläche im Bundesstaat Texas ist in Privatbesitz. Wie recht er hatte, leuchtete mir ein, nachdem ich im Laufe der Jahre mehrfach vor Ort war. Wer Marfa besucht, kommt wegen der Kunst und hat sich in vielen Zeitungsberichten und Reiseblogs in den sozialen Medien darüber informiert, dass sich die Stadt mit ihren weniger als 2000 Einwohnern an den Kunsttourismus angepasst hat. Man kann in Marfa fast alle Annehmlichkeiten der heutigen Zeit

the public annually for a Ranch Day event that involves, food, music, and a talk on the history and ecology of the region. For a first-time visitor to this rugged borderland, one of the more surprising aspects is that climate and landscape are vastly different from that of Marfa.

In the opening paragraph of the chapter *Sequence of Pools* in the 1989 book *Donald Judd Architektur*, Judd writes:

> In West Texas there's a great deal of land but nowhere to go. The land is closed to the people from the towns. There are no parks with facilities. On the other hand, as small as the towns are, most of the people are thoroughly urban and are not interested in the land.[2]

Judd's quote still rings true today. Over 95% of the land in the state of Texas is in private hands. His statement especially makes sense after visiting the area frequently in person over the years. The visitor to Marfa is prepared and made aware of its art by the many magazine articles and social media travel blogs that describe a town with less than 2,000 citizens that has adapted to the art tourism. Today one can expect most contemporary conveniences in Marfa. But once one travels into the rugged borderland area most modern amenities are few and far between. For Judd, the ideal way to experience the land was to own part of it.

In Marfa, Judd transformed former military buildings, warehouses, and homes among other structures into exhibition spaces for his art and the art of others whose work he considered significant. Other buildings such as a former grocery store Judd transformed into his Art Studio and the former Marfa National Bank building, he transformed into this Architecture Studio. During Judd's lifetime he used these carefully adapted spaces for himself in which he would work and think. Judd's context in Marfa, except for the former Fort D.A. Russell—now The Chinati Foundation located on the southern edge of Marfa—is indeed a small urban one and Judd treats his alteration of buildings as such. At the Block, one of his first acts of design was to build an adobe wall around the existing structures, to afford more privacy and shield them from the main road to the south and from the feed mill to the north. This is an urban planning move. At Ayala de Chinati, this is very different—Judd's context is open land.

vorfinden. Aber sobald man in das schroffe Grenzgebiet weiterreist, werden moderne Annehmlichkeiten immer rarer. Nach Judds Auffassung kann man das Land am besten erleben, wenn man einen Teil davon besitzt.

In Marfa verwandelte Judd ehemalige Militärbauten, Lagerhäuser und Wohngebäude in Ausstellungsräume für seine eigene Kunst und die Werke von Künstlern, die er als bedeutsam erachtete. Andere Bauten, wie einen ehemaligen Lebensmittelladen, transformierte er in ein Kunststudio und das ehemalige Gebäude der Marfa National Bank machte er zu einem Architekturstudio. Zu Lebzeiten nutzte Judd diese sorgfältig adaptierten Räume selbst zum Arbeiten und zum Nachdenken. Mit Ausnahme des Forts D. A. Russell am südlichen Ortsrand von Marfa, wo heute die Chinati Foundation beheimatet ist, betrachtete Judd Marfa immer in einem Kleinstadtkontext und passte seine Eingriffe in die Gebäude dementsprechend an. Bei der Umgestaltung des Blocks errichtete er als Erstes eine Mauer aus Lehmziegeln rings um die vorhandenen Gebäude, um einerseits etwas mehr Privatsphäre zu schaffen und sie andererseits von der Hauptstraße im Süden und dem Futtermittelwerk im Norden abzuschirmen. Das ist ein übliches Vorgehen im Städtebau. Bei Ayala de Chinati verfolgte er einen ganz anderen Ansatz, denn hier bildeten die offenen Weiten den Kontext.

1972 lebte Judd zum ersten Mal ein ganzes Jahr in einem gemieteten Haus in Marfa. Danach mietete er die Casa Lujan, die einst der Familie Lujan gehört hatte und die er irgendwann zu kaufen beabsichtigte.[3] Wie bei so vielen Gebäuden in Marfa sind Größe und Aufteilung der Casa Lujan eher bescheiden. Das Haus steht auf einer kleinen Anhöhe, umgeben von ein wenig Land. Am beeindruckendsten ist wohl die spektakuläre Aussicht nach Norden, wo man bis in fünfzig Meilen Entfernung nichts als Ranchland sieht. Anfangs lebte Judd inmitten von Marfa, doch bald zog es ihn an den östlichen Stadtrand, weil er die Nähe zur Natur suchte. In einem Telegramm an seine Mutter aus dem Jahr 1946 schrieb er, dass er sich von dieser Region im westlichsten Teil von Texas aufgrund der Natur, der Landschaft so angezogen fühlte.[4]

Bei Ayala de Chinati spielt diese Landschaft die Hauptrolle. Judds Vision, beim Umbau der Ranchgebäude nach seinen

In 1972 Judd lived his first full year in a rented house in Marfa. After that, Judd rented Casa Lujan, a house once owned by a family named Lujan and Judd at some point considered buying[3]. As with many structures in Marfa, Casa Lujan is rather humble in its size and layout. The house is situated on a gentle knoll with some surrounding land. The most impressive aspect is the spectacular vista to the north where one can see uninterrupted ranchland for fifty miles. After initially living in Marfa Judd was drawn to the eastern edge of the town because this placed him in closer proximity to the land. Referring to a telegram to his mother in 1946, Judd described far West Texas saying that it was the country, the land, that attracted him to the region in the first place.[4]

At Ayala de Chinati, the landscape is center stage. Judd's vision to protect the land, adapting the ranch structures for his purposes, took careful planning and great physical effort to realize. All construction materials, except for the rock from the nearby mountains, had to be carried to these remote sites, and the electricity for modern construction power tools came from gasoline powered generators that the construction workers brought with their pick-up trucks. This is a very different construction reality than that in nearby Marfa and yet another one than at 101 Spring Street in New York City where Judd first owned and adapted a historic cast iron building for his family and himself in 1968.

101 Spring Street served as a template of Judd's architectural ideas for his buildings in Marfa and Ayala de Chinati. Judd arranged the five-story cast iron structure from 1870 with two basements vertically. He gave each floor a specific designated purpose. He applied that same concept in Marfa at the Block but rather than organizing vertically he employed the concept to designate specific functions for the spaces horizontally. He altered structures, modified existing spaces, and expanded them laterally. Judd delineated boundaries with adobe walls, creating courtyards, narrow and wide outdoor spaces within close proximity of each other and covered most of the ground surfaces in raked gravel. He dotted certain areas with desert plants, pergolas, gardens, trees and his furniture; all carefully planned and placed in their respective locations. While

Vorstellungen den Grund und Boden zu bewahren, erforderte sorgfältige Planung und große körperliche Anstrengungen bei der Umsetzung. Alle Baustoffe, außer dem Gestein aus den nahen Bergregionen, mussten zu den entlegenen Farmhäusern transportiert werden. Der Strom für die elektrischen Werkzeuge und Baumaschinen wurde von benzinbetriebenen Stromaggregaten erzeugt, die von den Bauarbeitern per Kleintransporter mitgebracht werden mussten. Die Gegebenheiten auf diesen Baustellen unterschieden sich sehr stark von denen in Marfa und noch mehr von denen in der Spring Street 101 in New York, wo Judd schon zuvor ein Gusseisen-Gebäude besaß, das er 1968 für sich und seine Familie umbaute.

Das Objekt Spring Street 101 diente Judd als Vorlage für seine architektonischen Ideen für die Häuser in Marfa und Ayala de Chinati. Judd gliederte dieses fünfstöckige Gusseisen-Bauwerk mit zwei Kellergeschossen, erbaut im Jahr 1870, in der Vertikalen. Jeder Etage wies er einen bestimmten Zweck zu. Dasselbe Konzept wendete er auf den Block in Marfa an, dort jedoch wurden die Bereiche in horizontaler statt vertikaler Richtung mit den speziellen Funktionen verknüpft. Er modifizierte den Baukörper, veränderte die vorhandenen Räume und erweiterte sie in die Breite. Mittels Lehmziegelwänden zog er Grenzen, erzeugte Innenhöfe in Form von schmalen und weiten Räumen im Freien, die in enger Nachbarschaft zueinander liegen, und er ließ das Erdreich großflächig mit Kies bedecken. Punktuell platzierte er Wüstenpflanzen, Pergolen, Gärten, Bäume und seine Möbel; die Orte dafür wurden allesamt sorgfältig geplant. Während die Spring Street 101 den Beginn von Judds Architekturadaptionen darstellt, markiert Las Casas das Ende seines architektonischen Wirkens in Texas. Das Gusseisen-Gebäude in Manhattan ist der vollständigste von Judds Eingriffen in die Architektur. In Ayala de Chinati und Marfa blieben hingegen viele seiner Ideen unvollendet, in erster Linie, weil er unerwartet verstarb, aber was die Ranchhäuser anbelangt auch wegen deren abgeschiedener Lage.

Die Holzarbeiten in der Spring Street 101 sind meisterhaft. Grund dafür ist die größere Vielfalt an Materialien, Holzarten und Handwerkern, die Judd in der urbanen Umgebung von Manhattan zur Verfügung stand. Die Handwerker, meist Schreiner,

101 Spring Street marks the beginning of Judd's built architectural adaptions, Las Casas marks the end of Judd's realized architectural work in Texas. The Manhattan cast iron building is the most complete of Judd's architectural interventions. At Ayala de Chinati and in Marfa many of Judd's architectural ideas remain unfinished, mostly because of his premature passing but especially at the ranch houses because of their remote locations.

At 101 Spring Street, the craftsmanship of the woodwork is exceptional. The urban environment of Manhattan offers a larger variety of materials and selection of woods and craftsmen, often carpenters, working for Judd who were familiar with Judd's expectations in finish and quality of the work he expected. The urban context was a different one compared to the remoteness of Ayala de Chinati where most materials and construction tools had to be carried onto the site. The craftsmen had to be well skilled and adaptable not only with their tools but also aware of desert wildlife where a rattle snake bite could be fatal because of the remoteness.

In his essay *On Furniture*, Judd writes of his interest in designing furniture and makes it clear that after a failed attempt to adapt one of his artworks into a coffee table, his three-dimensional artwork could not be modified as furniture. Art and architecture, although related, required different approaches for Judd. He described his first piece of furniture in Marfa, a bed for his children for one of the rooms at the rented Casa Lujan, in the following way:

> The bed was designed so that the lumberyard could cut the few different lengths to size and I could then nail them together in place. I liked the bed a great deal, and in fact the whole house, for which I made other furniture. Later, in a large place in town, I designed desks and chairs for the children using the same method of construction. More furniture developed from this beginning, now made better, but still simply, by Celedonio Mediano.[5]

This is significant because Judd understood that the context mattered, and that Marfa did not offer the same readily availability of construction materials as at 101 Spring Street in New York

kannten seine Ansprüche an Arbeitsausführung und Qualität und konnten sie erfüllen. Der Großstadtkontext bot völlig andere Voraussetzungen als das entlegene Ayala de Chinati, wo die meisten Werkstoffe und Bauwerkzeuge angeliefert werden mussten. Die Handwerker brauchten Geschick und Einfallsreichtum. Sie mussten nicht nur mit ihren Werkzeugen umzugehen wissen, sondern auch mit wilden Tieren, denn der Biss einer Klapperschlange kann in dieser Gegend tödlich sein.

In seinem Essay *Über Möbel* schreibt Judd von seinem Interesse am Möbeldesign und erklärt darin unumwunden, dass einer seiner Versuche, ein dreidimensionales Kunstwerk in einen Tisch zu verwandeln, gescheitert war. Auch wenn Kunst und Architektur miteinander verwandte Disziplinen sind, erfordern sie nach Judds Auffassung völlig unterschiedliche Herangehensweisen. Sein erstes Möbelstück in Marfa, ein Bett für seine Kinder, das in einem der Zimmer im gemieteten Anwesen Casa Lujan stand, beschrieb er folgendermaßen:

> Das Bett war so konzipiert, dass die Schreinerei die wenigen unterschiedlichen Längen zurechtschneiden und ich sie dann an Ort und Stelle zusammennageln konnte. Mir gefiel das Bett sehr gut, eigentlich das ganze Haus, für das ich auch noch andere Möbel gebaut habe. Später habe ich in einem größeren Haus in der Stadt nach der gleichen Konstruktionsmethode Tische und Stühle für die Kinder entworfen. Aus diesen Anfängen entwickelten sich weitere Möbel, die zwar von Celedonio Mediano verbessert wurden, aber immer noch sehr einfach sind.[5]

Bedeutsam ist diese Aussage, weil Judd verstand, dass der Kontext wichtig ist und dass in Marfa das Baumaterial nicht im gleichen Maße verfügbar war wie in New York City für sein Haus in der Spring Street 101. In Westtexas entwickelte sich Kiefernholz zu seinem bevorzugten Material für den Möbelbau. Ein Modul basierte auf Schnitthölzern der Größe 2" × 12" (3,8 × 28,6 cm), 4" × 4" (8,9 × 8,9 cm) und anderen amerikanischen Standardmaßen für Bauhölzer, die vor Ort beschafft werden konnten. Judds Möbel- und Architekturentwürfe strahlen eine rohe, elegante Geradlinigkeit aus, die von der Architektenschaft meiner Ansicht nach häufig missverstanden oder zumindest fehlinterpretiert

City. In west Texas his preferred furniture material became pine wood. The module was based on a 2" × 12" and 4" × 4" and other standard American dimensioned lumber sizes that could be sourced locally. There is a raw, elegant, straightforwardness in Judd's furniture and architecture which in my view is often misunderstood or at the very least misinterpreted by the architecture community. Whenever Judd could find excellence in craftsmanship, he would use it in all three disciplines of art, furniture design, and architecture. Judd moved with ease among those three disciplines. Judd's architectural adaptions at 101 Spring Street show the high level in craftsmanship because the SoHo environment of the sixties and seventies in Manhattan one could draw from a large pool of skilled craftsmen. The same was true for Eichholteren in Switzerland. Eichholteren was the name of an old Inn near Küssnacht, in the Canton of Lucerne, Switzerland. Judd transformed the former Inn for his purposes between 1989 and 1992 in collaboration with Swiss architect Adrian Jolles. Unfortunately, Judd's architectural interventions were removed after his passing, but photographs of the project show how Judd could adapt to different cultural contexts whether in Switzerland or in the remote desert mountains of Texas. Judd respected the cultural tradition of each place while adding his unmistakable architectural design. In Switzerland the name of the country itself stands often as a synonym for precision and quality. Judd's architecture reflects that. At the Texas ranch houses a raw directness where a porch column and beam are nailed together is normal, rather than predrilled and fastened with weather resistant Phillips-screws, tapping into the pioneer culture of the European settlers and the frontier of the American West. Judd recognized that Switzerland offered a similar rich culture of manufacturing and craftsman expertise that he found with the Bernstein Brothers for his artwork in New York. But in Marfa, especially at Ayala de Chinati, it was important that the architectural work would be realized, and hence the different tectonic quality some perhaps would argue was of inferior quality. Personally, I see it as a strength of Judd's approach in how he accomplished his alteration. It is more important that the ranch houses were preserved and modified, and his architectural vison gets realized, compromising

wird. Wo auch immer Judd höchste Handwerkskunst finden konnte, nutzte er sie auch in allen drei Fachrichtungen: Kunst, Möbeldesign und Architektur. Er verstand es, sich mühelos in diesen drei Disziplinen zu bewegen. Judds architektonische Adaptionen in der Spring Street 101 zeichnen sich durch ein hohes Maß an Handwerkskunst aus, was daraus resultiert, dass es in den sechziger und siebziger Jahren des vorigen Jahrhunderts in SoHo unglaublich viele geschickte Handwerker gab.

Dasselbe galt für das ehemalige Hotel Eichholteren in der Nähe von Küssnacht im Schweizer Kanton Luzern. Dieses renovierte Judd zwischen 1989 und 1992 gemeinsam mit dem Schweizer Architekten Adrian Jolles. Leider wurden Judds Veränderungen an dem Gebäude nach seinem Tod wieder entfernt, aber Fotos des Projekts belegen, wie gut er sich an unterschiedliche kulturelle Kontexte, sei es in der Schweiz oder im texanischen Wüstengebirge, anzupassen vermochte. Er respektierte die kulturelle Tradition jedes Ortes und verlieh ihm dennoch seinen unvergleichlichen architektonischen Touch. Die Schweiz gilt oft als Synonym für Präzision und Qualität. Judds Architektur spiegelt genau das wider. Bei den texanischen Ranchhäusern dagegen ist eine rohe Direktheit völlig normal, bei der die Stützen und Querbalken der Veranda zusammengenagelt werden statt vorgebohrt und mit witterungsbeständigen Schrauben verbunden. Auf diese Weise knüpfte er an die Praktiken der europäischen Einwanderer und deren Besiedlung des amerikanischen Westens an. Judd erkannte, dass die Hersteller und Handwerker in der Schweiz ähnlich spezialisiert waren wie die Bernstein Brothers, die er in New York für die Umsetzung seiner Kunstwerke entdeckt hatte. In Marfa jedoch, insbesondere in Ayala de Chinati, stand im Vordergrund, dass die Bauarbeiten überhaupt realisiert wurden, weshalb manche Betrachter den Standpunkt vertreten, die architektonische Qualität dort sei minderwertiger. Für mich persönlich liegt die Stärke von Judds Vorgehen darin, dass er seine Umbauten überhaupt verwirklichte. Denn dass die Farmhäuser bewahrt und verändert wurden und dass seine architektonische Vision realisiert wurde, auch wenn dafür Abstriche bei der Qualität der Ausführung nötig waren, war viel wichtiger, als wenn es Judds Farmhäuser gar nicht gegeben hätte. Nur wenige Architekten erkennen in einer zweckmäßigen

perhaps on the quality of the craftsmanship, compared of having no Judd ranch houses at all. Few architects see a utilitarian pioneer ranch as an opportunity to bring in a level of sophistication and architecture—but Judd did. In Manhattan Judd's highly skilled carpenters helped him realize artwork, furniture, and implemented his renovation of 101 Spring Street. The great variety of historical photographs of Judd working at 101 Spring Street shows the many different stages and arrangements that the furniture and artwork went through at Spring Street during Judd's lifetime.[6]

Judd's approach to his architecture in Marfa and at Ayala de Chinati is raw, direct, and implemented with great clarity. Kitchen items such as pans, pots, and plates are visible, and not hidden from the user. Whenever quality hardwood was available, Judd would use it—such as for the children's loft and bathroom/closets on the fifth floor of 101 Spring Street or the bath room, kitchen shelves, puppet theater, and the small mezzanine which could be used as a sleeping loft during Judd's life time.

Judd values the honesty and history of a simple homestead, a warehouse or former military structure. To me, this is what often is underappreciated in Judd's approach of adapting the structures he acquired. In a formal architect's education students spend a large amount of time studying the technical, more engineering-related aspects of the architecture discipline. Possibly because Judd was not formally educated as an architect, he does not suffer from what is perhaps best described by the French as a *"déformation professionelle"* a term that can be loosely translated as: *professional deformation* or *job conditioning*. For example, in today's architectural education design often gets clobbered with technical and material aspects of architecture as well as building codes and construction norms. Furthermore, when it comes to the architecture idea, the concept, the goal often is to create architectural design where high end materials and lofty concepts are far from buildable reality. To me, besides Judd's obvious natural talent, this is exactly why Judd's architecture is filled with such clarity and why he was able to make such an impact in the field of architecture because he was not formally educated as an architect.

Ranch aus der Pionierzeit das Potenzial, Raffinesse und Baukunst einziehen zu lassen – Judd erkannte es. In Manhattan konnte er bei der Realisierung seiner Kunstwerke und Möbelstücke sowie bei der Renovierung seines Hauses in der Spring Street 101 auf die Unterstützung hochqualifizierter Schreiner vertrauen. Die Vielzahl historischer Fotografien, die Judd bei der Arbeit an diesem Gebäude zeigen, geben einen Einblick in die verschiedenen Stadien und Arrangements der Möbel und Kunstwerke im Laufe seines Lebens.[6]

Judds Architekturansatz in Marfa und Ayala de Chinati ist geradeheraus, direkt und mit enormer Klarheit umgesetzt. Küchenutensilien wie Pfannen, Töpfe und Teller sind sichtbar und werden nicht versteckt. Wann immer hochwertiges Hartholz zur Verfügung stand, setzte Judd es auch ein, beispielsweise für den Loft mit Badezimmer/Wandschrank für die Kinder im fünften Stock der Spring Street 101 oder für das Badezimmer, die Küchenregale, das Puppentheater und das kleine Zwischengeschoss, das zu Judds Lebzeiten als Schlafraum genutzt werden konnte.

Judd schätzte die Ehrlichkeit und die Geschichte eines einfachen Gehöfts, einer Lagerhalle oder eines ehemaligen Militärkomplexes. Diese Tatsache wird nach meinem Dafürhalten oft nicht ausreichend gewürdigt, wenn Judds Umgestaltung der von ihm erworbenen Gebäude bewertet wird. Im Architekturstudium wird viel Zeit darauf verwendet, die ingenieurtechnischen Aspekte des Fachgebiets zu vermitteln. Vielleicht liegt es auch daran, dass Judd nie eine formelle Ausbildung zum Architekten absolvierte, dass er nicht unter dieser *déformation professionelle* litt, wie es auf Französisch so treffend heißt. Gemeint ist damit eine *professionelle Umformung* oder auch *Berufsprägung*. Heutzutage wird im Architekturstudium der Entwurfsprozess häufig mit technischen und materiellen Aspekten, aber auch mit Baurichtlinien und -normen überfrachtet. Was die architektonische Idee anbelangt, besteht das Ziel meist darin, einen Entwurf zu erschaffen, der auf hochwertigen Baustoffen und hochtrabenden Konzepten basiert, aber fern jeder Realisierbarkeit ist. Abgesehen von Judds offenkundigem natürlichem Talent liegt für mich der Grund, warum seine Architektur so klar wirkt und warum er so bedeutsam für das

At the Block, Judd places on the raw adobe wall his untitled, 1966, a horizontal series of four 34 × 34 × 34-inch cubes in stainless steel with amber acrylic sheets—a bold move, especially when considering that the quintessential gallery settings in the modern era are tall bright white walls. Having had the opportunity to visit this space many times over the years, the most southern room at the West building at the Block is my favorite room containing Judd's artwork and furniture. That former military structure built in steel and adobe, covered in corrugated iron, and flooded with natural light through a clerestory is as powerful in its spatial experience as any of the recent high-tech museums around the world, and it was built for a fraction of the cost.

Minimalist architects often refer to Judd's art when it comes to their sources of inspiration for their own work. Architect John Pawson often goes to great lengths creating kitchen cabinets where no door hinge, doorknob, or drawer-handle is visible so as not to interrupt the row of cabinet surfaces. A spare, recessed lip must suffice to pull the drawer or swing the cabinet door open. High-end kitchen appliances are barely noticeable and artfully covered with the same material as the cabinets. In the discipline of architecture, minimalism is often regarded and practiced with the intent of designing spaces which are devoid of the signs of the appliances, light sources, and especially modern appliances which radiate luxury and are costly in the making. This is in stark contrast with Judd's kitchen at the Block, in the former Quartermaster Building. There, Judd placed a standard gas stove and a dishwasher next to open kitchen shelves. The open pantry area houses a typical white refrigerator and a floor to ceiling open pine wood shelf across from a low-slung open shelf with a series of frying pans directly hung from the wall. Judd followed the same approach at Casa Morales and Perez. At the latter, Judd also relocated the bathroom facilities outside of the main ranch house and Quartermaster house at the Block. While this might be an inconvenience, on the practical side it allowed Judd to install new plumbing and a new waste management system rather than renovate the old one. Also, I like to imagine, that going outside in the middle of a clear cool summer night with the stars shining from high in the

Fachgebiet der Architektur wurde, darin, dass er kein studierter Architekt war.

An die unverputzte Lehmziegelwand im Block hängte Judd sein Werk ohne Titel,1966, eine horizontale Reihe aus vier Edelstahlwürfeln mit 86 Zentimetern Kantenlänge und bernsteingelben Acrylplatten; ein kühner Schritt, wenn man bedenkt, dass die typischen Galerien der Moderne hohe weiße Wände besaßen. Ich hatte im Laufe der Jahre mehrmals die Gelegenheit, diesen Ort zu besuchen, und der südlichste Raum im Westgebäude des Blocks, der Judds Kunstwerke und Möbel enthält, gefällt mir am besten. Das ehemalige Militärgebäude aus Stahl und Lehmziegeln, mit Wellblech verkleidet und von natürlichem Licht durchflutet, das durch ein Fensterband einfällt, strahlt eine ebenso mächtige räumliche Wirkung aus wie jedes moderne hochtechnisierte Museum und wurde für nur einen Bruchteil der Kosten erbaut.

Fragt man minimalistische Architekten nach den Inspirationsquellen für ihre Arbeit, verweisen diese häufig auf Judds Werke. Der Architekt John Pawson gibt sich größte Mühe, dass an den von ihm entworfenen Küchenschränken keine sichtbaren Scharniere, Türknäufe oder Schubladengriffe die Ansicht der Schrankoberflächen stören. Eine zierliche versenkte Griffmulde muss zum Öffnen ausreichen. Moderne Küchengeräte sind kaum wahrnehmbar und kunstvoll mit demselben Material verkleidet wie die Schränke. In der Architektur versteht man unter Minimalismus meist die Intention, Räume zu entwerfen, die frei sind von Geräten, Lichtquellen und insbesondere modernen Einrichtungsgegenständen, die Luxus ausstrahlen und teuer sind. Ganz anders als Judds Küche im Block, im einstigen Haus des Quartiermeisters. Denn dort ordnete Judd einen gewöhnlichen Gasherd und einen Geschirrspüler direkt neben offenen Küchenregalen an. Die offen gehaltene Vorratskammer beherbergt einen weißen Kühlschrank sowie ein über die gesamte Raumhöhe offenes Kiefernholzregal an der einen Wand und an der anderen hängen ein niedrigeres Regal und ein ganzer Satz Pfannen. Denselben Ansatz verfolgte Judd auch in der Casa Morales und der Casa Perez, wobei er in der letztgenannten Ranchhaus ebenso wie im Haus des Quartiermeisters im Block sogar das Badezimmer aus dem Haupthaus verbannte. Was unpraktisch

west Texas sky was a pleasure rather than an inconvenience for Judd.

To me Judd's approach to architecture is an extraordinarily positive one. It fills me with great hope for the future of architecture and young architects everywhere, that with enough imagination and careful arrangement of space, straightforward, humble materials, architecture can happen at reasonable costs in very rural places such as the remote Chinati Mountains—and if it can happen there, it can happen anywhere.

1 Keller, David W. *In the Shadow of the Chinatis. A History of Pinto Canyon in the Big Bend.* College Station. Texas A&M University Press 2019.

2 *Donald Judd. Architektur,* Stockebrand, Marianne. Ed. 3rd ed. (Ostfildern near Stuttgart, Cantz, 1992), p. 33.

3 *Donald Judd. Architektur,* Stockebrand, Marianne. Ed. 3rd ed. (Ostfildern near Stuttgart, Cantz, 1992), p. 29 and 33.

4 Flückiger, Urs Peter. *Donald Judd Architecture in Marfa, Texas.* Birkhäuser 2007, p. 25.

5 *Donald Judd. Architektur,* Stockebrand, Marianne. Ed. 3rd ed. (Ostfildern near Stuttgart, Cantz, 1992), p. 134–135, and Reprinted as "On Furniture" in *Donald Judd Writings,* ed. Flavin Judd and Caitlin Murray (New York: Judd Foundation/David Zwirner Books, 2016), 452.

6 Judd Foundation. *Donald Judd Spaces.* DelMonico/Prestel, Munich 2020 p. 13–92.

klingen mag, bot ihm ganz praktische Vorteile, denn so konnte er die Wasser- und Abwasserleitungen komplett neu verlegen, statt die alten reparieren zu müssen. Ich könnte mir auch vorstellen, dass es für Judd sehr angenehm war, inmitten einer klaren kühlen Sommernacht in Westtexas zum Baden nach draußen unter den weiten Sternenhimmel zu gehen.

Judds Einstellung zur Architektur hat für mich etwas außerordentlich Positives. Für die Zukunft der Architektur und junge Architekten erfüllt es mich mit großer Hoffnung, dass man mit ausreichend Fantasie, sorgfältig arrangierten Räumen und bescheidenen Materialien eine Architektur zu vernünftigen Preisen selbst in sehr ländlichen Gegenden wie den Chinati Mountains erschaffen kann – denn was dort gelingt, kann überall gelingen.

1 David W Keller. *In the Shadow of the Chinatis. A History of Pinto Canyon in the Big Bend.* College Station. Texas A&M University Press 2019.
2 Donald Judd. *Architektur,* Marianne Stockebrand. Dritte Ausgabe, (Ostfildern bei Stuttgart, Cantz, 1992), S. 33/31.
3 Donald Judd. *Architektur,* Marianne Stockebrand. Dritte Ausgabe, (Ostfildern bei Stuttgart, Cantz, 1992), S. 29 und 33.
4 Urs Peter Flückiger. *Donald Judd Architecture in Marfa, Texas.* Birkhäuser 2007, S. 25.
5 Donald Judd. *Architektur,* Marianne Stockebrand. Dritte Ausgabe, (Ostfildern bei Stuttgart, Cantz, 1992), S. 134–135/127–130, und Judd Donald. *Donald Judd Writings.* Flavin Judd und Caitlin Murray. Hrsg. Judd Foundation und Zwirner Books, New York, 2016. S. 452.
6 Judd Foundation. *Donald Judd Spaces.* DelMonico/Prestel 2020, S. 13–92.

101 Spring Street, New York, view to northeast.

101 Spring Street, New York, Blick nach Nordost.

JUDD FOUNDATION

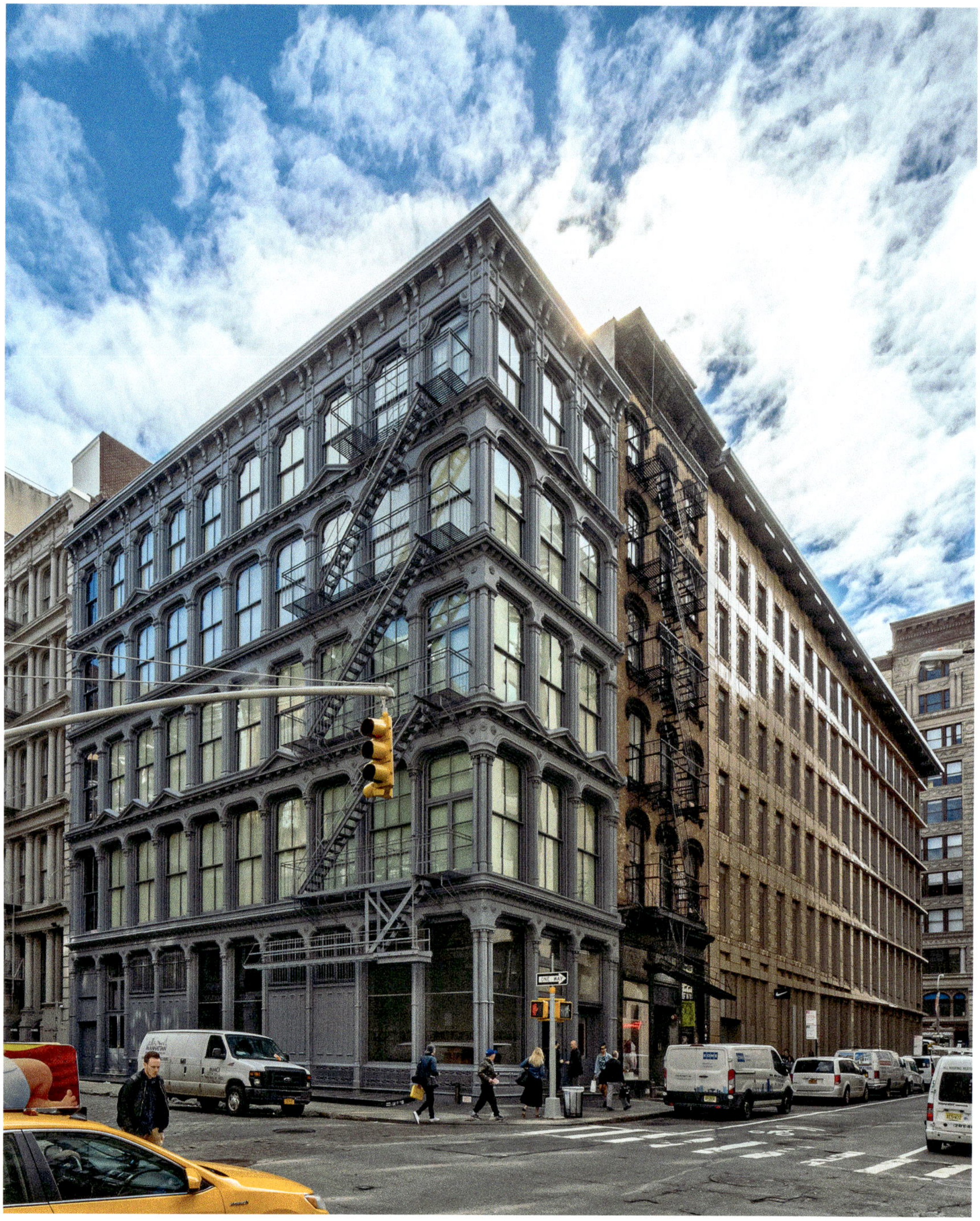

101 Spring Street, first floor, Installation view of Donald Judd, *Prints: 1992,* and untitled, 1974, view to north.

101 Spring Street, Erdgeschoss, Installationsansicht von Donald Judd, *Prints: 1992,* und untitled, 1974, Blick nach Norden.

101 Spring Street, first floor, Installation view of Donald Judd, *Prints: 1992,* and bed, view to east.

101 Spring Street, Erdgeschoss, Installationsansicht von Donald Judd, *Prints: 1992,* und Bett, Blick nach Osten.

JUDD FOUNDATION

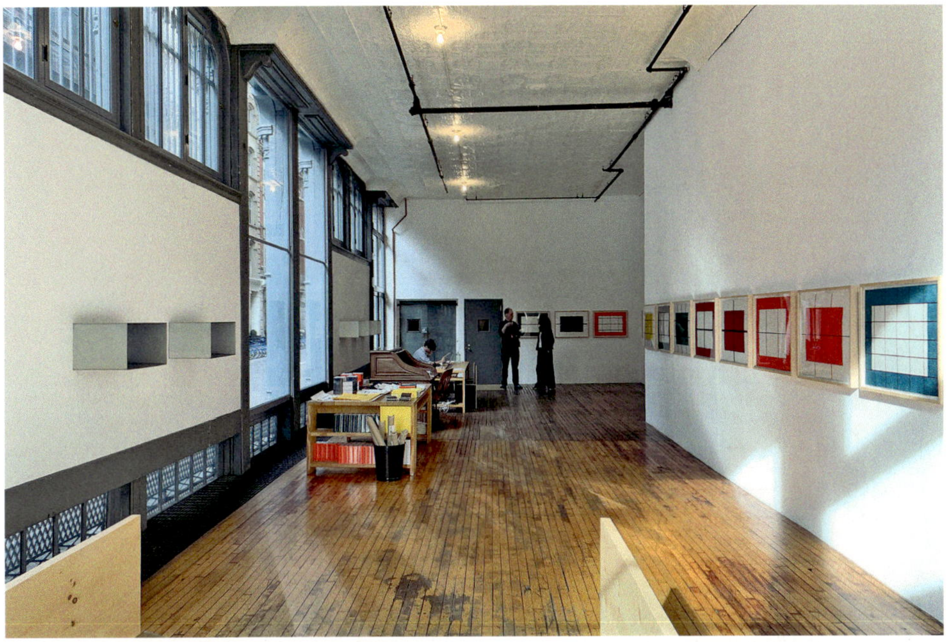

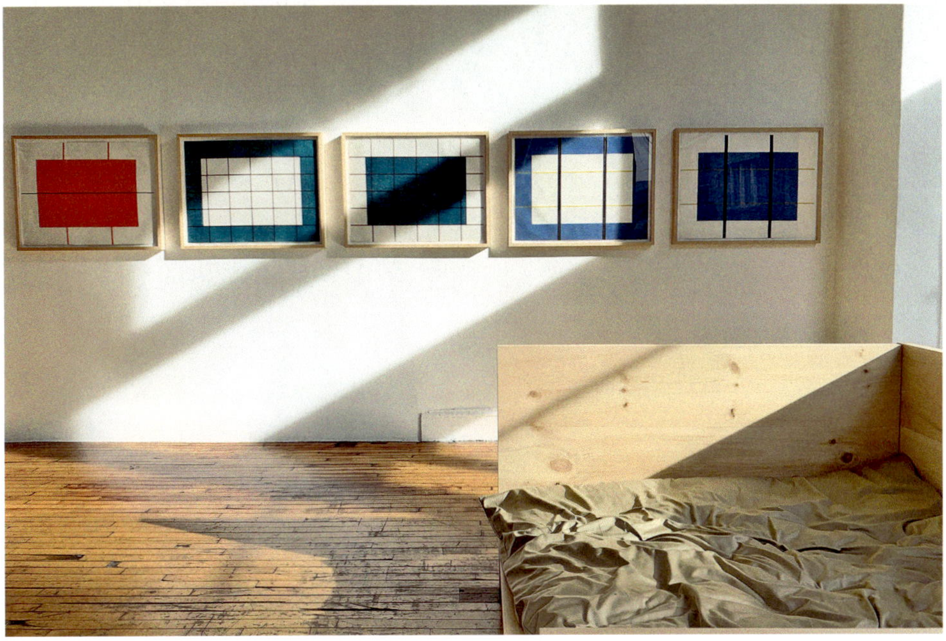

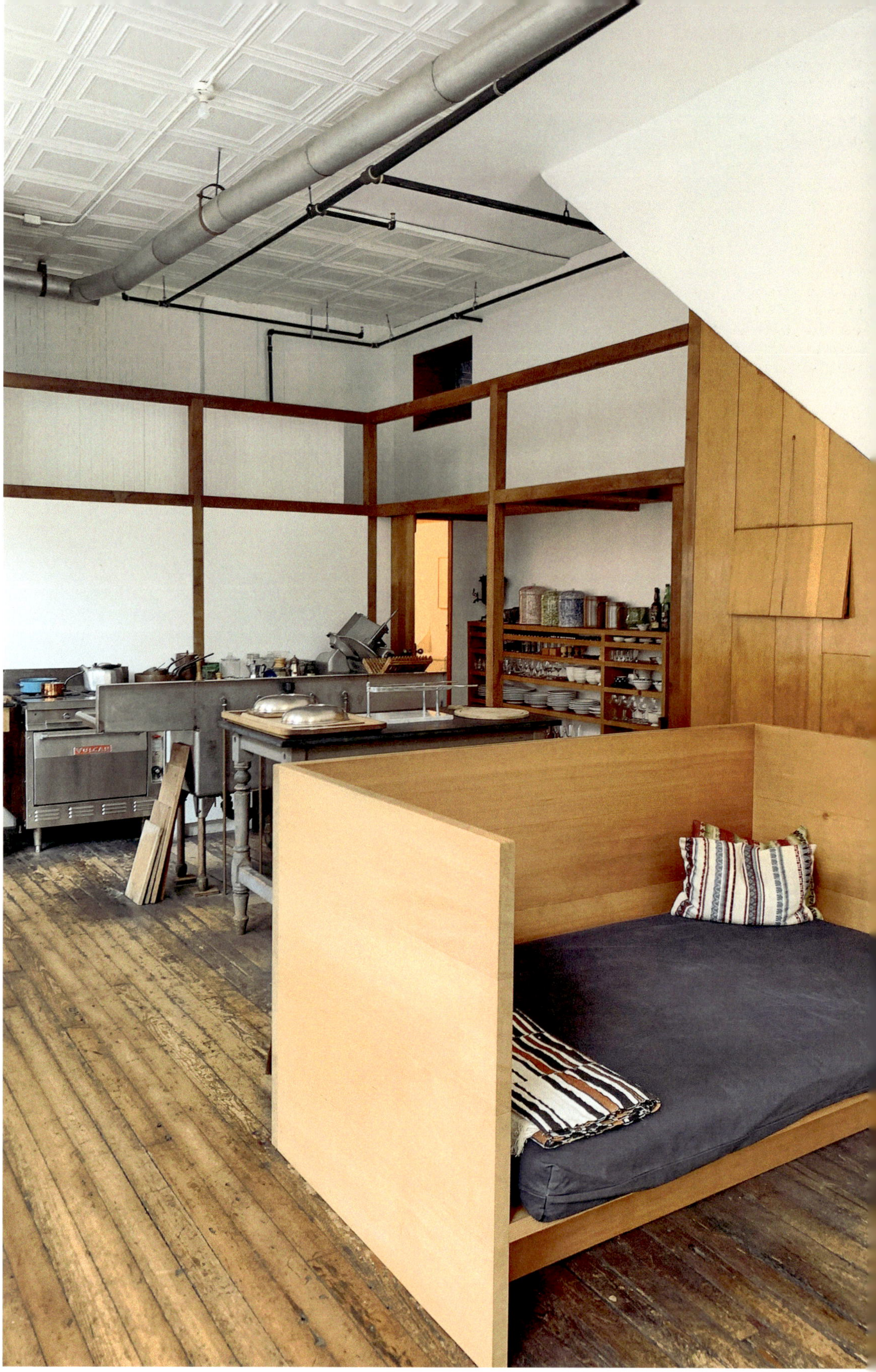

101 Spring Street, second floor, kitchen with puppet theater and bed by Donald Judd, view to northeast.

101 Spring Street, erster Stock, Küche mit Puppentheater und Bett von Donald Judd, Blick nach Nordost.

JUDD FOUNDATION

101 Spring Street, second floor, David Novros, no title / 101 Spring Street, 1970, view to east.

101 Spring Street, erster Stock, David Novros, ohne Title / 101 Spring Street, 1970, Blick nach Osten

101 Spring Street, second floor, with table and chairs by Donald Judd, *Abstract Painting, Red,* 1952, by Ad Reinhardt, view to north.

101 Spring Street, erster Stock, mit Tisch und Stühlen von Donald Judd, *Abstract Painting, Red, 1952,* von Ad Reinhardt, Blick nach Norden.

JUDD FOUNDATION

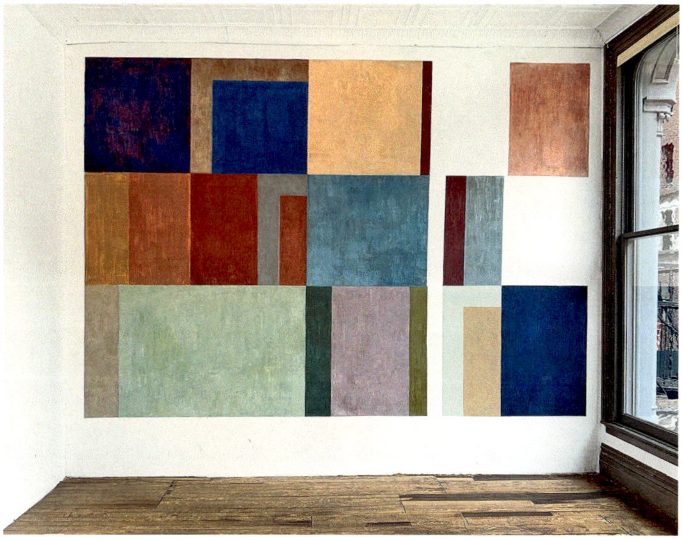

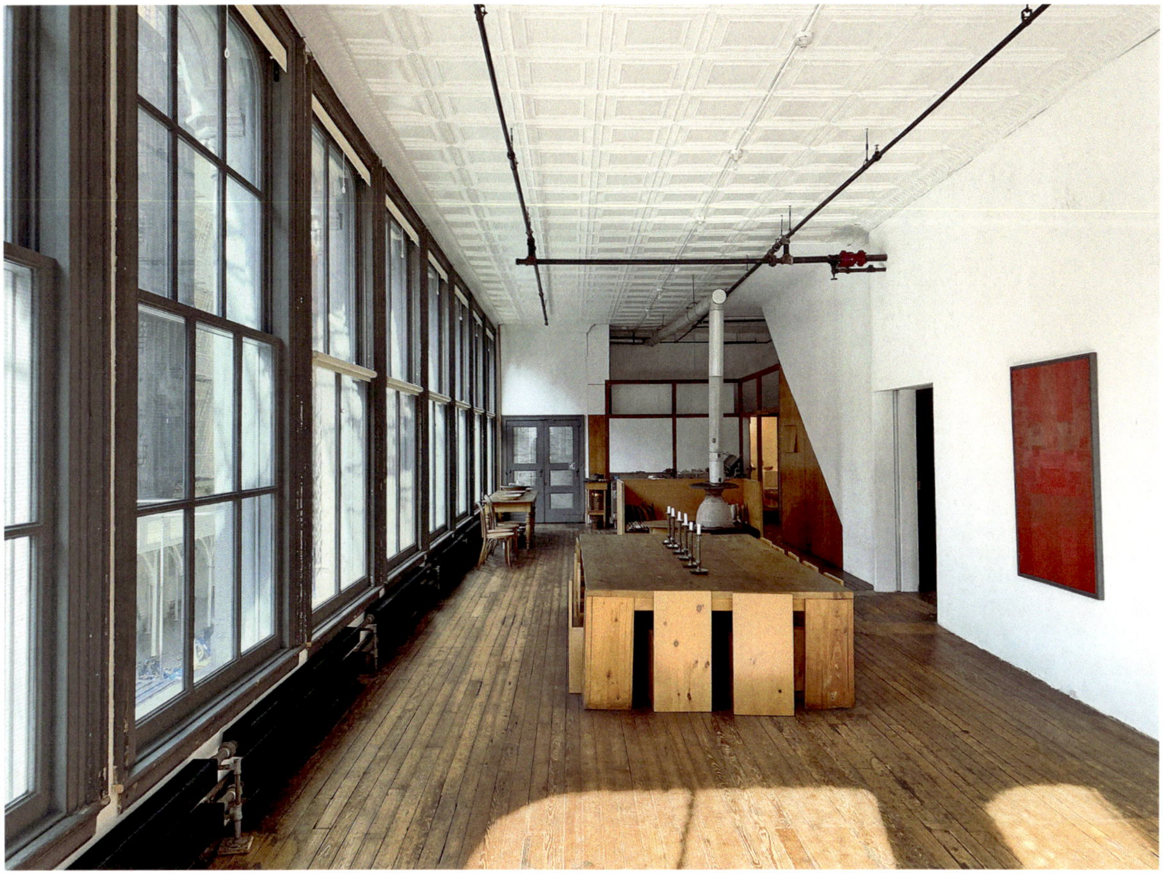

101 Spring Street, third floor, chairs, table and stools by Alvar Aalto, untitled, 1969 by Donald Judd, view to north.

101 Spring Street, zweiter Stock, Stühle, Tisch und Hocker von Alvar Aalto, untitled, 1969 von Donald Judd, Blick nach Norden.

JUDD FOUNDATION

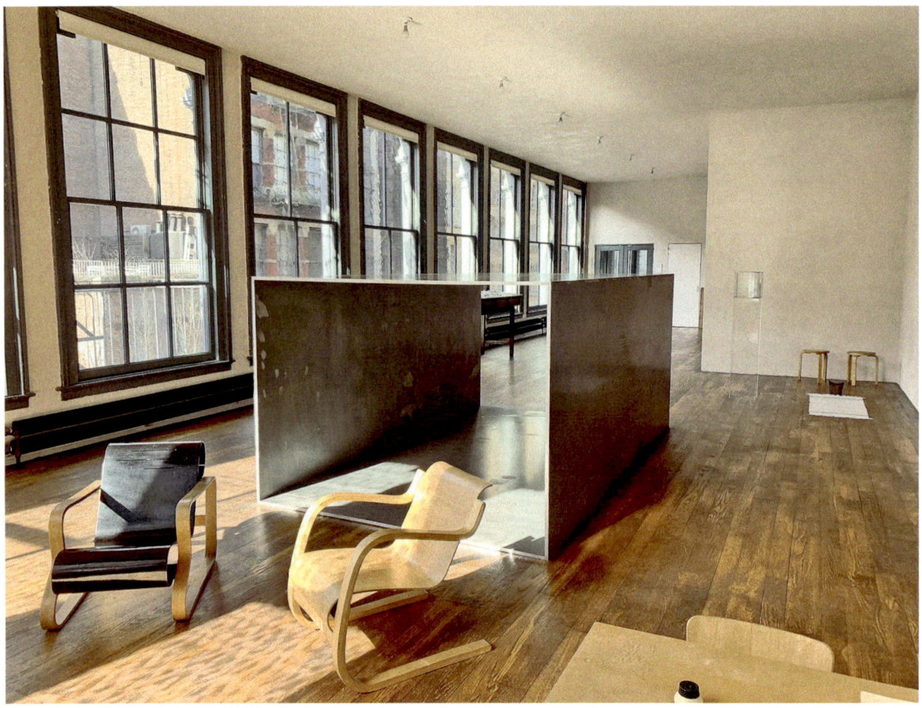

101 Spring Street, third floor, untitled, 1966 and untitled, 1969 by Donald Judd, view to south.

101 Spring Street, zweiter Stock, untitled, 1966 und untitled, 1969 von Donald Judd, Blick nach Süden.

JUDD FOUNDATION

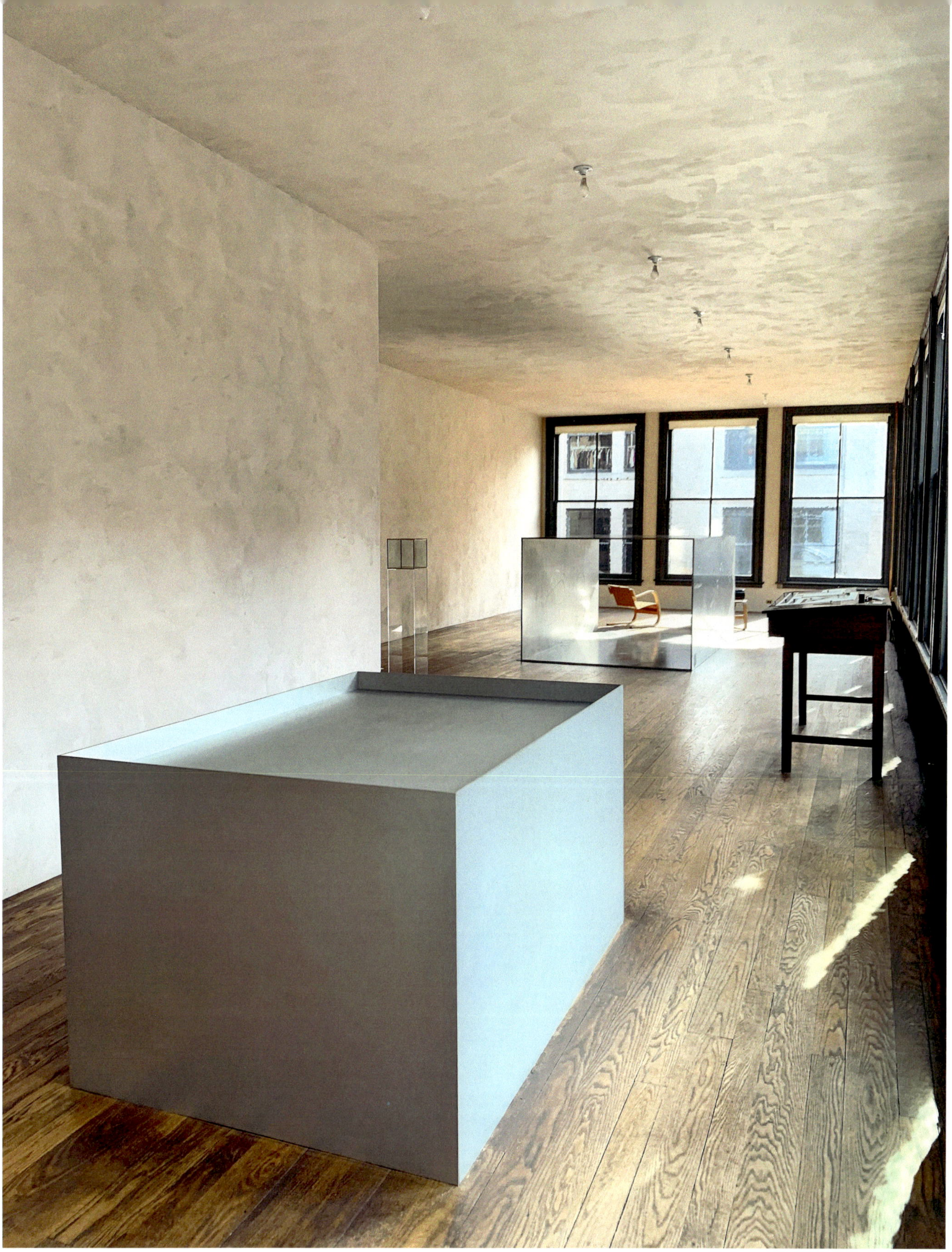

101 Spring Street, fourth floor, furniture by Donald Judd, chairs by Gerrit Rietveld, painting by Frank Stella, *Gur II,* 1967

101 Spring Street, dritter Stock, Möbel von Donald Judd, Stühle von Gerrit Rietveld, Gemälde von Frank Stella, *Gur II,* 1967

JUDD FOUNDATION

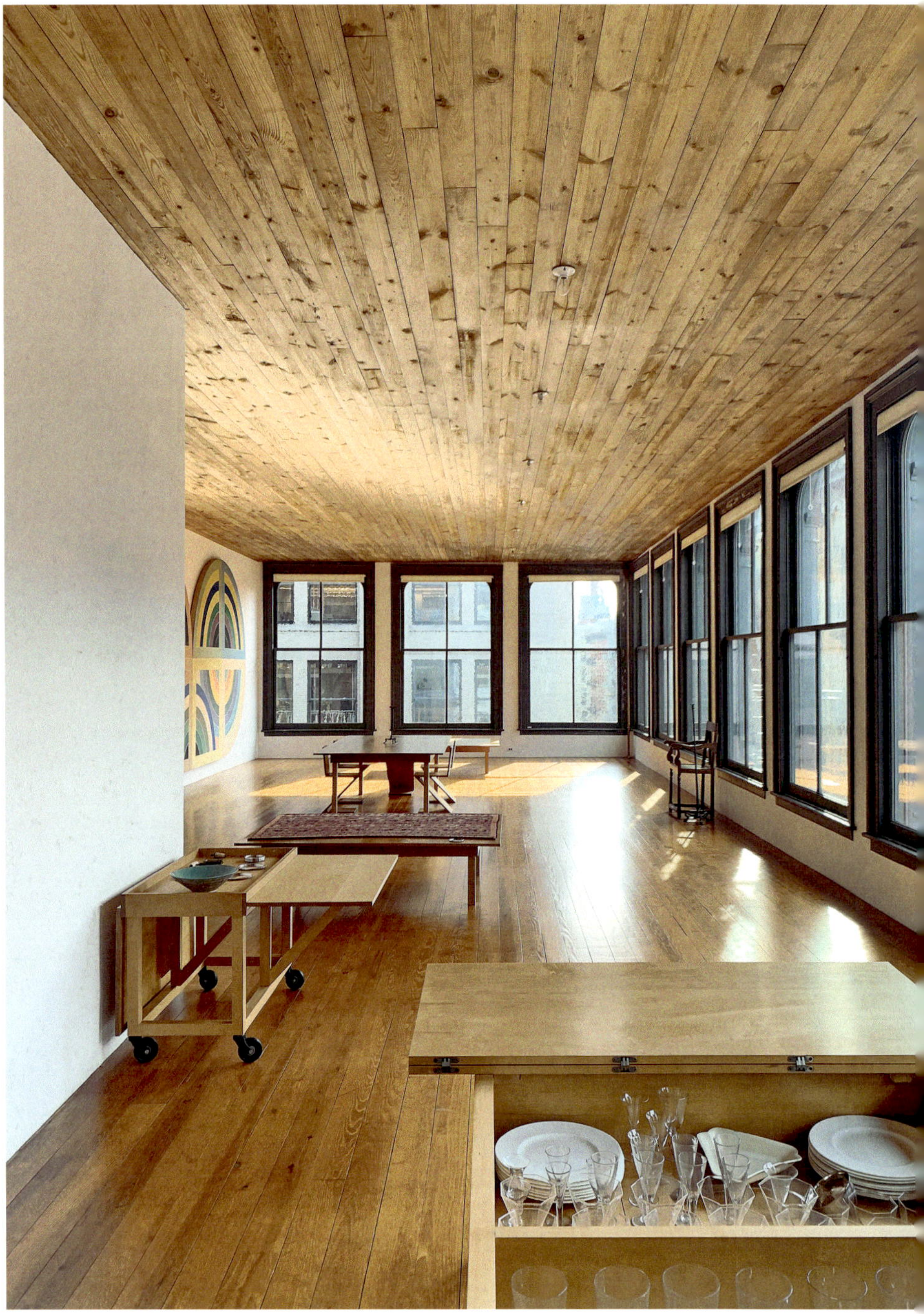

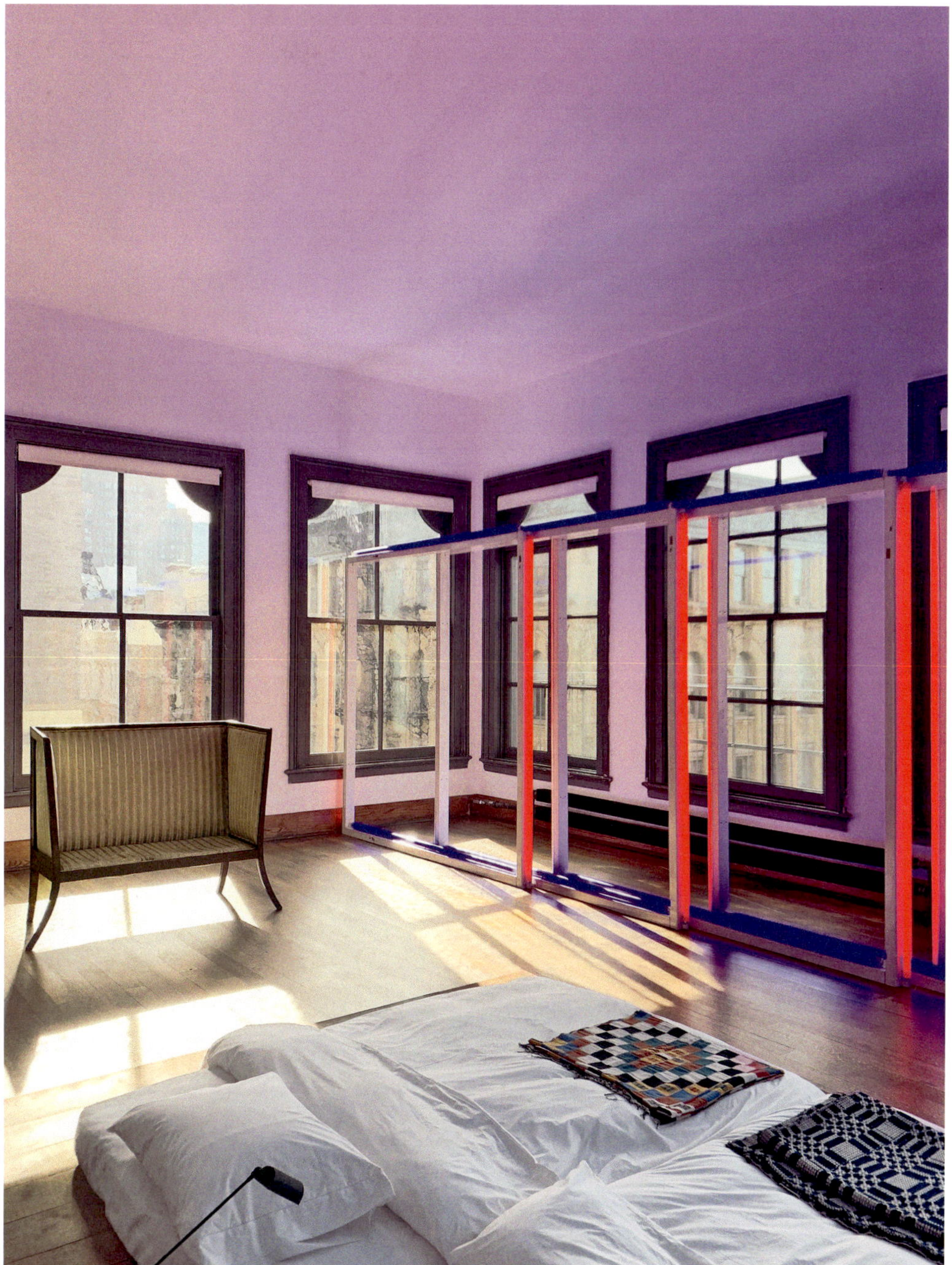

101 Spring Street, fifth floor, antique sofa, untitled, 1970 by Dan Flavin and bed by Donald Judd, view to southwest.

101 Spring Street, dritter Stock, historisches Sofa, untitled, 1970 von Dan Flavin und Bett von Donald Judd, Blick nach Südwesten.

JUDD FOUNDATION

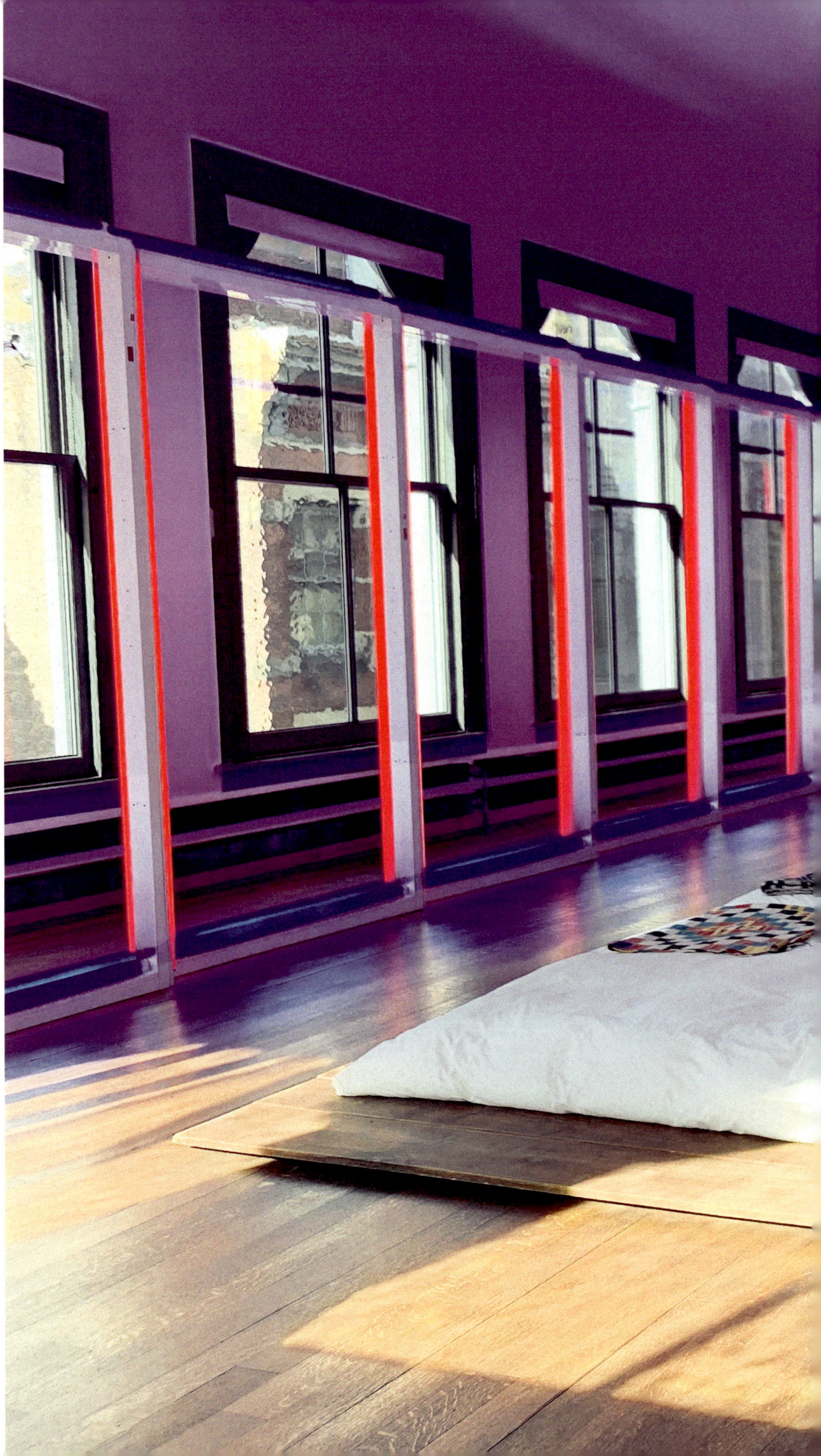

101 Spring Street,
fifth floor,
artworks by
John Chamberlain, *Mr. Press,*
Dan Flavin, untitled, 1970,
Donald Judd, untitled, 1963
and untitled, 1962,
Lucas Samaras, *Box #48*.
Bed by Donald Judd,
view to northwest.

101 Spring Street,
vierter Stock,
Kunstwerke von
John Chamberlain, *Mr. Press,*
Dan Flavin, untitled, 1970,
Donald Judd, untitled, 1963
und untitled, 1962,
Lucas Samaras, *Box #48,*
Bett von Donald Judd,
Blick nach Nordwesten.

JUDD FOUNDATION

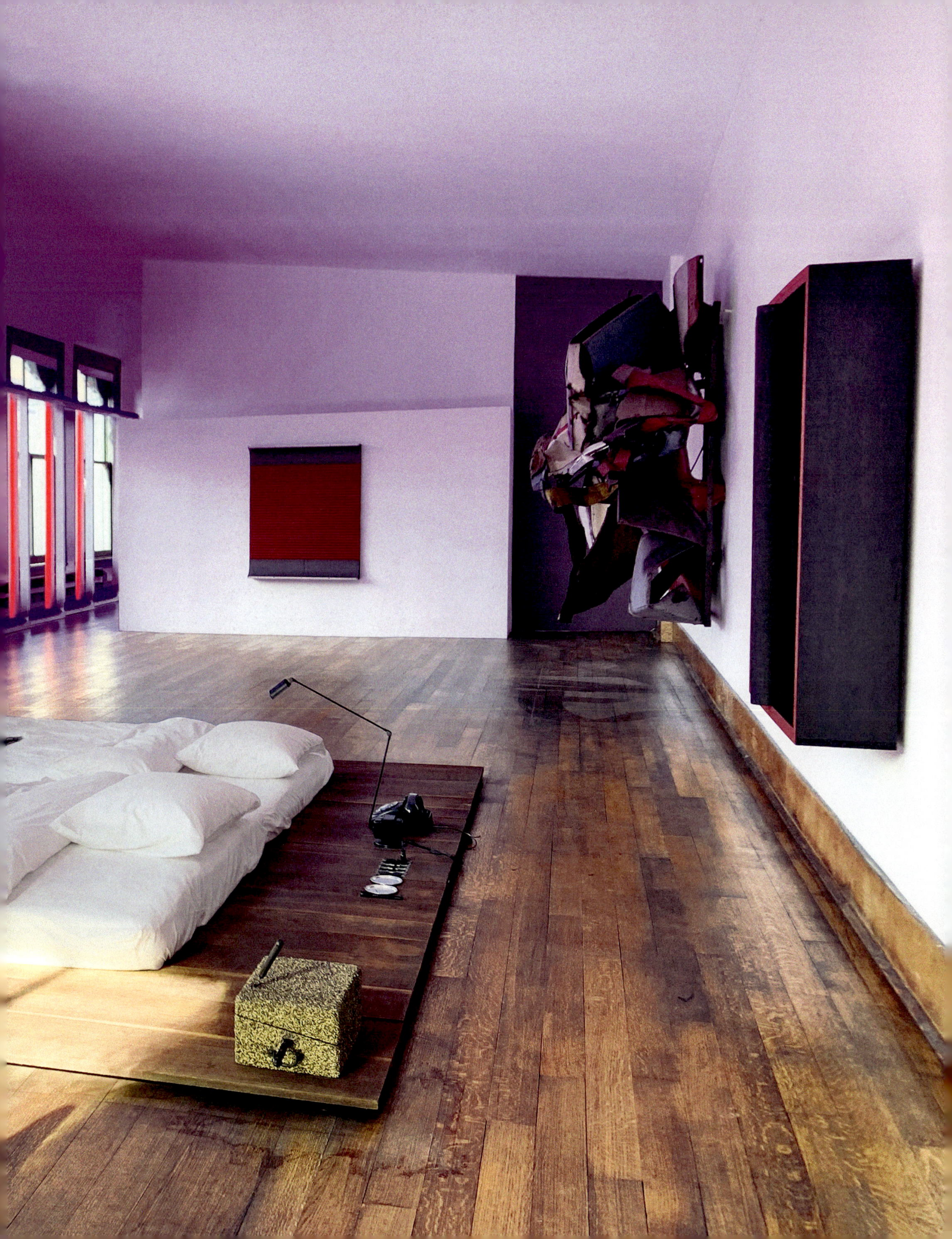

1 **101 Spring Street Site plan**
101 Spring Street Lageplan

2 **101 Spring Street Section B-B**
101 Spring Street Gebäudeschnitt B-B

3 **101 Spring Street Section A-A**
101 Spring Street Gebäudeschnitt A-A

4 **101 Spring Street Mezzanine floor, plan**
101 Spring Street Grundriss Zwischengeschoss

5 **101 Spring Street first floor, plan**
101 Spring Street Grundriss Erdgeschoss

6 **101 Spring Street second floor, plan**
101 Spring Street Grundrisse erstes Geschoss

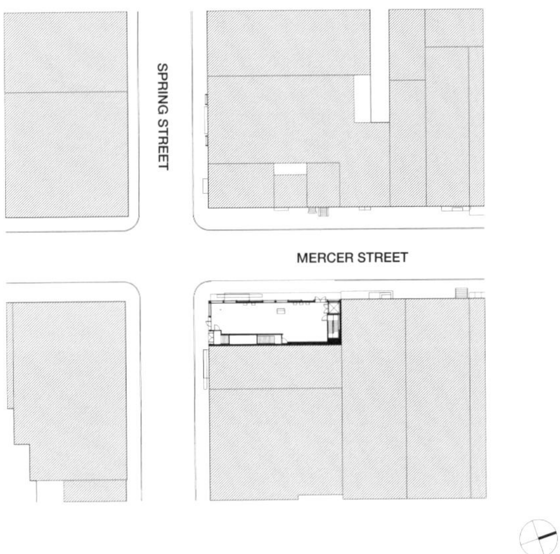

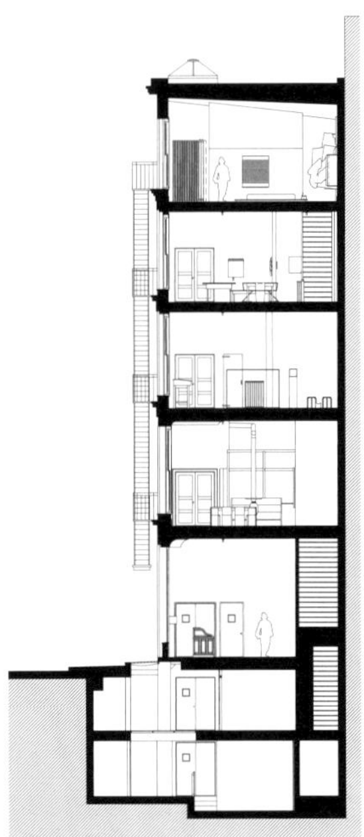

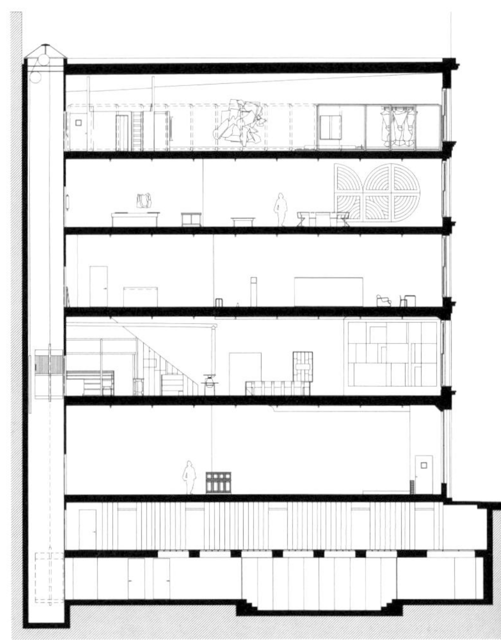

FEET 12 24 36
METERS 4 8 12

ARTWORKS
KUNSTWERKE

1 Carl Andre, Manifest Destiny, 1986

2 Donald Judd, untitled, 1974

3 David Novros, no title / 101 Spring Street, 1970

4 Ad Reinhardt, Abstract Painting, Red, 1952

5 Honoré Daumier, Le Salon de 1857, later printing

FURNITURE
MÖBEL

A Antique Writing Desk and Chair
Historischer Schreibtisch und Stuhl

B Donald Judd, Table and Chairs
Donald Judd, Tisch und Stühle

C Donald Judd, Single Daybed 32
Donald Judd, Single Daybed 32

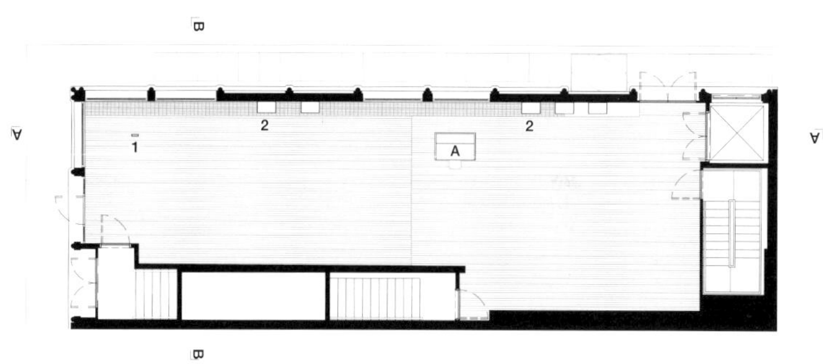

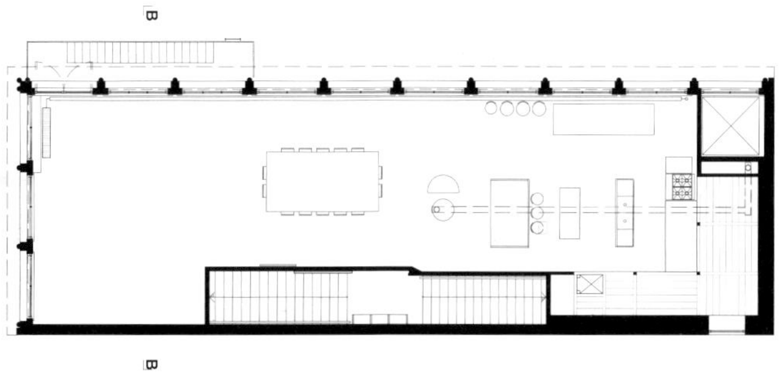

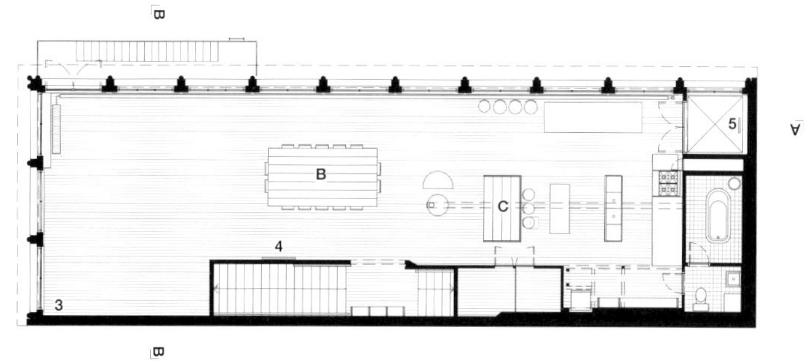

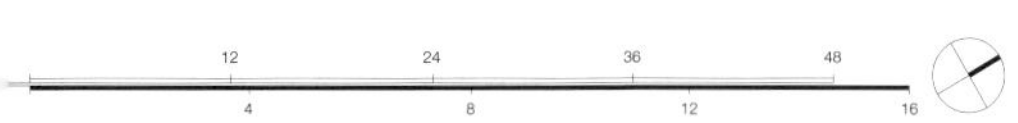

1 **101 Spring Street third floor, plan**
101 Spring Street Grundriss zweites Geschoss

2 **101 Spring Street fourth floor, plan**
101 Spring Street Grundriss drittes Geschoss

3 **101 Spring Street Mezzanine floor, plan**
101 Spring Street Grundriss Zwischengeschoss

4 **101 Spring Street fifth floor, plan**
101 Spring Street Grundriss viertes Geschoss

5 **101 Spring Street first basement, plan**
101 Spring Street Grundriss erstes Untergeschoss

6 **101 Spring Street second basement, plan**
101 Spring Street Grundriss zweites Untergeschoss

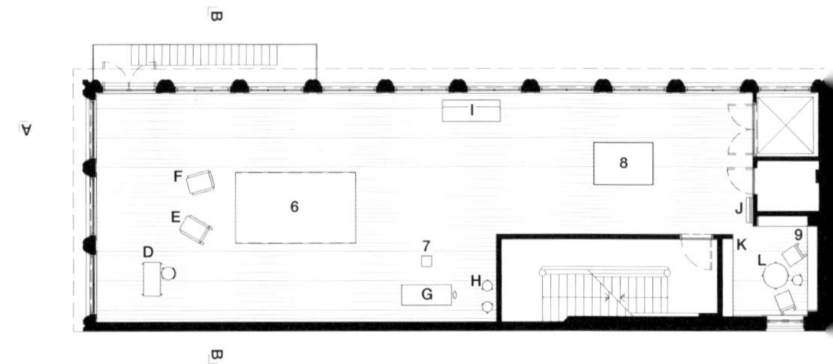

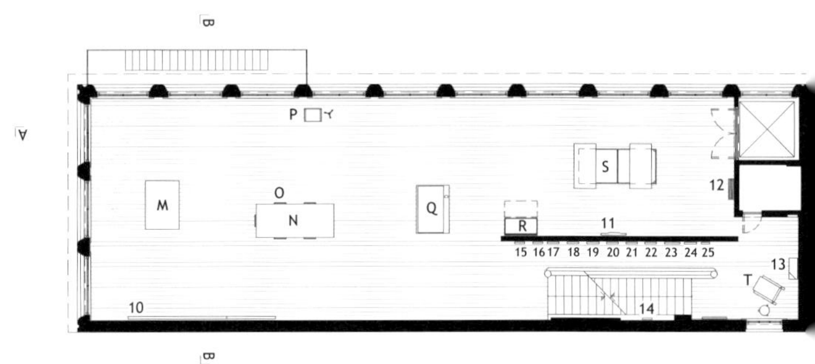

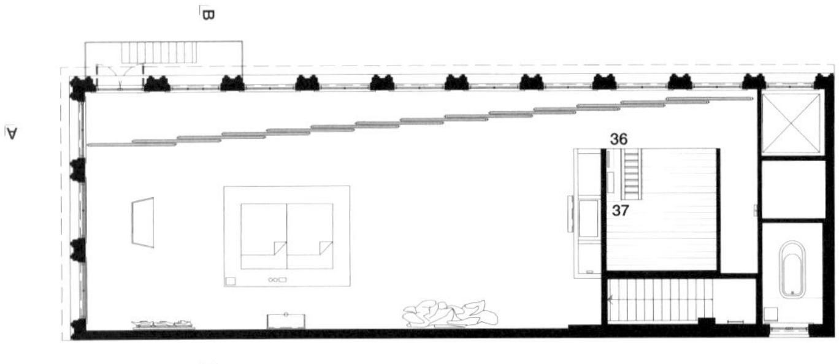

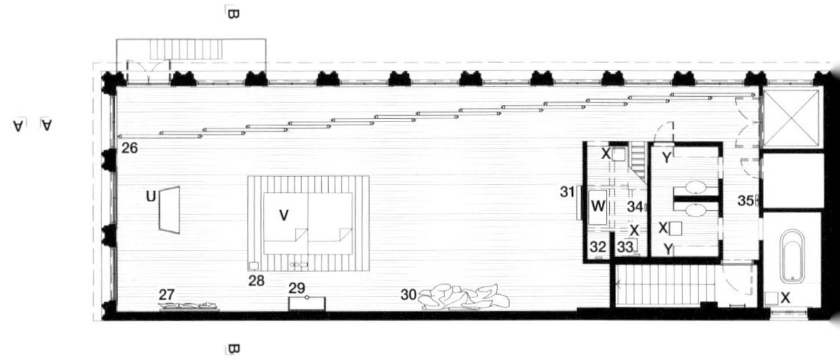

FEET 12 24 36 48
METERS 4 8 12 16

ARTWORKS
KUNSTWERKE

6 Donald Judd, untitled, 1969
7 Larry Bell, untitled, 1970
8 Donald Judd, untitled, 1966
9 Ad Reinhardt, Abstract Painting, 1960
10 Frank Stella, Gur II, 1967
11 Claes Oldenburg, Red Sausages, 1961
12 Dan Flavin, icon III (blood) (the blood of a martyr), 1962
13 Dan Flavin, icon VI (Ireland dying) (to Louis Sullivan), 1962-1963
14 Frank Stella, Study for Leo Castelli, 1963
15 Dan Flavin, ICON I THE HEART ICON III THE MYSTERY, 1962
16 Dan Flavin, ICON VI 1962-1963 (TO LOUIS SULLIVAN), 1964
17 Dan Flavin, from proposition two of diagram one for May 15, 1964, 1964
18 Dan Flavin, from proposition three of diagram one for May 15, 1964, 1964
19 Dan Flavin, variations on a theme of June 1, 1964, 1964
20 Dan Flavin, a right angle triangle, 1964
21 Dan Flavin, a right angle triangle, 1964
22 Dan Flavin, an isosceles triangle, 1964
23 Dan Flavin, extension of nominal 3 (to William of Ockham), 1964
24 Dan Flavin, form #1 of December 19, 1963 (in pink), 1964
25 Dan Flavin, (cool white and daylight) from no. 5 of March 2, 1964, 1964
26 Dan Flavin, untitled, 1970
27 Claes Oldenburg, Soft Ceiling Lights at La Coupole, 1964–1972
28 Lucas Samaras, Box #48, 1966
29 Donald Judd, untitled, 1962
30 John Chamberlain, Mr. Press, 1961
31 Donald Judd, untitled, 1963
32 Kurt Schwitters, Auweise, 1920
33 Stuart Davis, Detail Study for Cliché, 1957
34 Jean Arp, Multiple Femme V, 1956
35 Marcel Duchamp, In Advance of the Broken Arm, 1915/editioned replica 1964
36 Claes Oldenburg, Mickey Mouse, 1963
37 H.C. Westermann, 2063 AD, 1963

FURNITURE
MÖBEL

D Alvar Aalto, Table and Chair
Alvar Aalto, Tisch und Stuhl
E Alvar Aalto, Armchair 31
Alvar Aalto, Sessel
F Alvar Aalto, Armchair 41 “Paimio”
Alvar Aalto, Sessel 41 „Paimio“
G African Head Rest with Mat
Afrikanische Kopfstütze mit Matte
H Alvar Aalto, Stools
Alvar Aatlo, Stühle
I Writing Desk
Schreibtisch
J Donald Judd, Woodcut Blocks
Donald Judd, Holzschnittblöcke
K Donald Judd, Bookshelf
Donald Judd, Bücherschrank
L Alvar Aalto, Table and Chairs
Alvar Aalto, Tisch und Stühle
M Donald Judd, Table
Donald Judd, Tisch
N Donald Judd, Table
Donald Judd, Tisch
O Gerrit Reitveld, Zigzag Chairs
Gerrit Rietveld, Zickzack-Stuhl
P Antique Armchair and Lamp
Historischer Sessel und Lampe
Q Donald Judd, Table
Donald Judd, Tisch
R Donald Judd, Cart
Donald Judd, Cart
S Donald Judd, Serving Table
Donald Judd, Serving Table
T Alvar Aalto, Chair and Stool
Alvar Aalto, Sessel und Hocker
U Antique Sofa
Historisches Sofa
V Donald Judd, Bed
Donald Judd, Bett
W Table
Tisch
X Donald Judd, Chair
Donald Judd, Sessel
Y Donald Judd, Shelves
Donald Judd, Regal

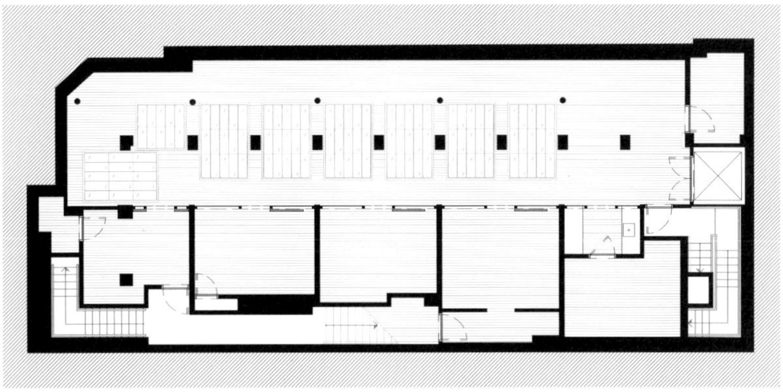

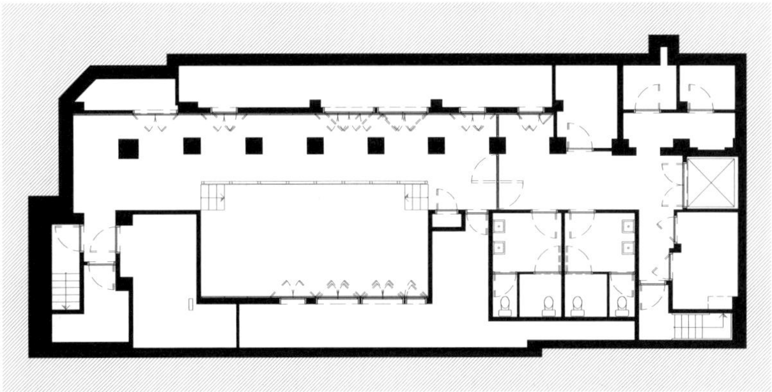

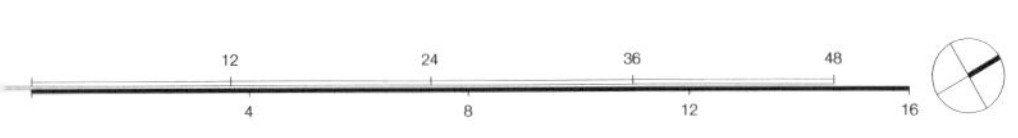

„DIE MEISTEN GEBÄUDE
HATTEN KEINE DÄCHER MEHR,
ÜBERALL LAG SCHUTT HERUM,
UND DAS LAND WAR VERWÜSTET.
AUS EINIGEN DER BARACKEN
HATTE MAN KITSCHIGE WOHNUNGEN
MIT DAZU PASSENDEN GÄRTEN
GEMACHT. EIN MILITÄRGEBIET,
VERSCHÖNERT MIT EINER KONSUM-
KITSCH-LANDSCHAFT:
DAS IST SCHWER ZU SCHLAGEN."

Donald Judd. Architektur,
Ostfildern, 3. Auflage, 1992, S. 68.

“MOST BUILDINGS WERE WITHOUT ROOFS, THERE WAS TRASH EVERYWHERE AND THE LAND WAS DAMAGED. SOME OF THE BARRACKS HAD BEEN TURNED INTO KITSCH APARTMENTS WITH COMPATIBLE LANDSCAPING. MILITARY LANDSCAPE OVERLAIN WITH A LANDSCAPE OF CONSUMER KITSCH IS HARD TO DEFEAT.”

Donald Judd. Architektur
(Ostfildern, 3rd edition, 1992), p. 72.

Donald Judd,
Biografische Notiz[1]

Donald Clarence Judd wurde am 3. Juni 1928 in Excelsior Springs, Missouri, geboren. 1971 zog er nach Marfa, Texas, wo er zunächst ein Haus mietete und 1973 sein erstes Gebäude erstand, das er anschließend sukzessive veränderte. Judd erwarb weitere Gebäude in Marfa und in der Umgebung der Stadt und baute sie mit sparsamen Eingriffen so um, dass Wohn- und Arbeitsbereiche sowie Ausstellungsräume für seine Kunstwerke und die anderer Künstler entstanden. Donald Judd starb am 12. Februar 1994 in New York.

Chronologisches Verzeichnis der architektonischen Werke:
Das folgende Verzeichnis der gebauten Werke von Donald Judd beruht auf Informationen, die in verschiedenen Publikationen verfügbar sind.[2] Es basiert auf Informationen, die zum Zeitpunkt der Veröffentlichung dieser Publikation zugänglich waren.

1940/50 Ideen für Häuser in Missouri/Nebraska

1968 Erwerb von Spring Street 101, New York, mit nachfolgender Renovierung und Transformation. Gusseisen-Gebäude aus dem Jahr 1870 nach einem Entwurf von Nicholas Whyte. New York.
Judd Foundation.

1971 Arroyo Grande, Hofhaus, Arroyo Grande bei El Rosario, Baja California, Mexiko; nicht ausgeführtes Projekt.

1972 Casa Lujan, Marfa, Texas; Judds Veränderungen nicht erhalten.

1972 La Catorcena, Marfa, Texas; nicht ausgeführtes Projekt.

1973–94: La Mansana de Chinati/Block, Renovierung und Transformation zweier ehemaliger, später als Lagerhäuser genutzter Flugzeughangars sowie eines zweigeschossigen Hauses mit Erweiterungen durch Baderäumlichkeiten, Bürogebäude, eine Pergola, ein Wasserbecken und weitere projektierte Gebäude. Marfa, Texas.
Judd Foundation.

1976 Casa Morales, Renovierung und Transformation eines Ranchhauses (Teilgebäude der größeren Ranch Ayala de Chinati) südwestlich von Marfa.
Judd Foundation.

Donald Judd,
Biographical Note[1]

Donald Clarence Judd was born June 3, 1928 in Excelsior Springs, Missouri. In 1971 Judd first rented a house in Marfa, Texas, and in 1973 he purchased his first building in town, modifying it subsequently. Judd acquired additional structures in Marfa and the surrounding area, altering them to accommodate his living and working quarters as well as his art and that of other artists. Donald Judd died February 12, 1994 in New York.

Chronological Index of Donald Judd's Architectural Work:
This index of Donald Judd's architectural work is based on information available through publications.[2] This index of Donald Judd's architectural work is based on information at the time of publication.

1940/50 Ideas for houses in Missouri/Nebraska

1968 Purchase of 101 Spring Street, New York with subsequent renovation and transformation. Cast-iron building originating from 1870 designed by Nicholas Whyte.
New York. Judd Foundation.

1971 Arroyo Grande, courtyard house, Arroyo Grande near El Rosario, Baja California, Mexico; unbuilt project.

1972 Casa Lujan, Marfa, Texas; Judd's modifications no longer in existence.

1972 La Catorcena, Marfa, Texas; unbuilt project.

1973–94 La Mansana de Chinati/the Block, renovation and transformation of two former hangars, later used as warehouses, and a two-story house, with additions of bathroom facilities, office buildings, a pergola, pool and other projected buildings. Marfa, Texas.
Judd Foundation.

1976 Casa Morales, renovation and transformation of a ranch house, part of the larger ranch Ayala de Chinati, located southwest of Marfa.
Judd Foundation.

c. 1978 Sequence of Pools, Marfa, Texas; unbuilt project.

Ca. 1978 Reihe von Wasserbecken, Marfa, Texas; nicht ausgeführtes Projekt.

Ca. 1978 Horti Conclusi, Hofhäuser für Westtexas; nicht ausgeführte Projekte.

1979–86 Artillerie-Hallen, Renovierung und Transformation zweier Geschützunterstände, Teile des ehemaligen Fort D. A. Russell. Marfa, Texas. The Chinati Foundation.

1980–84 Arena, Renovierung und Transformation eines Hangars, der später als Turn- und Reithalle benutzt wurde; Teil des früheren Fort D. A. Russell. Marfa, Texas. The Chinati Foundation.

1980–86 Chamberlain-Gebäude, Renovierung und Transformation eines ehemaligen Lagerhauses. Marfa, Texas. The Chinati Foundation.

Ca. 1980 La Misión del Sagrado Corazón, Plan zur Renovierung einer bestehenden Kirche aus Lehmziegeln, Ruidosa, Texas; nicht ausgeführtes Projekt.

1983–87 Casa Perez, Renovierung und Transformation eines Ranchhauses (Teilgebäude der größeren Ranch Ayala de Chinati) südwestlich von Marfa. Judd Foundation.

1984 Providence, Projekt für die Erneuerung des Platzes vor dem Rathaus von Providence, Rhode Island, zusammen mit Lauretta Vinciarelli; Wettbewerbssieger; nicht realisiert.

1986 Cleveland, Projekt mit Lauretta Vinciarelli, Claude Armstrong und Donna Cohen: städtebaulicher Entwurf für eine Landparzelle zwischen der Stadt Cleveland und dem Erie-See, Cleveland, Ohio; nicht realisiert.

1986–2001 Bahnhof Ost, Basel, Planung: Gesamtleitung: Hans Zwimpfer, Generalplaner: Project Group Bahnhof Ost; Leitung: Rudolf Zimmer, Architektur und Planung: Zwimpfer Partner Architekten, Buergin Nissen Wentzlaff Architekten (bis 1995), Hans Zwimpfer, Edi Buergin, Timothy O. Nissen, Ernst Zimmer, Lucien Brom, Pascal Essigmann, Christian Geser, Jaqueline Goetschy, Mirco Morassi, Tobias Nissen, Markus Ruetimann, Modellbau: Sidney Bannier. Quelle: Hans Zwimpfer, Peter Merian Haus Basel: an der Schnittstelle von Kunst, Technik und Architektur. At the Interface between Art, Technology, Architecture, Birkhäuser, Basel 2002.

1987 Betonbauten, 10 Gebäude für drei Gruppen von Werken Donald Judds auf dem Gelände des ehemaligen Fort A. D. Russell; zum Teil gebaut, doch unfertig. Marfa, Texas. The Chinati Foundation.

1987 Ausstellungsraum, Renovierung und Transformation einer früheren Militärbaracke in einen Ausstellungsraum auf dem Gelände des ehemaligen Fort A. D. Russell. Marfa, Texas. The Chinati Foundation.

1988 Sezession, Projekt für eine Einfriedung hinter dem Haus der Sezession, Wien; nicht realisiert. Judd Foundation.

1988 Belley, Projekt für den Kreisverkehr in Belley, Chambéry, Frankreich; nicht realisiert.

c. 1978 Horti Conclusi, courtyard houses for West Texas; unbuilt projects.

1979–86 Artillery Sheds, renovation and transformation of two artillery sheds, part of former Fort D. A. Russell. Marfa, Texas. The Chinati Foundation.

1980–84 Arena, renovation and transformation of a hangar that was later used as gymnasium and riding hall; part of former Fort D. A. Russell. Marfa, Texas. The Chinati Foundation.

1980–86 Chamberlain Building, renovation and transformation of a former warehouse. Marfa, Texas. The Chinati Foundation.

c. 1980 La Misión del Sagrado Corazón, proposed renovation of an existing adobe church, Ruidosa, Texas; unbuilt project.

1983–87 Casa Perez, renovation and transformation of a ranch house, part of Ayala de Chinati; southwest of Marfa. Judd Foundation.

1984 Providence, project for the renewal of the square in front of City Hall in Providence, Rhode Island, with Lauretta Vinciarelli; winning competition entry; unbuilt project.

1986 Cleveland, project with Lauretta Vinciarelli, Claude Armstrong, and Donna Cohen for urban design for a plot of land between the city of Cleveland and Lake Erie, Cleveland, Ohio; unbuilt project.

1987 Concrete Buildings, ten buildings designed for three groups of work by Donald Judd, on the site of former Fort D. A. Russell; partially built, but unfinished. Marfa, Texas. The Chinati Foundation.

1986–2000 Bahnhof Ost, Basel, Planning: Overall project management: Hans Zwimpfer, General planning: Project Group Bahnhof Ost; Direction: Rudolf Zimmer, Architecture and planning: Zwimpfer Partner Architekten, Buergin Nissen Wentzlaff Architekten (until 1995), Hans Zwimpfer, Edi Buergin, Timothy O. Nissen, Ernst Zimmer, Lucien Brom, Pascal Essigmann, Christian Geser, Jaqueline Goetschy, Mirco Morassi, Tobias Nissen, Markus Ruetimann, Model making: Sidney Bannier. Source: Zwimpfer, Hans. Peter Merian Haus Basel: an der Schnittstelle von Kunst, Technik und Architektur. At the Interface between Art, Technology, Architecture (Birkhäuser, Basel 2002).

1987 Exhibition Space, renovation and transformation of a former military barracks into an exhibition space, on the site of former Fort D. A. Russell, Marfa, Texas. The Chinati Foundation.

1988 Sezession, project for enclosure in the back of the Sezession, Vienna, Austria, unbuilt project.

c. 1988 Locker Plant, renovation and transformation of a former butcher's shop into a studio and exhibition space. Marfa, Texas. The Chinati Foundation.

1988 Belley, project for a traffic circle in Belley, Chambéry, France; unbuilt project.

1989 Architecture Studio, renovation and transformation of a former bank building, Marfa, Texas. Judd Foundation.

Ca. 1988 Schlachterei, Renovierung einer ehemaligen Metzgerei und Transformation in ein Studio und Ausstellungsräume. Marfa, Texas.
The Chinati Foundation.

1988–94 Las Casas, Renovierung und Transformation der Ranch Las Casas, Ayala de Chinati, südwestlich von Marfa, Texas.
Judd Foundation.

1989 Architekturstudio (*Architecture Studio*), Renovierung und Transformation einer ehemaligen Bank, Marfa, Texas.

1989–92 Eichholteren, Renovierung und Transformation eines früheren Hotelrestaurants, zusammen mit Adrian Jolles, Eichholteren, Küssnacht am Rigi; Judds Veränderungen sind nicht erhalten.

1990 Architekturbüro, Renovierung und Transformation einer ehemaligen Pension und eines Lebensmittelgeschäfts, Marfa, Texas.
Judd Foundation.

1990 Kunstatelier, Renovierung und Transformation eines ehemaligen Lebensmittelgeschäfts, Marfa, Texas.
Judd Foundation.

1990 Print Gebäude Renovierung und Transformation eines ehemaligen Hotels, Marfa, Texas.
Judd Foundation.

1990 Haus Cobb, Renovierung und Transformation eines früheren Wohnhauses, Marfa, Texas.

1990 Whyte-Gebäude, Renovierung und Transformation eines früheren Nutzbaus, Marfa, Texas.
Judd Foundation.

Ca. 1990–91 Ranchbüro, Renovierung und Transformation eines früheren Eisenwarengeschäfts, Marfa, Texas.
Judd Foundation.

1992 Bregenz, Büro- und Archivgebäude für das Kunsthaus Bregenz, zusammen mit Adrian Jolles, Bregenz, Österreich; nicht ausgeführtes Projekt.

1992 Gerlingen, Entwurf für einen öffentlichen Marktplatz, Gerlingen, Deutschland; nicht ausgeführtes Projekt.

1992 Fußbodendesign, Palais Lange Voorhout, Den Haag.

1992–97 Drei Brunnen, Steinberggasse, Winterthur.

1992–94 [Business Center] Bahnhof Ost Basel, zusammen mit den Architekten Zwimpfer & Partner, Bürgin, Nissen und Wentzlaff, Basel.

1993 Raum für Barockmöbel, Österreichisches Museum für Angewandte Kunst, Wien.

1 Eine ausführliche Bibliographie ist enthalten in: Nicholas Serota (Hg.), *Donald Judd*, London 2004, S. 246–270.

2 Als Quellen wurden benutzt:
Archiv im Gerichtsgebäude des Bezirks Presidio (Presidio County Courthouse), Marfa, TX (Urkunden vom Autor persönlich eingesehen).
Donald Judd, Architektur, 3. Auflage 1992, Ostfildern 1992.
Ders., Räume Spaces, Ostfildern 1993.
Nicholas Serota (Hg.), *Donald Judd*, London 2004.
Adrian Jolles, Adrian Meyer, *Donald Judd Eichholteren*, Ostfildern-Ruit 1997.
Peter Noever (Hg.), *Donald Judd, Architecture Architektur*, Ostfildern-Ruit 2003.

1989–94 Las Casas, renovation and transformation of the ranch Las Casas of the Ayala de Chinati, southwest of Marfa, Texas.
Judd Foundation.

1989–92 Eichholteren, renovation and transformation of a former hotel and restaurant, with Adrian Jolles, Eichholteren, Kuessnacht am Rigi, Switzerland; Judd's modifications no longer in existence.

1990 Architecture Office, renovation and transformation of a a former boarding house and grocery store; Marfa, Texas.
Judd Foundation.

1990 Art Studio, renovation and transformation of a former grocery store, Marfa, Texas.
Judd Foundation.

1990 Cobb House, renovation and transformation of a former house, Marfa, Texas.
Judd Foundation.

1990 Print Building renovation and transformation of a former hotel, Marfa, Texas.
Judd Foundation.

1990 Whyte Building, renovation and transformation of a former utilitarian structure. Marfa, Texas.
Judd Foundation.

c. 1990–91 Ranch Office, renovation and transformation of a former hardware store, Marfa, Texas.
Judd Foundation.

1992 Bregenz, office and archive building for Kunsthaus Bregenz, with Adrian Jolles, Bregenz, Austria; unbuilt project.

1992 Gerlingen, design of a public marketplace, Gerlingen, Germany; unbuilt project.

1992 Floor Design, Paleis Lange Voorhout, The Hague, The Netherlands.

1992–97 Three Fountains, Steinberggasse Winterthur, Switzerland.

1992–94 East Train Station Basel, collaboration with the architects Zwimpfer/Partner and Buergin Nissen Wentzlaff, Basel, Switzerland.

1993 Space for Baroque Furniture, Österreichisches Museum für Angewandte Kunst, Vienna, Austria.

1 A comprehensive biography is published in Serota, Nicholas (ed.). *Donald Judd*, Tate Modern (London, 2004), pp. 246–270

2 Sources are:
Archive at the Presidio County Courthouse, Marfa, TX (firsthand research by the author).
Donald Judd. Architektur, 3rd ed. (Ostfildern, 1992).
Donald Judd. Räume Spaces (Ostfildern, 1993).
Serota, Nicholas (ed.). *Donald Judd*, Tate Modern (London, 2004).
Jolles, Adrian and Meyer, Adrian. *Donald Judd Eichholtern* (Hatje Cantz Publishers, 1997).
Noever, Peter. *Donald Judd. Architecture Architektur* (Ostfildern-Ruit, Hatje Cantz Publishers, 2003).

Anmerkung zu den Zeichnungen

Sämtliche Zeichnungen, die in dieser Publikation enthalten sind, wurden in der Zeit von 2001 bis 2006 und 2016 bis 2020 vom Verfasser oder von Studenten des College of Architecture der Texas Tech University unter Anleitung des Verfassers angefertigt. Die Abmessungen aller abgebildeten Gebäude und baulichen Anlagen wurden vor Ort vorgenommen und sind so genau wie möglich wiedergegeben. Die Zeichnungen zeigen die Gebäude, baulichen Anlagen, Kunstwerke und Möbel, wie Donald Judd sie installiert hat, in ihrem heutigen Erhaltungszustand. In der grafischen Tabelle zu jeder Zeichnung sind Größe, Maßstab und Proportion sowohl in Fuß als auch in Metern angegeben. Der Nordpfeil gibt jeder Zeichnung die richtige Orientierung. Schnittabbildungen baulicher Details sind schwarz hinterlegt, unabhängig von ihrem Baumaterial und unabhängig davon, ob Gebäude oder Strukturen aus festen Lehmziegelmauern errichtet sind oder aus einem Rahmen aus Holzgerippe mit Luftraum. In den Schnittzeichnungen des zweigeschossigen Gebäudes, des Chamberlain-Gebäudes, des Whyte-Gebäudes und in Ayala de Chinati von Las Casas und Casa Perez ist auch der Dachboden mit schwarzer Hinterlegung dargestellt, um den räumlichen Charakter der „Box“ zu betonen. Zwei Ausnahmen von diesem Darstellungsmuster sind zu erwähnen: die zwei Artillerie-Hallen. Judd hatte geplant, die Flächen der Stirnseiten des gewölbten Raums der Dachkonstruktion in beiden Hallen zu verglasen, mit der Absicht, dem Betrachter den Eindruck von Licht und Raum innerhalb der Dachkonstruktion zu vermitteln. Aus diesem Grund ist dieser Raum in den Schnittzeichnungen der Artillerie-Hallen als Leerraum dargestellt.

Über den Autor

Urs Peter „Upe“ Flückiger ist Professor am College of Architecture an der Texas Tech University in Lubbock, Texas, USA, wo er außerdem auch sein Architekturbüro betreibt. Er arbeitete für verschiedene Architekturbüros in der Schweiz, unter anderem für das von Mario Botta in Lugano, und war in New York City im Büro von David Rockwell (Rockwellgroup) angestellt. Im Jahr 1998 nahm er seine Lehrtätigkeit am College of Architecture an der Texas Tech auf. Seinen Masterabschluss in Architektur erwarb er am Virginia Polytechnic Institute und an der State University in Blacksburg, Virginia. Flückigers Design- und Forschungsschwerpunkte sind der ökonomische und ökologische Wohnungsbau, Minimalismus in der Architektur, „design build“ sowie die Moderne vom 20. Jahrhundert bis heute. Nach seiner eigenen Designphilosophie entwarf und baute er 2004 mit der Künstlerin Carol Fitzgerald Flückiger ihr gemeinsames Wohnhaus mit Studio. Neben dem vorliegenden Buch ist er auch Autor von *Wie viel Haus? Thoreau, Le Corbusier und die Sustainable Cabin* (Birkhäuser 2016). Die spanische Ausgabe *¿Cuánta casa necesitamos? Thoreau, Le Corbusier y la cabaña sostenible* wurde 2019 veröffentlicht (Gustavo Gili 2019). Seine Designforschung wurde in zahlreichen Büchern, Zeitschriften und Zeitungen publiziert. Für seine Lehre, Forschung und seine Entwürfe wurde Flückiger mit diversen Preisen ausgezeichnet. Wenn er einmal weder über Architektur nachdenkt noch die Zeit mit seiner Familie genießt, liebt er es, mit klassischen, luftgekühlten Zweizylinder-BMW-Motorrädern durch die High Plains von Westtexas.

A Note about the Drawings

All drawings in this publication were prepared by the author or by students at the College of Architecture at Texas Tech University during the period 2001– 2006 and 2016–2020. Measurements of all the buildings and structures illustrated herein were taken on site and are represented as accurately as possible. The drawings show the buildings, structures, artwork and furnishings as Donald Judd installed them and as they are preserved today. The graphic scale for each drawing provides the size, scale and proportion in both imperial and metric measurements. An arrow pointing north gives each drawing proper orientation. Sectional representations of building elements are poched in black irrespective of their building material and whether or not the building or structure is constructed in solid adobe walls or wood stud framing with airspace. In the sectional drawings of the Two-story Building, the Chamberlain Building, the Whyte Building, and at Ayala de Chinati: Las Casas and Casa Perez, the attic space is also represented with a black poche in order to emphasize the spatial quality of the "box". Two notable exceptions to these conventions of representation are the two Artillery Sheds. Judd planned for both ends of the Quonset roof structure of the two Artillery Sheds to be closed by glass, the intended effect being that the viewer would sense light and space within the Quonset roof structure. Therefore that space in the sections of the Artillery Sheds is represented as void space.

About the Author

Urs Peter "Upe" Flueckiger is a Professor in the College of Architecture at Texas Tech University in Lubbock Texas, USA, where he also maintains his architectural practice. He worked for several architectural firms in Switzerland including the office of Mario Botta in Lugano and in New York City in the office of David Rockwell (Rockwellgroup). In 1998 he joined the faculty of the College of Architecture at Texas Tech. He holds a Master of Architecture degree from the Virginia Polytechnic Institute and State University in Blacksburg, Virginia. His design and research interests are economical ecological housing, minimalism in architecture, design build, and modernism in the 20th century to the present. In 2004 he and artist Carol Fitzgerald Flueckiger designed and built their current house and studio, basing it on Flueckiger's design philosophy. In addition to this book, he is the author of *How much House? Thoreau, Le Corbusier and the Sustainable Cabin* (Birkhäuser 2016). In 2019 a Spanish edition of *How Much House?* entitled *¿Cuánta casa necesitamos? Thoreau, Le Corbusier y la cabaña sostenible* was published (Gustavo Gili 2019). His design research work has been published in numerous books, journals, and magazines. For his work Flueckiger has received multiple teaching, research, and design awards. When he is not thinking about architecture or playing with his family, he loves riding classic BMW "airhead" motorcycles across the High Plains of West Texas.

Dank 2. Auflage

Das vorliegende Buch ist wie ein architektonisches Werk ein zugleich individuelles und kollektives Unternehmen. Ohne die Hilfe und den Beistand der unten genannten Personen und Organisationen wäre mir die Realisierung dieser 2. Auflage nicht möglich gewesen.
Ein besonderer Dank gebührt Flavin Judd, Artistic Director, Rainer Judd, President, Caitlin Murray, Director of Archives & Programs, sowie Richard Griggs, Chief Operating Officer, von der Judd Foundation, die mir die Veröffentlichung dieses Buches erst ermöglicht haben, indem sie mir im Laufe der Jahre immer wieder Zugang zu den Judd-Gebäuden in Marfa und New York gewährten und wertvolle persönliche Einblicke in Judds Schaffen vermittelten.
Mein Dank geht an Andrea Walsh und Emma Whelan von der Judd Foundation für ihre Überwachung und Koordinierung der Bildrechte sowie an Randy Sanchez und Rico Roman von der Judd Foundation, die mich mehrfach sicher nach Ayala de Chinati gefahren und mir den Zugang zu den Ländereien und Häusern ermöglicht haben.
Besonders danken möchte ich der Direktorin der Chinati Foundation, Jenny Moore, die uns auch dieses Mal die Nutzung der Bildarchive ihrer Stiftung erlaubte, sowie der Archivarin der Judd Foundation, Hannah Marshall, für ihre Unterstützung bei der Recherche.
Ich bedanke mich zudem bei W. Mark Gunderson für sein erkenntnisreiches Vorwort zu dieser 2. Auflage mit dem Titel „Proportion aller Belange“ und insbesondere dafür, dass er sich über all die Jahre stets Zeit zum Zuhören und Diskutieren sowie für den gemeinsamen Gedankenaustausch über Judds Werk nahm.
Danke auch an Pedro Espinet, Landon Wade und Margaret Ragain, die während ihrer Studienzeit am College of Architecture der Texas Tech University an den CAD-Adobe-Illustrator-Zeichnungen mitwirkten.
Ich danke meinen ehemaligen Studenten Dylan Bemberg und Ryan Bemberg, die mittlerweile zu Kollegen und Freunden wurden und die auch dieses Mal wieder gemeinsam mit mir an der Vermessung und den Zeichnungen von 101 Spring Street in New York und allen folgenden Schritten arbeiteten. Ebenso möchte ich meiner früheren Studentin und jetzigen Kollegin und Freundin Stephanie Bunt danken, die die Lagepläne von Ayala de Chinati zeichnete und die Konturen der Landschaft integrierte.
Ein herzlicher Dank geht an Florian Holzherr und Eugene Binder, die uns erneut ihre hochwertigen Fotografien für diese 2. Ausgabe zur Verfügung stellten sowie Elizabeth Felicella zur Casa Perez. Ohne ihre Aufnahmen wäre dieses Buch nicht realisierbar gewesen.
Ich danke David W. Keller, dem Autor von *In the Shadow of the Chinatis*, der sein Wissen über die Geschichte des Pinto Canyon mit mir teilte. Nancy Sparrow, kuratorische Assistentin in den Alexander Architectural Archives, der Architecture and Planning Library der University of Texas gewährte mir mehrfach Zugang zu den Tonaufnahmen von Donald Judds Vorlesung an der School of Architecture in Austin, Texas, aus dem Jahr 1992.
Es gibt noch einige weitere Personen, ohne deren Unterstützung diese 2. Auflage nicht möglich gewesen wäre – Clifton Ellis, Saif Haq, Trish Hart, Victoria McReynolds, Ana Mendoza, Denny Mingus, Robert D. Perl, Chris Taylor, Hillary Veeder, Lesley Nall Washington und Jim Williamson, die alle in unterschiedlichen Funktionen am College of Architecture der Texas Tech University tätig sind. Sehr dankbar bin ich auch all jenen, die Donald Judd kannten oder mit ihm gearbeitet haben und mir in unseren Gesprächen sehr hilfreiche Einblicke in und Perspektiven auf Judds Werk ermöglichten. Dazu gehören Robert Arber aus Marfa, Donna Cohen aus

Acknowledgements 2nd Edition

This book, like a work of architecture, is both an individual and collective undertaking. Without the support and help of the people and organizations below the 2nd edition of this book would not have been possible.
A special thanks is due to Flavin Judd, Artistic Director, Rainer Judd, President, Caitlin Murray, Director of Archives & Programs, and to Richard Griggs, Chief Operating Officer, of the Judd Foundation, who all made this book possible by giving me access many times to the Judd buildings in Marfa and New York as well as valuable personal insights into Judd's work over the past several years.
A thank you goes to Andrea Walsh and Emma Whelan from the Judd Foundation for overseeing and coordinating the image rights, as well as Randy Sanchez and Rico Roman from the Judd Foundation for driving me multiple times safely to Ayala de Chinati and giving me access to the land and the buildings.
Special thanks also go to Jenny Moore, Director of The Chinati Foundation, for letting us make use of The Chinati Foundation photo archives once more, and Hannah Marshall, The Chinati Foundation Archivist for her research assistance.
I am indebted to W. Mark Gunderson for his insightful foreword to the 2nd edition entitled: *Proportion of Concerns* and for generously giving his time to listen, discuss, and exchange our thinking on Judd's work in countless conversations over the years.
Thanks also go to Pedro Espinet, Landon Wade, and Margaret Ragain who all worked at some point on the CAD/Adobe Illustrator drawings of the Ranch houses Morales and Perez while being students at the College of Architecture, Texas Tech University.
I thank my former students, now colleagues and friends, Dylan Bemberg and Ryan Bemberg who once more worked with me on measuring and drawing 101 Spring Street in New York and its many iterations. Former student, now colleague and friend, Stephanie Bunt who drew the site plans with contour lines of the landscape at Ayala de Chinati.
A heartfelt thank you goes out to Florian Holzherr and Eugene Binder who once more let us use their high-quality photography for this 2nd edition and Elizabeth Felicella for Casa Perez. Without their photography this book would not have been possible.
There are several people whose support was instrumental in making this 2nd edition of this book become a reality—Clifton Ellis, Saif Haq, Trish Hart, Victoria McReynolds, Ana Mendoza, Denny Mingus, Robert D. Perl, Chris Taylor, Hillary Veeder, Lesley Nall Washington, and Jim Williamson, all in their respective functions at the College of Architecture at Texas Tech University. I am also grateful to the people who had either worked with Donald Judd or have known Judd and with whom I had conversations over the years and who were helpful with their insights and perspectives on Judd's work. These people are Robert Arber, Marfa; W. Mark Gunderson, Architect, Fort Worth; Adrian Jolles, Architect, Switzerland; and Michael Roch, Director of Education and Curricula at The Chinati Foundation.
I am enormously grateful to Annette Gref and Katharina Kulke whom I have worked with for years on multiple projects with Birkhäuser Basel, for the coordination and the oversight of this book. It is not self-evident to have a longstanding working relationship in our fast-paced world. I would like to thank Lisa Knapp for the copy editing and Floyd Schulze for his astute eye when designing the second and expanded edition of this book.
Last but not least a heartfelt thank you goes to my family, Carol and Lucas, who kept being supportive when my moods were gloomy.

Gainsville, W. Mark Gunderson, Architekt aus Fort Worth, Adrian Jolles, Architekt aus der Schweiz, und Michael Roch, Director of Education and Curricula bei der Chinati Foundation.
Überaus dankbar für ihre Koordination und Betreuung dieses Buches bin ich Annette Gref und Katharina Kulke vom Birkhäuser Verlag in Basel, mit denen ich seit mehreren Jahren diverse Projekte realisieren durfte. Eine derart langfristige Arbeitsbeziehung ist in unserer schnelllebigen Welt nicht selbstverständlich. Zudem möchte ich Lisa Knapp für das Lektorat und Floyd Schulze für seinen scharfsinnigen Blick auf die Gestaltung der zweiten und erweiterten Auflage dieses Buches danken. Nicht zuletzt danke ich von Herzen meiner Familie, Carol und Lucas, die mich auch dann stets unterstützten, wenn es um meine Laune nicht zum Besten stand.

Abbildungsnachweis:

Fotografie S. 12 /13, S. 112 oben rechts: Fotograf unbekannt. Quelle: Mit freundlicher Genehmigung des Marfa and Presidio County Museum, Marfa, Texas.
Fotografien S. 20, S. 23, W. Mark Gunderson
Fotografien S. 61 unten links, S. 76 Mitte links, S. 77 Mitte links und unten links, S. 90 unten rechts, S. 92 Mitte, S. 93 unten rechts, S. 94 unten links und rechts: Fotograf unbekannt. Quelle: Mit freundlicher Genehmigung der Chinati Foundation Archives.
Fotografien S. 126 /127, S. 132 /133, S. 134/135, S. 136 /137, S. 138 /139, S. 148 /149, S. 150 /151, S. 152 /153, S. 154 /155, S. 156, Fotograf: Urs Peter Flückiger.
Fotografie p. 157, Fotografin: Elizabeth Felicella.
Fotografie S. 166 /167: Fotograf: Eugene Binder.
Fotografien S. 169, oben links, S. 178 /179, S. 180 /181, S. 182 /183, S. 194/195, S. 196 /197, S. 198 /199, S. 200 /201, S. 202 /203, Fotograf: Urs Peter Flückiger.
Fotografie S. 216: Fotografin: Julie M. Finch. Quelle: Judd Foundation, mit freundlicher Genehmigung von Julie M. Finch.
Donald Judd Art © 2021 Judd Foundation/Artists Rights Society (ARS), New York.
Alle anderen Fotografien stammen von Florian Holzherr.
Mit freundlicher Genehmigung der Chinati Foundation.

Photographic Credits:

Photograph p. 12 /13, p. 112 top right: Photographer unknown. Source: Courtesy of Marfa and Presidio County Museum, Marfa, Texas.
Photographs p. 20, p. 23, W. Mark Gunderson
Photographs p. 61 bottom left, p. 76 center left, p. 77 center left and bottom right, p. 90 bottom right, p. 92 center, p. 93 bottom right, p. 94 bottom left and right: Photographer unknown. Source: Courtesy of The Chinati Foundation Archives.
Photographs p. 126 /127, p. 132 /133, p. 134/135, p. 136 /137, p. 138 /139, p. 148 /149, p. 150 /151, p. 152 /153, p. 154 /155, p. 156: Photographer: Urs Peter Flückiger © Judd Foundation.
Photograph p. 157, Photographer: © Elizabeth Felicella. Courtesy Judd Foundation.
Photograph p. 166 / 167: Photographer: Eugene Binder.
Photographs p. 169 top left, p. 178 /179, p. 180 /181, p. 182 /183, p. 194/195, p. 196 /197, p. 198 /199, p. 200 /201, p. 202 /203: Photographer: Urs Peter Flückiger © Judd Foundation.
Photograph p. 216: Photographer: Julie M. Finch. Source: Judd Foundation Archives, Marfa, Texas. Courtesy of Julie M. Finch.
All other photographs are by Florian Holzherr.
Courtesy of The Chinati Foundation.
Donald Judd Art © 2021 Judd Foundation/Artists Rights Society (ARS), New York.
Dan Flavin p. 59, 201, 202–203: © 2021 Stephen Flavin / Artists Rights Society (ARS), New York
Frank Stella p. 58, 200: © 2021 Frank Stella / Artists Rights Society (ARS), New York
Ad Reinhardt p. 197: © 2021 Estate of Ad Reinhardt / Artists Rights Society (ARS), New York
John Chamberlain p. 102–105, 202–203: © 2021 Fairweather & Fairweather LTD / Artists Rights Society (ARS), New York
David Novros p. 197: © 2021 David Novros / Artists Rights Society (ARS), New York
Richard Long p. 93: © 2021 Richard Long / Artists Rights Society (ARS), New York
David Rabinowitch p. 90: © David Rabinowitch
Larry Bell p. 198, 199: © 2021 Larry Bell
Lucas Samaras p. 202: © 2021 Lucas Samaras

Copy editing English/Lektorat Deutsch: Elisabeth Schwaiger/Ruth Lisa Knapp

Translation from English into German/ Übersetzung ins Deutsche: Ute Spengler/Christiane Böhme-Wilk

Project management/Projektkoordination: Annette Gref, Katharina Kulke

Production/Herstellung: Amelie Solbrig

Layout, Covergestaltung und Satz 1. Auflage/ Layout, cover design and typesetting 1st edition: Muriel Comby

Layout, Covergestaltung 2. Auflage/Layout, cover design 2nd edition: Floyd E. Schulze

Typesetting 2nd edition/Satz 2. Auflage: Sven Schrape

Paper/Papier: Magno Volume, 135 g/m²
Printing/Druck: Grafisches Centrum Cuno GmbH & Co. KG, Calbe
Image editing/Lithografie: LVD Gesellschaft für Datenverarbeitung mbH, Berlin

Library of Congress Control Number: 2021940217

Bibliographic information published by the German National Library

The German National Library lists this publication in the Deutsche Nationalbibliografie; detailed bibliographic data are available on the Internet at http://dnb.dnb.de.

This work is subject to copyright. All rights are reserved, whether the whole or part of the material is concerned, specifically the rights of translation, reprinting, re-use of illustrations, recitation, broadcasting, reproduction on microfilms or in other ways, and storage in databases.

For any kind of use, permission of the copyright owner must be obtained.

ISBN 978-3-0356-2161-7

© 2021 Birkhäuser Verlag GmbH, Basel
P.O. Box 44, 4009 Basel, Switzerland
Part of Walter de Gruyter GmbH, Berlin/Boston

9 8 7 6 5 4 3 2
www.birkhauser.com

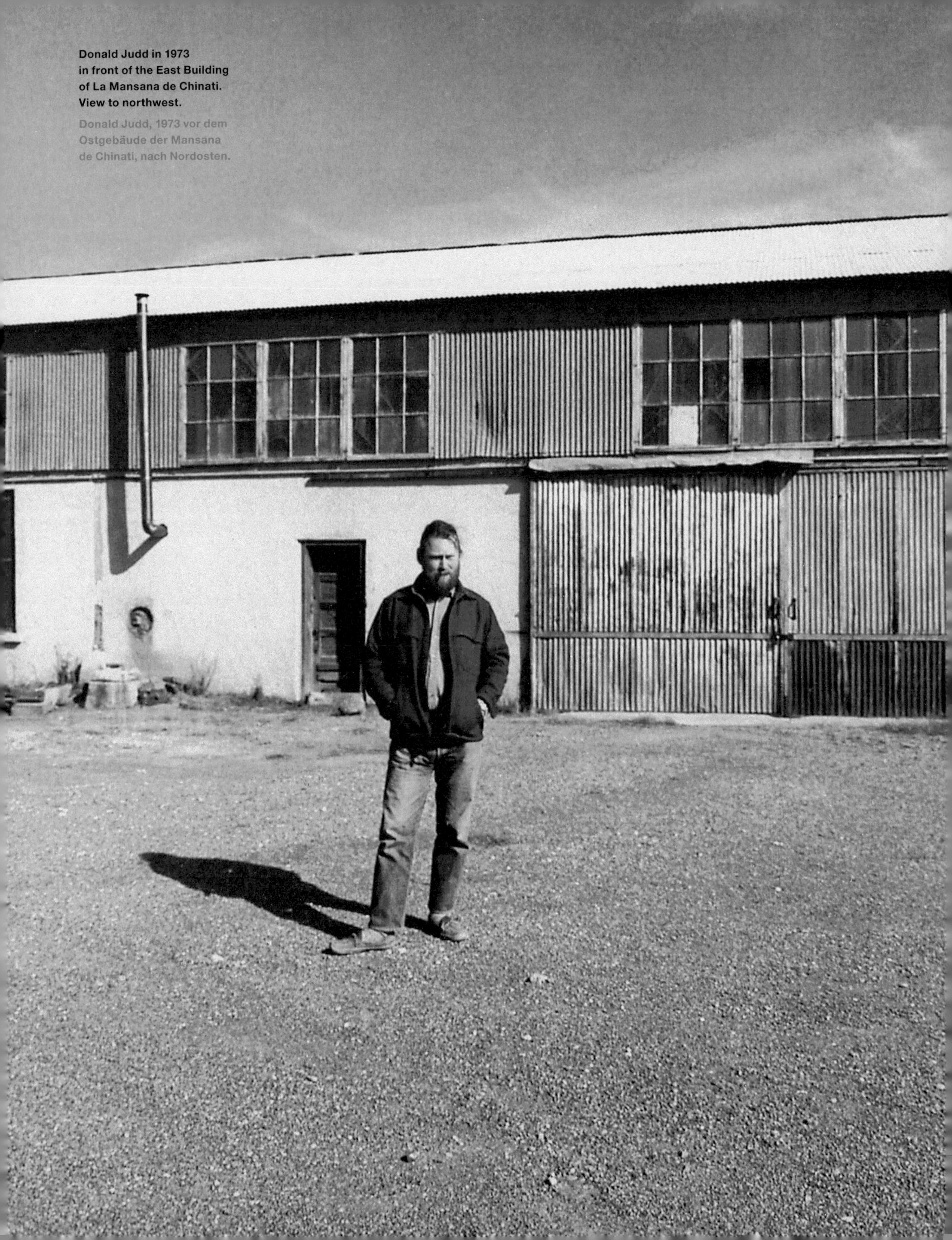

Donald Judd in 1973 in front of the East Building of La Mansana de Chinati. View to northwest.

Donald Judd, 1973 vor dem Ostgebäude der Mansana de Chinati, nach Nordosten.